DEFEAT IN THE WEST

By MILTON SHULMAN

With An Introduction By

MAJOR GENERAL SIR IAN JACOB, K.B.E., C.B.

E. P. DUTTON & COMPANY, INC.

New York   *1948*

INTRODUCTION

By Major General Sir Ian Jacob, K.B.E., C.B.

THE historian of the future will have an unprecedented opportunity. Not only will he have very complete documentation of the second World War on the Allied side, but he will have the entire political and military archives of Germany to study, since these have fallen intact into our hands. But the ground to be covered in writing a comprehensive history of the war is so extensive that many years must elapse before definitive volumes can be presented to the public. In the meanwhile the world does not stand still, and it is most desirable that interim studies of the great events of the past few years should appear and that in this way some of the lessons that are there to be learnt should be revealed before it is too late to make use of them. This book is just such a study. It describes in admirably lucid fashion the German defeat in the West as seen from the losing side; it traces the causes of that defeat, and it throws a lurid light on Hitler, on the German character and on the strengths and weaknesses of the Wehrmacht. There is no doubt about the essential accuracy of the picture that emerges. Further research may lead to modification of the details, but the main facts and the conclusions that can be drawn from them are likely to remain unchallenged.

Major Shulman was in an excellent position to gather the material for this book. It was his duty as a member of the Intelligence Staff of the Canadian Army to make a detailed study of the German Army before D-Day. He then made close personal contact with it throughout the operations in France, Belgium, Holland and Germany. Finally he was given the task of interrogating a large number of the senior Commanders who had fought for Germany against the Allies in the West, including such notable figures as von Rundstedt, 'Sepp' Dietrich and Student. Major Shulman has made the most of his opportunities, and the result is an absorbing tale of what happened "on the other side of the hill."

Those of us who were closely concerned with the higher direction of the war on the Allied side frequently speculated on the extraordinary mistakes that were made by the Germans. Why was the British Army allowed to escape at Dunkirk? Why did not the enemy attempt the capture of Malta, the key to the Mediterranean campaign and the thorn in Rommel's flesh, which so tapped his life-blood that he was prevented from driving home his victories? Why did the German armies on the various fronts never make strategic retreats? Why did they throw good money after bad in Tunisia? These and many other questions we asked ourselves. Some of them are directly answered by Major Shulman; the answers to others can now be deduced from the evidence that he has assembled. As Shulman says, it is at the fateful but clumsy feet of Adolf Hitler that we must lay the wreath of German defeat. Hitler, discipline, and ignorance, combined to make the immense sacrifices of the Wehrmacht ineffectual. But the supreme question that has to be answered is, How did one man so master Germany that when he was clearly leading the country to total destruction, when he was issuing impossible orders to formations hundreds of miles away in the line of battle, and when at all costs he should have been overthrown, no force was found with the spirit and cohesion to do the job? The answer lies in the state of degradation to which a nation, wedded to brute discipline and accustomed to military domination, can be reduced by an autocratic régime. Germany is a country that has never known truly democratic existence. The Germans have always responded with alacrity to the call to discipline, to self-sacrifice and to war. Autocratic leaders have always found it easy to fasten their militaristic chains on the docile and patriotic people of the Fatherland. The tradition of the Prussian military caste has thus been firmly established for many years, and has been gladly accepted by the men and women of German race. Its power and luster was in no way diminished by the outcome of the first World War. The myth of the "stab in the back" was cultivated to make the Germans believe that their army had not been defeated. The Wehrmacht, who knew the truth, and saw that Hitler gave promise of restoring their military glory, supported him in his rise to power. But their discipline and their ignorance made them incapable of withstanding his stupidities or of overthrowing him. There is now a real danger that a fresh myth may be built up by the Wehrmacht to put the blame for defeat on other shoulders than those of the German General Staff. "Hitler's interference" may take the place of "the stab in the back." Major Shulman's account shows clearly that although Hitler's intuition was the greatest single factor in Germany's defeat, the Wehrmacht contained in itself fatal weaknesses which led to its utter defeat in battle in the West as in the East.

Future generations of Germans may again be taught to believe that the Wehrmacht embodied everything that was glorious in German history. It is essential that the truth about its overwhelming defeat, along with all the other ghastly details of the Nazi era, should not be allowed to disappear, least of all from the consciousness of the German race. Major Shulman performs a valuable service in bringing that truth so vividly to light.

The outstanding lesson that we must learn is that at all costs Germany must remain disarmed and demilitarized, incapable of selling her power to the highest bidder. The effects of militarism ingrained for generations, coupled with the debauchery of the last twelve years, will not easily be eradicated. Constant vigilance will be needed. The urgency of this lesson is apparent when one sees the rapid growth of natural sympathy for the German people in their sufferings. We must never allow the Germans to profit by this sympathy to build up once more the ruthless war machine that so nearly achieved the domination of Europe. Another time there might not be a Hitler to misdirect the strategy, and the General Staff might eradicate its weaknesses. The really formidable power of a nation of soldiers would then be fully developed with fatal results to civilization.

CONTENTS

LIST OF ILLUSTRATIONS

PLATE I. Field Marshal Werner von Blomberg with Colonel General
Hans von Seeckt
At a ceremony in Berlin in March 1935 are Field Marshal von
Mackensen, Hitler and Field Marshal von Blomberg, Colonel
General von Fritsch, Göring and Admiral Raeder
Inspecting a guard during manœuvres in August 1938 are Colonel
General Blaskowitz, Field Marshal von Rundstedt, Field Marshal
von Brauchitsch and Hitler

PLATE II. Colonel General Franz Halder, Chief-of-Staff of the German
Army, September 1938 to September 1942
Field Marshal Fedor von Bock, Commander Army Group 'B' in
France (1940) and Army Group South in Russia (1941-42)
Colonel General Werner von Fritsch, Commander-in-Chief of the
German Army, February 1934 to February 1938
Hitler and his field marshals, August 1940: Field Marshal Keitel,
Field Marshal von Rundstedt, Field Marshal von Bock, Reichs-
marshal Göring, Adolf Hitler, Field Marshal von Brauchitsch, Field
Marshal von Leeb, Field Marshal List, Field Marshal von Kluge,
Field Marshal von Witzleben and Field Marshal von Reichenau

A STUDY IN VICTORY AND DEFEAT

PLATE III. Victorious Generals: Field Marshal von Rundstedt, Com-
mander Army Group 'A' in France (1940), Army Group South in
Russia (1941), Commander-in-Chief West (1942-45); Field
Marshal von Leeb, Commander Army Group 'C' in France (1940),
Army Group North in Russia (1941); Field Marshal List, Com-
mander Army Group 'A' in the Caucasus (1942)
Defeated Generals: Field Marshals von Rundstedt, von Leeb and
List as prisoners-of-war

PLATE IV. Field Marshal Erwin Rommel, Commander 'Afrika Korps'
(1941-43), Army Group 'B' in France (1944)
Colonel General Kurt Student, Commander Army Group 'H'
(1944-45), Commander-in-Chief German Airborne Troops
(1943-45)
Adolf Hitler congratulating Admiral Raeder, Field Marshal von
Brauchitsch, Field Marshal Keitel and S.S. Reichsführer Himmler
at Berlin in April 1941

PLATE V. S.S. Brigadeführer (Major General) Kurt Meyer, Commander
12 S.S. Panzer Division 'Hitler Jugend'
General Günther Blumentritt, Chief-of-Staff to the Commander-
in-Chief West (1942-44), Commander Twenty-fifth Army and
First Parachute Army (1945)

Field Marshal Rommel in May 1944 inspecting 21 Panzer Division led by Lieutenant General Edgar Feuchtinger

PLATE VI. S.S. Oberstgruppenführer (Colonel General) Joseph 'Sepp' Dietrich, Commander Fifth Panzer Army and Sixth S.S. Panzer Army
Colonel General Heinz Guderian, Commander-in-Chief East (1944), Chief-of-Staff of the German Army, July 1944 to May 1945
Field Marshal Walter Model, Commander Army Group North and Army Group Center in Russia (1944), Army Group 'B' in France (1944-45)
Colonel General Ludwig Beck, Chief-of-Staff of the German Army (1936-38), and military leader of the 20 July assassination plot against Hitler

PLATE VII. Field Marshal Günther von Kluge, Army Group Center in Russia (1943), Commander-in-Chief West (July-August 1944)
Field Marshal Albert Kesselring, Commander-in-Chief South (1942-43), Commander-in-Chief South-west (1944-45), Commander-in-Chief West (March-May 1945)
Colonel General Alfred Jodl signing the surrender terms on behalf of the German Supreme Command at Rheims on 7 May 1945. At the extreme right is Admiral Hans von Friedeburg

PLATE VIII. Wehrmacht (rear view), Nuremberg, September 1936
Wehrmacht (*front view*), The Elbe, May 1945

(These plates, which are all in one Section, will be found following page 144.)

MAPS

PREFACE

To write the story of the Allied victory in World War II, while not an easy task, is a relatively straightforward one. The documents have all been carefully preserved, the official reports are being written, the personalities are available to contribute their dispatches and memoirs. The historian or reporter needs only to dig amongst the files, find the relevant facts, and present his version of them. To write the story of the German defeat in World War II, at this early stage, is unfortunately a little more complicated. Documents have been destroyed, lost and hidden. Personalities are dead, disappeared or in prisoner-of-war camps. They produce no official reports, no autobiographies, no historical publications. Whatever is therefore written about the Wehrmacht less than two years after its final defeat must of necessity be incomplete. Much is still to be obtained from those Germans alive to tell the tale, and much will yet be derived from the mountains of documents waiting to be translated, classified and analyzed. It will be many more years before a complete history of Germany's part in the last war will be written.

Having thus sweepingly apologized for what this book does not contain, let me hasten to add what it does contain. Ambitiously enough this volume was begun with a threefold object — to tell the story of the defeat of the German Wehrmacht in the West, to suggest some of the causes that brought about that defeat, and finally to show how men, both great and small, react to the overwhelming, psychological experience of defeat itself. Supplementary to this hydra-headed purpose, but seriously influencing the book's final shape, was the desire to present it in terms intelligible to the reader whose military vocabulary had been acquired only by the reading of newspapers.

How I have gone about so diverse a task can best be seen by a cursory examination of the Table of Contents. The first section of the book is concerned primarily with examining the causes of the defeat of the Wehrmacht by tracing the story of German militarism from Versailles to Stalingrad. The second, and largest, section of the book is a relatively detailed account of the battles in the West from the invasion of Normandy to the surrender at Rheims. In this latter part I have included the letters, diaries, exhortations and propaganda written by men about to lose, in an attempt to depict the suffering, disillusionment and despair that must be faced by a modern armed force before it goes down to defeat.

For the student of military affairs some explanation as to my source material might be in order. As an intelligence officer serving at the headquarters of First Canadian Army it was my responsibility to read and collate the intelligence summaries and reports issued by Allied formations in Northwest Europe, and from them estimate the strength and location of enemy forces opposing the Canadian army. A list of these Allied intelligence documents is contained in the bibliography at Appendix 'B.' The bulk of the German papers quoted in this book were derived from this source.

Following the surrender of the German armed forces I was given the task of interviewing senior German officers who had fought in Germany and France, with the object of acquiring from them their version of what had transpired in the West. This information was to be used to supplement the official historical record of Canadian participation in World War II. The names of the German officers with whom I have spoken in this regard are listed in Appendix 'A.' To forestall any objections as to the reliability of statements made by captured enemy officers, I would like to point out that I have included in this volume only such statements as have appeared to me to be accurate on the basis of the available documentary evidence and on an examination of the attendant military circumstances.

While it is true that those who have suffered defeat will tend to excuse their mistakes by blaming someone else, and German generals were no exception to this rule, nevertheless it was possible for me to cross-check most of what they told by comparing it with statements from other German officers, and by the study of contemporary documents. As a matter of fact, most senior officers of the Wehrmacht were eager to relate the stories of their military careers. There were two main reasons for such generous co-operation. In the first place, they were anxious to explain their own particular, personal rôle to posterity. Since it would be a very long time before German historians would be able to hear their tales, they felt that an Allied version of their experiences was, at least, better than no version at all. The second reason was undoubtedly the sheer relief from boredom afforded by an opportunity to speak to someone other than the regular inmates of their own prisoner-of-war camp.

On the whole I believe it is fair to say that the statements of these men were reasonably truthful. Knowing that it was relatively easy for their interrogators to verify most of the facts, there was little to be gained in lying. Thus they usually told their story as they had seen it, with an occasional coloring of the account so that they personally would appear in the most favorable light. If the facts were much too damaging from their own particular standpoint they merely refrained from discussing them. Whatever juggling that may have been done with the truth was done in the form of acts of omission rather than those of commission.

In these pages I have endeavored sedulously to follow the thin, middle path of literary effort that appeals to both the serious student and the casual layman. The text has been freed, as much as possible, of detailed references to military formations or technical strategical problems which would be of little interest to the non-specialist reader. But for those who are interested in the minutiæ of military history, a number of notes and references have been appended.

The folly of war as an instrument for the settlement of national disputes is acknowledged by every intelligent man. Just how senseless and futile an expedient it really is can usually best be judged by those who have lost rather than by those who have won. There were no more fervent worshippers of Mars than the officers of the German Wehrmacht. They represented the disciplined, military mind carried to its logical, uncurbed end. It would be foolish not to recognize that similar minds still exist, not only amongst the defeated, but amongst the victors as well.

It is important therefore to realize what pathetic and petty figures these men really were who masqueraded behind their gaudy uniforms and strutted before the world as conquerors. It is important because we hear today, on all sides, similar narrow and pompous men advocating the use of force to resolve all social and political problems. Because they have been victors once, they are convinced they will be victors always. If moral considerations alone are not capable of curbing such views, perhaps the sobering prospect of defeat might. For it is sometimes forgotten by those who talk glibly of another war that every war entails the risk of defeat. And if there are any who are still in doubt as to what defeat in the twentieth century really means, the rubble of German cities and the plight of the German people should provide a vivid object-lesson.

That lesson would be more impressive still if it could but be appreciated that the pain and destruction suffered by the Third Reich in the second World War is but a fraction of the pain and destruction that awaits both those who win and those who lose a third World War.

DEFEAT IN THE WEST

Part I ⸗ THE CAUSES

Chapter I

MEN MAKE WARS

THIS is a story of defeat. It tells of men who fought, who were beaten and who fled. As such it is a gray story. There is no pink mist of glory to color the deeds of the vanquished such as so often envelops the tales of the victors. Defeat brings with it disloyalty, cowardice, brutality, inefficiency and death. Sometimes, but not as often, it displays courage and faith. Usually it produces truth. The winners can afford to conceal their failures; the losers are eager to explain theirs.

Rarely in history has an armed force been as thoroughly beaten as was the German Wehrmacht in the years from 1939 to 1945. The record of that defeat has been left in the exhortations, the oaths, the orders, the diaries, the letters, the speeches and the confessions of the men who suffered it. And it is in these words, from the mouths and the pens of German soldiers from private to field marshal, that the real account of the military collapse of the Third Reich can be found. For they disclose not only the errors and mistakes by which Germany blundered to defeat, but they also reveal the reactions of a modern armed force to defeat. How men accept victory is a tale often told. How they accept failure is less often told for it is seldom as heroic or as significant. The story of why Germany lost World War II and how it felt to lose it, as it was told and felt by those who were a part of the defeated Wehrmacht, is the purpose of this book.

It is inevitable that the physical and spiritual demands made on men who are losing are far more exacting than they are on those who are winning. In the same way that we can only be certain of the amount of air a rubber balloon can hold by pumping into it sufficient air to burst it, a man's faith and ability can only be truly tested when he has been subjected to enough pressure to destroy that faith and ability. If this be true then it follows that a defeated Wehrmacht should provide a better picture of its real worth than a victorious one would have done. For here one should be able to see just how capable were the men who made it up, and what sacrifices they were willing to make for the cause for which they fought.

It is obvious that men make wars. The corollary that men lose wars is a truism that is often forgotten. The popular tendency at the moment is to identify all man's military achievements with the machine. The aeroplane, the tank, the battleship, radar and the atom bomb amongst others are all credited by various proponents with having been the decisive factor in winning the war for the Allies. It seems to be felt, in some quarters, that given enough aeroplanes, or enough battleships or enough atom bombs, any power could guarantee for itself ultimate victory in a future war. But the story of Germany's defeat in World War II convincingly destroys such theories.

Germany had sufficient machines to have assured victory for herself more than once during this war, yet she failed. This view has been expressed over and over again by leading military personalities in the Wehrmacht. They propound it every time they talk about Germany's greatest military mistakes—and each general suggests a different one. Some say it was allowing the British to escape at Dunkirk, others the failure to invade England in 1940, others the refusal to invade Spain and seize Gibraltar, others the attack on Russia, others the failure to push on and take the Suez when Rommel was at El Alamein, others the stupidity at Stalingrad, and still others the disastrous strategy adopted at Normandy. At each of these decisive phases, except perhaps the last, Germany had sufficient material strength to have enabled her to defeat her immediate enemy or to have prevented that enemy from defeating her.

Yet why did the superior power of these machines not prevail? Because the men who controlled them lacked either the courage or the faith or the imagination or the ability to make them prevail. It is a fundamental principle of war that to win battles superiority of machines and men must be brought to bear at the right time and the right place. German strategists failed to carry out this tenet time and time again. Why, then, did these men who guided Germany's destiny make blunder after blunder until victory became impossible? In the answer to that question, rather than in the quantity and quality of machines, is the real reason for the fall of Germany in World War II.

The causes of the defeat of the Reich were substantially either political or military. The evidence and judgment of the Nuremberg Tribunal has done much to clarify the political reasons behind Germany's collapse. The military reasons, while obviously subordinate to political events, have not been given the same searching scrutiny and therefore still remain relatively obscure. The discriminating and scientific study of psychologists, sociologists and soldiers will undoubtedly produce the answers. But what evidence have we now on hand to help the historians and students of the future? The men of the Wehrmacht themselves. And their evidence is both interesting and important.

If men make wars, what manner of men were these who led the armed forces of the Reich to its worst defeat in history? What fundamental causes forced the military leaders of Germany to act as they did for five years of war? Why did a group of men with more training, more experience and more passion for the art of warfare than any other contemporary group of similarly trained men fail to ensure the victory that was so often within their reach? It is suggested that at least three weaknesses existed in the framework of the Wehrmacht which combined to produce a defeated, rather than a victorious, Germany. These weaknesses might be summed up in three words — Hitler, discipline and ignorance. Let us discuss each in turn.

Chapter II

HITLER

The incredible situation of the political head of a state personally directing the tactical moves of an armed force fighting on fronts as far removed from each other as France, Italy and Russia was the military position revealed in Germany when the curtain of war was lifted in Europe. Brooding over a large-scale map in Berlin, Hitler had for five years made every important decision taken by the Wehrmacht. This fact was both the strength and the weakness of German military power. It gave to Germany astonishing victories in the early years; it was the prime factor in Germany's ultimate defeat. It was Adolf Hitler's genius that brought military success to the Wehrmacht. But it was from that self-same success that failure in far greater measure stemmed. Look which way you will, there is only one ultimate place to lay the wreath of German defeat — at the fateful but clumsy feet of Adolf Hitler.

How was it possible that a man, whose military career ended at the rank of corporal, was nevertheless able to command over 300 divisions in battle? How was an untrained visionary able to accept and reject the advice of field marshals as he alone saw fit? The story of the struggle between National Socialism and the German army provides the answer. Once the Reichstag had been dissolved and a

fascist dictatorship had become a political reality, the one organization still able to furnish effective opposition to National Socialism
was the officer corps. Hitler was determined to either convert it or
break it. He partially, but not completely, achieved the conversion.
He definitely succeeded in breaking it. But by forcing the German
General Staff to yield to him, Adolf Hitler subjugated and rendered
impotent the only body of men capable of shielding and saving him.
With the National Socialist victory over the traditional military hierarchy, Germany's fate was sealed. For it convinced the Führer that
he was a soldier.

Before the war began it is extremely doubtful that Hitler considered himself a military leader. But on climbing the ladder to total
domination of the Reich he was forced to make political decisions
which involved important military considerations. Up until February
1938 the General Staff had still to be treated with the caution and
regard due to a dangerous adversary. But in that month by the dismissal of Field Marshal von Blomberg, the Minister of War, and
Colonel General von Fritsch, Commander-in-Chief of the German
army, the officer corps was relegated to the rôle of a tool, to be wielded
by Adolf Hitler in the shaping of a National Socialist Germany. By
this move the Wehrmacht had been purged of the leaders of the
aristocratic Prussian army who resented Hitler, not so much for his
ambition, as for his being a crude Austrian paper hanger whose coarse
methods they could not stomach.

One of the first political matters before the Führer that contained
serious military problems was the crisis of the Sudetenland in 1938.
A number of senior officers were concerned that Hitler's policy
towards Czechoslovakia would bring about a war with France.
Colonel General Ludwig Beck, Chief of the General Staff, along
with a number of others compiled a report showing that German
military strength could not possibly stand up to the large French
armies then in existence, and recommended that the aggressive attitude of Hitler be modified lest it lead to war. In the summer of 1938
Beck was dismissed. The Four-Power Conference at Munich thoroughly vindicated Hitler's view that the Sudetenland affair would
not set off a major war. Such 'unjustified' opposition confirmed in
Hitler's mind his opinion that the officer corps was a reactionary
group that was neither as courageous nor as able as himself.

Then followed Poland where again a political and a military problem were combined. Politically Hitler was completely wrong in his
assumption that England would not go to war over the Polish Corridor. But in the military sphere he again confounded his military

advisers by a lightning victory over Poland during which the French provided no trouble in the West. By now Hitler was prepared to rely on his own intuition in military matters, although he still pretended to listen to the advice of the experts about him. The feasibility of launching an attack against Norway was questioned by the General Staff and once more Hitler proved it could be done. In the plan to invade the Low Countries and France, Hitler again insisted that the offensive be taken and actually changed the military plan by which the forces were to carry out this large operation. There was deep resentment amongst senior officers against such brash and reckless behavior, but when France collapsed those who had opposed his plan could only shake their heads and admit that he had been right.

These matters will all be discussed at greater length in a subsequent chapter, but they are reviewed here to explain the stages by which Hitler's domination in military affairs became complete. He had proved brilliantly successful in his ability to recognize merit in military theories. He adopted Colonel General Guderian's radical new theories on armored warfare and encouraged their adoption in the face of a traditional backwardness in regard to technical improvement on the part of the General Staff. He was able to pick out the bold plan and force it to a successful conclusion without the reserve and caution of the expert. Staff officers began to admit that it was his recklessness and dash which were behind the German strategic moves of the time. They even began to believe that he possessed some inexplicable intuition which enabled him to guess right when the cold logic of the facts seemed to indicate he was wrong. What was worse, Hitler began to believe all this himself. A huge propaganda campaign in the press and radio extolled the Führer as the greatest military genius of all time. This thunderous eulogy, besides convincing the German public, also convinced Hitler that he was another Alexander or Napoleon. From then on he was always right. Whenever his senior officers cautioned him against any course of action, he always had the perfect answer, "Remember Czechoslovakia! Remember France!"

With the fall of France Hitler's military career had reached its zenith. The next five years were all downhill. He made mistake after mistake, but like a losing gambler at a gaming-table he kept frantically tossing the dice hoping that the winning number would turn up again. It never did. But he never really believed that his luck had left him. The abandonment of the plan to invade England in 1940, the declaration of war against Russia, the fiasco at Stalingrad, the childlike strategy in France, were all the personal decisions of the

Führer. They were often made in the face of the most strenuous opposition of the commander on the spot, and were rarely supported by any logical military considerations.

As failure followed failure Hitler became more morose and alone. He began to suspect that he was being betrayed by those under him, and he came to rely more and more on his own judgment even in the most minor matters. On one occasion Hitler, quite oblivious of what he was doing, ordered a concentration of armored units in a town in Russia. The result was a fantastic number of tanks in a very small sector. In the confusion that followed, Hitler ordered the court-martial of the corps commander concerned. It was pointed out to the Führer that he, himself, had planned the manœuvre. "Where did you read that?" snarled Hitler of the officer who had made the observation. "In the war diary," came the reply. That ended the matter. But on the same day the historical section of Hitler's headquarters was told that in future no reference was to be made to Hitler's operational orders in the war diary, nor was his interference in operations ever to be referred to even by implication. Six stenographers were henceforth employed to take down all discussions, briefings and orders in the operations room and to type out one copy only. This, in the special large type designed for Hitler's farsightedness, was kept locked in his own personal safe to which he alone had access. This transcript of the conversations held in the operations room often came in useful to Hitler when dealing with recalcitrant generals.[1]

From broad, sweeping decisions involving major strategy, Hitler was soon delving into detailed tactical matters which concerned relatively minor formations and unimportant sectors. His belief in his own infallibility was so firm that if an operation like the order to capture Moscow failed, his only explanation for the failure was the incompetence or the cowardice of the commander conducting the operation. It rarely occurred to him that the strategical plan might have been impossible in the first place. As a result he not only made the big decisions but tried to ensure that the methods by which they were carried out conformed with his own views. By the time the Allies were ready to invade the Continent every senior German officer was so hamstrung with restrictions and threats from Berlin that any initiative could only be exercised on the very lowest levels. In Normandy this interference reached such a stage that operational orders began to arrive from Berlin setting out, not only the units to be involved in an attack, but the sectors they were to occupy and the routes they were to use. By the time the Germans had been forced back to the Rhine, Hitler had taken over personal and complete com-

mand of all fighting in the West. On the 21 January 1945 Field
Marshal von Rundstedt issued the following top secret order.[2]

Supreme H.Q. West, G-3 No. 595/45.   21 *Jan*. 45.
                                                   Top Secret.
s/v Rundstedt.

The following order by the Führer is quoted in its original text:

1. The Commanders of Armies, Corps and Divisions will be personally
responsible for all of the following types of decisions or intentions reaching
me early enough to enable me to exercise my influence on such decisions
and for a possible counter-order to reach the front-line troops in time:

  (i) any decision involving an operational movement,
 (ii) any projected attack of divisional size or larger which is not covered
      by general orders issued by Supreme Headquarters,
(iii) any offensive action on an inactive front exceeding normal patrol
      activity and apt to draw the enemy's attention to that sector,
 (iv) any projected movement of withdrawal or retreat,
  (v) any contemplated abandonment of a position, a fortified town or a
      fortress.

2. The Commanders of Armies, Corps and Divisions, the Chiefs-of-
Staff and every single General Staff officer or staff officers will be personally
responsible to me to see to it that any report addressed to me directly or
through channels will contain nothing but the blunt truth. In the future I
will drastically punish any attempt at veiling facts, whether done on purpose
or through negligence. . . .

                              /s/ ADOLF HITLER.

To such a pass had come the proud German officer corps. Their
field marshals and generals virtually could not move their troops
backwards or forwards without first obtaining the permission of the
corporal they had despised. Never had military commanders been
so stripped of authority nor so ruthlessly and contemptuously treated.
It was the price they had to pay for helping to sabotage the Weimar
Republic in order to satisfy their ambitions for a nationalist, militant
Germany. In their eagerness to destroy democracy they spawned
a child destined to commit parricide.

It is interesting to speculate on what might have occurred had the
political head of a democratic state attempted to interfere with or
override his military leaders. Let us assume that Churchill had insisted that Field Marshal Montgomery attack at El Alamein two
months before the latter thought it advisable. In the first place Field
Marshal Alanbrooke, Chief of the Imperial General Staff, would
probably have approached Churchill on Montgomery's behalf and

suggested that the field commander knew best. If this failed, a meeting of the Chief-of-Staff Committee representing the heads of all the services would have asked Churchill to back down. Meanwhile someone might have approached Attlee, as Leader of the Opposition, or some other member of the War Cabinet to ask him to use his influence in getting the Prime Minister to reverse his decision. By that time, Churchill would undoubtedly have seen he was wrong and yielded, but probably not before some newspaper had hinted at differences of opinion within the War Cabinet and awkward questions had been asked in the House. All this would have brought heated and eloquent denials of any dissension and the operation would have gone on as originally planned.[3]

This would be the cumbersome and irritating process of democracy at work. Not so imaginative and dramatic as the bold wave of the dictator's hand galvanizing a nation into disciplined action. But it provided those restraints that prevented a single man's mistakes from catapulting a state into disaster. The virtue of the democratic method is that judgments reached under the illumination of free discussion are usually both comprehensive and sound. There is seldom the need to reverse a decision as so often happens when that decision is based on intuition alone. True, a democracy will often be slower to act than a dictatorship. But in the long run, as most German generals will now agree, it is by far the wiser way.

Chapter III

DISCIPLINE

WITHOUT discipline an army cannot function. Too much discipline, on the other hand, is likely to strangle it. The German army had too much discipline. Both its officers and men obeyed blindly and without question the orders of their superiors. This they continued to do even when faith in victory had gone and logic told them their efforts were useless. Very rarely did a subordinate revolt against a command or refuse to obey a senior officer. Even when circumvention of a command was the only sane course to take — particularly towards the end of the war when Hitler took over complete control — military leaders always managed to obey the letter of the order even though they avoided its spirit. So ingrained was the German soldier's submission to authority that any sidestepping of this kind was always accompanied by a rationalization in which the officer concerned justified his conduct as having literally conformed to the orders he had received. It was only by the knowledge of the fact that he had not disobeyed a command that his professional soldier's conscience could be clear. It was of secondary importance that he had acted humanely and had thereby saved men's lives.

It was this rigid discipline within the Wehrmacht that enabled the army to fight on for so long. But it was this same discipline that prevented it from taking the necessary steps to overthrow the forces driving Germany to destruction. Months before the war was over the bulk of senior officers realized that to go on was senseless. Yet so powerless had they become, and so incapable were they of opposing the political authority, that the best they could produce in the way of a real protest was a bungled assassination plot a bare nine months before the end of the war.

Since the Versailles Treaty had restricted the new German army to only 100,000 men, its new leaders were determined to make up in quality what they lacked in quantity. Setting themselves up as a caste apart, they formed a small, select inner circle of military experts with a moral and social code of their own. The commander and chief designer of this clique, Colonel General Hans von Seeckt, firmly believed that an efficient army must be completely divorced from politics. This view tended to isolate the professional soldiers from contemporary civilian thought. Although born to protect the Weimar Republic, it soon became obvious that the officer corps was in no way in accord with the principles of social democracy sponsored by the foundling government. In fact most of the officers were contemptuous of such principles as being weak and un-German. The army became a vocation and its officers came to owe their allegiance to it rather than to the government which it was supposed to serve. When Hitler abolished the constitution of the Weimar Republic, the German officer corps acquiesced in this political murder by doing nothing to prevent it. They believed that their ambition to enlarge the army and free themselves from the humiliating bonds of Versailles was far more likely to be achieved through Adolf Hitler than through the democratic Reichstag. Their loyalty followed their ambition.

To maintain such allegiance an iron discipline was imposed within the officer corps which brooked nothing but subservience to authority. Orders of a superior were to be obeyed without question, and any break from tradition was seriously frowned upon. Not only was their military life strictly supervised, but their personal life was also subject to an unrelenting social code. This adherence to a rigid standard of customs and morals was used by Hitler with startling results in his struggle to subject the German General Staff to his will.

The marriage of Field Marshal von Blomberg to a woman of questionable reputation created the crisis by which Hitler was able to rid himself of both von Blomberg and von Fritsch, both of whom had strenuously opposed him. A less publicized instance when Hitler took advantage of the officer corps' impeccable moral code was in the case of the divorce of Field Marshal von Brauchitsch. The rule was that if an officer was divorced because of his own misconduct he would be expelled from the corps. Von Brauchitsch fell in love with another woman and he asked his wife to provide the necessary grounds so that he could divorce her. She refused. He went to Hitler with his problem. The Führer told the wife that it would be advisable for her to do as she had been asked, and he also made a financial settlement with her. The result was an expensive moral obligation which was owed to Hitler by one of the leading members of the officer corps. Hitler did not hesitate to remind von Brauchitsch of this debt on subsequent occasions.[1]

This high standard of social conduct was demanded even during the war. It was always the aim of the German General Staff to create all officers in the same mould so that their reactions would be unvaried and therefore reliable. Even as late as April 1943 a school for artillery officer cadets published an order on behavior in society which contained items such as these:[2]

(1) *Paying a Visit.*
Visiting hours 11.30-13.00 hours on Sundays, 17.00-18.00 hours on week-days. Never later and never in the afternoon. . . .
On entering a room carry hat in left hand. On taking a seat lay the hat down. . . .
Coming and going: Length of visit should be about ten minutes. Do not look at your watch. No reason should be given for termination of visit. On leaving do not turn your back on the company when opening the door.

(2) *Entertainments.*
Wine: White wine to be drunk from tall glasses, red wine from short glasses.
Dances: First dance and quadrilles always with dinner partner. Never dance continually with one and the same lady.
Flowers: To be unwrapped in the hall. Never presented with the paper round them. In presenting flowers hold the stalks downwards. . . .

(3) *General.*
At races, the officer himself must never approach the totalizator. . . .

That these methods succeeded in producing loyalty and discipline within the army is undoubted. But these automatic and impersonal creatures of the officer corps were so obsessed with the omnipotence of authority that they were hypnotized by its very presence. To live was to obey. There was no other end in life. To challenge the Supreme Commander of the armed forces, Adolf Hitler, was unthinkable. And in any event their training prevented them from even knowing how.

Since it was improbable that opposition to the political authority would come from within the officer class of the army, the question remains whether some such initiative might not have come from the rank and file. The Russian Revolution of 1917, although its initial impetus came from civilian sources, showed that modern armies may turn against the constituted authority even in defiance of their military leaders. It was confidently expected by many military leaders that disintegration of the forces in the field would follow in the wake of an unsuccessful war. This result was based upon the historic examples of Austria in 1918 and Russia in 1917. But it is fair to say that although the Wehrmacht suffered a military defeat such as has not been equaled in modern history, at no time was there any suggestion of an organized revolt amongst the men in the ranks. This, despite the fact that they were badly led in a hopeless cause, and suffered catastrophic casualties and incredible hardships. The combined ingredients of Prussian discipline and Nazi propaganda produced this result. The reason that the German soldier did not revolt is not to be found in his loyalty. He did not revolt because he was bullied, threatened, drugged and duped so intensely and so persistently that his powers to resist or object were utterly destroyed. It was discipline and ignorance, not loyalty, that kept the German soldier in the field until May 1945.

For this achievement the officer corps must take their due share of credit. Being prepared to obey blindly themselves, they also demanded obedience of those whom they led. The German, ever since the days of Frederick the Great, has feared and respected the military class. It was therefore natural that a conscripted German soldiery should very easily accept the discipline demanded by a cult of professional soldiers. The philosophy of complete submission to a leader had, indeed, been strengthened by the advent of National Socialism and its theory of the 'Führerprinzip.' The officer corps made a fetish of discipline and therefore killed any latent resistance that might have sprung from the ranks of a soldiery raised by universal conscription.

The 'Duties of the German Soldier' proclaimed by Hindenburg

in 25 May 1934, and re-issued unaltered in 1942, was to be known by heart by every soldier. The first four paragraphs of this catechism ran as follows:

(i) The Wehrmacht is the arms-bearer of the German people. It protects the German Reich and Fatherland, the people united in National Socialism, and its living space. The roots of its strength lie in its glorious past, in German nationhood, German soil and German labor. Service in the Wehrmacht is honorable service for the German people.

(ii) The soldier's honor is embodied in the unconditional surrender of his person for people and Fatherland even to the sacrifice of his life.

(iii) The highest soldierly virtue is martial courage. It demands hardiness and determination. Cowardice is disgraceful, hesitation unsoldierly.

(iv) Obedience is the foundation of the Wehrmacht, confidence the basis of obedience. . . .

The individual is nothing; the state is all. This was the creed to which both National Socialism and the German armed forces subscribed. If obedience was 'the foundation of the Wehrmacht' then it follows that discipline was the means by which that foundation was built. The officer corps ensured that the discipline they cherished so much in themselves was also rooted in the men who served under them. It was achieved by a rigorous insistence on military form and bearing which never relaxed even when the inevitability of defeat was all about them. Thus in 1944 in France it was possible for a Colonel Göllnitz to issue a German district order, a part of which read:

Again and again I meet soldiers in the department of Eure who, as cyclists, do not keep their legs stiff when saluting. This is against orders when the bicycle is free-wheeling and the journey is not uphill.

Or for a Major General Conradi to drive through the streets of Krivoi Rog in Russia and force all soldiers who failed to salute him or who were improperly dressed to run behind his car. It was said that there were always thirty to forty soldiers running after the general's car. After two or three kilometres Conradi would stop, take down the names of the defaulters and put them all on a charge.

Instances of this kind could be cited again and again. But let us compare what effect such actions as the two mentioned above would have had on a democratic army. In England an incredible clamor was raised by press and public when it was discovered that an officer was insisting that his men shout "Ho de ho" each time he cried "Hi de hi."

And in America the slapping of a private soldier by General Patton created a crisis which almost forced General Eisenhower to fire his most successful commander.

The difference lies, of course, in the fact that while Englishmen and Americans are prepared, if necessary, to give up their lives for their ideals, they are never ready to give up their dignity as human beings. A fascist state like Germany was the perfect breeding ground for an army which thrived on discipline. For there was never any danger of interference with the army's methods from an indignant civilian population. And National Socialism demanded as much obedience as did the Wehrmacht. Once the German soldier had learned to obey instinctively and blindly it mattered not who gave the orders. The German General Staff, like Frankenstein, had built a monster of discipline which later helped destroy its master. They themselves could do nothing but follow the commands of their Führer, and the soldier they had created in their own image was as helpless as they were. There being no opposition from those who led the German armies, and none from those who formed them, the Austrian corporal was able to play madly at war with the sure knowledge that whatever he ordered would always be obeyed.

Chapter IV

IGNORANCE

THAT even Prussian discipline will disintegrate if sufficiently pummeled was shown by the attempt to assassinate Hitler on July 20, 1944. Although the active participants in this revolt were relatively few in number, it proved that Hitler had not acquired absolute obedience from all those who surrounded him. It is less a mystery that such a revolt occurred than that so few men took part in it. It is doubtful if any other government in modern times could have made so many mistakes and still have raised no more overt opposition than this ineffectual bomb plot against Hitler.

Once it is conceded that discipline is not an absolute thing and can be broken, then why were there so few generals involved in the affair of July 20? For if, as they now assert, they had the interests of their country at heart, why did they not oppose Hitler when it became obvious that he was leading Germany to destruction? Because when it did become obvious to them months before the end, it was then far too late. If discipline and loyalty to an oath prevented the German officer from rebellion, it was ignorance that cemented that discipline and loyalty so hard that it was almost impossible to crack. Rarely in modern warfare has there been a group of commanders so uninformed about both their own troops and those of their enemy as were the generals of the Wehrmacht in the second World War. It is because this ignorance played so vital a part in maintaining the discipline which kept Adolf Hitler in power, that it is included here as one of the major causes of the final defeat of Germany.

It is a primary principle of military tactics that a commander, in order to carry out his plan, must know as much as possible about his own troops and as much as is available about the enemy. In the Wehrmacht it was a deliberate policy to give a commander as little information as possible about his own side, and what was attainable about the other side was seldom adequate or seldom accurate. It is interesting to consider the circumstances which brought about such a state of affairs.

The war was hardly a few months old when a fortuitous event occurred which had far-reaching repercussions on the activities of German commanders. On the night of January 9, 1940, a German plane lost its way in a thick fog and landed at Mechelen-sur-Meuse in Belgium. The plane was on its way to Cologne from the headquarters of the Fourth Army in Münster. One of its passengers, a Major Rheinberg of the Luftwaffe, was carrying detailed plans for the invasion of the Low Countries. These papers revealed the part that the German air force and German parachutists were to play in the proposed attack. When the plane landed, Rheinberg ran behind a hedge and desperately tried to set fire to the documents, but a Belgian soldier snatched them away. Subsequently when he was being questioned at a Belgian headquarters Rheinberg again tried to destroy the papers by seizing them from off the commandant's desk and throwing them into a coal stove. But a quick-witted Belgian soldier plunged his hand into the red-hot stove and retrieved them before they had been badly damaged. From the scorched documents it was possible to piece together a fairly complete picture of the entire German plan for the invasion of the Low Countries.[1]

As a result of this incident a large-scale revision of the invasion plans had to take place. But a much more important result was an order which came from Berlin stating that under no circumstances was any commander to be informed of any operation which did not immediately concern him.[2] As the war progressed the terms of this order were taken more and more literally. A divisional commander knew only that which affected his own particular division. He would only be informed of what the divisions on his flanks were doing if their actions involved his operation. This restriction went all the way up the line from division to corps, to army, to army group. And it even held true for commanders-in-chief of the various fronts. Thus Field Marshal Kesselring in Italy never knew what reserves were available to Field Marshal von Rundstedt in France, and neither knew what was happening in Russia or how many reinforcements were still left in Germany.

Not only was an officer not to know of what was happening on other sectors, but he was to make no attempt to find out. The appalling lack of knowledge of the average senior commander of affairs which did not affect him operationally is sometimes incredible. No one was ever sure of what anyone else was doing and orders were carried out with nothing but the tactical information required for the immediate job. Divisions held fast in Normandy with no knowledge that the front on their left had been torn open and that they were being encircled; the Luftwaffe carried out sorties without notifying the troops over whom they flew, so that the men on the ground spent time and ammunition trying to knock down their own planes; officers in Italy were shocked to find that the vaunted Atlantic Wall was made of tissue paper and that Paris was empty of plentiful reserves. Colonel General Student, commander of Army Group 'H,' flanking the Ardennes offensive, knew nothing of the offensive until eight days before it occurred,[3] while divisional commanders only heard of it when it was announced over the German radio.

Compare this with Allied methods where Field Marshal Montgomery told every man under his command of his intentions twenty-four hours before the battle of El Alamein. Or try to imagine, if you can, General Bradley, commanding Twelfth Army Group in France, not being told that Montgomery was to carry out the parachute drops at Nijmegen and Arnhem until a few days before the operation was to take place. The constant and speedy flow of information between commanders about daily operations and future intentions was the lifeblood of Allied operations in Northwest Europe. Even relatively junior officers were aware of the broad strategical position at all times. This curtailment of news about their own troops in the German armies is therefore all the more difficult to understand.

It had two immediate results. It meant that no matter how high a rank was held, no officer in the field could approach Hitler and suggest a proposed operation was impracticable because of lack of

resources. Since no one, other than a small group of Hitler's immediate advisers, knew the true overall picture, no officer could produce
a reasonable argument against a future operation since he would not
have the required facts or statistics to support his contentions.

The second result of this policy of officially maintained ignorance
was that, not having any other information to rely upon, all officers
turned to Dr. Goebbels for their news. They listened faithfully to
his assurances that the German armed forces were strong and intact,
that the Allies were suffering catastrophic losses and that important
secret weapons were on the way. A man like General Alfred Schlemm,
commander of First Parachute Army, admits that when he heard
of the assassination attempt of 20 July he recoiled with indignation
at the news. Here, he reasoned, was another stab in the back by
traitors on the home front. What reason was there for such treachery
when the situation was stabilized in Italy, when the Allies were being
bled white in Normandy, when the Russians were being held in
the East and when plentiful reserves were in hand? So thought
Schlemm.

"I realize now how ignorant I was of the truth," Schlemm says
today.[4] "I see now that all the assurances of Goebbels were nothing
but lies, and that by July 1944 the war was already well lost. Hitler
alone knew this and he kept it from us. Had I known then what
I know now I would have had every sympathy with the assassins."

In addition to being kept in ignorance of what was happening on
their own side of the line, German commanders were woefully mis-
directed as to what was happening on the enemy's side. This was
due more to inherent defects in the training and methods of the
Wehrmacht than it was to design. It combined with the policy of
limiting operational information to produce one of the most badly-
informed groups of generals that ever conducted a major war. For
one of the most surprising, and at the same time most reassuring, post-
war revelations has been the fact that German military intelligence
was astonishingly inaccurate and ineffectual.

The omnipotence of the Fifth Column and the cunning of the
German agent have for years been the favorite topic of the adventure
novelist and the movie thriller. Both before and during the war the
shadow of a super-spy organization centralizing the work of such
dreaded agencies as the Gestapo, the Abwehr, the Sicherheitsdienst,
the Auslands organization, threatened the world with its ramifications and power. It should come, therefore, as a pleasant shock to
discover that seldom has a body of men been so overrated as the
German Secret Service under Admiral Canaris at Berlin. If it was the

ultimate function of the thousands of agents employed by the Nazis
to provide information which could be used by their military leaders
to conduct the war, they singularly failed in their purpose. Rarely
was an armed force so badly served by its intelligence service as
was the Wehrmacht during World War II.

The list of blunders is almost as long as the list of decisions that
had to be made. Even the German victories were won by disregarding
military intelligence rather than by heeding it. One common denomi-
nator that characterized almost all German generals was their astonishing ignorance of the strength and intentions of their enemies during the various campaigns of the war. There was hardly an important
battle that was not marred by faulty intelligence. The Czechs would
fight for the Sudetenland; the French were too strong behind the
Maginot Line; the English were too powerful to attack after Dunkirk; the Russians could not stand up to modern mechanized warfare;
the defenders of Stalingrad were too weak to stage a counter-offensive; the Anglo-American invasion of the Continent would come in
the Pas de Calais rather than Normandy. These are only some of the
wrong guesses made by the intelligence organization before whose
reputation the whole world had trembled.

The failure of German intelligence can be attributed to two main
factors. The first is the methodical Teutonic mind obsessed with
detail but never developing the ability to distinguish the true from
the false. Having successfully used the secret attaché case-champagne
bottle technique of the romantic spy story in their Fifth Column
activities on the Continent, they carried these methods over into the
military sphere. Agents by the score, masquerading behind false
beards and forged passports, worked feverishly in every capital city
of the world. The information they gathered flooded into Berlin where
it was tabulated, card-indexed and filed in the most thorough Germanic manner. But the German never learned to evaluate sources.
Every item that was received was kept, even if it was originally false,
until if it was reported often enough, it somehow became true through
the sheer force of repetition. Volume became more important than
reliability; the more facts the greater their accuracy. The result was
a fund of innumerable details neatly catalogued but having little real
worth because they had never been properly sifted.

A typical example of this process is the following excerpt from
an intelligence report sent by Army Group Southwest to the Tenth
and Fourteenth Armies in Italy.[5] It deals with the interpretation of
the words 'Blighty establishment,' which in this instance was simply
a soldier's expression to describe establishments which could be

found in formations stationed in England. Here is how German intelligence goes about it:

According to a prisoner's statement, the support battalion, recently incorporated in the English infantry division, is known in the jargon of the soldier as 'Blighty establishment.' The meaning of this designation is as yet not entirely clear. There are two possible derivations:

(a) The Indian word 'Bilati' meaning village or home, which during the World War turned up in the soldier jargon as 'Blighty' and was used to designate a wound warranting the return of the injured man to England.

(b) Blight meaning mildew, poisonous vapor or 'to blight,' *i.e.* destroy.

Since the transformation of the machine-gun battalion to a support battalion, the unit has been allotted 106.7 mm. mortars (4.2 inch chemical mortars), it seems reasonable to assume that the derivation discussed under (b) is applicable.

It is requested that interrogators determine whether the English designation 'Blighty establishment' is related to the aforementioned allotment of chemical material to the support battalion.

Here the plethora of facts available to the intelligence staffs provided them with so many irrelevant items that the odds were soon against their picking out the important and most reliable one. It is little wonder that the rigid Teutonic mind dominated by its card-indexes and blinded by its catalogues hit upon the wrong answer so often, and usually got the right one only by disregarding its intelligence altogether.

The second reason for the failure of German intelligence was the professional soldier's distaste for the opinions of those who handled the paper war. Having been reared in an atmosphere which held nothing but contempt for the civilian and his clerical associations, it was natural that the average officer viewed with suspicion any opinions of the men who did their fighting from behind desks in Berlin. As a result the German commander tended to replace intelligence appreciations with appreciations of his own. This meant that instead of weighing the facts and from them determining what the enemy might do, he placed himself on the other side and decided what he would do in their place. Since problems which were considered important to a German general were probably not nearly so important to an Allied one, such guesses as to enemy intentions could at best be only half right.

After the Canaris organization had made some stupid mistakes early in the war it found difficulty afterwards in having its views accepted even when it was right. In addition the generals in the flush of their first victories began to feel that intelligence could be disregarded without seriously affecting the battle. They never got into the habit of taking it seriously again, even when they were losing, at which time intelligence becomes not merely useful but essential.

A lieutenant colonel who was head of the German intelligence section called 'Foreign Armies West' describes this attitude on the part of the old-line generals in these words:

> My appreciation (that the Dieppe raid in August 1942 was not the fore-runner or part of a serious Allied invasion effort) was not approved by General Zeitzler, the Wehrmacht Chief-of-Staff and therefore not published. The reason for this was that General Zeitzler, as former Chief-of-Staff in France, had expected a large-scale invasion of France, in spite of the appreciations of my department which expressed the opposite view. . . .
> Our appreciation that the British could not mount a large-scale offensive at a time when they were deeply committed in North Africa was also ignored. The Dieppe landing strengthened both Zeitzler and Keitel in their convictions. Both in France and in the rear, I was present at conferences in which my chief tried to persuade the High Command of the actual object of the operation. When my paper was laid before the Chief-of-Staff for approval he said, "The Foreign Army West section seems to spend too much time producing papers. It should occupy itself with more constructive work."
> Towards the end of 1943 my chief and I were summoned at least once a month to conferences of the Joint General Staff of the Wehrmacht. We were always surprised at the completely illogical under-estimation of the Anglo-American forces, and the equally illogical over-estimation of the potentialities of the German defense force in France, Norway and the Balkans. Formations were continually being transferred to other theatres. Consequently my chief agreed to step up our estimate of the number of British divisions in order to counter this all too optimistic tendency of the Joint General Staff. . . .[6]

Now to recapitulate briefly what these first few chapters have been trying to say. There were many occasions during World War II when Germany, had she taken another course, could have been victorious. On each of these occasions the German nation was in possession of sufficient material resources to win. Yet it failed. The reason for its failure lies in the fact that the German military leaders who were responsible for conducting the war were unable to use effectively their superiority when they had it. There were three fundamental weaknesses in German military leadership. First they allowed Hitler to become not only the supreme political but the supreme military authority in the land. Secondly, their discipline and personal code prevented them from revolting against the head of the state, and they impressed this discipline so deeply upon the rank and file that they, too, were unable to organize any active opposition to Hitler. And thirdly, this discipline was never subjected to any serious strain because officers and men were kept so sublimely ignorant of what was taking place on both sides of the line that they never knew enough to resist.

In the early years of the war too much ignorance, too much discipline and too much Hitler were responsible for the mistakes that robbed Germany of the victory that she almost, but not quite, achieved. In the last year of the war when victory was no longer possible, and only the shadow of ultimate defeat remained, these same three factors brought to Germany needless destruction, despair and death. Because this is a story of defeat, emphasis will naturally be placed upon the final year of the war when defeat was no longer a prospect but a reality. But before one can fully understand what brought about the collapse of the Wehrmacht, it is essential to know what the Wehrmacht really was and how it came into being. Having done that let us then consider the fatal steps by which Germany brought about her own defeat, and finally how a year of defeat was suffered by the German armies in the West.

One other thing must be said before proceeding any farther. The furnace in which the defeat of the German armies was forged was the vast Russian theatre. There, two-thirds of the total German armed strength was constantly engaged and systematically destroyed. Lack of space prevents anything more than very sketchy references to these great battles. But it can reasonably be said that the story of the German defeat in the East does not in any material way differ from the story of the German defeat in the West. It may have been more extensive and more bitter, but it could hardly have been more final or more complete.

Chapter V

THE WEHRMACHT IS REBORN

THE war was over but peace had not come to Germany. It was November 1918. A disgruntled army officered by men who were sure they had not been beaten, but had been stabbed in the back by those at home, had just completed an orderly withdrawal in the West while still holding on to what they had conquered in the East. A Socialist government, partially trying to demobilize a huge, disaffected army, found the task too much for it. It called upon Field Marshal von Hindenburg, the head of the German armed forces, for help in the technical problems of bringing the troops back from the front. Von Hindenburg's staff carried out the assignment with the ease born of experience and training, and thus averted the chaos which would otherwise inevitably have overrun the country. But by this act a new government had admitted its reliance upon the officers of the old school and had thereby linked the Imperial General Staff with the Republic.

Instead of this association becoming weaker in the ensuing months, it became stronger. The shaky Socialist government was being threatened on all sides, but most persistently by groups of demobilized soldiers and sailors led by Communists. To meet this threat, the government had two alternatives — either to organize a citizen army of its own, officered by men it could trust, or call upon the professional soldiers still loyal to the traditions of the old Imperial régime. It chose the latter. The reasoning of the government is summed up in the following words of Herr Noske, the majority Socialist leader at the time.

"It is our misfortune," he wrote, "that no leader has risen from the ranks of the N.C.O.s or the common soldiers, despite the fact that power was everywhere in their hands. I have been obliged to fall back on the officers. Certainly many of them are monarchists, but when one is faced with reconstruction, one must have recourse to professionals. An army without discipline is a monkey's grimace. Between a bad Socialist officer and a good Conservative officer I choose the second." [1]

Thus instead of the liquidation of the old officer corps, it was hurriedly revived under the name Free Corps with a mandate by the Socialist government to repress all opposition. This it successfully did.

The Spartacus Revolt in Berlin in January 1919, led by Liebknecht, was suppressed by mortars and flame-throwers. In February working-class rebels in Bremen and the Ruhr were overwhelmed. In March the Free Corps used tanks and planes against another uprising in Berlin. An attempt to set up a Soviet government in Bavaria led to the killing of over 1000 civilians in Munich. Quickly joined by unemployed adventurers and men grown fond of soldiering, the Free Corps, all of whom were volunteers, became increasingly more aggressive and more brutal in their suppression of disorders. And what was worse; they developed an *esprit de corps* of their own and an allegiance to their officers which was completely divorced from any sense of loyalty to the government. As a matter of fact, their only political faith was contempt and hatred for the Socialist movement which had overthrown the German Empire they had served.

From quelling street riots, the Free Corps soon graduated into full-blooded battles against the Russians in the Balkan States and the Poles in Poland, who were both trying to seize German territory, so that the Peace Conference would be faced with a *fait accompli*. It was from this group of irresponsible, swashbuckling men that the bullying gangs of the latter day Hitlerite S.A. and S.S. drew their most promising leaders. The influence of the Free Corps on the future of Germany may best be judged by listing some of its members: Göring, Hess, Roehm, Rommel, von Manstein, von Küchler, Ramcke, Bormann, Frick, Dietl, von Epp — to mention but a handful. It is unquestionable that the Free Corps was one of the two important elements that not only formed part of, but also helped determine the character of, the Wehrmacht of World War II. The other element was the 100,000 army.

The immediate post-war future of the armed forces of the German Republic was laid down in the regulations contained in Part V of the Treaty of Versailles. Under them, general conscription was abolished and the Imperial army was to be replaced by a force of 100,000 volunteers, who agreed to serve, if other ranks for twelve years, and if officers for twenty-five years. The sole purpose of this army was to maintain the internal security of Germany. The navy was reduced to an impotent size, and no air force whatever was to be permitted. The General Staff was to be dissolved.

Yet instead of stifling the military ambitions of Germany as was its design, the Versailles Treaty encouraged them. For not only did it set up a small clique of men whose profession was soldiering, and could be nothing else, but by its very restrictions it imbued this group with yearnings to put into practice the art which they had so thoroughly mastered. Anyone, therefore, who promised them aid in freeing them from the bonds of Part V of the Versailles Treaty was bound to receive their implied support.

The Free Corps and the 100,000 army together furnished the leaders of a resurgent Wehrmacht. It can be safely said that with but few exceptions, every man who attained the rank of a German general in World War II, received part of his early military training as a junior officer or N.C.O. in one or the other of these two organizations. Most of them saw service with both. The better type of men were enlisted with the 100,000 army. The bully and the adventurer who loved the crude brutality of the Free Corps, later found full scope for his ambitions in the ranks of the S.S. and the Brownshirts.

A very common misconception, which might well be cleared up, is the view that the German General Staff was a mystic, military order confined to a small clique of master minds. Actually every officer in the German army was eligible for membership in the General Staff. If his ability warranted it, he was sent on a rigorous two- to three-year course dealing with the technical problems of warfare, after which he tried a series of competitive examinations. Once accepted into the General Staff it meant that he was then capable of performing the complicated administrative tasks required at the headquarters of various formations.

Except for the occasional training trips he was obliged to take, a series of lectures which he attended one afternoon a year, and the scarlet band down his trouser leg, there was nothing to distinguish the General Staff officer from the regular officer serving in the field. Of course, a man with General Staff training was more likely to get ahead because of his more extensive military education, but a large proportion of German officers attained general's rank without ever being accepted for the rigorous academic course of the staff college.

The General Staff influence on the army lay in the strictness and aloofness of its traditions. These had been laid down by Colonel General Hans von Seeckt, who was Chief of the Army Command until October 1926. He maintained that the army must be completely divorced from politics, and to carry out this principle it was forbidden for a soldier to vote, to belong to a political party or to take part in political demonstrations. The result of such a policy was that the army began to owe its allegiance, not to any civil government which happened to be in power, but to itself. When a conflict arose between its own immediate interests and those of the government it was serving, it was naturally more likely to sacrifice the interests of the government. Such a situation presented itself with Hitler's coming to power. The promise of an unrivaled military force free from the restrictions of Versailles was the reward set before the officer corps, for their non-intervention during the last days of the German Republic. Having no ideological attachment to the government which had nurtured them in the post-war years, the officer corps did not find it difficult to yield to the temptations offered by National Socialism. They sat by and did nothing while the Weimar Republic slowly bled to death.

It is fair to say that the great bulk of the German General Staff participated in Hitler's rise to power merely as spectators. In a struggle between the democratic elements of the Republic and the fascist elements of the National Socialists, the conservative Prussian officer could find himself sympathetic with neither side. He was not prepared to lift a finger to help maintain a politically left Reichstag, and while the nationalist sentiments of Hitler held a definite appeal, his ardor for National Socialism was dampened by the coarseness of Nazi leaders and Nazi methods. It was with mingled contempt, indifference and superiority that the officer corps learned, on 31 January, 1933, that Adolf Hitler had become the new Chancellor of the German Reich.

Then began the real struggle for power within Germany. The one group of men still able to provide effective opposition to National Socialism was the officer corps. Hitler knew this well and he was resolved either to convert it or break it. First he tried the former plan. An intensive propaganda drive, especially designed to meet the nationalist and military ambitions of the General Staff, was carried out in the army. Lectures by Goebbels, Rosenberg and others were delivered to the entire officer body, and all manner of subtle flattery was attempted. It had only limited success.

The first concrete alignment between Hitler and the General Staff took place during the blood purge of June 1934. Roehm who was the leader of the S.A. or 'Brownshirts' had attempted to undermine the General Staff by constantly objecting to its lukewarm attitude to National Socialism. He had actually accused it of plotting to gain political power. Hitler, upon the advice of Himmler, decided to back the officers in this dispute, and ordered the murder of Roehm and his associates. The army assisted in quelling the riots amongst the Brown-shirts, only to find when the shooting was over that some of their own number, like Generals von Schleicher and von Bredow, had been eliminated as well.

The uneasy partnership into which the General Staff had entered, in order to rid itself of a rival, became more uneasy in the ensuing months. The National Socialists refused to absolve the generals murdered during the riots of participation in the Roehm conspiracy. Their propaganda efforts became even more strident and more crude than before. Their interference in economic and military affairs became more persistent and more irksome. Then followed a severe blow — the death of Hindenburg in August 1934. Twenty-four hours later Adolf Hitler was appointed Supreme Commander of the German armed forces, and the entire officer corps delivered their oath of allegiance to him.

Chapter VI

HITLER VERSUS THE GERMAN GENERAL STAFF

Just over six months had passed when, on 16 March 1935, Hitler made official and public what had been going on secretly ever since he came to power. With a stroke of the pen he declared Part V of the Treaty of Versailles invalid, reinstituted general conscription, ordered the army to be increased to over five times its size and announced the existence of the German air force. The War Ministry was reorganized and the activities of all the armed forces were co-ordinated under it. The War Ministry subsequently was renamed the Oberkommando der Wehrmacht (O.K.W.) and the service heads were called Commanders-in-Chief of the army (O.K.H.), the navy (O.K.M.) and the air force (O.K.L.). Hitler was Supreme Commander of the Wehrmacht, and he appointed Field Marshal von Blomberg as his War Minister, while Colonel General von Fritsch became the Commander-in-Chief of the army.

The next few years were busy ones for the officer corps. The rearmament programme as laid down by Hitler, outdistanced even the most ambitious plans of the military leaders. Hardly had one budget been approved when it was replaced by a larger one. More divisions were formed, more planes built, more war factories were put into production. The German General Staff viewed this trend with considerable satisfaction, although they were a little perturbed that the speed of the program might result in its being inefficiently carried out. There was also cause for concern in the growing strength of the National Socialists. The old Imperial traditions were being replaced by strange Nazi ones, and the pressure to convert the new Wehrmacht to the 'new order' was greatly increased. Under the leadership of their Commander-in-Chief, von Fritsch, the General Staff opposed these overtures and continued to remain aloof and superior in their relationships with the political upstarts governing the country. The

views of the officer corps during these important years are clearly outlined in an attempted defense of the General Staff written by General
Walter Warlimont, Chief of the Joint Planning Staff of the Wehrmacht.[1] As the deputy to Colonel General Alfred Jodl, Hitler's principal adviser on planning and strategy, Warlimont, perhaps more than
any other officer, was in a position to witness the struggle between
the army and the National Socialists. Discussing the reactions of the
General Staff to these events, Warlimont has this to say:

"Though it would be entirely wrong to interpret the attitude of
the General Staff towards rearmament as a consent to preparations
for war, it certainly should not be denied that every General Staff
officer was anxious to take leave of the wooden cannon and the paste-
board tank — a measure of liberation from a shameful imposition. It
was also the General Staff who asked for aircraft and heavy guns
as a necessary part of German armament. . . .

"The substitution of the swastika for the recently regained black,
white and red flag was a slap in the face, and it meant nothing to us
that the color scheme remained the same — a fact Hitler used to
emphasize. We found the swastika strange and un-German. In addition, we disavowed the claims that National Socialism was responsible for the new Wehrmacht, and were openly pleased when Colonel
General von Fritsch, in a public address (Bremen, 1936), declared
that it was the 100,000-man army and its officers who alone had kept
up military spirit and knowledge.

"We accepted without fully understanding, the consequences of
the Nuremberg Laws, which entailed the dismissal of capable popular
officers and their sons. . . . Simultaneously, it was learned that National
Socialist bosses were personally enriching themselves through such
proceedings, and this widened the breach between the party and the
new army. Gradually the General Staff officer found it necessary to
acquire some sort of a stabilizing influence and he began to look
to Hitler, in contrast to his followers, as the new hope for Germany.
In addition to the rearmament program, the peaceful reoccupation
of the Rhineland enhanced Hitler's personal reputation within the
officer corps, since this move corresponded to the fundamental policy
of the army. . . ."

But despite Warlimont's protests that all this was not to be interpreted as 'preparations for war' there is sufficient evidence to show
that that was what it undoubtedly was and, also, that the leaders
of the Wehrmacht were entirely aware of Hitler's future plans for
the military machine that was being assembled so feverishly. It is true
that they protested against some of these plans, but never because
they were ideologically opposed to war or Hitler's ambitions. Their

advice was always based on strict military principles, rarely on humanitarian ones. If they opposed one of Hitler's decisions it was because they thought it impracticable — not because they thought it immoral. Warlimont himself unwittingly displays this frame of mind in his discussion of Germany's armed intervention in the Spanish Civil War which had begun in July 1936.

"On returning from Spain in December 1936," he writes,[2] "I was ordered for the first and only time before the war to attend and take part in a conference of Hitler's. I then succeeded — supported by von Fritsch and von Blomberg, but opposed by the ambassador to Spain, Faupel — in convincing the Führer that it would be unwise to send several large units of the German army to Spain. Hitler's explanation at this time was that the German soldier in Spain had not been called upon, as he believed, to offer his life in the fight against Bolshevism, but rather that, by his interference in Spain, German foreign policy would be strengthened for other political aims — such as the rearmament program. At that time I considered this a smart political move, but I could not help feeling shocked that German soldiers who had died in Spain had been so grossly deceived. . . . "

But the most concrete evidence that the leaders of the Wehrmacht were well aware of Hitler's aggressive intentions, and that the armed forces were not merely being strengthened for a defensive rôle within the borders of the Reich, is contained in a document headed 'Notes of a Conference held in the Reich Chancellery on 5 November 1937.'[3] Here at a select meeting, confined to Hitler, the War Minister von Blomberg, the three service heads — von Fritsch, von Raeder and Göring — the Foreign Minister von Neurath and a Colonel Hoszback, the Führer outlined his ideas on future German expansion. His statements on this occasion were to be regarded as his last will and testament in case of his death.

The fundamental problem facing Germany, Hitler began, was *Lebensraum* (living space). Since Germany's future could not be assured by either economic self-sufficiency or by an increased share in the world's commerce and industry, the need for living space was imperative. Consequently, "the question for Germany was where the greatest possible conquest could be made at the lowest cost." But since both England and France could not tolerate a strong Germany, it would only be possible to acquire living space by the use of force. And this was "never without risk." If, however, this was the only solution, the only questions to be decided were "when and how" force would be used.

Hitler pointed out three occasions when he felt Germany's aggressive moves could be made with the least risk. The first occasion was the period 1943-45. By then the rearming of the army, navy and air force would be practically complete; the equipment and material of the armed forces would then be modern, but from that time on would be increasingly out of date; and it would be difficult to maintain the secrecy of special weapons indefinitely. As other nations would have started to rearm by this date, a decrease in relative power could be expected. Although the actual situation in 1943-45 could not be predicted; nevertheless, Germany would lose more than she would gain by waiting any longer and it was therefore the Führer's "irrevocable decision to solve the German space problem no later than 1943-45."

The second occasion when Germany could act with comparative safety was a serious political crisis in France preventing the employment of the French army against Germany. That would be the moment for action against Czechoslovakia. The third occasion was if France became involved in war against "another state," in which case, again, Czechoslovakia could be attacked.

Hitler then assessed the probable behavior of France, England, Poland and Russia in the event of German action against Czechoslovakia and Austria. Britain was far too concerned, said Hitler, with her own Empire problems to become involved in a long European war, and France would not fight without British support. Poland, with Russia in her rear, would not dare engage a victorious Germany. Only Russia might act, and if so, then Germany would have to meet such a threat by speedy military operations.

Hitler also felt that the civil war in Spain was to Germany's advantage, since it maintained tension in the Mediterranean and might even lead to war between Italy, on the one hand, and France and Britain on the other. If such a war did develop, then Hitler was prepared to exploit this opportunity by lightning action against Austria and Czechoslovakia.

Throughout this entire discourse in which the ruthless, aggressive aims of National Socialism were clearly revealed, not a solitary murmur of a moral protest was heard from any of the military personages present. The only matters that worried von Blomberg and von Fritsch were strategical ones. They were rather sceptical of Italy's ability to hold the combined forces of France and Britain, and they were not as convinced as the Führer, that Britain would not intervene on the Continent. But aside from these military considerations they could apparently see nothing wrong with the predatory ambitions of Hitler so coldly outlined to them. Despite the fact that events enabled Hitler to follow a course different from that set out in this remarkable document, it clearly shows the common knowledge of aggressive aims shared by the political and military leaders of the Reich. The minutes of this meeting should decisively destroy any future claims by the German General Staff that they were simple soldiers merely being faithful to their oaths and that they did not realize whither the policy of rearmament was leading them.

The central figure in the next phase of the struggle for power between Hitler and the Wehrmacht was Colonel General Werner von Fritsch, Commander-in-Chief of the army. A haughty aristocrat, stocky and square-faced in appearance, he was Conservative, hard and aloof. His conscious arrogance, heightened by an ever-present monocle, made of him a perfect model for all those fictionized, heel-clicking German officers so loved by romantic novelists. Utterly contemptuous of the Nazis, their leaders and their methods, he did not hesitate to show his disdain even towards the Führer himself. He personified and epitomized the last ditch stand of the German officer corps against complete domination by Hitler.

He was outspoken in his opposition to many of Hitler's wishes and, on occasions, was tactless and even rude when dealing with the Führer. Thus when Hitler appeared at Saarbrücken, to receive the homage of his people following the successful occupation of the Rhineland, the atmosphere of awed respect shown to the Führer by Himmler, Hess and others was suddenly broken by the abrupt appearance of a high-powered Mercedes in the town square. Out jumped von Fritsch, gave Hitler a stiff military salute, obviously ignored the proffered hand of greeting, uttered a hasty perfunctory report, saluted again, turned on his heels, marched stiffly to the car and drove off. Conduct such as this inevitably led him into conflict with the party leaders, particularly Himmler. It was the latter who finally succeeded in bringing about his downfall.

The occasion which brought this hidden conflict to the surface was the marriage of War Minister von Blomberg to an unknown stenographer. Von Fritsch, who had begun to suspect that von Blomberg was coming more and more under Hitler's influence, decided that von Blomberg had outlived his usefulness. He also resented the fact that von Blomberg had let down the General Staff by taking unto himself a bride of such lowly origin. He collaborated with Himmler in producing a police dossier of the woman's past which showed that not only was the wife of the War Minister of common birth, but that she had been a prostitute as well. When Hitler, who had attended the wedding as a witness and thus given the affair his blessing, was shown this dossier, he flew into a terrible rage and immediately dismissed von Blomberg. To prevent von Fritsch from receiving the

War Ministry appointment, Himmler then produced for Hitler evidence which purported to prove that von Fritsch was a homosexual. The 'proof' had been secured from an ex-convict party member and had obviously been arranged by Himmler himself. Faced with such immoral conduct on the part of his two most senior army officers, Hitler's solution was the removal from office of both von Fritsch and von Blomberg. This date, February 4, 1938, marked another turning-point in Germany's pre-war history, for now the chief obstacles to the political indoctrination of the army had been removed. Such opposition as still remained amongst officers of the German General Staff could easily be disposed of.

The infamy of the methods adopted to remove von Fritsch is revealed in a series of letters[4] written by him to his sweetheart, Baroness von Schutzbar-Milchling, a cousin of Dr. Meissner who was then German Secretary of State. When von Blomberg was dismissed, von Fritsch seems to have suspected that he was somehow also involved. Early in February he wrote:

... of my own affair I don't know very much. Only that the resignation of von Blomberg has some connection with me. I have the impression that the Führer ... has decided, during my absence, to remove me very shortly. ...

The proceedings at his trial for homosexuality were described to the Baroness in a letter from Berlin, dated 23 March, 1938:

... the trial I demanded began on the 3rd. Because of the events in Austria it was postponed until the 17th, and completed on the 17th and 18th. The verdict read: "Proven not guilty as charged, and acquitted." The judges were Göring, Brauchitsch, Raeder and two senior members of the Judge-Advocate's Department. In view of the facts, this verdict was inevitable. Finally, which was rather miraculous, they managed to find the fellow who had been dragged out to testify against me. Even Göring was forced to admit that after the proceedings no one would believe in my guilt. As a climax, at the very end, the star witness, on whose testimony everything was fabricated, admitted that all his statements were given under duress and were pure lies. ... The background of this whole affair has become quite clear to me; but I am powerless to defend myself. ...

But despite his acquittal, Colonel General von Fritsch was relieved of his command and reduced to the rank of a colonel.

On 4 September, 1938, he wrote again:

... Dr. Meissner (Secretary of State) has undoubtedly told you about it in poignant terms. Perhaps he has also told you that I gave Herr Hitler my word of honor that the accusations were untrue. Herr Hitler has lightly tossed aside the word of honor of the then Commander-in-Chief of his army, in favor of the word of an honorless scoundrel. He has also not found a single word of apology for me. It is this, above all that I cannot countenance. ...

Although the latter part of von Fritsch's story does not fit chronologically in the narrative, it is worth relating. In August 1939, on the eve of war, von Fritsch had this to say to the Baroness:

> . . . For me there is neither in peace nor in war any part in Herr Hitler's Germany. In this war I will accompany my regiment only as a target, because I cannot stay at home. . . .

And shortly afterwards from the Polish front came an intimate personal letter to the Baroness which ended ". . . This will be my last letter. . . ."

Many accounts of the death of von Fritsch have been told. The most common one was that he had been shot in the back by some of Himmler's men. The true story is told by one of von Fritsch's adjutants.[5] He went to Poland as a company commander of the regiment which bore his name. When the battle outside Warsaw was at its height, he walked out with his adjutant far ahead of his troops. Things became so hot that the adjutant finally took cover and shouted out to Fritsch: "Duck, Colonel, duck." Von Fritsch refused to stop. In a few seconds he was severely hit in the thigh and in a matter of minutes bled to death unattended. So died the once Commander-in-Chief of the German army. With him died the last formidable and active opposition to Hitler's Reich. He left behind him an officer corps, groveling and helpless before the man whom they had, at first, disdained, but who had finally broken them.

A few months later, in June 1938, a final feeble effort to resist Nazi domination was made. This foray was led by Colonel General Beck, the army Chief-of-Staff, a capable and efficient officer very highly regarded in the General Staff. Hitler, at a conference of senior officers, had presented a plan for the invasion of Czechoslovakia in the event that political negotiations failed to solve the Sudeten crisis. Beck took the lead in drafting a warning memorandum opposing Hitler's prospective course of action. Not only was the military plan considered unfeasible, but, in addition, it was stated that an act of aggression of this kind would bring in against Germany the combined might of France, United States and Great Britain. Against such a force Germany would have no chance. Beck, also, repeated his opinion that not earlier than 1943 could Germany be sufficiently rearmed to carry out a defensive war against France.[6] Most of the responsible officers in the Wehrmacht, including men like Field Marshal von Rundstedt, endorsed this memorandum. Hitler's reaction was violent and decisive. He dismissed Beck, issued a call to arms without consulting the General Staff, and carried on with his plans for Czechoslovakia. Beck did not, like von Fritsch, decide that suicide was the only thing left for him. He plotted a more tangible protest and died by his own hand only after the assassination attempt of 20 July 1944 had failed. But more of that later.

Now what was the result of this spate of dismissals in the hierarchy of the Wehrmacht? Its most important result was the firm entrenchment of Hitler's position as the dominant force in the state, not only in the political but in the military field as well. Hitler found it distressingly easy to find replacements amongst the General Staff for these men he had removed. And because they came on Hitler's terms, rather than their own, their authority was commensurately decreased. Field Marshal von Keitel replaced von Blomberg as head of the Wehrmacht, but his power was considerably curtailed since Hitler, who had formerly been merely the nominal Supreme Commander as the political head of the state, now took over the immediate direction of military affairs as his own personal responsibility. In other words, to adopt again a familiar analogy, he exerted the combined power of President Roosevelt and Secretary of War Stimson rolled up into one.

To succeed von Fritsch as Commander-in-Chief of the army, Hitler chose Field Marshal von Brauchitsch, an abler and more polite man than his predecessor. Although very popular with the General Staff, Hitler nevertheless hoped that von Brauchitsch would be more amenable to the Führer's policies. Von Brauchitsch lasted a little over three years, when a disagreement over strategy in Russia in December 1941 resulted in his dismissal. Hitler's appetite for military power now having been thoroughly whetted, he assumed, in addition to all his other responsibilities, the post of Commander-in-Chief of the army. This unprecedented step gave to Hitler the swollen authority of a Supreme Commander, a Minister of War and an army Commander-in-Chief, or, to return to our analogy, the combined responsibility of Roosevelt, Stimson and General Marshall. Having made of himself a martial trinity of such dimensions, Hitler had irrevocably underwritten his personal responsibility for Germany's defeat.

The ease with which Hitler was able to fill the vacancies of his higher military establishments is a sad commentary on the idealistic pretensions of the German General Staff. On no occasion did they present a unified front against the aggressive policies of Hitler which they believed were leading their country to disaster. The best they could produce were isolated protests by isolated individuals whom Hitler was able to handle and destroy one at a time. The bulk of the General Staff excused their docile acceptance of these events on two grounds. The first was that military obedience, traditional discipline and faithfulness to their oath prevented them from rebelling against the political authority and, conversely, bound them to accept the posts offered them when their comrades had been dismissed. The second ground was that their obligation to the German people and the world forced them to remain within the Wehrmacht and attempt to maintain the influence of the General Staff. Rashly to have opposed National Socialism would only have meant an end on the gallows or in a concentration camp, which would then have left Germany to the mercy of stark and undiluted Nazism. It seems never to have occurred to them that a strong, united stand on the part of all military leaders, opposing the Führer's aggressive policies, might have effectively curbed Hitler's ambitions, and at the same time made it impossible for him to wreak vengeance on them as individuals.

This failure to combine against Hitler was probably due to a third reason, which General Staff officers never volunteer themselves. It is that ambition is a most effective solvent of ideals. When it can be rationalized as loyalty too many men will be tempted to adopt the camouflage in order to achieve their personal desires. To discipline, add fear, a pinch of idealism and a generous helping of ambition and you will have the recipe that rendered the German officer corps impotent and encouraged Hitler to proceed with his mad plans for world conquest.

Chapter VII

THE PHONEY WAR

MUNICH saw the justification of all of Hitler's arguments. Britain and France yielded to German pressure and the Sudetenland was returned to the Reich. The officers who had shown such alarm about Hitler's strategy were discredited and discomfited. More than a little abashed they sat back and watched the next political moves without daring to interfere. And by now they were beginning to be much more amenable to Hitler's direction. The Führer's political victories had been more successful in converting the officer corps than all the propaganda efforts of Goebbels. General Warlimont puts it this way: [1]

The occupation of Czechoslovakia in the spring of 1939 was an almost purely political matter — the military part of it being of a more or less routine nature. Nevertheless, it is interesting to note that those of the General Staff who had been against this move now appeared to have been wrong. From a psychological viewpoint it was now easier to guide the General Staff in preparing for action against Poland. In addition the regaining of Danzig and the reunion with East Prussia was an aim of all Germans, even the General Staff, as Foch had foreseen after the Versailles Treaties. The separation effected by the corridor, and the intransigent attitude of Poland when approached on the subject of the revision of the German eastern border placed Germany under a restraint unparalleled in history.

How easy it had become "to guide the General Staff in preparing for action against Poland" was only too evident by subsequent events. On 3 April 1939, a directive was issued by the Supreme Command to the armed forces, which, after referring to military preparations already ordered for the occupation of Danzig, went on to discuss 'Fall Weiss,' the code name for the German invasion of Poland. This directive stated that: "The Führer has added the following directions to Fall Weiss: (1) Preparations must be made in such a way that the operations can be carried out at any time from 1 September 1939 onwards. (2) The Supreme Command of the armed forces has been directed to draw up a precise timetable for Fall Weiss and to arrange by conferences the synchronized timings between the three branches of the armed forces."

But if this were not enough to convince the General Staff that Hitler's course was set for aggressive war, the important conference held in the Führer's study in the Reich Chancellery on 23 May 1939 should have provided final proof. Like the minutes of the meeting of 5 November 1937, when Hitler set forth his current views on the action to be taken against Czechoslovakia, the report of this conference sets out the Führer's intentions in regard to Poland.[2] Some fifteen representatives of the army, navy and air force were present at this conference, including Göring, Raeder, von Brauchitsch, Keitel, Halder and Warlimont. After analyzing the political situation Hitler claimed that the quarrel with Poland was not over Danzig at all. It was a question of acquiring more living space for Germany and of securing her food supplies.

"Poland sees danger in a German victory in the West," said the Führer, "and will attempt to rob us of that victory. There is therefore no question of sparing Poland, and we are left with the decision: to attack Poland at the first suitable opportunity. We cannot expect a repetition of the Czech affair. There will be war. Our task is to isolate Poland. The success of the isolation will be decisive. . . . The isolation of Poland is a matter of skilful politics. . . ."

Hitler then went on to consider the possibility of Great Britain and France coming to Poland's assistance. If, therefore, the isolation of Poland could not be achieved, Hitler believed that Germany should attack Great Britain and France first, or at any rate should concentrate primarily on the war in the West in order to defeat Great Britain and France quickly. As to Russia's actions in the event of an attack on Poland, Hitler said, "It is not impossible that Russia will show herself to be disinterested in the destruction of Poland." He concluded his remarks by emphasizing that a war against the Western Powers might well be of "ten to fifteen years duration," and that plans would have to be made accordingly. And as at the Führer's conference on Czechoslovakia, his military advisers listened to all this with not a dissenting voice, and finally left the meeting to busy themselves with their preparations for the next war.

But there seems to have been no unanimity of opinion amongst senior officers as to Germany's capacity to conduct a full-scale war in the autumn of 1939. Von Brauchitsch, as Commander-in-Chief of the army, apparently felt that Germany could handle France, Britain and Poland. But he warned against adding Russia to the list. The danger of a two-front war was conceded by everyone. Hitler accepted von Brauchitsch's view in this instance and did not press his claims against Poland to a military decision until he had secured his Russian frontier. The result of this reversal in political strategy was the Russo-German pact which enabled Hitler to proceed with his plans in the West.

Not all generals were as sanguine about Germany's ability to hold both France and Britain as von Brauchitsch. Amongst those who were apprehensive about a lengthy war were such important men as Generals von Schweppenburg, Warlimont, von Salmuth, Felmy and von Wühlisch.[3] Hitler realized that this fear existed in the ranks of the General Staff and tried to abate it by logical and convincing arguments proving that France and Britain would not interfere if Germany forced Poland to yield. On the 22 August 1939, Hitler announced to an assembled meeting of generals and General Staff officers his definite decision to make war against Poland. There was much head-shaking amongst the officers when the meeting was over, but, bound to their military oaths, they all hurried back to their troops to make plans for the big day.

The lightning campaign in Poland fulfilled the most optimistic hopes of both Hitler and his generals. The Führer's interference in the preparatory planning was not of any great moment, nor did it seriously affect operations which achieved success on every side. Not only was victory quick in the East, but it was attained with only negligible interference from Germany's enemies in the West. Opposing the Maginot Line the Germans gambled with some twenty-three divisions to hold any offensive action on the part of the French. The

French did nothing and Poland was overwhelmed. In a story of the defeat of Germany the Polish campaign has little place.

But once Poland had given in, the General Staff seems to have returned again to its cautious approach to military operations. A memorandum was drawn up by the Deputy Chief-of-Staff of the army, General Heinrich von Stülpnagel, showing that an offensive war against France was impossible. General Warlimont was busy assembling facts to prove that economically Germany was only capable of protecting her borders. Even von Brauchitsch, whose original advice was optimistic, now strenuously opposed a large-scale offensive in the West. The latter's objections seem to have been based on the view that the time was not yet ripe for a grand assault, and that a period of proper preparation should expire before the Western Allies were tackled. Hitler's plans were completely different. Attack immediately, defeat France before winter and quickly end the war — that was the way Hitler wanted it done. Hitler's failure to have his way in this regard resulted in the so-called 'phoney war' which dragged through the winter months of 1939-40. The activities that went on behind the German lines during this static period of war while the world comfortably settled down in expectation of long, dreary years of trench warfare, are related in some detail by General Warlimont.

"Following the collapse of the Polish armies," he writes,[4] "the Führer returned to Berlin and as early as September 1939 assembled in the Reich Chancellery, the Commanders-in-Chief of the army, navy and air force and the Chief of the Wehrmacht, together with their closest advisers, to announce his decision to attack and crush France before the end of autumn 1939. (Hitler used slips of paper with jottings as reminders, and burned them in the open fireplace after the conference.) The preparations were to be concluded within six weeks, by early November. I no longer remember the details of Hitler's operational instructions; they aimed at turning the Maginot Line at its strongest-built parts in the north, by repeating the World War I advance through Belgium, but this time including the Maastricht corner of the Netherlands. No objections were raised.

"Again the deployment of troops according to these orders had to be improvised, since no plans existed. While the troops were moving west without any important interference, the army General Staff arrived at the conclusion that the first order to cross the Franco-German border would have to be given seven days before X-Day. General Brauchitsch arrived at the Reich Chancellery and demanded to see the Führer in private. It was a Sunday early in November 1939. By chance I was present in the Reich Chancellery, representing General Jodl, who was ill. Hardly half an hour later Brauchitsch left, and Keitel was called in to the Führer. Keitel told me later that Brauchitsch had reported on conversations with his army commanders during a trip to the West which he had just concluded; in a written reply Brauchitsch attempted to convince the Führer that his intention to attack France was impracticable — at least at the time intended, the autumn of 1939.

"However, when he reached the point in his report alleging that the aggressive spirit of the German infantry in Poland had lagged seriously behind that of World War I, Hitler was deeply offended because of his pride in the National Socialist education of German youth, rudely interrupted Brauchitsch, and forbade him to continue his report.

"The Führer's indignation over Brauchitsch's statements was so great and enduring that it was forgotten to decide whether the opening of the campaign should be ordered. After the Führer's departure I asked Keitel about it, pointing out that the order would have to be released by one o'clock in the afternoon. Keitel then rushed after the Führer, and returned with the decision that the order ought to be given at once, presumably setting 12 November as X-Day. When I thereupon telephoned the order to Brauchitsch's headquarters, I was asked for a written confirmation, since the order was incomprehensible to them in view of the report which the Commander-in-Chief of the army had just rendered to the Führer. . . .

"When the order to march had to be suspended two days later because bad weather was forecast, a period of increased distrust began. It is a meteorological fact that weather is always bad during this season in Central Europe — especially in the West; the most exact and detailed weather reports were submitted daily by the armies in the West; they supplemented reports by the air force, which had not yet become an object of Hitler's suspicion; and yet Hitler was not satisfied that it really was the weather situation and not the opposition openly voiced by Brauchitsch which further delayed the opening of operations. The series of intervals of first three then five days from one decision to the next led to a lasting restlessness, diverted attention and effort from more important problems and steadily undermined the small stock of confidence which the General Staff had in the Supreme Command. Furthermore, there seemed to be a leak which had several times let the enemy know of these decisions.

"It was about this time that I made an attempt of my own to influence the course of events by initiating negotiations with the Western Powers through the King of the Belgians. It was not until mid-

December when the system of postponing the day of attack every few days was finally abandoned, that other operational details could be considered. . . ."

Thus it was that even in the very earliest days of the war Hitler began to influence and direct military operations. In 1939, however, he was still susceptible to argument. The opposition of his generals and the weather had been sufficient to cause him to reverse his decision about attacking before the winter. But as the war grew older he began to rely less and less on those who advised him, until finally he shut himself off completely from everyone and acted autocratically upon his own intuition alone.

The invasion of Norway was predominantly a naval operation. Only a relatively small part of the army was involved. The General Staff seemed to have frowned upon the idea as much too risky, but Hitler, fearing an attempt by England to set up air and naval bases in Norway, insisted that the invasion be launched. Again, in a tale of defeat, the brilliant success of the Norwegian campaign can find little place. But for the sake of continuity it might be worth while to present the German reasons for this assault on 9 April 1940. Admiral Krancke, who in 1940 commanded the *Admiral Scheer* and who in 1943 was responsible for organizing the naval defenses of Western Europe, had written a short account of the German naval point of view. He had this to say about Norway.[5]

"The danger that England would, as in 1918, close the entrance routes to the Atlantic, and perhaps settle forces in Norway in order to obtain bases there for the air force, led to our decision to counteract this measure by occupying Norway and thus gain access to the Atlantic. It was hoped that we should be able to achieve our military aims without any extensive military operations and without making war on Norway, and at the same time without encroaching upon her political freedom. When we got reports that England had similar intentions, and the total disregard for Norwegian territorial waters in the case of the *Altmark* made it quite clear what Norway's relations with England were, the operations for the Norwegian campaign were prepared. It is true that this operation required only small land forces, but it was possible only with the co-operation of the entire German navy and the High Command. The High Command was in no doubt about this; but here was a task for the German vessels which was strategically worth while.

"How right this decision was, was proved when, immediately after the English mines had been laid in Norwegian territorial waters, a similar invasion was undertaken by the English, but was broken off

when the German ships were sighted. The orders, captured later in
Lillehammer, gave full confirmation of this. The success of the Norwegian campaign, in spite of temporary reverses in Narvik, obviated
the danger of being hemmed in with mines or threatened from Scan-
dinavia or Denmark."

But the view that the Allies intended to occupy Norway before
the Germans did has been soundly rebutted by the unanimous verdict
of the tribunal at Nuremberg. For it is there pointed out that when
the final orders for the German invasion of Norway were issued, the
diary of the Naval Operations Staff for 23 March 1940, records that:
"A mass encroachment by the English into Norwegian territorial
waters . . . is not to be expected at the present time." And another
entry by Admiral Assmann on 26 March states "British landing in
Norway not considered serious." Summing up its discussion of the
events that led to the attacks against Norway and Denmark, the
judgment at Nuremberg concludes: "In the light of all the available
evidence it is impossible to accept the contention that the invasions
of Denmark and Norway were defensive, and in the opinion of the
tribunal they were acts of aggressive war."

Chapter VIII

VICTORY — AND DEFEAT

WITH the abandonment of the decision to launch a full-scale attack in
the West before the winter of 1939, Hitler began to look again at the
plan which was designed to break the Maginot Line. It had been
prepared by the General Staff under the direction of von Brauchitsch
and his Chief-of-Staff, Halder. No fewer than four army groups were
involved, with Army Group 'B' under von Bock on the right wing
opposite the Low Countries, Army Group 'A' under von Rundstedt in
the center facing the Ardennes and Army Group 'C' under von Leeb
on the left wing opposite the Saar. In reserve was a panzer army group
led by von Kleist. The whole force totaled some 150 infantry divisions
and 10 armored divisions.

The original plan was a modified version of the classic von Schlief-
fen operation which, itself modified, had almost proved successful in
the early days of World War I. Under this plan the main assault rôle
was to be carried out by von Bock's Army Group on the right wing
by means of a wide out-flanking movement through the Low Countries. But before it could be put into practice an alternative proposal
had been presented to the Führer. The originator of this new plan
was General von Manstein, Chief-of-Staff to von Rundstedt of Army

Group 'A.' It suggested that instead of the decisive blow being struck in the north against Belgium, it be shifted to the center of the front and be made through the Ardennes.

Von Manstein presented formidable arguments to back up his alternative plan. An attack through the Low Countries would be too much like the 1914 operation to achieve surprise; in Belgium the Germans would have to fight their main battle against the British who would prove more obstinate than the French; the flat land of Holland and Belgium was crossed by innumerable canals and rivers making difficult the deployment of large armored forces. In favor of his own proposal von Manstein contended that the disadvantages of using tanks in the hilly and wooded country of the Ardennes would be offset by the complete surprise of such a move. Once out of the close country and across the Meuse River at Sedan, the rolling farmlands of Northern France would be perfect for the rapid advance of the German armor.

Von Brauchitsch and Halder were both very lukewarm about von Manstein's scheme. Halder was particularly opposed to it, perhaps more because he did not get on well with von Manstein than because the plan was unfeasible.[1] But the more Hitler studied it, the more he liked it. Finally the Führer decided that the original plan was to be shelved and von Manstein's suggestions adopted instead. Naturally such a decision created resentment amongst the senior officers who had devised the first operation, and also amongst the officers in von Bock's Army Group who had been delegated to a secondary rôle while von Rundstedt's Army Group was given the prima donna part. Unable to vent their feelings on Hitler himself, the High Command felt it necessary to show their disapproval of von Manstein, particularly since he had approached the Führer himself with his plan rather than using the normal army channels. They removed him as von Rundstedt's Chief-of-Staff and gave him command of a corps which played no part in the scheme he had evolved. It was thus no happy and harmonious family of officers that began the offensive in the West on the 10 May 1940.

The military personality that dominated both the first year of the war and the last year of the war was undoubtedly that of Field Marshal Gerd von Rundstedt. To him was given the task of leading the German soldier to his most glorious victory and to his most abysmal defeat. In him was personified the traditional, Conservative, exclusive, aristocratic professional soldier upon which the General Staff liked to believe its members were modeled. As such his background is worth recording.

Von Rundstedt has a face that is ageless. A straight firm nose, long

thin lips and determined blunt jaw, give the impression of a sculp-
tured bust, immutable and relentless. The tiny wrinkles and serried
lines that striate the skin help to create this effect of chiseled rock. The
eyes, however, bright and restless, reveal the presence of warm blood.
The occasional limited smile coupled with a dry, restrained wit con-
firms the fact that this man is human after all. If stone predominates
in the Field Marshal's physical appearance, it probably betrays what
has taken place in the spirit as well. This transformation to granite can
hardly be wondered at, for only ossification could have withstood the
buffeting of howling events that assailed him from all directions.

Born in 1875 of an aristocratic Prussian family steeped in military
tradition, Gerd von Rundstedt was already sixty years old when the
second Great War began. By 1932 he had been given the most important field command in Germany — commander of Army Group 'I'
which controlled Berlin and Brandenburg. In this post he was in
charge of the military forces for whose control political elements
played a desperate game of murder and intrigue. He obeyed like
an automaton the orders he was given by the political leaders of
the day. He questioned neither the contents nor the authority of any
orders. Thus his troops brought about the forcible dissolution of the
Social Democratic government of Prussia because von Rundstedt
was told to do so by Chancellor von Papen; his men stood idly by as
Hitler took over power, dismissed the Reichstag and destroyed the
Weimar Republic because President von Hindenburg did not object;
and he did nothing during the blood purge of June 1934 when Roehm,
the Storm Troop leader, and General von Schleicher of the Wehrmacht were both murdered, because the Führer had so ordered.
Here was the non-political soldier following his creed. Whether von
Rundstedt would have obeyed so automatically had the course of
revolution been reversed and a republic taken over from a monarchy
or a fascist form of government, no one can say. For while it may be
true that von Rundstedt despised the manners and aspirations of the
Nazis, he had never felt any great respect for the Weimar Republic or
its leaders. To him it was merely choosing a lesser evil. The promise
of a Germany free of the shackles of Versailles, and the prospects
of a powerful Wehrmacht, were probably enough to tip the scales in
favor of Hitler.

The next few years were happy ones for a general — to increase
and overhaul the army as quickly as possible. He laid emphasis on
the modernization and improvement of the weapons and training of
the infantrymen. He also saw the need for the close co-operation
between armor and infantry, but always insisted that the latter were
the most important element in any battle. His theories contributed

immeasurably to the efficient war machine that swept all before it in the early days of the war.

The dismissals of von Fritsch and von Blomberg in 1938 created the first break in von Rundstedt's acquiescence in Hitler's actions. He protested to the Führer about the shabby treatment of von Fritsch, but received no satisfaction. When Beck presented his criticism of the proposed invasion of Czechoslovakia, von Rundstedt was one of the men who endorsed the memorandum. Following the occupation of the Sudetenland in the autumn of 1938, von Rundstedt, having guessed wrong, asked that he be permitted to retire on the grounds of old age. This he was enabled to do, but in August 1939, just before the war began, he was called back to command an army group on the Polish front. Unable to resist the call to arms, and true to what he felt was his patriotic duty as a soldier, he donned his field uniform once again.

Brilliantly successful in his operations in Poland, in May 1940 he was poised on the edge of the Ardennes ready to carry out the rôle which Hitler's personal decision had entrusted to him — the leading part in the conquest of France. How well he performed that part has already been judged by military experts. The breaking of the Maginot Line will always remain as a classic example of the use of armor and infantry in the offensive. Von Manstein's plan worked exactly as predicted. The Allied forces on the left advanced to meet von Bock's Army Group in Belgium only to find that von Rundstedt's tanks had penetrated the Ardennes and crossed the Meuse at Sedan. The French, caught completely unawares in the good tank country west of the Meuse, could do nothing to halt the drive of the panzer formations to the Channel coast. And as the German armor drove forward, its positions were quickly taken over by motorized infantry which held the ground captured by the tanks. These tactics revolutionized military thinking and taught the Allies the principles which they subsequently used to defeat their teachers. The Allied left wing, comprising the bulk of the British army, was caught against the Channel and could not break through the tightly held salient carved out by von Rundstedt. The Allied position thus having been cut in two and all attempts to pry open the trap having failed, there remained only one course open — the evacuation of the British from Dunkirk. Up until now victory had tumbled upon victory in breathless profusion. Now was time for defeat. Hitler suffered his first at Dunkirk. And what better authority for this statement than von Rundstedt himself.

"To me," remarked the Field Marshal rather ruefully,[2] "Dunkirk was one of the great turning-points of the war. If I had had my way the English would not have got off so lightly at Dunkirk. But my hands were tied by direct orders from Hitler himself. While the English were clambering into the ships off the beaches, I was kept uselessly outside the port unable to move. I recommended to the Supreme Command that my five panzer divisions be immediately sent into the town and thereby completely destroy the retreating English. But I received definite orders from the Führer that under no circumstances was I to attack, and I was expressly forbidden to send any of my troops closer than ten kilometres from Dunkirk. The only weapons I was permitted to use against the English were my medium guns. At this distance I sat outside the town, watching the English escape, while my tanks and infantry were prohibited from moving.

"This incredible blunder was due to Hitler's personal idea of generalship. The Führer daily received statements of tank losses incurred during the campaign, and by a simple process of arithmetic he deduced that there was not sufficient armor available at this time to attack the English. He did not realize that many of the tanks reported out of action one day could, with a little extra effort on the part of the repair squads, be able to fight in a very short time. The second reason for Hitler's decision was the fact that on the map available to him at Berlin the ground surrounding the port appeared to be flooded and unsuitable for tank warfare. With a shortage of armor and the difficult country, Hitler decided that the cost of an attack would be too high, when the French armies to the south had not yet been destroyed. He therefore ordered that my forces be reserved so that they could be strong enough to take part in the southern drive against the French, designed to capture Paris and destroy all French resistance."

Hitler's successes as a strategist were now beginning to bear their blighted fruit. Despite the assurance of a man like von Rundstedt that he was capable of carrying on against the English at Dunkirk, his opinion was tossed aside by the Führer in favor of his own judgment and intuition. Thus a little man studying a map hundreds of miles away from the battle, by rejecting the advice of his most brilliant commander, changed the course of history. The 'miracle of Dunkirk' seems even more fore-ordained than it ever appeared before.

Hardly was the ink dry on the armistice documents signed at Compiègne declaring the unconditional surrender of the armed forces of France, before the Supreme Command was busy on its most ambitious and most important future operation — the invasion of England. While the Germans gleefully sang "Wir fahren gegen England" (We're Marching Against England), the planning staffs were not as confident as the song writers. The sudden victory had taken them all by surprise. Having prepared themselves for a slow campaign of attrition in the West, their speedy success had far outdistanced their most optimistic plans. Now they were faced with an entirely new problem for which they had no precedents. Being an essentially land-bound army the narrow expanse of Channel waters presented a formidable obstacle to which they could not quickly adjust themselves. But it was realized that the resistance of England might eventually become a serious menace, if not eliminated, and thereby they made plans to deal with it. Hitler ordered von Rundstedt to prepare his Army Group for the prospective invasion. The operation was given the rather transparent code-name of 'Sea Lion.'

The General Staff seems to have been divided about the feasibility of a cross-Channel invasion. Some pressed their convictions that it should be attempted, but the majority of officers, still conservative, felt that the moment was not opportune. Shipping and proper equipment for a sea-borne invasion would take a long time to assemble. The English would bitterly resist any landings, and it was not known just how strong their land forces still were. That the Royal Air Force and Royal Navy would provide formidable opposition was not forgotten. To be successful the enterprise had to be sure of three conditions — complete air superiority, favorable weather, and protection of the flanks of the invasion zone by mining and naval forces. On the assumption that these three conditions would prevail the General Staff prepared its plans. These plans only remained consistent in their broad outlines; frequent alterations in detail made it impossible to describe any one operation as the 'invasion plan.' All that can be provided is some idea of how the project was to be carried out.

Colonel General Franz Halder, who replaced Beck as the army Chief-of-Staff, and whose final years of the war were spent in a concentration camp for having disagreed with Hitler about operations in Russia, has provided a general outline of operation 'Sea Lion.' Extracts from his account give the following overall scheme: [3]

"It was planned to use three armies for the invasion of England and they were stationed along the Channel coast from Le Havre to Holland. These three armies were to form the army group led by von Rundstedt. A large number of army and navy units were working at the time in the estuaries of the Rhine, Meuse and Scheldt, building transport craft, landing craft and landing equipment, and preparing other measures supplementary to those taken by the engineers on the French coast. Special training courses for engineers and armored forces were also taking place on the Friesian Islands, as well as special courses for the assault troops on the French coast in the areas of the

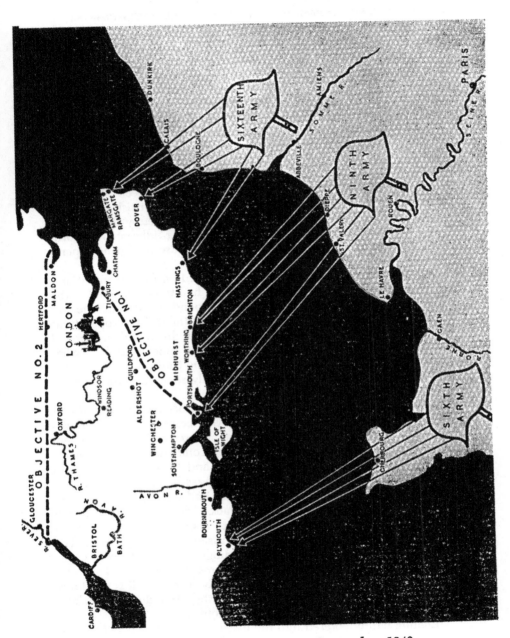

THE INVASION THAT NEVER CAME -- *September,* 1940.

Sixth and Ninth Armies. Even at the time it was hardly possible to form a clear picture of all these preparations.

"The total strength of the German forces to be utilized in 'Sea Lion' must first of all have been twenty-four to twenty-six divisions, including motorized formations. This number was ample, as it would take several weeks for these divisions to complete the crossing. Should further forces or staffs be needed during this period, it would have been easy to train them, as no military forces were facing the Germans on the Continent. The problem was purely that of transport across the sea.

"The intention of von Rundstedt's Army Group was approximately as follows: To land on the English south coast between Dover and Portsmouth (both exclusive), to destroy opposing British forces and to advance step by step northwards in order to occupy the area between the south coast and a line drawn through Midhurst-Guildford-North Downs, which area was required as a base for further operations.

"No orders were issued nor could be issued on further intentions, because the critical phase of the operation had to be expected in the area given above and all further tasks depend on its outcome. An additional hindrance to further planning was the fact that operations affecting wider areas had to be carried out by strong motorized formations, and it was quite uncertain how quickly and in what strength these motorized formations could be transported across the sea. Their supply lines had also to be firmly secured before further strategical tasks could be envisaged. . . .

"The general outline of further tasks was the occupation of Southern England approximately up to the line Gloucester-Oxford-Hertford-Maldon. I cannot recollect if these actual names were ever mentioned, but I use them only to indicate the area comprising the narrowest waist of England between the Thames and Severn estuaries and including London. It was this area which was being considered. . . .

"The limitation of landing areas in east and west was really undesirable but was inevitable because of lack of means to attack Dover and Portsmouth from the sea, or even to neutralize them. Sufficient craft were also lacking to stage the first assault on a larger front. The original intention of extending the landings to the west up to Lyme Bay had therefore to be abandoned. Dover was to be taken by a surprise attack from the land immediately after the first landings. Portsmouth was also to be taken from the land during the later strategic extension of the area of operations. . . .

"London hardly entered into the discussions, as it was outside the first objective. . . . I was of the opinion that our comparatively weak forces (relative to the tasks in hand) would allow us only to isolate the capital from the remainder of the country. This necessitated the surrounding of London from the north as soon as the River Thames had been crossed west of the city with sufficiently strong forces. . . .

"The operation was to be carried out in three phases. Phase I dealing with the initial crossing was to be done in three waves. The first wave was to be formed of fast landing craft, some crossing under their own power, others lowered from sea-going ships outside the coast defense zone. The second wave was to consist of the main body of landing craft, some of which could move slowly under their own power, some of which had to be towed. The third wave was to consist of large sea-going vessels which could carry the bulk of the troops as well as their supporting tanks, engineers, signal units, etc. . . .

"Phase II provided for the crossing of the panzer and motorized divisions from the Dutch area and of further infantry divisions from the French coast. Phase III provided for the crossing of further infantry divisions and of large supplies to form a supply base. The details of Phase II and Phase III could be worked out only after it had become clear to what extent sea-going vessels would be available after the completion of the initial landings."

Thus it can be seen that the plan had been worked out in considerable detail. A scheme had even been evolved for the establishment of a 'Control Commission' for civilian administration in Britain.

On August 1, 1940 Hitler issued the following directive.

The Führer and Supreme Commander of Armed Forces.

Führer's Headquarters,
1 August 1940.

Directive No. 17

For prosecuting air and sea war against England.

I have decided to carry on and intensify air and naval warfare against England in order to bring about her final defeat.

For this purpose I am issuing the following orders:

1. The German air force with all available forces will destroy the English air force as soon as possible.

The attacks will be directed first against airborne aircraft, their ground and supply organization and then against industry, including the manufacture of anti-aircraft equipment.

2. After gaining temporary or local air superiority, air attack will be continued on harbors, paying special attention to food storage depots and particularly food storage depots in London.

In view of our own intended operations, attacks on harbors on the south coast must be kept to a minimum.

3. Attacks on warships and on merchant shipping will be of secondary importance to those against enemy air power except when specially favorable opportunity targets present themselves, or additional effect may be provided within the framework of attacks quoted in para. 2, or where supplementary training is necessary for air crews.

4. The intensified air war will be so planned that adequate forces may be diverted at any time for favorable opportunity targets.

Moreover, fighting strength must be maintained at disposal for the operation 'Seelöwe' (Sea Lion).

5. I am reserving terror attacks as reprisals.

6. Intensification of the air war can begin on 5 August 1940. It is for the air force staff to choose the exact time, in accordance with the completion of preparations, and according to weather conditions. The navy will at the same time announce the planned intensification of naval war measures.

HITLER.

About a month later, on September 3, 1940, an order was sent out by Field Marshal Keitel setting the tentative invasion date as 21 September. It was not a firm date, by any means, and the troops would be given ten days' advance warning — that is on September 11 — if this day was subsequently confirmed.[4]

Yet despite the definite character of these activities there seemed to be no enthusiasm for the operation. Hitler himself appeared particularly hesitant. A great part of the blame for this lukewarm atmosphere can be traced to the estimates of English strength prepared by German military intelligence. Von Rundstedt has admitted that England at this time was a 'Sphinx.' No reliable information was to hand and all that was received by the planners were the bad guesses of the intelligence staffs. They warned of the strength of the Royal Air Force and of the omnipotence of the Royal Navy. Their description of the British soldier, based on the experience of the battle of France, was extremely flattering. In part they described him thus:

The English soldier was in excellent physical condition. He bore his own wounds with stoical calm. The losses of his own troops he discussed with complete equanimity. He did not complain of hardships. In battle he was tough and dogged. His conviction that England would conquer in the end was unshakeable.

The English soldier has always shown himself to be a fighter of high standard. Certainly the territorial divisions are inferior to the regular troops in training, but this is compensated for by their morale. In defence the Englishman took any punishment that came his way. During the fighting, Fourth Army Corps took fewer English prisoners than in the engagements with French or Belgians. On the other hand, the losses on both sides were bloody and high.[5]

But if German intelligence was right about the quality of the English soldier, it was incredibly wrong about the quantity of them. The operation order of von Rundstedt's Army Group 'A' at the beginning of September 1940 deals with the enemy in the following paragraph: [6]

(1) Enemy: The deployment of the English army as at the beginning of September is appreciated as follows:

(a) Employment of seventeen divisions for coastal defense. Close collaboration of these divisions with the coastal defense, the air force and the navy.

(b) Twenty-two divisions in the London area as a tactical and operational reserve. Their task will be to repulse enemy penetration by counter-attack. . . .

With a potential force of thirty-nine enemy divisions against them no wonder the General Staff were hesitant about committing a mere twenty-six divisions in an invasion across the Channel. The fact that no such fantastic force existed in England at the time has already been told by Winston Churchill.[7] Barely a hundred tanks and two or three equipped divisions was the best England could have mustered in those days. Men with pitchforks and stout hearts ready to defend their homes, Britain possessed by the millions. But to estimate that the troops, who had been forced to leave their equipment on the beaches of Dunkirk, still numbered thirty-nine divisions each containing 15,000 men possessing adequate weapons to fight, was sheer nonsense. The much overrated German intelligence service was beginning to reveal its true worth.

One of the most sceptical of all was von Rundstedt himself. Although ordered to command the operation, he was most unenthusiastic about its prospects.

"The proposed invasion of England was nonsense," said von Rundstedt,[8] "because adequate ships were not available. They were chiefly barges which had to be brought from Germany and the Netherlands. Then they had to be reconstructed so that tanks and other equipment could be driven out of the bows. Then the troops had to learn how to embark and disembark. We looked upon the whole thing as a sort of game, because it was obvious that no invasion was possible when our navy was not in a position to cover a crossing of the Channel or carry reinforcements. Nor was the German air force capable of taking on these functions if the navy failed.

"Perhaps we might have come over; but how things would have gone as regards reinforcements and supplies is another matter. There was another difficulty as well. These barges had to be towed, and that could only be done at high tide. If anything had happened *en route* causing me to lose one or two hours, we would have been caught in an ebbing tide and then been stranded off the English coast. I was always very sceptical about the whole affair. I must admit that serious preparations were made, but we only had very few paratroops at the time — one airborne division.

"I have a feeling that the Führer never really wanted to invade England. He never had sufficient courage. He used to say: 'On land I am a hero, but on water I am a coward.' Hitler definitely hoped that the English would make peace overtures to him. It was useless to attempt an invasion later on, since by then the English had become much too strong."

The military objections to an invasion of England in the late summer of 1940 may or may not have been valid. Had the German General Staff known the true strength of the land forces available in Britain at the time, it is probable that they might have urged a different course. But such military protestations had rarely interfered with Hitler's decisions before, and they bore little weight in influencing him on this occasion. The real reason for Germany's failure to cross the Channel lay in Hitler's supreme confidence in his ability to come to political terms with England. That the English would continue to resist after the fall of France was to him unthinkable. All the evidence points to this explanation for what would otherwise remain a completely illogical and inexplicable series of events.

Von Rundstedt's statement that Hitler was waiting for the English to make "peace overtures to him" is substantiated by General Günther Blumentritt, who was von Rundstedt's Chief-of-Staff during the battle of Normandy. Completely opposite to von Rundstedt in both appearance and personality, Blumentritt possessed those qualities which von Rundstedt lacked. Where the Chief was taciturn, Blumentritt was loquacious; where von Rundstedt was frigid, Blumentritt was genial; where von Rundstedt thought in generalities, Blumentritt was patient with details. Dark-skinned, broad and expressive, his face contrasted sharply with the pale, thin, impassive face of von Rundstedt. Together they made an excellent team. Had they been permitted to fight the war their own way, it might well have gone on longer.

In 1940 Blumentritt was senior operations officer on von Rundstedt's staff and his account of the days following the fall of France is most revealing. According to Blumentritt,[9] life at St. Germain, where Army Group 'A' was located, was a conqueror's paradise. The atmosphere was saturated with the prospects of peace and everyone felt that further serious fighting was unlikely. True the Army Group was supposed to be planning the invasion of England, but no one took

it very seriously. Von Rundstedt himself never attended the headquarters where the planning was being done, nor did he visit the
areas where invasion equipment was being assembled, nor did he
inspect the troops being trained for the operation.

The explanation for this attitude, Blumentritt claims, lay not only
in the military difficulties surrounding the invasion, but in the political
background of the days just before and immediately after the fall
of France. The senior officers felt that Hitler was relying on bluff
to achieve a great many of his ends. This impression had first been
created during the events of 1939-40 when the troops in the Rhineland had been alerted for an offensive into France no fewer than
eleven times. While some of these alerts were undoubtedly due to
Hitler's quarrels with the General Staff, already described, Blumentritt believed that some of them were also designed to keep the Allied
forces guessing. With deception as one of Hitler's chief weapons it
was natural that many of them felt that the invasion preparations
were merely being used to frighten England into submission.

"Hitler's order preventing us from attacking the English at Dunkirk
convinced many of us that the Führer believed the English would
come to terms," said Blumentritt, "I have spoken to some Luftwaffe
officers and they also say that Hitler forbade them from conducting
an all-out aerial attack against the shipping at Dunkirk. This attitude
of the Führer's was made clear to me at a round-table conference
he had with a small group of officers following the break-through
into France. It was at Charleville when Hitler came to visit Army
Group headquarters. He was in an expansive mood and discussed
with us his political ideas of the moment. He told us that he was
exceptionally pleased with the way the offensive was going, and that
everything had worked out beyond his wildest expectations. Once
France was defeated there was only England left.

"Hitler then explained that in his opinion there were two fundamental established institutions which, for the time being, must be
recognized as essential cornerstones in the framework of Western
civilization — the Catholic Church and the British Empire. The power
and strength of these two forces must be accepted as *faits accomplis*,
and Germany must see that, for the moment, they be maintained.
To achieve this purpose he proposed to make peace with England
as soon as possible. Hitler was willing to grant England most generous
terms, and he would even desist from pressing his claims for German
colonies. Of course, England's armed forces would have to be disbanded or seriously decreased in size. But in return for such a concession, Hitler was prepared to station as many as ten German divisions in England to aid the British government in maintaining the

security of the United Kingdom. Having heard these theories of the Führer, we can hardly be blamed for believing that the invasion of England was never contemplated as a serious operation."

If there is still some speculation as to Rudolf Hess's mission to England, this attitude of the Führer's may shed some light on the mystery. Apparently Hitler was not the only one in the Nazi hierarchy who believed in England's readiness to discuss terms with Germany. The shortsighted ability of the German to see only what he wants to see was never better illustrated than in this fantastic misappreciation by Hitler and his advisers of what was going on in the mind of the average Englishman. It was a miscalculation that shadowed them from the moment they decided to attack Poland to the day they signed the armistice terms at Rheims.

This confidence of Hitler's in England's speedy capitulation was further demonstrated by a series of decrees issued in the late summer of 1940. First Hitler ordered a gigantic victory parade to be held in Paris; then all soldiers who had served in World War I were dismissed from the service to help in agriculture and other peacetime occupations; then an order was published demobilizing fifty German divisions and directing the men back into civilian life; and finally there was an extensive planned decrease in the production of the materials of war. Coupling these events with the Führer's frame of mind, in regard to England, and the scepticism of the General Staff as to the military feasibility of the operation, it cannot be wondered at that when the following order arrived from Berlin on October 12, 1940, no one was very surprised:

Führer's Headquarters,
12 October 1940.

1. The Führer has decided that from now on until the spring, preparations for landing in England will be maintained purely as a military and political threat.

Should the intention of a landing in England in spring or early summer 1941 be renewed, the necessary state of preparedness will be ordered in sufficient time beforehand. Until then the military groundwork for a later landing will be further improved.

2. All measures concerning the relaxing of the state of readiness for attack must be regulated from the following viewpoints:

(*a*) The English must retain the impression that from now on we are preparing to land on a large scale.

(*b*) At the same time, however, German domestic economy will be relieved of a burden. . . .

(Signed) KEITEL,
C.-*in*-C. *Armed Forces.*

But, in addition to the decision not to invade England, Hitler made another decision in these days which was destined to doom him to defeat. According to General Warlimont,[10] Hitler announced at a conference called by General Jodl in late summer 1940 that he intended to invade Russia. Thus, at the height of his greatest victory, the Führer prepared the way for his greatest defeat.

Now what of the General Staff during these triumphant days? Hitler spared them no honors. In a speech on July 19 to the Reichstag, he showered so much praise upon his senior officers that they were both flattered and grateful. And simultaneously the Goebbels propaganda machine turned on all its taps to pour out to the German public thousands of words about 'Hitler the General.' Thus in the mind of the average German was built up a picture of an invincible group of Teutonic military geniuses over whom floated the guiding spirit of the master-genius of them all — Adolf Hitler. Cowed by these honors and this propaganda the generals meekly bowed before their Supreme Commander. General Warlimont sums up this disintegration of the spirit of independence and opposition within the General Staff in the following words:

"Thinking back I cannot therefore help believing even today that the fortune and success of the French campaign, together with the honors awarded to high-ranking generals combined to silence temporarily the opposition in the General Staff — a fact of which Hitler may well have been aware when he decided to invade Russia. The Commander-in-Chief of the army and his General Staff had for the first time let themselves be reduced to mere executive assistants of Hitler; now they were kept on that level. The final decline of the General Staff had begun. The longer the war went on the more unfortunate became the situation on the fronts, and the more the art of strategy degenerated, while the organization of the Supreme Command gradually dissolved. In the General Staff, which faced this development powerless and without a leader, the unanimous opposition of former times made way for the formation of mutually opposing and ever more suspicious groups. The Party, however, proceeded to extend its power over the Wehrmacht itself, and left it finally to its horrible fate, unique in German history."

And so ended the first year of war. It had given the German nation three glorious victories — Poland, Norway and France. But it had also given it three defeats, far from obvious at that time, but far more significant — Dunkirk, the failure to invade England and the decision to go to war with Russia. Thus even the years of victory lay the foundations for ultimate defeat.

Part III ⁊ THE MISTAKES

Chapter IX

THE EARLY MISTAKES – GIBRALTAR AND CRETE

Towards the end of World War II it was popular, amongst the bombed-out, blacked-out populations of German cities, to whisper satirical jokes about their plight. One of the more popular was the story of the uneducated German peasant being given his first lesson in geography. Standing before a large map of the world, his instructor was pointing out the size and location of the various countries of the world.

"These big areas colored pink," said the teacher, indicating the United Kingdom, Canada, India, Australia and the other parts of the Empire, "belong to England."

"Ja, Ja," nodded the peasant, "England."

"And this large piece of land," said the instructor pointing to the United States, "is America."

"America," repeated the farmer thoughtfully, "Ja, Ja, America."

"And this huge territory in the east," went on the instructor waving his stick to show the vast extent of the U.S.S.R., "is Russia."

"Hm," muttered the peasant, "I see. Russia."

"Now in the center here," continued the teacher pointing to Europe, "this small bit of land in the middle — that's Germany."

The peasant was silent for a moment while all this knowledge sank in. As if to confirm all these facts he walked to the map and pointing out each country in turn, repeated what he had just been told. "England — America — Russia and this little piece in the center — Germany."

"Yes, that's right," said the teacher.

Another moment's silence followed while the peasant concentrated on the map. Then looking up he asked in wonderment, "Has anyone told the Führer?"

While the story had its point in 1945, at the end of 1940 it would have had none at all. For at that time the Third Reich was dominating all of Europe and part of Asia, having conquered France, the Low Countries, Norway, Poland, Austria and Czechoslovakia, having as allies the signatories to the Tripartite Pact — Italy, Japan, Hungary

54

and Roumania — and having the sympathetic support of the so-called neutrals, Finland and Spain. Officially resisting this allegiance of might was only the British Empire, represented at that moment by a small, untrained, badly-equipped force trying to reassemble itself along the southern coast of England. Well might some uninformed peasant, looking at a war-map of those days, have asked "Has anyone told Churchill?"

Yet at this peak in their glory, while Germans dined in Paris, goose-stepped in Oslo and danced in Vienna, the man who had brought it about was busy planning the undoing of it all. And there was no one left to utter a word of caution, restraint or advice. The German General Staff, mellowed by their victories and subdued by their internal defeats, were quite content to follow the Führer wherever he now chose to lead them. Having clung to a rocket in its dazzling ascent they had to hang on while it plunged to earth as well.

The early triumphs — political and military — had been achieved primarily through following the calls of Hitler's intuition. Austria, Czechoslovakia, Poland, Norway, France, had been the vindication of the Führer's personal policy and philosophy. They convinced both the German people and their leaders that Adolf Hitler was infallible. And, what is more, they also convinced Adolf himself. Having deprived themselves of the right and power to object, because of their faith in one man, the German nation could now only sit by and watch that one man make mistake after mistake after mistake — until what should have been inevitable victory recoiled into inevitable defeat.

Mistake Number One, as we have already seen, was the failure to advance against the British at Dunkirk. This was Hitler's decision alone. Mistake Number Two was the abandonment of the plans to invade England. This error was due to bad military judgment on the part of German operational and intelligence staffs, and equally bad political foresight on Hitler's part as to the temper and determination of the British people. These were only the beginning. From September 1940 to September 1943 there were far more to come — and bigger and better ones.

Having abandoned the immediate prospect of an invasion of England, the Führer looked about him for an alternative plan for throttling the Empire. Although already convinced that war with Russia was necessary, he had not yet decided whether it would be wiser to hold off this attack until after he had brought England to its knees. The chief protagonist of first handling England and then taking on Russia was Reichsmarshal Hermann Göring. As early as September 1940 Ribbentrop had discussed the prospects of Spain's entry into the war with Serrano Suñer, the Spanish Foreign Secretary. According to minutes of a talk between Ribbentrop and Mussolini at that time, the Spaniards wished to invade and conquer Gibraltar by themselves, but in order to make sure of the outcome, Germany had promised to provide Franco with special weapons and troops.[1]

On 12 November 1940, Hitler issued an order to the commanders of his army, navy and air force, stating that "political steps to bring about an early Spanish entry into the war have been taken (Operation Felix). Gibraltar will be taken and the British will be prevented from gaining a foothold at another part of the Iberian peninsula or in the Atlantic islands." Officers in plain clothes were to be sent to investigate the situation around Gibraltar and prepare to take over aerodromes. Hitler assured his commanders of "the secret co-operation of the Spaniards" in preventing the British from breaking out of the Rock to improve their positions. The Spaniards were also to aid in keeping the German plans secret.[2]

All during the winter of 1940 Göring pressed for the adoption of his plan to deprive Britain of access to the Mediterranean. But it was a far more ambitious scheme than merely sending a few troops to aid Franco to capture Gibraltar on his own. Actually the Reichsmarshal envisaged a concerted thrust against both the east and west entrances to the Mediterranean. Three army groups were to be involved in this huge offensive. The first, led by Field Marshal von Rundstedt, was to strike through Spain, capture Gibraltar, move into Morocco and advance along the African coast to Tunis. The second army group, under Field Marshal von Bock, was to move through Italy into Tripolitania. The third army group, under Field Marshal List was to drive through Greece and the Balkans, capture the Dardanelles and Ankara and continue on to the Suez.[3]

"When the encirclement had been successfully completed," explained Göring, "it was proposed to offer Britain the right to resume peaceful traffic through the Mediterranean if she came to terms with Germany and joined us in a war against Russia."

According to Göring the original plan for the move through Spain was practically complete. Fifteen infantry and armored divisions had been assembled along the Pyrenees, and 600 88-millimetre guns were to carry out an intensive bombardment of the Rock. In addition a division of paratroops was to be dropped on Gibraltar, should resistance be greater than expected, and heavy siege guns were to destroy the batteries and emplacements on the Rock.[4]

"The attack on Gibraltar had been so fully prepared," said Göring, enthusiastically, "that it could not have failed. We would then have pushed through to Casablanca and Dakar, which would have foiled the deployment of American forces in North Africa. Aircraft and U-boats from these bases could have harassed the American convoys, and with the Mediterranean closed we could have struck across Tripoli to Suez, and the long Italian coastline would have been no longer endangered."

By late 1940 Hitler had not made up his mind which was more urgent — the final elimination of Britain or war with Russia. That Russia would eventually have to be dealt with was a decision that he had already taken. But he was not certain as to whether an offensive in the East should be attempted while England was still resisting. Hitler had become suspicious of Russia's intentions during the visit of Molotov to Berlin in November 1940. At that conference, claims Göring, Hitler had been disturbed by the Russian Foreign Minister's talk of Russian aims in the Daradanelles and the possibility of an attack on Roumania from Bessarabia. The Führer also felt that since Britain had not capitulated despite the fact that she was now alone, she must have come to some secret agreement with Russia. It was therefore necessary, Hitler told Göring, to anticipate a quick and sudden stab in the back from the Soviets.

These fears culminated in a directive which was issued in December 1940 ordering the commanders of the German armed forces to prepare a lightning campaign against Russia to be undertaken before England had fallen. Thus, early in 1941 the Wehrmacht was busy with two huge planning programs — Göring's against the British lifeline in the Mediterranean and Hitler's against Russia. According to Göring, the final decision as to which of these operations would be attempted first, was not reached until March, 1941. It was then that things finally came to a head. The unilateral invasion of Greece by Italy had embarrassed the Supreme Command, particularly since the prestige of Germany's Axis partner was being badly shaken by the bitter Greek resistance. When British divisions were sent from Africa to Greece, thus threatening to drive Italy back to the Adriatic, it brought British troops in dangerous proximity to the Balkans.

The last straw was the overthrow of the Yugoslav Regent, Prince Paul, on 27 March, two days after he had signed the Tripartite Pact. This convinced Hitler that Moscow was encouraging Yugoslav resistance to Axis domination, and the presence of British troops in Greece tended to confirm his suspicions of an Anglo-Russian secret arrangement.[5] He then decided that Germany could not afford to wait any longer as far as Russia was concerned. Göring's plan for a knockout blow against England's position in the Mediterranean had to be abandoned, and all efforts were concentrated on the coming struggle in the East. The invasion of Yugoslavia and Greece on 6 April was designed to clear the decks for action against Russia. History has decisively shown how disastrous that decision was for Germany. Second guessing, after it was all over, Field Marshal Wilhelm Keitel nodded in agreement with history's verdict.

"Instead of attacking Russia," he said,[6] "we should have strangled the British Empire by closing the Mediterranean. The first step in the operation would have been the conquest of Gibraltar. That was another great opportunity we missed."

And that was Lost Opportunity or Mistake Number Three.

The defeat of Greece and Yugoslavia had left an unpleasant aftermath from the German point of view. The bulk of the British forces had succeeded in escaping from the mainland and were now ensconced south of the Peloponnesos, on the island of Crete. Before proceeding with his offensive against the Russians, Hitler decided that it was essential to eliminate this potential base for future British operations against the Balkans. At first he had considered it impossible to conquer Crete by an assault from the air. But he was finally convinced of its feasibility by Colonel General Kurt Student, the commander-in-chief of the German paratroops. Strangely enough, this victory at Crete, which was intensely studied by Allied strategists as a model of airborne tactics, was considered, by the Germans themselves, to be their first serious set-back.

Colonel General Student, with his dominant forehead, pale face and high-pitched voice looked like a prosperous business executive rather than the intrepid leader of the daring paratroops. His successful use of paratroops in Holland and in cracking the Maginot Line at Eben Emael had brought him into close proximity to the Führer, who admired these exploits. His rise within the Wehrmacht was due primarily to his undoubted loyalty and close, personal associations with Hitler. Amongst many members of the German General Staff it was felt that his position was due more to his party connections than to his ability. According to General Eugen Meindl who led the glider troops into Crete, "Student had big ideas but not the faintest conception as to how they were to be carried out."[7]

On 20 May a force consisting of a parachute division, a mountain division suddenly converted to an airborne rôle, and a glider formation, began the assault in Crete. On the first day the operation went very badly. Military intelligence had again blundered in their assessment of enemy strength by failing to point out to the planners that the defenders of Crete possessed about twenty-five tanks. Thus, landing without any anti-tank weapons, the first wave of paratroops were badly cut up. In addition, the gliders landed in between the first and second defense lines, rather than behind them as planned, and reinforcements setting out by sea from Greece were attacked by the British fleet and suffered severe casualties. However, the invaders managed to hold on to the airport at Maleme and after a bitter ten-day struggle succeeded in forcing the English, New Zealand and Australian troops to evacuate the island.

"The Führer was most displeased with the whole affair," admitted Student.[8] "Our losses at Crete were very high for that time. We had been lucky so far, as the whole French campaign had not cost us as many lives as a single battle in 1870. It was the same with the Balkan campaign, excluding Crete. Crete alone cost us 4000 killed and missing out of 20,000 men thrown in."

In view of the mistakes and losses that were still to come, this rebuff at Crete would seem to have been a relatively minor one. However it had two significant repercussions. Since the Crete affair had been scheduled to take no more than three days, the ten days needed to overcome the tenacious resistance of the British had been far too long. For it meant that the opening of the offensive against the Russians had to be set back another week. In view of the early Russian winter of 1941 this delay deprived the Germans of still more good campaigning weather just when they needed it most.

The second, and more serious, result of the battle of Crete was the fact that it made Hitler super-cautious and distrustful of all future German airborne operations. Student had a number of other plans for operations in the Mediterranean. "After Crete I proposed that we should make an attack on Cyprus in order to obtain a jumping-off ground for an air attack and paratroop attack on the Suez Canal," he said. "But Hitler rejected it because of the losses we had received in Crete."

Another parachute operation planned by Student was a proposed drop on Malta to take place in September 1942. The Führer had at first given his approval and all the details were almost completed. The attack was to be carried out by two German parachute divisions, an Italian airborne division and an Italian parachute division, roughly about 40,000 men. This was to be accompanied by a seaborne landing on the island after the paratroops had seized a bridgehead. "In July I flew to Berlin for a final conference," said Student.[9] "When I went in to see the Führer he simply turned it down flat. 'The affair will go wrong and will cost too many lives,' he said. I also had the impression that he didn't trust the Italians at all."

Whether Cyprus or Malta would have been logical operations in those early years, it is difficult to say. Had Hitler been prepared to throw his men into battle with the same abandon as he was willing to do in the subsequent battles in Russia and France, it is likely that he would indeed have been successful. The seizure of Malta, Crete and Cyprus by 1942 would have seriously affected British activities in North Africa and would have undoubtedly delayed Italy's eventual collapse. In a less telling way it might have achieved something of the results expected from Göring's large-scale offensive towards the Mediterranean. The decision to abandon further airborne activities in the Mediterranean because of the lessons of Crete, although not as serious or as conclusive as the others, might, nevertheless, well be listed as Mistake Number Four. Bad intelligence, bad generalship and bad intuition brought it about.

Chapter X

THE GREATEST MISTAKE — RUSSIA

ON 18 December 1940, nine copies of a secret directive were issued to the chiefs of the various German services. The document was signed by Hitler and initialled by Keitel and Jodl.[1] It began as follows:

"The German armed forces must be prepared to crush Soviet Russia in a quick campaign before the end of the war against England (case Barbarossa).

"For this purpose the army will have to employ all available units with the reservation that the occupied territories will have to be safeguarded against surprise attacks.

"For the Eastern campaign the air force will have to free such strong forces for the support of the army that a quick completion of the ground operations may be expected and that damage of the eastern German territories will be avoided as much as possible. This concentration of the main effort in the East is limited by the following reservation: That the entire battle and armament area dominated by us must remain sufficiently protected against enemy air attacks and that the attacks on England and especially the supply for them must not be permitted to break down.

"Concentration of the main effort of the navy remains unequivocally against England also during an Eastern campaign.

"If occasion arises I will order the concentration of troops for action against Soviet Russia eight weeks before the intended beginning of operations.

"Preparations requiring some time to start are — if this has not yet been done — to begin presently and are to be completed by 15 May 1941.

"Great caution has to be exercised that the intention of the attack will not be recognized. . . ."

That was Mistake Number Five — and the greatest one of all.

Actually the planning of the attack on Russia had begun many months before the issue of this directive. Field Marshal von Paulus has testified at Nuremberg that he was told of the proposed offensive on 3 September 1940, when he became Quartermaster-General of the General Staff. Colonel General Franz Halder, who was Chief of the army General Staff at the time, handed the plan, in so far as it had already been prepared, to von Paulus and asked him to examine it. The forces required were between 130 and 140 divisions, and use of Roumanian territory was envisaged.

"Objectives of the attack," said von Paulus, "were first the destruction of the Russian army on the western boundary of the Soviet Union; second, an advance into Russia of such depth that it would not be possible for the Russians to carry out air attacks on the Reich; and third, attainment of a line runnñing from Archangel to the Volga."

These objectives remained unchanged in the order issued on 18 December 1940. On 3 February 1941, Hitler gave his final approval of the Barbarossa plan, but he did not set a definite date for the attack. On 28 March, hearing of the uprising in Yugoslavia, the Führer told von Paulus of his intention to invade Yugoslavia. "Objectives were to secure our flank for the operation against Greece," said von Paulus, "secure the Belgrade-Nish railway line, and above all, make sure that we had our right shoulder free when we attacked Russia." [2]

The original date for the invasion of Russia had been tentatively fixed for mid-May, as this was the earliest possible time, in view of the weather, for large-scale operations in Russia. But on 1 April von Paulus was told that this date had been set back about five weeks until the second half of June. While the Balkans were being cleared a huge deception scheme was instituted in Norway and on the French coast to create the impression of invasion preparations against England.

On 6 June 1941, D-Day for the attack was finally set as 22 June. This order, signed by Keitel, shows that six divisions had been withdrawn from the West for the operation, leaving a force of 42 divisions facing England. Available for the first phase of the Russian invasion on 22 June 1941 were 121 divisions of which 29 were either armored or motorized.[3] Before very long this figure had been raised to almost 200 divisions on the Eastern front.

It is beyond the scope of this book to deal comprehensively with the Russian campaign. But since defeat in the East was the prelude to final defeat it is necessary to analyze the factors that helped bring it about. These follow the familiar pattern already seen at work in the early mistakes — but on a much larger scale. Military intelligence was worse, Hitler was more domineering and the generals were more impotent.

The majority of German senior officers admit that they were hopelessly ill-informed about the strength and ability of the Russian forces that they would be meeting. "Information concerning Russia was comparatively scanty," said Colonel General Franz Halder, who as von Brauchitsch's Chief-of-Staff was responsible for most of the detailed planning of the campaign.[4] "We had in our possession the captured archives of Holland, Belgium, Greece, Yugoslavia and even of the French General Staff, but none of these countries was any better informed about the Russians than we were. The information concerning the troops we should first meet on the border was fairly correct, but we had no statistical data as to the future potentialities of this vast state. Of course, during our first six months' advance we found out a lot more."

Just how badly informed the Germans were is best revealed by the following excerpts from an intelligence report issued to the 22 Infantry Division on the eve of its taking part in the invasion of Russia. The report is dated 8 June 1941 — two weeks before the attack on Russia began. To aid in showing the inadequacies of this appreciation, some contrasting comments by German generals who fought the Russians will follow the relevant extracts.

Discussing the Russian armored troops the report had this to say:

"Experiences in Finland showed that Russian tank crews attack spiritedly. Battle training, especially co-operation of units with other arms, was insufficient. Tank maintenance was completely unsatisfactory. The numerous breakdowns are an especially difficult problem as the majority of troops are not capable of making repairs.

"In Finland it was only static warfare. The Russian tank troops are not capable of coping with the demands of a modern war of movement of close formations over great distances.

"In 1939-40 deficiencies in organization and training have come to light and lead to the conclusion that the Red Army, in its present state of development, is not fully adapted to modern demands and is not capable of standing up to a fast, modern, boldly-led enemy. By too large-scale manœuvres in recent years, the battle training of the individual fighting man and of small units has been neglected. . . ."

Now compare this with the opinion of Colonel General Joseph 'Sepp' Dietrich, who was later to lead the Sixth S.S. Panzer Army in the Ardennes offensive of December 1944. After commanding 1 S.S. Panzer Division in the battle for Rostov, the attempt to relieve Stalingrad, and the recapture of Kharkov, Dietrich had this to say of Russian tank troops: [5]

"The Russians completely fooled us in Finland. When we invaded we thought they had no tanks and suddenly we were confronted with over two thousand T-34s. The T-34 was at that time the best fighting tank in existence. It had ample gun-power, was amazingly fast and was well-armored. They were skilfully used and efficiently maintained. The mechanical ability of the Russian was astounding. . . ."

The report then goes on to discuss the merits of Russian officers.

"After the execution of Tuchatschewski and the purge of summer 1937 there remained only a few leading commanders. Among these, People's Commissar for Defense Timoshenko undoubtedly belongs. Replacements from inexperienced year classes will not be able to free themselves from doctrinaire restrictions and will impede the execution of bold decisions. . . ."

It needs no German general to indicate how incorrect that assessment turned out to be. One needs only to list the names of Zhukov, Koniev, Rokossovsky, Cherniakovsky, Malinovsky and Tolbukhin as some of the "inexperienced" commanders who managed to "free themselves from doctrinaire restrictions" and who were not impeded in their "execution of bold decisions." The report continues:

"Corps commanders down to lieutenants show the greatest weaknesses. Extraordinarily young: colonels (35-40 years) lead divisions, majors (30-35 years) lead regiments. Company commanders, etc. are almost all only lieutenants or second lieutenants. There is a lack of experience and initiative. . . ."

How quickly these green officers learned their trade is indicated by the following statement of General Alfred Schlemm who commanded a corps in the battle for Smolensk and Vitebsk, and later took over First Parachute Army in the West: [6]

"The Russian ability to manœuvre large tank forces came as a complete surprise. Their operations were well-planned and efficiently carried out, and they were not afraid to improvise or experiment. . . ."

Only when dealing with the Russian private soldier did the report come anywhere near the truth. Of these it said:

"The private soldiers are hard, unpretentious, willing, brave. No longer the 'brave Muzhik' as known in the World War. His intelligence and tutorial adaptability have grown. Modern training can, in the course of time, make him an independent fighter, and give him a mastery of technical warfare. . . ."

If one is seeking for a reason for the failure of the Germans in Russia this final overall appreciation of the opponent they were to meet in two weeks' time should help provide the answer. Who could but fail to be confident when facing an enemy as riddled with weaknesses as the one described in this intelligence report?

"A gradual improvement in the Red Army is to be expected, but not for some years yet. Large parts of the army in the provinces will make very slow progress. The Russian national characteristics — sluggish, unwieldy, doctrinaire, indecisive, lacking in responsibility — have not altered. Leaders of all ranks will not be suited, within a measurable space of time, to lead large formations competently, and are poorly qualified for the operations of a large-scale attack, quick decisions and independent action within the framework of the whole.

"The troops, as a mass, and by virtue of the number of modern weapons, will fight bravely. They are not equal to the demands of modern attack. The initiative of the individual fighter will frequently be found wanting. . . .

"The weakness of the Red Army lies in the clumsiness of its leaders of all ranks, its adherence to the doctrinaire, its training unequal to modern demands, its reluctance to assume responsibility and its appreciable lack of organization in all its parts. . . ."

Was there ever more profound twaddle? Here was German military intelligence making the most important assessment of an enemy it had ever been called upon to make, and it produced something no better than one of Dr. Goebbels's propaganda efforts. It can, therefore, hardly be wondered at that Hitler undertook the Russian venture with a light heart and with an optimistic expectation of a quick and easy victory. It is true that all German generals were not so sanguine as their Führer about the outcome of a Russian campaign. The constant fear of another disastrous war on two fronts still dominated much of their thinking, and there was, therefore, a tendency to steer clear of further entanglements in the East before the situation in the West was cleared up. Von Brauchitsch, Halder and von Rundstedt were all unenthusiastic, not on any moral grounds, but purely because of the military difficulties involved. They did not feel that defeating Russia was beyond their capabilities. They only thought that it would not be as easy as it looked to Hitler. Von Rundstedt was particularly concerned about an early start since he realized what problems a Russian winter might give them.

"I was called away as Commander-in-Chief West at the beginning of April 1941," said von Rundstedt,[7] "to take over Army Group South in Russia. The troops to be involved had begun to move east long before this date. The plans for the campaign had been prepared during the winter by Halder in Berlin. In January, Halder came to me in France and, since my Army Group was to be involved in the attack, some members of my staff carried out an exercise based on Halder's views. I said to them at that time 'Gentlemen, if you are going to conduct a war in Russia you must remember that campaigning weather ends early there. Once winter comes it becomes very difficult. One must start operations in Russia as soon as the swampy period is over, which is usually in May.' The Balkans campaign brought about a delay and we began at least four weeks after we had planned. That was a very costly delay. I was never enthusiastic about the Russian campaign, in any case, since I felt we could reach an understanding with them. But Hitler was convinced that if we did not strike, the Russians would do so before us."

General Blumentritt, who had been sent to Warsaw to act as Chief-of-Staff of the Fourth Army in November 1940, verified the luke-warm attitude of von Rundstedt towards the coming attack and also indicated why the Germans were suspicious of Russian intentions at the time. "When I first arrived in the East," said Blumentritt,[8] "our divisions were strung thinly along the Russian border with sectors from eighty to one hundred kilometres in size. No offensive operation seemed likely then. But soon there came reports of a tremendous Russian build-up of armed forces in the southern sector. Rumors of war were rife during that winter of 1940-41. A Lithuanian colonel, planted in the Red Army near Riga by Admiral Canaris, the Wehrmacht's senior intelligence officer, confirmed these stories of growing Russian strength. It was no surprise, therefore, when an operation order visualizing action against the Russians was received at our headquarters in January 1941."

The original plan for the Russian campaign was based upon a lightning dash into the interior followed by vast encirclements west of the Dnieper in which the bulk of the Russian armies would be swallowed in one big gulp. "I was told that the war with Russia would be over in ten weeks, and long before the winter would affect us," said von Rundstedt. "The Führer based this estimate on the belief that once we had reached the Dnieper River all the Russian forces opposing us would have been wiped out. He felt that after the initial big defeats the Russians would give in." [9]

But apparently Hitler had been reading his intelligence reports much too carefully. For the Russians were neither as incompetent, nor as slow, nor as clumsy as he had been led to believe. Along the Minsk-Moscow highway, driving towards the Russian capital, was the strongest German army group under Field Marshal von Bock. In three and a half weeks it had covered more than 450 miles from Byelostok to the outskirts of Smolensk. But while it had made satisfactory territorial gains, it had failed in its main object — the destruction of the Russian armies. Three times von Bock attempted huge encircling movements — at Slonim, at Minsk and at Smolensk — and three times the "clumsy" Russians succeeded in escaping the pincers. Although it was still only 16 July, the Germans were no longer finding the going easy. The country was now dwindling off into dirt roads, small bridges and forests and swamps. Torrential rains made the roads impassable, and the Russians, recovering from their surprise, were offering stiffer and more able resistance. At Smolensk on the Dnieper, still some 200 miles west of Moscow, the first serious halt to German progress was made. Not until 7 August 1941, after three weeks of bitter fighting, was Smolensk finally cleared, and then only at the expense of heavy and unexpected German casualties.

Von Rundstedt's Southern Army Group was not having the startling success of its neighbor to the north. By the first week in August these troops had only reached Zhitomir, which was still over eighty miles west of Kiev and the Dnieper. Unable to push straight east, von Rundstedt diverted a large force southeast where Russian opposition was much weaker. Here, after a decisive victory at Uman, the Germans poured into the lower valley of the Dnieper and by the end of August had captured the industrial region of Dniepropetrovsk and were besieging Odessa. But despite these undoubtedly grievous blows to the Russian effort, the Germans were still far from having eliminated Russian opposition. The ten weeks of campaigning had gone by and still substantial Russian forces were fighting along the entire front — west of Leningrad, east of Smolensk and west of Kiev. Von Rundstedt was now beginning to discover how badly the Russians had been underestimated.

"I realized soon after the attack was begun that everything that had been written about Russia was nonsense," said the Field Marshal.[10] "The maps we were given were all wrong. The roads that were marked nice and red and thick on a map turned out to be tracks, and what were tracks on the map became first-class roads. Even railways which were to be used by us simply didn't exist. Or a map would indicate that there was nothing in the area, and suddenly we would be confronted with an American-type town, with factory buildings and all the rest of it."

Having failed to destroy the Russian armies west of the Dnieper, Hitler decided to postpone his original plan of an advance towards Moscow, and instead made another attempt to bag the Russian troops west of Kiev. Von Bock's tanks were to move south and von Rundstedt's tanks to move north with the two arms of the pincer meeting behind Kiev. The manœuvre was brilliantly successful. Marshal Budenny's force was wiped out, and over 600,000 Russian prisoners taken. But Kiev did not fall until 20 September and the Russians were still far from beaten.

Despite the increasing difficulties of maintaining his huge forces hundreds of miles from their supply bases, despite the threat of winter, and despite the fact that the Russians had not collapsed west of the Dnieper as planned, Hitler decided to push on to Moscow. On 2 October, with no fewer than sixty divisions assembled at Smolensk, this offensive, which Hitler described as "the greatest ever known," moved forward towards Moscow and victory. By 15 October advance German spearheads had reached Mozhaisk, about ninety miles west of the capital. And then Fate took a hand. Winter arrived at least one month ahead of schedule. The snow and frost arriving in mid-October instead of mid-November upset all German plans. The mud and mire stalled the tired mechanized troops. Fresh Russian forces began to appear in front of Moscow. Von Brauchitsch, as Commander-in-Chief, saw the dangers involved in pressing on with forces improperly equipped for winter warfare, and advised an immediate withdrawal to a defensive line where the troops could be properly sheltered for the winter. Hitler would have none of it. Having staked his reputation on the capture of Moscow he insisted that his armies fulfill his promises. On 2 December another lunge was directed against the city, but the bitter cold, the long nights, the black forests and the skilful stubbornness of the Russian defenders, held von Bock's forces out of Moscow.

Four days later, on 6 December, the first Russian winter counter-offensive began. Here again German military intelligence had failed. For as General Blumentritt admitted, this blow by the Russians under Zhukov came as a stunning surprise. "The Russians had carried out their preparations in the greatest of secrecy," he said, "and we were badly informed as to the resources and reinforcements that were still available to the Red Army." [11]

The failure to capture Moscow brought about another humiliation for the General Staff in its struggle with Hitler. Field Marshal von Brauchitsch, who had opposed the plan of continuing on to the east once winter had come, was dismissed from his post as Commander-in-

Chief of the army. To take his place came none other than Hitler himself. Having made himself Minister of War in the early days of his régime, having taken over command of the Wehrmacht when von Blomberg was dismissed, he now completed the martial trinity by making himself Commander-in-Chief of the army as well. Never was a Supreme Commander more supreme than Hitler in December 1941. As leader of the state, War Minister, chief of the armed forces and head of the army he could now declare war, decide how he was going to wage it, make the plans and carry them out all by himself. While it undoubtedly shortened the chain of command, it made it rather difficult for Hitler the Führer to dismiss Hitler the Wehrmacht chief when Hitler the army commander led his forces to disaster.

But von Brauchitsch was not the only senior officer to disagree with Hitler's strategy in Russia in the winter of 1941. Von Rundstedt, whose Army Group South had driven as far as Rostov, following the victory at Kiev, was also finding the Führer's strategy more than irksome.

"After accomplishing my first objective," said von Rundstedt,[12] "which was the encirclement and destruction of the enemy forces west of the Dnieper, I was given my second objective. It was to advance eastwards and take Maikop and Stalingrad. We laughed aloud when we received these orders, for winter had already come and we were almost 700 kilometres away from these cities. Hitler thought that with the frost making the roads hard we could advance towards Stalingrad very quickly. At the same time I was told to advance towards Maikop because oil was urgently needed and I was also expected to clean up the Crimea in order to deprive the Russians of their airfields in this area. With my forces split in these three drives, we nevertheless managed to get a tank force as far east as Rostov. This meant that I had a terribly long left flank with nothing to protect it. The Russians attacked at Rostov from the north and south about the end of November, and realizing that I couldn't hold the city I ordered it to be evacuated. I had previously asked for permission to withdraw this extended armored spearhead to the Mius River, about 100 kilometres west of Rostov. I was told that I could do this and we began to withdraw very slowly, fighting all the way. Suddenly an order came to me from the Führer: 'Remain where you are, and retreat no further,' it said. I immediately wired back 'It is madness to attempt to hold. In the first place the troops cannot do it and in the second place if they do not retreat they will be destroyed. I repeat that this order be rescinded or that you find someone else.' That same night the Führer's reply arrived: 'I am

acceding to your request,' it read, 'please give up your command.'
I then went home."

There is some difference of opinion amongst German senior officers
as to whether or not Hitler's decision to stand in front of Moscow
that winter was the correct one. While von Brauchitsch had favored
a withdrawal to a safe winter line, von Leeb and von Rundstedt had
gone even further and suggested that the German forces be withdrawn to their original starting line in Poland. However, a number
of officers like von Bock and von Tippelskirch believed that an
attempted retreat in mid-winter would have had disastrous repercussions. With the picture of Napoleon's retreat from Moscow to
haunt them as a horrible example, these generals felt that a retirement at this stage might easily have turned into a panic with disastrous results. But they all agreed that the German plight would
not have arisen in the first place had Hitler been content with his
successes west of the Dnieper once it was obvious that winter had
forestalled his prospects of a quick victory.

Until now the war had been comparatively easy for the Wehrmacht. Defeats had been few and victories inexpensive. The Russian
winter changed all that. The Führer in his confident dreams of an
early triumph had neglected to provide for an army stuck in the
Russian steppes for a whole winter. Sufficient winter clothing had
not been prepared, and even the clothes that were available could
not get to the front because of rail and road difficulties. Oils and
lubricants for winter transport had also been inadequate, causing
serious damage to mechanized equipment. The result was that frost
and snow took a terrible toll of men and material. Casualty lists soon
mounted into the tens of thousands. The Luftwaffe suffered heavy
losses as well in their attempts to supply the isolated garrisons
scattered along the huge front.

During the spring of 1942 the German forces were brought up to
strength by the intake of fresh recruits from Germany and by the
replenishment of lost equipment. Some 200-220 German divisions
were now available in the East although the strength of these new
formations had been brought down from 12,000-15,000 men to 8,000-
10,000 men. In addition the satellite divisions of Finland, Roumania,
Hungary and Italy contributed another sixty-five divisions of questionable fighting value. To help the new Army Commander, Adolf
Hitler, work out his flashes of tactical intuition was von Brauchitsch's
Chief-of-Staff, Colonel General Franz Halder. The Führer was not
happy about his assistant, whom he distrusted and resented. However, Halder was an able planner with a brilliant mind, and was, at
first, indispensable to Hitler in his task of leading troops in the field.

While the Führer, completely unperturbed by the losses of the winter, made grandiose plans for a summer offensive in 1942, Halder became increasingly concerned about the growing strength of the Russian forces.

"During the first six months of the Russian campaign it became evident to us how much we had underestimated the resources available within Russia," said Halder.[13] "From statements made by high-ranking prisoners-of-war and from other sources of information, we began to see, that even if we had destroyed all the Russian forces originally mobilized, that the manpower and material potential of Russia could still be colossal. When this potential became obvious we tried by every means to obtain a clear picture of the situation. By combining the information received from Finland, Roumania, Turkey and Japan it was conclusively proved to me, in the early summer of 1942, that from the end of 1942 onwards we would be dealing with much greater forces of Russian manpower and armaments than we had ever known before. I tried to explain these matters to Hitler in June but he flew into a rage. When I presented him with the figures of Russian tank production he went off the deep end. He was no longer a rational human being. I don't know whether he didn't want to understand or whether he really didn't believe it. In any event, it was quite impossible to discuss such matters with him. He would foam at the mouth, threaten me with his fists and scream at the top of his lungs. Any logical discussion was out of the question."

In May 1942 the Russian offensive at Kharkov was held and after clearing up their right flank by taking Sevastopol and crushing all remaining resistance in the Crimea, the Germans began their summer offensive towards the Caucasian oilfields. Striking hard along the corridor between the Don and Donetz rivers the attack, which began in mid-June, made rapid progress. In six weeks one force was well beyond Rostov, over 250 miles east of the start line, while another force was reaching the region of Stalingrad. But while the Germans made sweeping gains of territory, they again failed to trap the elusive Russian armies. "Our early advances were due to the fact that the Russians did not fight it out in this area," said Halder. "They evaded action and maintained their forces intact. This was something that Adolf Hitler could not believe."

By the end of August, German spearheads had penetrated 450 miles east of Rostov and reached the heart of the Caucasian oilfields. Here a break-down of transport left the German armor stalled for three weeks without fuel. Then instead of consolidating his gains in this region, which had been his prime and initial objective, Hitler began to cast longing eyes towards Stalingrad. Withdrawing forces from the

Caucasus, he switched them north towards Stalingrad in a feverish desire to take the city. The more bitterly the Russians fought in front of Stalingrad the more insistent Hitler became. The name of the city seemed to have some symbolic significance for him and he so weakened his Caucasian forces to reinforce the Stalingrad front, that what had, at first, been only a subsidiary effort now had grown into the main one.

In mid-September the Sixth Army under Field Marshal Paulus began the actual assault against Stalingrad. But it was soon evident that the Russian will to resist was as determined as Hitler's will to conquer. After three weeks of house-to-house fighting the Germans stopped their costly attacks against the fortified homes and factories of Stalingrad and settled down to an uneasy siege of the battered city. A few weeks before, however, Halder had recommended that the offensive towards Stalingrad be broken off since it was losing momentum. In a violent interview Halder was told who was running the campaign and was then dismissed. To take his place in implementing the whims of the Führer came Colonel General Kurt von Zeitzler, who managed to hold the thankless job of Hitler's army Chief-of-Staff until 20 July 1944, when the repercussions of the bomb plot against the Führer removed him from office.

The Russian winter offensive of 1942 came as an even greater surprise than the offensive of the winter before. Settling in for a long, cold siege of Stalingrad the Sixth German Army of Paulus was dumbfounded suddenly to find that on 19 November a twenty-mile hole had been torn in its northern flank. Although some officers, like Halder, had warned Hitler of the steadily increasing Russian strength, the bulk of them believed that the successful German summer campaign had taken the sting out of any immediate Russian effort. In any case Hitler refused to consent to a withdrawal of the forces surrounding Stalingrad, despite the obvious risk entailed in maintaining an extended salient hundreds of miles beyond his main line.

Here again German military intelligence produced the wrong answer. They gave no warning to Paulus of the vast Russian forces being assembled east of the Volga. In fact they assured him that there was no possibility of a serious counter-offensive. So confident were these reports that a weak corps consisting of two Roumanian divisions and one German division was given a sector on the Don near Kalach. It was commonly recognized that the quality of the Roumanian formations was low, since they were badly-trained and had few anti-tank guns. Nevertheless they were given a vital sector to hold as there seemed little to fear from the beaten and tired Red Army.

The Roumanians broke overnight before the tremendous Russian thrust. In two days the Russians had advanced over forty miles in the bend of the Don and taken Kalach. South of Stalingrad another arm of the encircling movement found equally unprepared and surprised troops. In a week almost 65,000 prisoners were taken and 1000 tanks captured or destroyed. By the end of November the gap between the Russian pincers had not yet been closed. But Paulus made no attempt to escape, for by then the decision had been made at Berlin that he was to hold and not withdraw. Instead a relief force attempted to break through the Russian ring from the south, but it was thrown back with terrible losses. By the end of the year the encirclement of the 250,000 men of the Sixth German Army was complete. All hope of escape was past. On February 2, 1942, Field Marshal Paulus with twenty-three of his generals formally surrendered his entire force.

"It was my task to attempt to supply the Sixth German Army by air," said Lieutenant General Wolfgang Pickert, a thin, loquacious Luftwaffe officer,[14] "but our resources were far too inadequate. We lost over 500 transport planes trying to bring in ammunition and food for the quarter of a million men encircled in the city. Food soon became so short that the troops had to eat horses that had been frozen in the snow for weeks. It was useless to attempt to break out once we had been surrounded because there was nothing behind us but hundreds of kilometres of open, frozen steppes. In any case we had been ordered by the Führer to hold Stalingrad. We always underestimated the Russians, but our intelligence was particularly bad in their estimates of Russian strength in the winter of 1942."

By April 1943 it was obvious that even Hitler could not win wars cheaply. What had been a glorious march to certain victory had suddenly been brought to a sobering halt. The six months' fighting in Russia since mid-November 1942 had cost the Wehrmacht almost 1,250,000 personnel casualities, 5000 aircraft, 9000 tanks and 20,000 guns.[15] Over a hundred divisions had been destroyed or ceased to exist as effective fighting units. Had the Führer's intuition been working properly it would have told him, then, that this was only a portent of far worse things yet to come.

Thus in Russia by the spring of 1943 the forces of self-destruction within the Wehrmacht could be seen busily at work. The campaign that had opened with every prospect of success was teetering on the abyss of failure. Each startling advance had ended up in a cul-de-sac; each brilliant plan had brought nothing but frustration. Despite victories of classic proportions and textbook perfection, the spectre of defeat had not vanished — in fact it had grown clearer and larger and nearer. The exponents of the offensive and the masters of blitz-krieg warfare were now talking gloomily of the defensive and of holding on to what they had.

One needed only to study what had happened in Russia to under-stand what had brought about this paradoxical state of affairs. The intuitive guesses of the corporal who outranked field marshals had suddenly gone wrong. The crystal ball that had revealed the way to victory over Czechoslovakia, Poland, Norway, France, had dimmed in the frosty atmosphere of a Russian winter. And clairvoyance could never be a substitute for sound, strategical reasoning when dealing with an enemy as virile and as cunning as the Red Army. Having made the blunder of attacking Russia in the first place, Hitler followed it up by wasting his strength in a futile attempt to capture Moscow and defeat the Russian winter at one and the same time. The next year, having failed to learn from experience, he had once more driven his armies forward only to be beaten again by Stalingrad and another winter.

The Führer's faulty and over-optimistic reasoning was abetted all along by incredibly bad information supplied to him by his intelli-gence service. They consistently underestimated the Russian ability to resist, to recover, to produce and to fight. They had predicted victory west of the Dnieper, had failed to believe the Russians capable of launching an offensive in the winter of '41, and had been taken completely by surprise at Stalingrad in '42. They had been encour-aged in their lighthearted prognostications by a Führer whose wishful thinking corresponded to their own. The prospect of instant dismissal if one suggested facts different from what Hitler wanted them to be, may have also discouraged many an officer from indulging too deeply in either pessimism or the truth.

And finally there was no one left to prevent the Führer from making as many and as stupid and as expensive mistakes as he alone saw fit. He was now all the important military authorities rolled up into one, and there was no man either above him or below him to check his mad desires. He had fired those offiecrs who disagreed with him, such as von Brauchitsch, Halder and von Rundstedt, and he had replaced others like von Leeb, von Bock and List when they failed to carry out his impossible orders. Discipline and the chance for rapid promotion kept the remainder of the German General Staff clicking their heels whenever the Führer barked. And all the while the men up front, suffering the real anguish and misery of the cold and the fire and the steel, could but wonder and obey, for they were too deluded and too ignorant to do anything else.

Chapter XI

THE DECISIVE MISTAKE — UNITED STATES

IF THE FIVE mistakes already discussed had not been sufficient in themselves to bring about the downfall of Hitler's Reich, Mistake Number Six made it inevitable. This decisive blunder was the decision to encourage Japan's participation in the war even at the risk of bringing in the United States on the side of Great Britain. On 27 September 1940, the signing of the Tripartite Pact between Germany, Italy and Japan made official what had been covertly in effect for some time. Under the terms of this ten-year military and economic alliance the Axis Powers agreed "to stand by and to co-operate with one another in regard to their efforts in Greater East Asia and regions of Europe respectively, wherein it is their prime purpose to establish and maintain a new order of things."

Actually, close liaison for subversive ends had been established between the Nazi authorities and Japan long before the war began. For as early as 31 January 1939, General Oshima, the Japanese Ambassador in Berlin, was plotting with Heinrich Himmler the assassination of the head of a so-called friendly state. In a document drawn up by Himmler recording a conversation of that date held with the Japanese Ambassador, Himmler reported that Oshima was undertaking, in collaboration with German subversive agencies, the long-range task of "the disintegration of Russia from the Caucasus and Ukraine." In furtherance of that ambitious aim Himmler also wrote that "Oshima had succeeded up to now in sending ten Russians with bombs across the Caucasian frontier. These Russians had the mission to kill Stalin. A number of additional Russians, whom he had also sent across, had been shot at the frontier." [1]

Nevertheless, despite such activities, there seems to have been little determined effort made on the part of Germany to seek Japan's participation in the war during its early phases. But once the decision to attack Russia had been made, the need to keep England occupied while the Wehrmacht busied itself in the East, made it desirable from the German point of view for Japan to take a hand in affairs in the Pacific. The steady flow of American goods across the Atlantic and the imminence of unlimited Lend-Lease aid to England probably stimulated the top secret directive issued by Field Marshal Keitel on 5 March 1941. It stated that "The Führer had ordered instigation of Japan's active participation in the war," and directed that, "Japan's military power has to be strengthened by the disclosure of German war experiences, and support of a military, economic and technical nature has to be given." The aim of such aid was declared to be to crush England quickly, and thereby keep the United States out of the war.[2]

During the later stages of the preparations for the attack against Russia, Japan was kept constantly informed of German intentions. Joachim von Ribbentrop, as Foreign Minister, seems to have carried out most of the negotiations designed to lure Japan into the war, but the Japanese were not easily convinced that what was best for Germany was necessarily best for Japan. Aiding von Ribbentrop in his encouragement of Japanese cupidity was Adolf Hitler himself. While the Führer would have preferred to have Japan concentrate her energies against Great Britain alone, he realized that any Japanese intervention in the Pacific might well provoke the United States into action. He was, nevertheless, willing to take that risk, feeling confident that American intervention would not be able to make itself felt before it was far too late to help England. This fatal miscalculation of Hitler's is clearly set out in a document captured from the files of the German Foreign Office. It consists of notes dated 4 April 1941 "regarding the discussions between the Führer and the Japanese Foreign Minister, Matsuoka, in the presence of the Reich Foreign Minister and the Reich Minister of State, Meissner, in Berlin." [3] In part the record of this conference reads:

"Japan would do her utmost to avoid a war with the United States. If Japan should decide to attack Singapore, the Japanese navy, of course, had to be prepared for a fight with the United States, because in that case America probably would side with Great Britain. He (Matsuoka) personally believed that the United States could be restrained by diplomatic exertions from entering the war at the side of Great Britain. Army and navy had, however, to count on the worst situation, that is on war against America. They were of the opinion that such a war would extend for five years or longer and would take the form of guerilla warfare in the Pacific and would be fought out in the south seas. For this reason the German experiences in her guerilla warfare were of the greatest value to Japan. It was a question how such a war could best be conducted and how all the technical improvements of submarines, in all details such as periscopes and such like, could best be exploited by Japan.

"To sum up, Matsuoka requested that the Führer would see to it that the proper German authorities would place at the disposal of the Japanese those developments and inventions concerning navy and army which were needed by the Japanese.

"The Führer promised this and pointed out that Germany too considered a conflict with the United States undesirable, but that it had already made allowances for such a contingency. . . . Germany has made her preparations so that no American could land in Europe. She would conduct a most energetic fight against America with her U-boats and her 'Luftwaffe' and due to her superior experience, which would still have to be acquired by the United States, she would be vastly superior, and that, quite apart from the fact that the German soldiers naturally rank high above the Americans.

"In the further course of the discussion, the Führer pointed out that Germany on her part would immediately take the consequences if Japan would get involved with the United States. It did not matter with whom the United States would first get involved, whether Germany or Japan. . . . Germany would strike without delay in case of a conflict between Japan and America, because the strength of the Tripartite Powers lies in their joint action; their weakness would be if they would let themselves be beaten individually. . . ."

Having thus assured Japan of his determination to back any course of action she might take, the Führer left Ribbentrop to complete the task of bringing Japan into the war. Hitler relied on Ribbentrop's judgment in foreign affairs, despite his failure correctly to assess the prevailing mood of England following the fall of France. Göring was not so confident of Ribbentrop's ability. "When I criticized Ribbentrop's qualifications to handle British problems," said Göring,[4] "the Führer pointed out to me that Ribbentrop knew 'Lord So and So' and 'Minister So and So.' To which I had replied 'Yes, but the difficulty is that they know Ribbentrop.' "

Probably the Japanese also "knew Ribbentrop" for, while carrying on conversations with him about the progress of the war, they never revealed to him their definite intention of striking at the United States. As late as 28 November 1941, the Japanese Ambassador in Berlin, Oshima, and Ribbentrop were holding discussions about the possibility of Japan's entry into the war.[5]

Intercepted diplomatic messages sent by Oshima to Tokyo reporting on these discussions, reveal that Ribbentrop urged Japan not to lose a golden opportunity of effecting the new order in Asia. If she hesitated then, said the German Foreign Minister, the military might of Britain and the United States would be concentrated against her. He insisted that Japan must make the decision to fight Britain and the United States. Ribbentrop then went on to reveal Germany's future plans. They were first to drive Stalin deep into Siberia by the spring of 1942 and after that to wipe out Britain's influence in the

Near East, Africa and the Mediterranean. Oshima then asked whether Germany also intended to launch a campaign against the United Kingdom itself. "Germany has, of course, made all necessary preparations," was Ribbentrop's classic answer. "However, she is in receipt of information which would seem to indicate that all is not well within England. For example, we hear that there is a split within the ranks of the Conservatives, that Churchill's influence is on the wane, and that Bevin, the chief of the Labor Party, is advocating revolutionary measures." After such a reply it is small wonder that Oshima thought better of revealing to Ribbentrop what Japan had up her sleeve.[6] Nine days later the Japanese bombed Pearl Harbor.

"The Japanese attack on Pearl Harbor came as a complete surprise, albeit a gratifying one," said Göring. "Hitler declared war on the United States because he was convinced that such a war was inevitable. The re-election of President Roosevelt was accepted by him as conclusive. Up to that time, the Führer had tried to avoid an open break with the United States, and the German navy had been ordered to allow American ships to move unmolested, although it was known that they were fully laden with war materials for England. Since Japan was the aggressor we had no treaty obligation to side with her, but Hitler felt a sense of gratitude towards the Japanese, and he may, therefore, have acted impulsively."[7]

Only future historians will be able adequately to judge whether Hitler's view of the inevitability of war with the United States was the correct one. Had he played his cards differently and attempted to restrict Japan's aggressive activities only to British holdings in the Pacific, it is a matter of conjecture whether Congress would have immediately gone to war. What President Roosevelt would have done had Japan attacked Singapore, Hong Kong and the Dutch East Indies on 7 December 1941, and left American possessions alone is a question that will never be answered. But it is fairly certain that such a course might well have delayed America's entry into the conflict for many months while Congress debated what to do next. And those months at the beginning of 1942 were very vital months indeed.

The Führer however preferred to believe that the support of a fully prepared Japan would far outweigh the opposition of an unprepared America. The tremendous industrial and military potential of the United States did not impress him. Göring had once said, "The Americans can't build planes: only electric iceboxes and razor blades." Hitler, apparently, shared that opinion. He was soon to learn otherwise.

Chapter XII

THE FINAL MISTAKE — EL ALAMEIN

ONCE HITLER had succeeded in pitting against the Reich the combined might of the British Empire, Russia and the United States, it is extremely doubtful that Germany could ever have won World War II. But had she taken advantage of the opportunities that presented themselves after Pearl Harbor, it is certain that she might have prolonged the war for many years to come, or even brought about a military stalemate in Europe. The one chance that still remained open to her in 1942 was the same chance that she had tossed aside in 1940. It was to try again to expel the British from the Mediterranean by sealing off both the eastern and western approaches to the sea. In July 1942 that opportunity was once more within reach, for a victorious German force had just reached El Alamein, a desert position within striking distance of Alexandria and the Suez Canal. With the Suez Canal in their hands innumerable possibilities would be opened up for the German Supreme Command. Having driven the British from North Africa the Germans could have then taken on Malta, Gibraltar and Cyprus to complete the task of clearing the Mediterranean, or advanced through the Middle East and in a gigantic pincer movement joined up with German forces driving through the Caucasus. Either of these moves would have prevented the débâcle at Stalingrad, would have made impossible the Allied landing in North Africa and would have kept Italy in the war. But the glittering opportunity of El Alamein, like so many others before it, was not grasped. That was Mistake Number Seven. The man who gave the Third Reich that one last chance to avert defeat was a German officer called Erwin Rommel.

Few generals in their lifetime have had as many words written about them as has Field Marshal Rommel. And seldom has there been more controversy about a man's accomplishments in the military field. On the one hand he was hailed as a military genius, and on the other he was berated as an incompetent upstart. While it was undoubtedly Hitler himself, supported by Goebbels, who began the Rommel legend, it was the Allied press, coupled with the respect shown his ability by the Eighth Army troops in the desert, that helped foster it beyond all reason. Strangely enough, it was the senior officers of the German General Staff who did most to discount Rommel's reputation and to ascribe his victories more to good luck than to any outstanding ability.

There was nothing striking about Rommel's physical appearance. He was of medium height and the only characteristic feature of his rather open face was a blunt, determined jaw. In the first World War Rommel, as a junior officer, had won the highest German decoration for valor, the Pour Le Mérite — an award equivalent to the Victoria Cross. Yet despite this distinction his academic ability was not considered of a high enough calibre to warrant his being trained as a General Staff officer. When Hitler came to power, however, Rommel was appointed to instruct the Führer's bodyguard in military tactics. This proximity to Hitler Rommel exploited vigorously and in the Polish campaign he was given a panzer division to lead. With the aid of Goebbels this formation's part in the French campaign was extensively publicized, as Rommel had now become the Führer's favorite general. In March 1941, after the Italians had been smashed in the Western Desert and thrown out of Cyrenaica, Rommel arrived at Tripoli with his famous Afrika Korps, consisting then of two well-equipped armored divisions.

The seesaw struggle that developed in North Africa in the next eighteen months has already been well, and often, told. Rommel's skill in twice driving the British back to the Egyptian frontier, and his elusiveness in evading annihilation when the British struck back, gained for him his unparalleled fame as a master tactician. Poised before El Alamein in July 1942, he boasted that he would be in Cairo in "three or four days." But here his luck ran out. His weary troops, far beyond their supply bases, found that General Auchinleck's defense was not as vulnerable as their commander had believed it to be. Checked after two successive attempts, the Afrika Korps paused for a rest before trying again. In the meantime Auchinleck had been replaced by Field Marshal Montgomery, who, after building up an adequate British force, hit out at El Alamein on 23 October 1942. Ten days later the Afrika Korps, for the last time, was in full retreat towards Tripoli. Rommel, who had been in a hospital in Germany, was rushed back to his post. But it was then far too late, and Germany had lost its final chance to reach the Suez.

What prevented the Germans from pushing on beyond El Alamein in July 1942? The complete inability of the German Supreme Command to recognize the significance of what a German victory at El Alamein might lead to. Curiously enough on this point Hitler and his military advisers seem to have been in complete accord. The North African campaign was viewed at Berlin as of secondary importance and neither the Führer nor the General Staff took it very seriously. The presence of German troops in Africa at all was merely a political gesture to appease Mussolini. According to General Ritter von Thoma, who succeeded Rommel in the desert, Hitler was quite confident as to the ability of the Italians to hold Africa by themselves. He, therefore, felt that the presence of one or two German divisions would be sufficient to bolster the Italians, and also keep Mussolini from changing sides.

This view was strenuously backed by Colonel General Franz Halder, the army Chief-of-Staff, who was against any German forces being involved in the Mediterranean. He consistently warned Hitler against the dangers of stretching their resources too far. In addition Halder had scant respect for Rommel's generalship and this may have influenced his desire to keep German troops out of Africa.

"As far as I was concerned the North African affair was largely a political decision," said Halder, discussing the reason for the small size of the force sent to Africa.[1] "We realized that it was important to Italy that the African coastline be prevented from falling into enemy hands, but with the English commanding the sea I insisted that the utmost we could send, and keep supplied, were three to four divisions. With so small a force all we could hope to do was to defend Italian territory for as long as possible. Of course if the opportunity for offensive action presented itself we would take it. But on the whole we regarded the matter as a fight for time. Sooner or later things were bound to turn out badly for the Italians, but the longer we could postpone that from happening — perhaps for years — so much the better. To achieve that purpose, the outlay of three to four divisions might not prove too costly.

"I last talked to Rommel about this subject in the spring of 1942. At that time he told me that he would conquer Egypt and the Suez Canal, and then he spoke of East Africa. I could not restrain a somewhat impolite smile and asked him what he would need for the purpose. He thought he would want another two armored corps. I asked him, 'Even if we had them, how would you supply and feed them?' To this question his reply was, 'That's quite immaterial to me; that's your problem.' As events in Africa grew worse Rommel kept demanding more and more aid. Where it was to come from didn't worry him. Then the Italians began to complain because they were losing their shipping in the process. If history succeeds in unraveling the threads of what finally went on in Africa, it will have achieved a miracle, for Rommel managed to get things into such an unholy muddle that I doubt whether anyone will ever be able to make head or tail of it."

As late as 3 October 1942, just a few weeks before Montgomery's attack at El Alamein, Rommel was still outwardly confident of the outcome of the African campaign. For on that day in Berlin he boasted to a group of foreign journalists: "Today we stand one hundred kilometres from Alexandria and hold the gateway to Egypt, with the full intention of getting there, too. We have not got so far with any intention of being flung back either sooner or later. You may rely on our holding fast to what we have got. . . ."

Whether these words were designed primarily to reassure those at home in the Reich or whether Rommel actually believed them is difficult to say. According to one of the divisional commanders who fought with the Afrika Korps, a Major General Johann Cramer, the supply situation at El Alamein was giving Rommel a great deal of concern. "El Alamein was lost before it was fought," said Cramer.[2] "We had not the petrol. Vast stocks of petrol and material were lying around in Italy and the Italians were supposed to bring them over, but they could not do it. Rommel for a long time had known that the campaign in North Africa was hopeless, not because we lacked weapons or reserves, but because of petrol shortage. He appealed to Hitler to end the campaign as soon as El Alamein was lost and thus save us much greater losses later on — which in fact we suffered at Cap Bon in Tunisia."

Thus General Cramer in a somewhat oblique manner confirmed General Halder's opinion that the North African venture would flounder on the problem of supply. While Rommel will undoubtedly be regarded by posterity as a brilliant tactician, his obvious weaknesses in the administrative field should deprive him of any lasting recognition as a great general. His personal defects in this regard were magnified by an unco-operative Supreme Command which refused to consider his theatre of operations seriously and therefore made little effort to maintain an adequate German force in the desert. Looking back at it now, it seems that the diversion of but two or three more properly equipped divisions to aid Rommel in July 1942 might well have paid the Wehrmacht handsome dividends. These divisions could easily have been spared from the idle formations in France uselessly watching the Channel coast at a period when it was obvious that Allied strength was not great enough to venture an essay against the Atlantic Wall. Again being wise after the event, Field Marshal Keitel acknowledged the mistake of El Alamein in these words:[3]

"One of the biggest occasions we passed by was El Alamein. I would say that, at that climax of the war, we were nearer to victory than any time before or after. Very little was needed then to conquer Alexandria and to push forward to Suez and Palestine. But we just were not strong enough at that particular point, due to the disposal of our forces and primarily the war against Russia."

The defeat of the Afrika Korps brought about three important results within a very few months — the expulsion of Axis troops from all of Africa, the elimination of a huge German force in Tunisia, and the opportunity for the Allies to assault the southern rim of the European continent. For, having tried to stand at El Alamein too long — Hitler, as usual, having prevented a withdrawal in good time — Rommel on 2 November was back-pedaling as hard as he could go in the direction of Tripoli. Too weak to attempt to hold any intermediate defense line in the desert, Rommel conducted a skilful, but hasty, retreat to the Mareth Line. This position had been built earlier by the French behind the Tunis-Tripoli frontier as protection against the Italians.

While Rommel was making this 1400-mile withdrawal in less than three months, the first large-scale Allied amphibious landing was successfully made on 8 November 1942 on the beaches of Casablanca, Rabat, Oran and Algiers in French North Africa. German military intelligence, whose ineptitude had already been well demonstrated by its misappreciations of British and Russian resources, continued its record of blunders in North Africa. Despite the many facilities for espionage in a Vichy-controlled French Africa, and despite the fact that an armada of 850 warships and merchantmen had to sail for many days in the open Atlantic before reaching its destination, the Germans nevertheless were taken completely by surprise when the landings were reported. Admiral Krancke, who was subsequently responsible for organizing the German naval defense of Western Europe, admitted that the navy was caught badly off guard by this Allied move. "Neither the preparations nor the transit of the landing barges were known to the German naval staff," said the Admiral.[4] "Consequently, U-boats were not put into operation off the African coast."

The result of the Allied landings was that the entire Axis force in Africa was sandwiched between the Eighth Army under Montgomery advancing from the east, and the newly-arrived Anglo-American force under General Eisenhower attacking from the west. In a forlorn attempt to retrieve a hopeless situation, Hitler finally undertook to do what he had refused to do early in 1942 when it would have been of some avail. He sent reinforcements of men and supplies to Africa. But whereas such a German force might, indeed, have reached the Suez Canal eight months before, in March 1943 it could only hold an uneasy bridgehead in North Africa and hope thereby to deny the Allies unfettered use of the Mediterranean. Under Rommel facing east, and Colonel General von Arnim facing west, the Germans held off the Allies until April 1943, when the Mareth Line was broken. Rommel, then, went back to Germany too ill to carry on. He left behind the entire Afrika Korps, now swollen to over 120,000 men under General von Arnim, to continue the useless struggle for another month. No serious attempts to evacuate these troops were made, for the Führer had decided that they would not withdraw and that they would resist to the last. It was an order that had already cost the Wehrmacht much in Russia, and was one that was destined to cost them much more before World War II had come to its end. On 13 May 1943, the complete Italian and German forces in Tunisia, numbering some 250,000 men, surrendered to the Allies. The Mediterranean was again an Allied sea, and Europe lay open for invasion and freedom.

For the next fifty-eight days Anglo-American forces made ready to strike at the underbelly of Europe. On 10 July 1943, Sicily was invaded. Two weeks later at a meeting of the Fascist Grand Council the first Axis dictator, Benito Mussolini, was dethroned and placed under arrest. These events, virtually ending Italy's participation in the war, were the culmination of a long and steady series of rebuffs, defeats and humiliations suffered by the Italian people in their partnership with Nazi Germany. Ever since Italy's sudden entry into the war on 10 June 1940, in an effort to acquire a jackal's share in what appeared to be certain victory, she had been a constant drain on Germany's war effort. Both Keitel and Jodl contend that Italy's help was undesired, but once she was committed she had to be supported. Mussolini's unilateral action in attacking Greece and Egypt had resulted in Germany's being involved in both the Balkan and African campaigns when she would have preferred to concentrate her efforts in Europe. But, as we have already seen, instead of making a concerted and serious attempt to aid Italy in the Mediterranean, Hitler and his staff half-heartedly undertook what they felt to be a secondary, and irritating, sideshow. As a result the opportunities to gain a decisive victory in the Mediterranean were lost, and German forces were frittered away because they were too weak to bolster the numerous, but badly-led, Italian armies.

By 1943 Italy's record in World War II was both inglorious and pathetic. She had been held and even pushed back by a Greek army far inferior in size and equipment; her navy had been hiding in port ever since its crippling defeat at Taranto on 11 November 1940; over 130,000 Italian prisoners had been captured by General Wavell's tiny force when it drove Marshal Graziani's army out of Egypt and Cyrenaica in early 1941; later in 1941 she lost Italian East Africa, including Eritrea, Italian Somaliland and Abyssinia; and finally the disaster in Tunisia completed the destruction of the Italian African Empire and of most of the Italian armed forces. The invasion of Sicily, where

Italian divisions merely laid down their arms before the Allied invaders, showed how unenthusiastic about the war the Italian people had become. When Hitler refused to send additional German reinforcements to Mussolini following the Sicilian landings, the Duce's prestige had fallen so low that nineteen of the twenty-six members of the Fascist Grand Council asked him to resign on 24 July 1943. To take his place as head of the government came Marshal Badoglio, openly pledging support to the Axis, but secretly starting negotiations with the Western Allies some three weeks later.

All this time German military intelligence had completely failed to divine either Allied or Italian intentions. The attack against Sicily came as a surprise. "We believed the Allies would invade Sardinia first," said Colonel General Student, who was commanding the German paratroops in Italy at the time.[5] The downfall of Mussolini came as a surprise. And finally the capitulation of Badoglio, secretly agreed to on 3 September but not announced until 8 September 1943, came as a surprise. "I did not know of the Italian surrender until I heard it announced over the wireless on 8 September," said Colonel General von Vietinghoff, commander of the Tenth German Army in Italy.[6] "Although we had suspected that something of the sort might happen, the actual event came as a great shock."

It is to the credit of the German General Staff that despite these three successive bad guesses on the part of their intelligence, they, nevertheless, managed to adjust themselves with commendable speed to each of these surprise blows. In Sicily, by acting quickly, they succeeded in delaying the Allied conquest of the island for thirty-eight days, which cut down the subsequent campaigning weather for operations in Italy. On hearing of Mussolini's eclipse, they promptly sent reinforcements to Italy both for the purpose of protecting the German troops already there and to safeguard the southern frontiers of the Reich. And finally when the surrender of Badoglio's government was announced, they ruthlessly took charge of a situation that could quite easily have become uncontrollable. German officers merely marched in on their neighboring Italian headquarters and ordered their ex-allies to lay down their arms. "We had no difficulty at all in dealing with the Italians," said von Vietinghoff.[7] "They were just as surprised as we were by the announcement of the surrender and they had not the faintest idea of what it was all about. I only know of one Italian divisional commander who refused to order his troops to disarm. He was shot, by the German escort who came to him, when he reached for his pistol. It is still not clear whether the Italian commander intended to defy us or merely hand over his weapon. This was the only case where there was any trouble."

The German plan, in the event of an Allied invasion of the Italian mainland, had been to carry out a slow withdrawal to the Apennines and evacuate Italy. Rommel, who was now commanding an army group in Northern Italy, had been the chief proponent of giving up Southern Italy as soon as possible. He believed that with Allied control of the sea, any line too far south would be in grave danger of being cut off by Allied landings behind it. But when it was discovered that there would be no danger from the Italians, who had meekly gone off to their homes, and when it was obvious that the Allied bridgehead at Salerno was being held, Field Marshal Kesselring, Commander-in-Chief in Southern Italy, decided not to retire just yet, but to hold south of Rome for as long as he could. Thus, according to von Vietinghoff, the original scheme to abandon Italy was revised and it was decided early in October to build a Winter Line based on the Abruzzi Mountains in the center, the Sangro River in the east and the Garigliano River in the west. Here, behind formidable geographical barriers, the Germans began their winter-long defence of Southern Italy which was to result in the bitter battles for Ortona, Cassino and Anzio before Rome finally was taken on 4 June 1944.

The unexpected stabilization of the Italian front was, however, the only bright gleam in the increasingly darkening horizon of Germany's future. Manpower was fast becoming a pressing problem and by mid-1943 boys of fifteen were being used to help man the anti-aircraft guns of the Reich. In addition, calls were being made upon the Luftwaffe and the navy to give up some of their personnel to help meet the terrible losses of the army. With childish petulance Göring would only consent to his air force personnel being used as ground troops if he still retained control of their activities. Thus there came about a series of private armies in the Wehrmacht, each with their own chain of command responsible only to the Führer. For, not to be outdone by Göring, Himmler also built up his own S.S. divisions, and Dönitz insisted that naval personnel were answerable only to him and not to any army authorities. Since all these independent groups were supposed to fight within the general framework of the army, the resultant quibbling and petty jealousies amongst them made a unified command almost impossible.

"With the heavy set-backs that started in the fateful month of November 1942," writes General Warlimont, discussing this period,[8] "the organization of the Supreme Command broke up more and more. Rommel retreated from El Alamein on 2 November; the surprise Anglo-American landings in French North Africa occurred on 8 November, and Stalingrad was encircled on 29 November. Göring stirred the fire, interfering with everything without scruple or responsibility. The misshapen Luftwaffe field divisions originated at that time, because Göring could not expect his air force men to change their blue-gray uniform for the field-gray of the army. . . . The peculiar position of the S.S. further increased the difficulties of command. In spite of their tactical subordination to the army, the ever-growing number of S.S. divisions used channels of their own, which could be depended upon to supply everything. In their estimation whoever accused the army, especially the General Staff, was right.

"Thus Hitler alone had an overall view of the whole situation. Now, more than ever, he amused himself by shifting divisions and smaller units, especially armored units, from one area to another, and trying to attend personally to every minute detail. This, naturally, prevented the timely discovery and consideration of important events which were pending — such as the armament of the United States, the air war of annihilation, the dangers in the Balkans and the decay of Italian power (co-operation with our allies was generally much neglected). However, Hitler was at least willing to read reports on such developments, but the constant submission of intelligence of the ever-growing Russian forces had already become impossible in Halder's time. Hitler simply refuted such information and regarded it as an expression of the General Staff's defeatist attitude. The method of self-deception was gradually extended to all fields; figures took the place of strength; orders were given, but no material existed to carry them out. Fanatical clinging to individual localities was supposed to prevent the loss of whole areas, while the substance of the army was wasted at a steadily increasing rate. . . ."

And thus the stage was set for defeat. Only three years before, in September 1940, Hitler, the master of a continent, could brandish his fists and mouth his threats at his only remaining enemy — a stunned and unprepared England only twenty miles away. Now, in September 1943, the ersatz Napoleon could watch his rapidly shrinking empire being besieged from the north, the south and the east by the advancing armies of his many and powerful enemies. For the transformation he had chiefly himself to blame. But he was ably assisted in bringing about the fall of the Third Reich by the officers of the Wehrmacht, who were too blind, too rigid, too disciplined, too uninformed, too weak, too frightened and too ambitious to prevent both themselves and their countrymen from taking the mad course their Führer had set for them.

Victory, in those early years, was within reach of the Third Reich time and time again. Yet on each occasion the wrong step was taken, the stupid decision made. Future generations of German apologists will try to explain away their defeat by moaning about the vast arsenals, the mighty factories, the immense riches of the powers assembled against them. They will neglect to mention that for three years Germany had all the might, all the material, all the experience, all the triumphs. They will fail to point out that against a continent geared for war stood only one island isolated by thousands of miles of water from those who wanted to help her. They will hide the fact that Germany undertook to go to war with countries that her leaders felt were unprepared enough or inexperienced enough to be beaten easily. It was men who made those decisions, not machines. It was Germans who blundered to defeat, no one else.

Look back at the mistakes that were committed by the Third Reich — at Dunkirk, Russia, El Alamein and elsewhere. Some were Hitler's decisions alone, in others he was supported by his General Staff, and in still others he was fooled by his own intelligence service. But even when the course adopted was patently absurd, even when the risk to be taken involved thousands of German lives, few leaders of the Third Reich, either military or political, were honest or brave enough to voice their disapproval or dissent. They carried out their orders, however stupid or brutal or costly or inhuman, and justified their conduct with the excuse that true Germans only obeyed — they did not think. Each mistake that led to Germany's ultimate defeat was compounded out of the same elements — a Führer who was guided by intuition rather than logic, a group of advisers who consistently underestimated and misappreciated the moral and physical capacity of their opponents, a military clique that allowed itself to be kept in the dark and was too disciplined or too self-seeking to protest even when it began to see the light. And again — because it cannot be repeated too often — these mistakes were man-made and they were made in Germany.

By the end of 1943 the German nation, as exemplified by its leaders, had decisively demonstrated that it possessed neither the wisdom, the courage nor the faith to achieve or deserve victory. It only re-mained for Time to bring about the inexorable end. In traveling the road to defeat Germany had reached the mountain-tops of dizzy suc-cess and then, unable to climb any higher, had been forced to make the tortuous descent to dismal failure. But before the Third Reich had reached the cold shadows of the valley of final defeat, her people were destined to suffer agony and despair and pain in far greater measure than anything the German nation had ever experienced before. For it was now no longer a question of whether Germany had lost her second Great War. The only question was: When?

Part IV ⸴ THE INVASION

Chapter XIII

THE ATLANTIC WALL AND THE MEN BEHIND IT

WITH the German failure to capture Moscow late in 1941, a two-front war had become an unpleasant reality. The entry of the United States into the conflict presented the possibility of an invasion of the Continent in the West. No longer was there freedom to take on one foe at a time without danger of a threat from behind. The eyes of the Supreme Command began to shift apprehensively from side to side. They could no longer face resolutely in only one direction.

Hitler looked about him for a man who could provide him with security in the West while his armies were still engaged against the Russians. The choice was obvious. The one general who had been consistently successful in all he had undertaken was the aloof, professional Field Marshal von Rundstedt. But in early 1942 the Marshal was in one of his periodic retirements. His quarrel with the Führer over the recommendation that Army Group South be permitted to withdraw from its advanced winter positions in the Caucasus had brought about von Rundstedt's resignation. The Field Marshal, however, was not destined to remain unemployed for very long.

Von Rundstedt had never underestimated the potential strength of the British. He had consistently warned the Supreme Command of the danger in the West. Knowing his interest in this theatre and playing upon the old man's loyalty to duty and the Fatherland, Hitler was able to convince von Rundstedt to take up the marshal's baton once again. In March 1942 he arrived at St. Germain, France, to take over the post of Commander-in-Chief in the West.

During 1942 Hitler still believed that victory over Russia was within reach. Despite the failure of his efforts to take Moscow, there had been cause for elation in the successful drive of the southern armies to the Don. He concentrated his main resources hoping to capture Stalingrad, only to find that what seemed like victory had suddenly become defeat. With the loss of the Sixth Army under Paulus at Stalingrad, the German forces in the East were forced to retire to the Dnieper River.

Preoccupied with the prospects of victory in Russia in 1942, Hitler paid scant attention to events in France. After Stalingrad the losses in the East had so weakened the Wehrmacht that all possibilities of an offensive policy in the West had to be abandoned. From the early part of 1943 onwards Germany was limited to a policy of strategic defense in Western and Southern Europe.

General Günther Blumentritt, who was appointed to act as von Rundstedt's Chief-of-Staff late in 1942, has provided an account of some of the problems that faced the Commander-in-Chief West in the months preceding the Allied invasion of the Continent.[1] According to Blumentritt the task of defending Western Europe was complicated by the formidable area involved. Stretching some thousands of kilometres in a vast semi-circle from Norway along the coast of Europe and through the Mediterranean to Greece, the possibilities of invasion zones were innumerable. With complete superiority of air and sea power, the British and Americans could choose the time and place not only for a main attack, but for any amount of feints as well. The German navy could offer little interference to any such operation, while the bringing up of reserves to threatened sectors was already hampered by Allied air power and the damaged state of the continental railways. Thus in the years 1942-43 the forefinger of High Command strategists moved around the map like an uncertain compass needle trying to point the way to the next Allied move.

The first area considered vulnerable to Allied attention was Norway, Denmark and, above all, the North Sea between the Elbe and the Ems. It was thought that landings in these northern regions would take place independent of a cross-Channel assault. Blumentritt said that there was a certain amount of doubt about Sweden's reliability, and it was feared that she might have been prevailed upon to grant air bases to the Allies.

When not casting its gaze northward, von Rundstedt's headquarters was keeping an apprehensive eye southwards. "Two or three times during 1943," said Blumentritt, "our attention was drawn by the Supreme Command to the possible threat of an Allied landing in Spain or Portugal. Information about Spain was obtained through attachés in Madrid and Vichy, and Spanish officers were often guests at the headquarters of the German Nineteenth Army in Southern France. We considered Lisbon, the northwest tip of Spain, the Balearic Isles and the Barcelona area as the most likely landing places.

"It was considered that such landings might be made in conjunction with an attack on the south or west coast of France. Countermeasures were prepared by the Commander-in-Chief West in the shape of an operation 'Ilona.' In the event of an Allied landing in Spain or Portugal, Ilona would be put into operation if Spain remained neutral or came in on the German side. . . . Ten divisions were concerned, and there were two lines of attack, one against the Barcelona area, and the main one, should there be an Allied landing in the west, along the line Valladolid-Salamanca where the decisive battle was expected to take place. . . . However, we never did take this threat to Spain very seriously at von Rundstedt's headquarters."

In early 1944 the attention of the Commander-in-Chief West was diverted again. This time to Southern France. Agents' reports flooded into von Rundstedt warning of imminent landings about to take place in the area of the Rhône delta and near the French-Spanish frontier. It was appreciated that if such an attack did take place, another landing around the mouth of the Gironde was to be anticipated. A pincer movement against Toulouse was to be expected, after which there would be an advance along the Canal du Midi to cut off Spain and join up with the growing Resistance Movement in the south of France.

But as the months passed each appreciation was discarded in turn and replaced by another until by the end of March 1944, it became obvious that the northern coast of France provided the most likely and most profitable results for an invasion attempt of the Continent. According to Blumentritt, Admiral Canaris's intelligence branch had only six agents in England about this time, but all of them confirmed the fact that an invasion was to be launched from Southern England.[2]

The possibility of Allied landings on the French Channel coast gave Field Marshal von Rundstedt his greatest concern. To deny a foothold to an invading force in this area, unwarranted reliance had been placed upon the Atlantic Wall. This line of fortifications girdling the coast of France was directly under the Commander-in-Chief West but its technical construction had been entrusted to the organization Todt. This latter organization was thoroughly National Socialist in its conception and had been responsible for the building of the Siegfried Line as well. The strongest parts of the Atlantic Wall were in Holland and the Pas de Calais, with relatively strong sectors in Normandy and Brittany. But on the southern coast of France these static defenses hardly existed at all, and faith had to be pinned on earthen fieldworks and the badly-trained divisions available in the region.

All along this coastal line like so many buttresses to a wall, a series of nodal points had been designated as 'fortresses.' These places were to have the biggest guns, the most cement and the best troops in France. They were to be defended "until the last drop of blood," and the fortress commandant was to be personally responsible with his head if this was not carried out. The instructions in regard to the handling of these bastions came straight from Berlin in a series of Führer's decrees. Dunkirk, Calais, Boulogne, Le Havre, Cherbourg, Brest, La Rochelle, Gironde, Toulon, were some of over a dozen fortresses that were named, and they punctuated the coastline of France like so many knots in a string.

But what Hitler, in his mania for fortresses, had forgotten, was that while the knots themselves might be strong and not readily broken, the weaker cord between could be easily snapped. Therefore — and changing the metaphor — while the fortresses formidably jutted their blunt jaws menacingly towards the sea, their backsides were vulnerable to a devastating kick. There were neither the men nor the materials to build these zones so that they provided all-round protection against the land as well as the sea. Thus they remained bristling in front and flabby behind.

Von Rundstedt was most unhappy about both the Atlantic Wall and this system of fortresses. "Strategically the value of these fortresses was insignificant," said the Field Marshal,[3] "because of their inability to defend themselves against a land attack. When the Führer's instructions for the defense of the fortresses was sent to me, I had the words 'defend to the last drop of blood' changed to 'defend to the last bullet' before I sent them forward to the troops. We subsequently lost over 120,000 men in these concrete posts when we withdrew from France. I always considered this to be a tragic waste of useful manpower.

"As for the Atlantic Wall itself," continued von Rundstedt, "it had to be seen to be believed. It had no depth and little surface. It was sheer humbug. At best it might have proved an obstacle for twenty-four hours at any one point, but one day's intensive assault by a determined force was all that was needed to break any part of this line. Once through the so-called Wall the rest of these fortifications and fortresses facing the sea were of no use at all against an attack from behind. I reported all this to the Führer in October 1943, but it was not favorably received."

If von Rundstedt was unhappy about the Atlantic Wall itself, he was bitter about the formations available in the West to man it. When he had first arrived in France in 1942 there were only some thirty

German divisions in all of France and the Low Countries. As the Russian adventure became more and more costly the threat of a second front in the West became correspondingly greater. Von Rundstedt was thus able to convince the Supreme Command to send him an increasing share of the total resources of the Wehrmacht. By June 1944 von Rundstedt had under command a nominal total of sixty divisions.

According to the Field Marshal only a few of these divisions could be considered first class. No more than fifteen of these sixty formations had either the equipment or the personnel to warrant their being classed as a division. Aside from the panzer and parachute divisions, which were still being sent the fittest troops and the most modern weapons, the bulk of the infantry divisions were miserable skeletons of fighting units. Sitting deep in their bunkers in the Atlantic Wall, they were equipped with a hodgepodge of foreign artillery, relied on horses and bicycles for their mobility, and were formed chiefly of personnel from older age groups and convalescents from the Russian front.

France had been turned into a vast training-center, where divisions destroyed on other sectors could come for rest, refitting and reorganization. Thus, many of these divisions were more real on paper than they were on the ground. "Often I would be informed that a new division was to arrive in France," said von Rundstedt,[4] "direct from Russia or Norway or Central Germany. When it finally made its appearance in the West it would consist, in all, of a divisional commander, a medical officer and five bakers."

To reform these shattered divisions which had left the bulk of their German personnel in Russian graves or Russian prisoner-of-war camps, the Supreme Command drafted so-called volunteers from amongst the peoples of the countries they occupied. There not being enough able-bodied Germans still capable of keeping a war machine and an industrial machine going at the same time, the infantry divisions in France were largely rebuilt by utilizing the huge reserve of non-Germanic manpower in Europe. Using this foreign element chiefly for supply and administrative duties, the infantry divisions in the West were liberally sprinkled with Poles, Hungarians, Yugoslavs, Roumanians, Czechs, Dutchmen, Alsatians, to mention but a few. These non-Germans usually made up at least ten per cent of a division's strength and in some divisions comprised about twenty-five per cent of the formation's personnel.

But the largest group of foreigners found in the Wehrmacht in the West were Russians. So many prisoners had been taken in the early victories in Russia, that it was decided in 1942 to make use of these troops rather than continue to feed them or exterminate them. Realizing that it might be dangerous to inject so large a foreign element into normal German divisions, the Supreme Command decided to form these Russian troops into separate units of their own which would be officered by Germans. With the aid of a Russian general, Vlassov, this huge recruiting drive was begun.

It might be of interest to make a chronological diversion at this point in order to describe the methods by which such Eastern or Ost battalions were formed. The experiences of an Armenian who deserted from 812 Armenian Battalion in Holland provide a typical example of what happened to thousands of his countrymen.[5] Having been captured on 12 November 1941, he was thrown into a German prison cage, where he suffered the kind of treatment made famous by the camps of Belsen and Buchenwald. For fifteen days he was forced to march towards the rear areas, living on a handful of wheat each day as his ration. Prisoners who dropped out of the line to steal potatoes from the fields en route were shot. In a camp near Minsk they were given verminous quarters, no blankets, and drinking water was obtained by scooping snow into a can and waiting for it to melt. Twenty to thirty men died every night due to the combination of hours of hauling wood, generous lashings with leather whips, and bad food.

Suddenly, in early 1942, there was a revolutionary change. Barracks were cleaned, men were deloused and food became more abundant. For six weeks they were forced to take exercise so that they could get their strength back. This was a gradual and slow process since by this time most of them were so weak and sick they could hardly walk. In May 1942 they were sent to a new camp in Poland where they discovered they were now part of four Armenian battalions which were being formed and trained to fight in the German army. Supplied with a mixture of German and Russian weapons, each battalion contained about a thousand men. All company commanders were German, but junior officers were Russian, usually of the émigré White Russian variety. Early in 1943 two of these Armenian battalions were sent to the West and the other two to the East.

By June 1944 over 75,000 of these Russian troops were stationed in France, chiefly employed in rear area duties. But some of the Eastern battalions were given operational rôles, usually as units in the normal German infantry divisions. Their fighting value to the Germans proved negligible, while the administrative problems they raised were staggering. The following order issued by 276 Infantry Division in Normandy gives some indication of the difficulties that plagued German staffs.

Infantry Regiment 987,
Personnel Branch.

Regimental H.Q.,
9 Aug. 44.

Subject: *Paybooks for volunteers in German units.*

In order to issue paybooks to volunteers in German units a nominal roll of such volunteers, separated according to their nationality, will be handed in to Regimental Headquarters by 11 Aug. 44.

The paybooks will be issued in eight different forms, *i.e.:*

 (i) For Russians, Ukrainians and White Ruthenians — Russian paybook.
 (ii) For Cossacks — Cossack paybook.
 (iii) For Armenians — Armenian paybook.
 (iv) For Aserbaijans — Aserbaijan paybook.
 (v) For Georgians (including Adschars, South Ossetans and Abschars)— Georgian paybook.
 (vi) For Adigis, Karbadins, Karatjers, Balkars, Kherkassians, North Ossetans, Ingus, Takjenen, Dagastares (Calmuckes, Awares, Lakes, Dargines, etc.) — North Caucasian paybook.
 (vii) For Turkemen, Usbeks, Kazaks, Khirgiz, Karakalpaks, Tadschiks — Turkestan paybook.
 (viii) For Volga Tartars (Kazan Tartars), Bashkires, Tartar-speaking Tschuwashi, Maris, Merdwiners, Udmuns — Volga Tartar paybook.

By order,

[Signature illegible],
Lt. and Regtl. Adjutant.

With troops such as these under command it can hardly be wondered at that von Rundstedt was sceptical as to his ability to thwart an Allied invasion. "The Russians constituted a menace and a nuisance to operations in France," complained the Field Marshal,[6] "while most of our own infantry divisions were filled with second-rate personnel. The armored and parachute formations alone contained young men, and there were too few of these. In fact there were insufficient troops in the West to carry out properly the rôle required of them. Once the various divisions were stretched along the huge coastal front, there was little left in the interior. So thin were troops on the ground that three infantry divisions patrolled the Atlantic coast from the Loire to the Pyrenees, a distance of almost 450 kilometres.

"To make matters worse, orders were constantly received from Berlin shifting these divisions about without any apparent justification. Thus one of our best equipped infantry divisions was sent to the Channel Islands late in 1941, and they were never returned to me during the entire course of the Western Campaign. So long was this formation stationed in Jersey, Guernsey and Alderney, that rumor had it that they were soon to receive arm-bands inscribed with the words 'King's Own German Grenadiers.' "

Chapter XIV

WATCHING AND WAITING

WITH the fortifications along the Channel so inadequate and with manpower strictly limited, measures had to be taken to give the Allies the impression that there was a sufficient force on hand to meet an invasion should it occur. A huge deception program, which has been described by General Blumentritt,[1] was undertaken, designed to build up the strength of Germany's western forces in the minds of her enemies. Intensive propaganda about the invincibility of the Atlantic Wall was carried on. This was aided by the laying of dummy mine-fields and by the circulation of maps and legends showing formidable concrete defenses and minefields. These latter were passed to the Allies by means of German agents in Paris and Switzerland.

In addition to inflating the ground defenses it was necessary, as well, to show more divisions in France than there actually were. This was achieved by various ingenious and complicated means. Local French authorities were told a new division was to arrive and orders were given for the preparation of billets. Then advance parties would reconnoiter the area, buildings would be taken over, and finally exercises would take place in the area, or reinforcements of another division would pass through the locality. This would give the impression of the arrival of a fresh division, which news in due course would reach England. Or if a division was being sent to France from the East, agents would report that two divisions were coming. So extensive did these deceptive measures become that it was necessary to keep a list of real and false divisions at von Rundstedt's headquarters to prevent the staff from becoming muddled. One column showed the facts about a dummy division, its supposed date of arrival and its presumed area of occupation, a second column provided the correct information. On maps the real divisions were shown in red, while fake divisions were marked in blue. Even the Japanese Ambassador at Vichy was supplied with some of these false maps designed to lull both him and his government into a sense of security as to the strength of German forces in the West.

Once it had been decided that the northern coast of France was to be the scene of the Allied invasion attempt, the next problem was to pick the most likely spot. Three areas were actually selected — one by Hitler, one by his advisers at Berlin and one by von Rundstedt. Von Rundstedt chose the Pas de Calais. In explaining his choice he counted out his reasons with the facility of a man who has argued this matter many times before.

"In the first place," he said,[2] "an attack from Dover against Calais would be using the shortest sea route to the Continent. Secondly, the V-1 and V-2 sites were located in this area. Thirdly, this was the shortest route to the Ruhr and the heart of industrial Germany, and once a successful landing had been made it would take only four days to reach the Rhine. Fourthly, such an operation would sever the forces in Northern France from those along the Mediterranean coast. Against the Pas de Calais being chosen was the fact that this area had the strongest coastal defenses, and was the only part of the Atlantic Wall that even remotely lived up to its reputation. I always used to tell my staff that if I was Montgomery I would attack the Pas de Calais." The staff officers at Berlin believed the Allies would attack farther west, between the Seine and the Somme, while Hitler suddenly decided it would be Normandy. General Warlimont described these differences at Berlin as follows:

"Up to May 1944 when Hitler first spoke of Normandy," he said,[3] "the staff was all prepared for a landing in the Channel zone between the Seine and the Somme, by Abbeville and Le Havre. Therefore the coastal defenses were mainly built up in that area. We were not quite convinced that Hitler was right in expecting the attack in Normandy, but he kept insisting on it and demanded more and more reinforcements for that sector."

With three divergent views as to the possible invasion area, it was impossible to concentrate all resources against any one contingency. Hitler's appreciation that the landings would take place in Normandy was sent to von Rundstedt approximately six weeks before D-Day, although no specific places were cited as potential danger zones. Von Rundstedt agreed that an invasion of Normandy might be attempted but he considered that it would coincide with a large-scale assault on both sides of Calais. The possibility of a diversionary effort on the French Mediterranean coast before the invasion in the north was also contemplated by the Field Marshal. But he felt that such an attack, if it did come, would be primarily designed to draw divisions from the Channel coast where the major operation would take place.

German intelligence seems to have been of little help in deciding

either when or where the invasion would come. The few over-
worked agents in England had nervously been passing on warnings
of an invasion since early April. When April had come and gone and
nothing had happened, they picked early May and then late May
for the attempt. The intelligence staffs having cried 'wolf' so often,
by June general opinion at von Rundstedt's headquarters was that
no invasion was now to be expected until July or August. The actual
day of the landing therefore came as a surprise.

From the few intelligence reports that did filter through from
England it was estimated that between fifty-five and sixty divisions
were assembled in England to take part in the invasion. This figure
was relatively accurate. But aside from this information nothing else
of importance seems to have been forthcoming from intelligence
channels. General Blumentritt has ruefully admitted[4] that even
demonstrations put on especially for the benefit of German agents
were never reported to von Rundstedt's headquarters. Such an effort
was the elaborate deception plan carried out by the invading forces
a few days before D-Day. A large number of ships were loaded with
troops and equipment as if they were about to sail. Some of them
actually left the coast. This large-scale manœuvre was done as obviously as possible, with only a paltry attempt at security. It was hoped
that these movements would be reported to the Germans in France
and that they would, in turn, set their counter-invasion plans in
motion. Allied agents in France were all set to report any such manœuvres of German formations. The Germans did not move a man.
The Allies were naturally rather disconcerted by this canniness on
the part of the German Command in the West. But Blumentritt now
confesses that this failure to react was not due to the cunning of von
Rundstedt's staff, but to their sheer ignorance of the whole affair.

Thus, with little reliable intelligence information to guide them,
the men responsible for the defense of France had to rely upon their
military judgment alone in making their appreciations. Normandy
was discounted as the most likely invasion spot, chiefly because of
its lack of good harbor facilities. Here again, German intelligence had
failed them for they knew nothing of the artificial port — Mulberry —
which was being secretly assembled in England to take care of this
deficiency. Reports of these large contraptions lying in the Thames
were made to Berlin, but estimates as to their function ranged anywhere from floating grain-elevators to substitute piers for use in a
captured harbour. Thus the only correct guess as to Allied intentions
was made in direct contradiction to all military reasoning. General
Warlimont explained it in these words:[5] "We generals calculated

along the lines of our regular, military education, but Hitler came
to his own decision, as he always did, on his intuition alone." And
Hitler's intuition said it would be Normandy.

Having decided that the main attack would be launched in the
Pas de Calais with a secondary effort between the Seine and Cherbourg, von Rundstedt attempted to deploy his troops in accordance
with his appreciation. However, he was constantly pestered by suggestions from Hitler, and by a difference of opinion with his most
senior subordinate commander, Field Marshal Erwin Rommel, whose
background and previous exploits in North Africa have already been
discussed.

The sixty divisions in France and the Low Countries on 6 June
1944 were shared between four army commands. Field Marshal
Rommel, as commander of Army Group 'B,' controlled two of these
armies, the Seventh and Fifteenth, while Colonel General Blaskowitz, as commander of Army Group 'G,' directed the remaining two
armies, the First and Nineteenth. Rommel's Army Group was responsible for the defense of the Channel coast and for this task he had
been allotted well over two-thirds of the divisions in the West.

There was a serious difference of opinion as to the strategy to be
adopted against an Allied invasion. This concerned itself with the
best method of deploying the ten armored divisions which constituted
von Rundstedt's mobile reserve. Rommel argued that these tank formations must be brought forward as close to the threatened coastal
areas as possible. He fervently believed that landings had to be
defeated on the beaches themselves, and that once an Allied bridgehead had been established it would be impossible to contain it. In
accordance with this theory he ordered his infantry divisions to concentrate no farther back than five kilometres from the coastline; he
issued detailed instructions on the building of costly and complicated
water obstacles and coastal fortifications along the north shores of
France; and he edged the panzer divisions under his command as
close to the water-line as he could.

Von Rundstedt agreed with the principle that an invasion had to
be smashed before it had secured a firm foothold on the mainland,
but he was not as eager to commit his reserves into battle too soon.
Not being too certain that the first landings would necessarily constitute the main Allied thrust, he preferred to hold his armor in hand
until Allied intentions were more clear-cut. His plan, therefore, was
to hold back a strong armored force some fifty to sixty kilometres
from the coast, and, at the decisive moment, release it in a full-blooded
counter-attack against the Allied bridgehead.

Since von Rundstedt held the senior command in France, normally his theory would have prevailed. But because Rommel had so much influence with Hitler, he was able to dilute von Rundstedt's plan with his own. The result of these differences was an unhappy strategical compromise which had disastrous consequences in the days immediately following the Allied landings. The infantry divisions were deployed thinly along the coast from Holland around to Marseilles acting as a sea-wall of manpower to keep out the expected flood. The size of the coastline and the shortage of infantry limited the thickness of this wall, and only in the Pas de Calais did von Rundstedt succeed in producing a second layer of infantry divisions.

The much discussed armored divisions were neither all forward nor were they all back. Six of the ten panzer divisions were placed north of the Loire, while the other four acted as a scattered reserve for the south and the southwest coast of France. Three panzer divisions were under Rommel's command, while the others, north of the Loire, were under von Rundstedt's direct command in a reserve formation called Panzer Group West.[6] This splitting of the mobile reserve produced the inevitable result. Rommel stationed his armor as close to the coast as he could, while von Rundstedt kept his farther back. When the invasion began there was, therefore, neither enough armor to push the Allies back off the beaches, in the first few hours, nor was there an adequate striking force to act as an armored reserve later on. No better design for a successful Allied landing could have been achieved than this failure to concentrate the armor in the West along one unified and determined course.

Being pressed by Hitler to be wary of Normandy, von Rundstedt had stationed his three strongest panzer divisions in the rectangle formed by the Seine and the Loire rivers. They were 21 Panzer Division, 12 S.S. Panzer Division 'Hitler Jugend' and Panzer Lehr Division. Together they constituted a striking force of almost 600 tanks. They contained the best trained and most fanatical troops in France. It was their task to deliver the counterblow which would put an end to any invasion attempt in Normandy. A co-ordinated counterblow never came. Instead it consisted of a series of isolated, independent jabs which the Allies were easily able to ward off. In the combination of events which made a strong, armored offensive impossible lies the most important reason for the comparative ease with which an Allied bridgehead was established and maintained in those early critical days.

One of these divisions, 21 Panzer, was under Rommel's direct command. Its commander, Lieutenant General Feuchtinger, had

been given definite instruction, that, in the event of an invasion, he
was not to make any move until he had been given his orders by
Army Group 'B.'[7] This meant that the moment a landing occurred,
21 Panzer Division could not be committed by either the corps or
the army immediately involved in the battle. The other two panzer
divisions, 12 S.S. 'Hitler Jugend' and Panzer Lehr, were to receive
their orders from a still higher authority than Army Group. They
were not to move until the Commander-in-Chief West, Field Marshal
von Rundstedt, had given the word. But as if this were not authority
enough, von Rundstedt has now revealed that while nominally he
had the power to commit these two formations, in actual fact he had
received instructions from Berlin that in the event of an invasion
neither of these divisions was to be moved until permission from
Hitler himself had been received! The delay created by this incredible
chain of command in the first vital hours of the invasion was one of
the chief reasons for the failure of the expected German counter-
attack.

Chapter XV

THE FIRST DAYS

LIFE was relatively serene amongst the German formations in France
on the evening of 5 June 1944. There had been no warning of any
untoward manœuvers on the part of the Allied forces in England and
all previous alarums of German agents had proved unfounded. The
invasion seemed weeks away. Rommel was visiting his wife in Stuttgart after a liaison trip to Berlin, and a large number of the divisional
commanders in Seventh Army, responsible for the defense of Normandy, had been called to Rennes to take part in an anti-invasion
exercise.

This tranquility was abruptly broken at von Rundstedt's headquarters with a report that the B.B.C. was broadcasting an unusually
large number of encoded messages to the French Resistance Movement. The contents of some of these messages, coupled with the large-
scale situation map of England kept by the intelligence staff which
showed only a few units along the southwest shore, but heavy con-
centrations in the Dover-Folkestone area, seemed to confirm von
Rundstedt's appreciation that an assault was imminent in the region
of the Pas de Calais. At eleven o'clock that night, Fifteenth Army,
east of the Seine, was given Alarm II which meant that all men were
to be near their vehicles and ready for any eventuality. Seventh Army

in Normandy was allowed to carry on its routine activities undisturbed and was never given any alert of any kind.

At ten minutes past midnight the Commander-in-Chief West received the first report that the invasion had begun. Symbolically enough, it was a false report — that paratroops and gliders had landed on the western side of the Cotentin Peninsula. It was not until nearly one o'clock in the morning that the news of paratroops near Troarn, east of the Orne River, was received. There was a determined effort to remain calm and objective at von Rundstedt's headquarters as the reports came flooding in. With the memory of Dieppe still on everyone's mind, it was imperative to appreciate whether this was merely a feint or the main attack. Von Rundstedt was eager to explain his actions during these first hours.

"I have been criticized because it was said that I delayed too long in committing my panzer divisions against the bridgehead," said the Field Marshal.[1] "Although Panzer Lehr and 12 S.S. Panzer Divisions were under my command I could not move them until I had received permission from Berlin.

"At four o'clock in the morning, three hours after I received the first reports of the invasion, I decided that these landings in Normandy had to be dealt with. I asked the Supreme Command in Berlin for authority to commit these two divisions into the battle. Berlin replied that it was still uncertain as to whether or not these first assaults were the main Allied effort or merely a diversion. They hesitated all that night and the next morning unable to make up their minds. Finally at four o'clock in the afternoon of 6 June, twelve hours after I had made my request, I was told I could use these panzer divisions. This meant that a counter-attack could not be organized until the morning of 7 June. By then the bridgehead was over thirty hours old and it was too late."

Seventh Army, led by Colonel General Dollman, was in the meantime trying to hold its positions with four weak infantry divisions and one armored division. At about five in the afternoon of 6 June the intentions of the Supreme Command were finally communicated to Dollman. They were reported in the following words in the meticulously kept telephone journal of the Seventh Army.[2]

16.55 hours.
*Chief-of-Staff of Seventh Army reports to Chief-of-Staff
Western Command.*

Chief-of-Staff Western Command (von Rundstedt's headquarters) emphasizes the desire of the Supreme Command (Hitler) to have the enemy in the bridgehead annihilated by the evening of 6 June, since there exists a

danger of additional sea- and airborne landings for support. In accordance
with an order by General Jodl, all units will be diverted to the point of
penetration in Calvados. The beach-head there must be cleaned up by not
later than tonight. The Chief-of-Staff declares that such would be impossible. The commander of Army Group 'B' (Rommel) states that 21
Panzer Division must attack immediately regardless of whether reinforcements arrive or not. The Supreme Command has ordered that the bad
weather conditions of the night of 6-7 June be utilized for the bringing up
of reserves.

And later on, at midnight of 6 June, the journal reports the following conversation of the Chief-of-Staff with the commanders of 21
Panzer Division and 716 Infantry Division. The latter formation was
the unfortunate occupant of the coastal sector protecting Caen and
received the full brunt of the Allied onslaught. It practically disappeared as a fighting unit within twenty-four hours.

24.00 hours. 716 Infantry Division is still defending itself at strong-
points. Communications between division, regimental and battalion headquarters, however, no longer exist, so that nothing is known as to the number
of strong-points still holding out or of those liquidated.... The Chief-of-Staff
of Seventh Army gives the order that the counter-attack of 7 June must
reach the coast without fail, since the strong-point defenders expect it of us.

Now with all this going on at the higher levels of the military
command, what was happening to the divisions that were actually
fighting the battle? The self-same hesitancy and uncertainty which
was harassing von Rundstedt was also limiting their activities. The
infantry divisions in the bunkers along the coast had been able to
offer little resistance to the combined naval, air and land assault and
surrendered in their thousands, trembling and exhausted by their
terrifying experiences. The costly under-water obstacles had been
largely swept away by the first wave of attacking infantry. The one
division in immediate reserve capable of affecting the battle was 21
Panzer Division. It contained about 170 armored vehicles and was
under the direct command of Rommel's Army Group 'B.' Its headquarters was at St. Pierre-sur-Dives about twenty-four kilometres
from the coast. Its commander, Lieutenant General Edgar Feuchtinger, a tall, wiry, well-built man with a slightly bent nose, which
gave him the appearance of a somewhat elderly pugilist, had this to
say: [3]
"I first knew that the invasion had begun with a report that parachutists had been dropped near Troarn a little after midnight on 6
June. Since I had been told that I was to make no move until I had
heard from Rommel's headquarters, I could do nothing immediately

but warn my men to be ready. I waited impatiently all that night for some instructions. But not a single order from a higher formation was received by me. Realizing that my armored division was closest to the scene of operations, I finally decided, at six-thirty in the morning, that I had to take some action. I ordered my tanks to attack the English 6 Airborne Division which had entrenched itself in a bridgehead over the Orne. To me this constituted the most immediate threat to the German position.

"Hardly had I made this decision, when at seven o'clock I received my first intimation that a higher command did still exist. I was told by Army Group 'B' that I was now under command of Seventh Army. But I received no further orders as to my rôle. At nine o'clock I was informed that I would receive any future orders from 84 Infantry Corps, and finally at ten o'clock I was given my first operational instructions. I was ordered to stop the move of my tanks against the Allied airborne troops, and to turn west and aid the forces protecting Caen.

"Once over the Orne River, I drove north towards the coast. By this time the enemy, consisting of 3 British and 3 Canadian Infantry Divisions, had made astonishing progress and had already occupied a strip of high ground about ten kilometres from the sea. From here the excellent anti-tank gun-fire of the Allies knocked out eleven of my tanks before I had barely started. However, one battle group did manage to by-pass these guns and actually reached the coast at Lion-sur-Mer, at about seven in the evening.

"I now expected that some reinforcements would be forthcoming to help me hold my position, but nothing came. Another Allied parachute landing on both sides of the Orne, together with a sharp attack by English tanks, forced me to give up my hold on the coast. I retired to take up a line just north of Caen. By the end of that first day my division had lost almost twenty-five per cent of its tanks."

The man chosen to conduct the counter-offensive of 7 June was Oberstgruppenführer (Colonel General) Joseph 'Sepp' Dietrich, commander of 1 S.S. Panzer Corps. Short and squat, with a broad dark face dominated by a large, wide nose, Dietrich resembled a rather battered bartender in appearance. He was a typical product of the Free Corps and the bullying gangs with which Hitler first made his advent on the German political stage. The first Great War interrupted his plans to become a butcher, and after four years of fighting he had attained the rank of a sergeant major. He spent the post-war years at a series of unsuccessful odd jobs and occupied his spare time as an enthusiastic adherent of the Nazi Party.

In 1928 he joined the S.S. as a full-time member and in five years

rose to the rank of Brigadeführer (Major General) as the Commanding Officer of Hitler's personal bodyguard. He led the first S.S. division 'Adolf Hitler' in the French, Greek and Russian campaigns, and
boasted that by 1943 only thirty of the original 23,000 men in his
division were still alive and uncaptured. In Germany the Goebbels
propaganda machine had made of 'Sepp' Dietrich an almost legend-
ary figure, whose exploits as a fighting man of the people rivaled, if
not surpassed, those of that other popular National Socialist personality, Erwin Rommel. Crude, conceited and garrulous, his meteoric
career was undoubtedly achieved more by his hard and ruthless
energy than by his military ability. Von Rundstedt's description of
Dietrich is admirable for both its accuracy and brevity, "He is decent,
but stupid."

On D-Day, Dietrich was in Brussels with the headquarters of his
formation, 1 S.S. Panzer Corps. He was directly under command
of von Rundstedt and had been immediately summoned to Paris. At
five o'clock on the afternoon of 6 June the corps was given its first
task. It would conduct an attack from the vicinity of Caen and drive
the British into the sea. For this purpose Dietrich was to use 12 S.S.
Panzer Division 'Hitler Jugend,' 21 Panzer Division, already on the
spot, and Panzer Lehr Division, which was to come up as soon as
possible. Dietrich immediately sent out his orders to Lieutenant General Feuchtinger of 21 Panzer Division and Brigadeführer (Major
General) Kurt Meyer of 12 S.S. Panzer Division. These two armored
formations would co-ordinate an attack to be launched together at
first light on 7 June.

Kurt Meyer of 12 S.S. Panzer Division (then only a regimental
commander) became the youngest divisional commander in the German army at the age of thirty-three. He was the perfect product of
Nazi fanaticism. Tall, handsome, with penetrating blue eyes, he knew
only what Hitler had told him, and believed it all. He was prepared
to die for his faith in National Socialism and he was utterly ruthless
in forcing others to die for it as well. Tried as a war criminal for
inciting his troops to murder Canadian prisoners-of-war, he was
sentenced to life imprisonment. In such a man the Nazi virus will
always live. It has become part of his lifeblood.

Meyer had neither the training nor the experience to lead 20,000
men and over 200 tanks into battle, but he possessed both a keen
tactical sense and the tenacity of a zealot, which enabled him to
perform the defensive rôle required of him at Caen. In the offensive,
however, he failed badly. Like Dietrich, he owed his position to his
loyalty and not his ability.

Feuchtinger, when he received his orders, suggested to Dietrich that two armored divisions were not enough to take on the well-entrenched British, and that they ought to wait until Panzer Lehr Division had arrived and do the attack with three formations. He was told, however, that only the two armored divisions were available and to co-ordinate his attack with 12 S.S. Panzer Division that night.

"About midnight, Kurt Meyer arrived at my headquarters," said Feuchtinger.[4] "He was to take over on my left and we were to carry out a combined operation the next morning. I explained the situation to Meyer and warned him about the strength of the enemy. Meyer studied the map, turned to me with a confident air and said, 'Little fish! We'll throw them back into the sea in the morning.'

"We decided to drive towards Douvres and 12 S.S. was to take up assembly positions during the night. Artillery fire was so great that a proper co-ordination of this attack was impossible. Meyer did make a short spurt with some fifty tanks, but was driven back. He never reached the start-line from which our combined attack was to begin. Allied anti-tank guns prevented him from getting into proper position."

The vagueness and pettiness that dominated the German generals at this time is well illustrated in the discussion that has followed on the failure of this counter-attack. Meyer vigorously denied that it was anti-tank gun-fire that stopped him from getting forward. "We failed to achieve more substantial results on 7 June," explained Meyer,[5] "because in the long drive to the front we had exhausted our petrol supply. I tried to replenish it, but it was impossible. I could, therefore, only use half my tank strength in the attack." Feuchtinger scoffed at this excuse. "If Meyer was really short of petrol, why didn't he mention it to me," he said, "I could have given him all he wanted if he had asked for it." Dietrich, the corps commander, when asked to choose between these two stories, supported Meyer. "It is easy for Feuchtinger now to say that he would have given Meyer petrol on 7 June," he said,[6] "but on that morning his answer to such a request would have been 'I haven't got any.'"

That such lack of harmony should exist at so vital a time seems difficult to imagine. But the explanation probably lies in the deep-rooted distrust and resentment of the average, regular army officer, like Feuchtinger, towards the political party S.S. officers, like Dietrich and Meyer. Whatever the real reason for the failure of this attack may be, it left two panting armored divisions on the northern outskirts of Caen, shaken, uncertain and waiting for more help before trying again.

By 8 June the German High Command in France was well aware of the immediate intentions of the Allies and also of the number of

English and American divisions involved. The circumstances by which this information was obtained are revealed in that day's entries in the telephone journal of Seventh Army: [7]

06.40 hours.

Chief-of-Staff Seventh Army to Army Group 'B.'

An English operational order has been recovered from the water. Contents will be transmitted by telegraph.

08.10 hours.

Chief-of-Staff Group 'B' to Seventh Army.

An urgent demand for information on the situation by order of Field Marshal Rommel, since the report telegraphed this morning has not yet come through.

(*a*) Extracts are given from the operation order of 7 American Corps according to which the following units are committed:
On the right: 7 American Corps with four divisions.
Mission: To attack northwards from the Carentan-Quinéville bridgehead and to take Cherbourg from the land side.
On the left: 5 English Corps with four English divisions and two American divisions in the Calvados sector.
Mission: To take Bayeux and join up with the 7 American Corps at Carentan.

(*b*) *Our own situation:*
Bayeux in enemy hands. . . . Attack by 1 S.S. Panzer Corps because of the situation in the air, was not possible until this morning. Direction of the attack: north and northwest of Caen, in the direction of the coast. Field Marshal Rommel interrupts and orders 1 S.S. Panzer Corps to initiate a point of main effort on the left as quickly as possible, using all three divisions.

It, therefore, appears that Rommel on 8 June did not yet know that the attack of 1 S.S. Panzer Corps had already proved abortive. Dietrich, whose reputation for inaccurate reporting to higher commands was notorious, had apparently failed to pass on the news of what had happened to 21 Panzer and 12 S.S. Panzer Divisions at Caen. But where was the third division, Panzer Lehr, all this time? Although only some ninety miles south of Caen at LeMans, it had not yet arrived seventy-two hours after the landings began! Its commander, Lieutenant General Fritz Bayerlein, a short, stocky, energetic man who had been Rommel's Chief-of-Staff in Africa, has given a colorful account of his division's entrance into the battle of Normandy.

"At two o'clock in the morning of 6 June, I was alerted," he said.[8] "The invasion fleet was coming across the Channel. I was told to begin moving north that afternoon at five o'clock. This was too early. Air attacks had been severe in daylight and everyone knew everything that could fly would support the invasion. My request for a delay until twilight was refused. We moved as ordered, and immediately came under an air attack. I lost twenty or thirty vehicles by nightfall. . . .

"We kept on during the night with but three hours' delay for rest and fuelling. At daylight, General Dollman, commander of Seventh Army, gave me a direct order to proceed and there was nothing else to do. The first air attack came about half-past five that morning, near Falaise. By noon it was terrible; my men were calling the main road from Vire to Beny-Bocage a fighter-bomber racecourse. . . .

"Every vehicle was covered with tree branches and moved along hedges and the edges of woods. Road junctions were bombed, and a bridge knocked out at Condé. This did not stop my tanks, but it hampered other vehicles. By the end of the day I had lost forty tank trucks carrying fuel, and ninety others. Five of my tanks were knocked out, and eighty-four half-tracks, prime-movers and self-propelled guns. These were serious losses for a division not yet in action. I was just east of Tilly on 6 June and ready to attack.

"My attack took Ellon, and I could have gone straight to the sea down the corridor between the American and British forces, splitting them apart. I was ordered to hold at Ellon because units on my right flank had been delayed. I was a day behind schedule myself, because of air harassment."

Thus 9 June arrived and still no co-ordinated armored attack had been possible. The Seventh Army telephone journal provides the appreciations of the High Command for that day: [9]

17.30 hours.

Conversation of Field Marshal Rommel with the Commander and Chief-of-Staff of Seventh Army at Army Headquarters.

Field Marshal Rommel . . . orders that the enemy must be prevented at all costs from:

(a) Getting the fortress of Cherbourg, and harbor, in his hands.

(b) Establishing the connection between both bridgeheads; that west of the Orne and that west of the Vire.

The Chief-of-Staff of Seventh Army expresses the opinion that the enemy, because of the increased resistance south of Montebourg, will commit more airborne troops, in order to take possession of Cherbourg rapidly. Field Marshal Rommel does not share this opinion, since the Supreme Command expects a large landing on the Channel coast within the next few days, and therefore the enemy will not have more airborne troops available. . . .

But it was not until 10 June that bad news in full measure began to flood into the headquarters of Seventh Army. The first part of the day's entries records such pessimistic sentences as these: "3 Parachute Division must be brought forward piecemeal because of lack of fuel" and "The advance units of 17 S.S. Panzer Grenadier Division are stuck in the St. Lô area because of lack of fuel." The first information that the counter-attack of Panzer Group West, of which 'Sepp' Dietrich's 1 S.S. Panzer Corps was the most important part, had failed, was noted in these words: "Panzer Group West has sustained enemy attack and is now engaged in local counter-attack. It is evident, from reports that Panzer Group West has been prevented from carrying out its basic mission."

Just how badly that "basic mission" had fared is vividly described by Fritz Bayerlein of Panzer Lehr Division.

"While I waited for support on my right flank, the British counter-attacked next day (10 June). They massed an unbelievable concentration of heavy artillery and I was glad when we finally were out of it. We pulled out of Tilly on 15 June and the British filled the gap. My chance to drive to the sea was lost. We pulled back south of Aunay, to regroup. We had lost about 100 tanks against the British. Half my striking force was gone. . . ." [10]

Recognition that the prospects of eliminating the Allied bridgehead were rapidly deteriorating was finally realized at Seventh Army. Instead of the usual orders for counter-attacks "to destroy and wipe out the enemy" the evening of 10 June saw this entry made:

The Chief-of-Staff Army Group 'B' presents the views of the Supreme Commander of the armed forces (Hitler) . . . that there should be neither a withdrawal, fighting to the rear, nor a disengagement rearward to a new line of resistance, but that every man will fight and fall, where he stands. . . .

With these words vanished the grandiose hopes of a brilliant German offensive and an early victory. The significance of the demand to "fight and fall" presaged the hard days ahead. It was the first of many similar orders issued in the West. And as defeat followed defeat such orders became more urgent and more demanding and more desperate. They succeeded in so terrifying the German soldier that when at last, he had ceased to fight because it was his duty, he continued to fight because he was afraid to do anything else.

Thus less than a week after the invasion had begun the German forces in Normandy were back on the defensive. Their short-lived opportunity to deny the Allies a foothold on the coast of France was over. The attempts to crush the landings had already cost them over 150 tanks and about 10,000 German prisoners-of-war. They were dazed, uncertain and weary. They could do nothing but sit back and wait for help to come. When it finally arrived it was far too little and much too late.

Chapter XVI

THE BATTLE OF THE BRIDGEHEAD

AT THIS point it might be wise to review briefly Allied invasion strategy. A bridgehead was to be established in Normandy between the Orne River and the Cherbourg Peninsula. This critical operation of cracking the crust of the Atlantic Wall was known as the 'break-in.' Then was to follow a tenacious holding of this ground by both the First U. S. Army and the Second British Army. Periodic thrusts forward were to be made in order to provide elbow-room for the masses of supplies and men that were to follow. For into this confined space was to be concentrated as well the additional forces of the Third U.S. Army and the First Canadian Army. During this stage it was planned to reach Avranches and capture the port of Cherbourg. This second phase of the battle was known as the 'build-up' and it was predominantly to be a defensive operation. When sufficient power had been concentrated to ensure a smashing blow into France, the third phase or 'break-out' was to be made with the object of reaching Paris and the Seine. This phase was to be started by an attack of General Patton's Third U.S. Army designed to drive south and sweep into Brittany. The original timetable visualized the 'build-up' period as taking anywhere from four to six weeks. It was planned to reach the Seine by D-plus 90 or about the first week in September.

Allied intelligence had warned that a major counter-attack could be expected within four or five days after the landings. By D-plus 20 it was appreciated that the Germans could have brought between twenty-five and thirty divisions against the bridgehead, and by D-plus 60 or early August that they might have as many as fifty divisions in the battle. Allied planning also continued on the assumption that once it was clear the Normandy bridgehead could not be contained, German strategy would take the form of a slow withdrawal to the Seine, using the intervening river lines of the Dives and the Touques as temporary stopping-places. A hard and bitter battle to cross the Seine in the fall was then envisaged by the Allied planning staffs.

How did the Germans comply with this appreciation? In the first place the major armored counter-attack fizzled out badly as we have already seen. Once it had failed, nothing more could be done until more troops had arrived. And here is where Allied air power proved decisive. Maintaining a non-stop air cover over the complete battle area, they harassed and delayed the movement of German reinforcements so effectively that no substantial force could make its way to Normandy in time to influence the bridgehead battle.

Most bridges on the Seine and Loire had been destroyed before the invasion began, thus isolating this rectangle of France. Then the Luftwaffe was so efficiently shot out of the air that after the first few days it only appeared in desultory raids carried out chiefly at night. With unhampered freedom of the air, the Allied planes bombed and swooped and hovered and pranged and strafed so many bridges, railway lines, marshaling yards, roads and rivers that movement in France by day became almost impossible.

The infantry divisions in the immediate area were quickly rushed to the scene of the conflagration. Most of these divisions had little motorized equipment and they therefore were forced to march hundreds of miles into battle. It was a common occurrence for these troops to cover on foot twenty to twenty-five miles every night for a week, and then take over front-line positions without an intervening rest of any kind. Some of the luckier formations had managed to beg, borrow or steal sufficient bicycles to supply the fighting men with this means of transportation to supplement their horse-drawn vehicles. Many a German prisoner was taken in these early days still breathless from the exertion of miles of vigorous pedaling with full kit and rifle on his back. One unit starting out at eleven in the evening of 6 June arrived near Caen at noon on 8 June, having madly cycled over sixty-five miles with no sleep, no food and no halts *en route*. Shoved into the line an hour later, they hardly had time to press a trigger before they turned up as bewildered and exhausted prisoners, just in time to have their dinner in Allied lines.[1]

The infantry divisions being so slow in getting to Normandy, it was necessary to call upon the panzer divisions outside the Seine-Loire area. It was hoped that these divisions, since they traveled on tracks and wheels, would make the journey much faster. We have already seen what happened to Panzer Lehr Division in its attempts to approach the battle zone. Two other panzer divisions trying to get to Normandy suffered much the same fate.

The tanks of one division left Abbeville by rail on 9 June intending to make the trip to the front by way of Paris. The locomotives were hit so many times by Allied fighter-bombers that the tanks finally had to finish the journey by road. It was not until 18 June that eighty of the 120 tanks that originally started, finally limped into the line around Caumont, having taken almost ten days to travel about 300 miles.[2] Another armored formation, 17 S.S. Panzer Grenadier Division needed five days to motor from Thouars, south of the Loire, to Périers in the Cherbourg Peninsula, a distance of about 200 miles. A staff officer of the division has provided a graphic account of that journey.

"On 7 June our division received orders to leave the marshaling area in Thouars and to move to the invasion front in Normandy. Everyone was in a good and eager mood to see action again — happy that the pre-invasion spell of uncertainty and waiting was snapped at last.

"Our motorized columns were coiling along the road towards the invasion beaches. Then something happened that left us in a daze. Spurts of fire flicked along the column and splashes of dust staccatoed the road. Everyone was piling out of the vehicles and scuttling for the neighboring fields. Several vehicles were already in flames. This attack ceased as suddenly as it had crashed upon us fifteen minutes before. The men started drifting back to the column again, pale and shaky and wondering how they had survived this fiery rain of bullets. This had been our first experience with the 'Jabos' (fighter-bombers). The march column was now completely disrupted and every man was on his own, to pull out of this blazing column as best he could. And it was none too soon, because an hour later the whole thing started all over again, only much worse this time. When this attack was over, the length of the road was strewn with splintered anti-tank guns (the pride of our division), flaming motors and charred implements of war.

"The march was called off and all vehicles that were left were hidden in the dense bushes or in barns. No one dared show himself out in the open any more. Now the men started looking at each other. This was different from what we thought it would be like. It had been our first experience with our new foe — the American.

"During the next few days we found out how seriously he was going about his business. Although now we only traveled at nights and along secondary roads rimmed with hedges and bushes, we encountered innumerable wrecks giving toothless testimony that some motorist had not benefited from the bitter experience we had had. After about five days we moved into our assigned sector east of Périers."

But if the mechanized formations were slow in reaching the front, they were energetic hares in comparison to the tortoise-like pace of the infantry units. Once the immediate battle area had been milked of all available infantry, it was necessary to call upon the divisions outside the Seine-Loire rectangle. These formations with nothing but their horses and their legs to propel them, took an interminable length of time to get into battle. One infantry division[3] in Southern France started to leave the vicinity of Bayonne on 12 June. The broken railways, the destroyed bridges and the French Maquis so delayed them that the last elements of the division finally arrived at Hottot in Normandy on 4 July. In other words, to make a journey of some 400 miles, which could normally be completed by rail in seventy-two hours, required no less than twenty-two days. The main body of the division had to march at least one-third of the distance on foot, averaging approximately twenty miles each night.

Since it was impossible to bring up sufficient infantry to resist the mounting pressure of the Allies, it was necessary to use the armored divisions in an infantry rôle. They, being the only troops immediately available, were forced to dig into the rich, brown soil of Normandy and hold their ground as tenaciously as possible. This, of course, prevented them from carrying out their proper function which was to have been the mounting of a large-scale armored counter-offensive.

'Sepp' Dietrich of 1 S.S. Panzer Corps constantly protested to Rommel about this wasteful use of his troops.[4] About a week after D-Day he reported that unless reinforcements arrived for his three armored divisions, he could not guarantee to hold his position around Caen for more than another three weeks. And three days later he said to Rommel again: "I am being bled white and I am getting nowhere." To which Rommel replied: "You must attack." Receiving this answer Dietrich raised his hands and moaned: "But with what? We haven't enough troops. We need another eight or ten divisions in the next day or two or we're finished."

The merit of Dietrich's observations was well-recognized by the Commander-in-Chief West. Ten days after the initial landings the Allies had swollen their bridgehead to include almost half a million men and 300,000 vehicles. Von Rundstedt realized the necessity of immediate action. He planned to pull the armored divisions out of the line and reassemble them for a counter-attack. This attack he wanted to direct against the Americans north of St. Lô, thereby splitting the British and American forces.

"To concentrate enough tanks for a decisive blow," said von Rundstedt,[5] "it was imperative that infantry be available to replace the armour that had been rushed up to hold the line. I recommended to Berlin that the fifteen or twenty infantry divisions in Southern France and along the Atlantic coast be pulled back and sent north of the Loire. With these divisions I planned to hold a position along the Loire and the Orne rivers, relieve the panzer divisions, and with them push forward with a counter-offensive. Such a policy, of course, meant the abandonment of all of France south of the Loire, and this decision was considered politically impossible at Berlin. With insufficient infantry at my disposal I was unable to remove the armored formations facing the Allied bridgehead."

The only other source of infantry in the West was Fifteenth Army which controlled some nineteen infantry divisions in Northern France and the Low Countries. At first von Rundstedt had been reluctant to use these troops which were largely bunched in the Pas de Calais opposite the Straits of Dover. He had refrained from thinning out this force because he had been informed that still another Anglo-American army group was assembled in southeast England awaiting embarkation. The view that a second landing at Calais would take place died hard. Hitler, von Rundstedt and Rommel all believed it was coming. This appreciation was helped along by a huge Allied deception plan which filled the harbors of southeast England with dummy boats, moved American and Canadian troops into the Dover-Folkestone area, transmitted a steady stream of fake wireless messages for German intercept units, and maintained a strategical bombing program east of the Seine, consistent with invasion intentions in that region. This ruse easily tricked the German intelligence staffs, who found a ready ear for their unimaginative prognostications amongst senior officers who had thought the invasion would come there in the first place.

After two weeks of waiting for these second landings to occur, von Rundstedt and his Chief-of-Staff, Blumentritt finally decided that the main Allied effort would be concentrated in Normandy, and that from an Anglo-American standpoint there was no need to risk another landing since the first had proved so successful. With this decision, they recommended to Berlin that the bulk of troops east of the Seine be moved into Normandy. Permission to do this was not granted. If the fear of a second landing died hard at von Rundstedt's headquarters, it almost attained immortality at Berlin. In rejecting von Rundstedt's request for divisions from Fifteenth Army, the Supreme Command said that they expected that main operations were soon to begin, even at this late date, in the Pas de Calais. In other words, Hitler, who had at first believed Normandy would be the Allied invasion choice, had now changed his mind and he insisted that the coastline opposite Dover be strongly manned. It was not until early August that Hitler finally abandoned the view that a second landing would take place in the Pas de Calais. By then it was too late to release divisions for action in Normandy, since Seventh Army, at that date, was beyond all help.

Thus, with insufficient infantry to put into the line, there remained little to do but cling desperately to each inch of ground while the Allies continued their feverish build-up in the bridgehead. No division could be moved out of position without an explanation being sent to Hitler, and every tactical change had to be ratified by Berlin. The conduct of the battle was no longer in von Rundstedt's hands. Every decision was made by the Führer himself. "I could have stood on my head," remarked the Field Marshal,[6] "but I would still not have been able to budge a division if Hitler disagreed with my judgment." As the situation worsened, and as there was no hope of obtaining assistance from the divisions in Southern France, von Rundstedt decided the only advisable course was to swing his forces back and take up a line along the Seine River, as Allied planning staffs had predicted he would.

In mid-June Hitler came to see the situation in France for himself by visiting the headquarters of the Commander-in-Chief West. At Soissons he held a conference with von Rundstedt and Rommel. After listening to the opinions of both field commanders that a retirement to the Seine was the only logical plan, he flatly rejected the proposal and ordered that Normandy be held at all costs. As an alternative course it was agreed to attempt von Rundstedt's plan of an armored counter-attack designed to drive a wedge between the British and American forces. For this purpose it was planned to use 'Sepp' Dietrich's 1 S.S. Panzer Corps of three or four panzer divisions, which was then busy holding its ground at Caen, together with two fresh S.S. panzer divisions[7] which were being rushed to Normandy from the Russian front. With this force of five or six armored formations, having a combined strength of almost 500 tanks, it was hoped to make a desperate try at regaining the offensive.

The fall of Cherbourg on 26 June meant the release of further American troops for the southern drive, and it was obvious that the stage for an Allied break-out was now set. When the Americans had first driven across the Cherbourg Peninsula some six days before, Hitler had frantically ordered reinforcements to be sent to the northern part of the peninsula to defend the port. "Instead of trying to pull the troops out of a hopeless trap," said von Rundstedt, "Hitler wanted to send more men into it. Of course, we paid no attention to the order."[8]

Meanwhile Eisenhower and Montgomery had decided to use the American armored troops to break out on the right flank, while the British would maintain pressure on the left flank near Caen so that the strongest German elements would be attracted and held there. Von Rundstedt realized that his forces were relatively weak on his western flank but he dared not reduce the number of men defending the vital Caen hinge, for if it snapped, the German armies west of the Seine were doomed. In fact at the end of June he sent another three panzer divisions against the British to supplement the four panzer divisions already there.

This new armored force which had just arrived from Belgium and Russia consisted of fresh, full-strength S.S. panzer divisions filled with young fanatical troops. It was their task to launch the counter-attack arranged between Hitler and von Rundstedt at Soissons. Although it had been originally hoped that 'Sepp' Dietrich's armor at Caen would also be able to participate in this operation, after three weeks of battle they had been so thoroughly weakened that it was decided to make the attempt by relying chiefly on the newly-arrived forces, with only minor assistance from Dietrich's tired troops.

Again the British were chosen to face the armored blow. In the neighborhood of Evrecy about 250 tanks and 100 guns were poised to try and gain the Caen-Bayeux road. The attack was to take place on 29 June under the leadership of Obergruppenführer (General) Paul Hausser, commander of 2 S.S. Panzer Corps. The general had this to say about that attack.

"It was scheduled to begin at seven o'clock in the morning, but hardly had the tanks assembled when they were attacked by fighter-bombers. This disrupted the troops so much that the attack did not start again until two-thirty in the afternoon. But even then it could not get going. The murderous fire from naval guns in the Channel and the terrible British artillery destroyed the bulk of our attacking force in its assembly area. The few tanks that did manage to go forward were easily stopped by the English anti-tank guns. In my opinion the attack was prepared too quickly. I wanted to wait another two days, but Hitler insisted that it be launched on 29 June."

Thus ended the second of the only two armored offensives made by the Germans along the entire Normandy front during the vital days of June 1944. Both had been directed at the British part of the line, as the Allied strategists had hoped, and both had been thoroughly beaten there. And in their being beaten were destroyed the only effective fighting troops available to the German High Command in the West. For no fewer than seven of the total of nine panzer divisions in Normandy had butted their tanks against the iron-wall defence put up by the British soldier. By the end of June these seven armored formations had lost over 350 tanks.[9] Personnel losses amongst their fighting troops ranged as high as twenty-five to fifty per cent, due to the costly battle of attrition created by the constant pressure of the British. The plan of attracting to the eastern side of the line the strongest German forces was paying magnificent dividends. In less than a month the bulk of von Rundstedt's armored might lay gasping in a semi-circle around Caen, weary and exhausted after their exertions and able to do little more than hang on stubbornly to the blood-soaked Normandy soil that their Führer refused to give up.

And while the British were taking their toll of German armor, the Americans were whittling down the strength of the German infantry. The break-through at Cherbourg had destroyed at least three infantry divisions as effective fighting units, and the first large batches of German prisoners-of-war were making their disconsolate way back to English prison camps. By the end of June well over 50,000 German prisoners had ceased to take any further active interest in the struggles of the Wehrmacht. Most of them had ended their military careers in the concrete bunkers built to protect the port of Cherbourg.

Chapter XVII

THE GERMAN SOLDIER STILL HOPES

THE reaction of the average German soldier to these disastrous events was stunned surprise. Having been assured by Goebbels that the Atlantic Wall was impregnable, they now could see how fragile it really was; having been told by Göring that American factories could only produce electric refrigerators and razor blades, they now faced an overwhelming superiority of material strength in planes, guns and tanks; having been promised a secret weapon by Hitler himself which would destroy the enemy in one swift, catastrophic Armageddon, they found instead an enemy growing stronger and bolder as each day passed. The one emotion which gripped them all was incredulity. They had not yet begun to despair. Having been doped so long by propaganda, the effects did not easily wear off. Much more time and much more suffering was needed before the German soldier finally awoke to the reality of events about him.

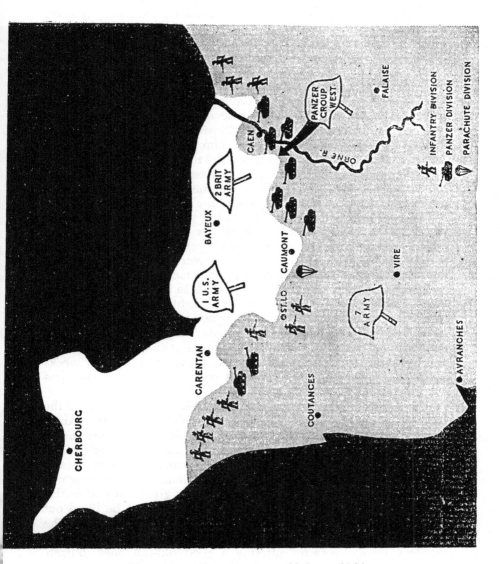

THE NORMANDY BRIDGEHEAD — 29 *June*, 1944.

A first-hand account of what German troops were experiencing in Normandy has been written by the paunchy, red-faced, forceful member of the German nobility, General Freiherr Heinrich von Lüttwitz, who was later to gain some rather dubious fame as the officer who received the contemptuous reply "Nuts" to his demand for the surrender of the American airborne troops at Bastogne in the Ardennes. Lüttwitz commanded 2 Panzer Division, which had been fighting in the vicinity of Caumont since early June until it was relieved in mid-July. In a top secret document dated 17 July 1944, von Lüttwitz passed on the following information to the new infantry division which was relieving him.

"... The incredibly heavy artillery and mortar fire of the enemy is something new, both for the seasoned veterans of the Eastern front and the new arrivals from reinforcement units. Whereas the veterans get used to it comparatively quickly, the inexperienced reinforcements require several days to do so, after which they become acclimatized. The average rate of fire on the divisional sector is 4000 artillery rounds and 5000 mortar rounds per day. This is multiplied many times before an enemy attack, however small. For instance, on one occasion when the British made an attack on a sector of only two companies they expended 3500 rounds in two hours. The Allies are waging war regardless of expense. In addition to this, the enemy have complete mastery of the air. They bomb and strafe every movement, even single vehicles and individuals. They reconnoitre our area constantly and direct their artillery fire. Against all this the Luftwaffe is conspicuous by its complete absence. During the last four weeks the *total* number of German aircraft over the divisional area was six. . . .

"Our soldiers enter the battle in low spirits at the thought of the enemy's enormous material superiority. They are always asking: 'Where is the Luftwaffe?' The feeling of helplessness against enemy aircraft operating without any hindrance has a paralyzing effect, and during the barrage this effect on the inexperienced troops is literally 'soul-shattering,' and it must be borne in mind that four-engined bombers have not yet taken part in attacking ground troops in this division's area. It is, therefore, essential for troops to be lifted out of this state of distress the moment the counter-attack begins. The best results have been obtained by the platoon and section commanders' leaping forward uttering a good old-fashioned 'hurrah' which spurs on the inexperienced troops and carries them along. The revival of the practice of sounding a bugle call for the attack has been found to answer the purpose, and this has been made a divisional order. An attack launched in this manner is an experience which new troops will never forget, and stimulates them into action again. . . ."

But, contrary to the fond hopes of von Lüttwitz, not all junior commanders in the West were the 'hurrahing' type. It was only their discipline and not their faith that kept many of them in the line. Thus it was quite common to find German officers surrendering only after they had assured themselves that their honor had not been compromised. The fact that they had sworn to fight to the last was interpreted by many officers as fighting until they found a way to stop which was not inconsistent with their oath.

On one occasion an infantry commander refused to surrender unless Allied troops had first thrown some phosphorus grenades into his position, as he had no answer to phosphorus. Six grenades were therefore produced and thrown, and, after inspecting the results of the subsequent explosion, the German officer, his honor apparently having been saved, quietly surrendered himself and his whole unit. Another instance of this kind of behavior was provided by the commander of the Cherbourg Arsenal who declined to give himself up until a tank was produced. A Sherman tank was accordingly driven up to the walls of the Arsenal and the general then considered he had been subjected to a tank attack. Not possessing adequate anti-tank defense, he now felt that he could surrender honorably and without having broken his pledge to defend to the end.

Realizing that the constant pressure of defeat might eventually effect the German soldier's faith in an ultimate German victory, Goebbels began an incredible propaganda campaign with a view to counteracting any such tendency. The gleaming hope held up to all Germans was the promise of new and more devastating secret weapons which would make a Teutonic victory inevitable. Glowing tales of the success achieved by the pilotless planes over England were followed by fervent assurances of still better weapons to come. The soldier in Normandy caught the occasional glimpse of the terrifying, ghost-like buzz-bombs, spouting red flames from their tails, and believed all he heard about its awe-inspiring potentialities.

It is a measure of the extent to which the average German's mind had been deprived of its ability to reason that he could believe the fantastic lies told to him by Goebbels and his assistants. One prisoner assured his interrogator that three more V-weapons were in the offing. The V-2, which would be used on or before 18 July against Allied fleets in the Channel, would force the invading armies out of France. The V-3 had an even more devastating effect, but the prisoner knew no details. The V-4 had a single and ambitious purpose. It was designed to sink the British Isles.[1]

Another prisoner captured in early July reported that his company commander had given them lurid details of the results of pilotless plane activity over England. All Southern England was aflame, he solemnly announced, and no fewer than 12,000,000 people had so far been killed.[2] And, astonishing as it may now sound, such tales were accepted by the vast majority of the rank and file as unassailable truth. He wrote letters to his family like the following, written by a sergeant in an infantry division.

"The R.A.F. rules the skies. I have not yet seen a single plane with a 'swastika,' and despite the material superiority of the enemy we Germans hold firm. The front at Caen holds. Every soldier on this front is hoping for a miracle and waits for the secret weapons which have been discussed so much."

There is little doubt that it was this dogged hope in a secret weapon, coupled with a mind disciplined to accept authority unquestioningly, that kept the German soldier confident and obedient in his fox-hole during the early days in Normandy.

With the fall of Cherbourg, the failure of the armored counter-attack and the growing strength of the Allies in the bridgehead, relations between the Commander-in-Chief West and the Supreme Command at Berlin, always cool even in the halcyon days, now became frigid. Von Rundstedt was fed up with the constant interference of Hitler and his staff, while there was a growing suspicion at Berlin that either von Rundstedt was not enthusiastic enough or that he was getting too old for his job. The Field Marshal was much more bitter and resentful towards Keitel and Jodl than he was towards Hitler himself. He referred to them as the two 'yes' generals and resented their failure to oppose Hitler's more mad military ventures. As a result he made a point of not speaking to them personally over the telephone unless the matter was exceedingly urgent. This task he delegated to Blumentritt, his Chief-of-Staff.

The mounting toll of death and disaster had its effect on the men in command. Tempers became badly frayed and disagreements became more frequent and more violent. On one occasion Keitel was complaining bitterly about the trend of events and implying that von Rundstedt had failed to do his part. "If you think you can do any better," von Rundstedt finally exclaimed in exasperation, "you had better come down here and lead this filth yourself."[3]

When Cherbourg had been captured and it was obvious that the armored attack of 29 June had failed, Keitel called up and in desperate tones asked: "What shall we do? What shall we do?" Von Rundstedt replied in his cool, impassive voice: "What shall you do? Make peace, you idiots! What else can you do?" and calmly hung up the receiver.[4] Blumentritt reports that twenty-four hours later, on 2 July, an order arrived from Berlin relieving von Rundstedt of his command. To take his place came stocky, colorless, sixty-one-year-old Field Marshal Günther von Kluge, who had directed the ill-fated armored offensive in the Kursk salient in Russia a year before. To have replaced von Rundstedt, the man who had achieved the most striking offensive successes of the war by von Kluge, whose reputation had been chiefly attained as the apostle of the 'victorious defense' in the East, was an omen of the times.

It is idle to speculate on what might have happened in Normandy had von Rundstedt been allowed to fight the battle his own way. His own views on the subject are rather philosophical. "I knew all along that the German position in France was hopeless," he said,[5] "and that eventually the war would be lost. But if I had been given a free hand to conduct operations, I think I could have made the Allies pay a fearful price for their victory. I had planned to fight a slow retiring action exacting a heavy toll for each bit of ground that I gave up. I had hoped that this might have brought about a political decision which would have saved Germany from complete and utter defeat. But I did not have my way. As Commander-in-Chief in the West my only authority was to change the guard in front of my gate."

It is safe to say that von Rundstedt's way was a much wiser one than Hitler's. Thousands of American and British lives are undoubtedly owed to the fact that he was unable to carry it out. A corporal had overruled the greatest living German soldier. For that the world can be truly grateful.

Part V ⨍ THE DECLINE

Chapter XVIII
JULY TWENTIETH

"Providence has preserved me from all harm, so that I may continue with the great work of victory." The words came from the familiar voice of Adolf Hitler to a world still reeling from the news that an attempt had been made to assassinate the German Führer. It was 20 July 1944. The announcement carried with it both hope and disappointment for all peoples at war with the German Reich — hope that at last the Germans themselves were prepared to rid themselves of the man who had brought them untold death and misery; disappointment that this first real manifestation of resistance to Nazism had proved such an obvious failure.

But the curtain was pulled aside for only a brief moment when this scene of dissension on the German political stage was revealed. In that glimpse the world could catch sight of the scurrying shadows of an anti-Nazi movement which they had ceased to believe existed. Then the house lights went down and once more the stage was dominated and directed by the cunning manipulations of Goebbels. By clamping down a rigid, carefully-controlled censorship of the circumstances surrounding the plot, by ruthlessly exterminating or interning all those even remotely associated with it, and by staging a dramatic well-regulated trial of the leading conspirators, the Nazis managed to befuddle and blind both Germans and non-Germans as to the true nature and significance of the putsch of 20 July. As a result, the affair has taken on the rather dubious attributes of an unimportant resistance movement, a revolt of disgruntled malcontents and a badly-managed *coup d'état* of army opportunists.

In reality it represented a far more important aspect of Nazi Germany. For in this assassination attempt were combined all those elements within Germany which were courageous enough to offer even token opposition to the Hitler régime. It was a revolt which came from the top, rather than the bottom, of German political life. It was made up chiefly of persons whose position in the contemporary life of the Reich represented both authority and prestige. Because of the select character of its participants the numbers actively involved were relatively small, but the breadth of German opinion which they represented was far beyond their quantitative strength. In nature and form the revolt was completely different from the Russian Revolution of 1917, where the impetus sprang from the workers and the common soldiers. The whole-hearted support of the masses themselves made possible the overthrow of the Czar. The plot of 20 July did not stem from the German people. They knew nothing of it. Nevertheless, it represented the one genuine, internal revolt against Nazi ideals. Its suppression may have had little effect on the average German soldier because he had not been taken into the confidence of the conspirators. But its repercussions within the hierarchy of the army command were significant. The full extent of the scope and implications of the conspiracy have only recently begun to come to light. There are still many aspects of it which have yet to be discovered, but the general outline of its main features has been well presented in a detailed report produced by the Strategic Services Unit of the United States Forces.[1] From this and other documents it is clear that the putsch of 20 July will occupy an increasingly prominent place in any honest history of the Third Reich.

The first elements to undertake clandestine opposition to Nazism were the members of intellectual and left-wing groups who refused to yield to the pressure of fear and ambition. Constantly shadowed by one of the most ruthless and vigilant police systems in history, this opposition was driven deeper and deeper underground as National Socialism embedded itself more firmly into the life of the German nation. And as success after success followed Hitler's leadership in both the domestic and foreign fields, these resistance groups dwindled in strength and enthusiasm until little remained of them but small discussion coteries which concerned themselves chiefly with keeping alive a philosophical, rather than a physical, opposition to Nazism. It was only after these civilian elements were able to enlist the support of the dissident, influential army officers that their opposition could take on a more active form. With their help, and the potential force they could command, the strength of the private S.S. troops surrounding Hitler could, to some extent, be neutralized. It was thus possible, for the first time, to formulate plans for an act of physical violence designed to overthrow the National Socialist régime.

The conspirators themselves represented a wide range of German opposition to Hitler. As the government continued to make enemies so did the group continue to grow. The only common policy which bound these diverse elements together was a negative rather than a positive, one. They all desired the end of Nazism in its current form. And each group within the conspiracy was motivated by different reasons in that desire. Some were intellectually opposed to the moral and philosophical program of National Socialism, others wished a return to a Conservative Republican form of government, others hoped to achieve a left-wing social revolution, others desired to salvage the power and prestige of the army. And within each group individuals participated for a variety of motives including personal ambition, patriotism, idealism, revenge, fear and jealousy. At least six distinguishable groups played a prominent part in the conspiracy. These were the civil servants, ex-Nazis, Social Democrats, churchmen, intellectuals and army officers. A brief discussion of each of these groups in turn will indicate how wide were the ramifications of a plot which included such divergent elements.

The civil servants constituted the most important civilian opposition to the Hitler régime. Having either held high government office, or being still in possession of it, they constituted a body of trained personnel whose talents could be usefully employed both in carrying out the mechanics of the revolution and in the establishment of the new government that was to follow. The leading figure in this group was Dr. Karl Goerdeler, former Lord Mayor of Leipzig and Reich Price Control Commissioner when the Nazis came to power. His connections were chiefly with industrialists and business men, although his opposition to Hitler brought him into contact with both military and left-wing circles. By 1938 he was convinced that Hitler's policies would lead Germany to economic disaster and it was this motive which dominated his activities. Politically he was Conservative, and after the war began he concentrated his efforts in the hope that the putsch might succeed in bringing about an occupation of Germany by the Western Powers alone. In the government that was to be set up following Hitler's overthrow, Goerdeler was to hold the important post of Chancellor.

Other conspirators from the civil-servant class included Count Friedrich von der Schulenberg, former ambassador in Moscow, and Ulrich von Hassell, former ambassador in Rome, both of whom had been dismissed from the German Foreign Office for disagreeing with the Führer's policies in regard to Russia and Italy; Hans Popitz, former Prussian Minister of Finance; the former Württemberg State President Eugen Bolz, and many others of a like standing in the political life of the Reich. The majority of these men agreed with Goerdeler in his Conservative political views. They hoped by destroying National Socialism to set up a parliamentary democracy similar to Great Britain and the United States, retaining and protecting

vested commercial interests, but willing to compromise with those
Socialist elements which were not too revolutionary in their demands
for reform.

The renegade Nazis who decided to abandon the losing cause of
National Socialism following the first great military defeats were
included in the plot since they could help undermine Nazi solidarity
as well as control certain elements of the Berlin police on the day
of the putsch. These turn-coats had no ideological pretensions in
shifting their allegiance but were motivated either by fear for their
own personal safety or bald political opportunism. Amongst the
prominent members of this group were Arthur Nebe, Chief of the
Criminal Department of Himmler's Security Services, and Professor
Jens Jessen, an economist of the University of Berlin.

It was inevitable that the remnants of the left-wing Social Democrat and Communist parties would maintain some semblance of
opposition to the Hitler régime. Knowing the enduring quality of
such opposition the Nazis concentrated their most determined efforts
on crushing it. By dissolving all left-wing parties, smashing the
trade unions, prohibiting strikes, imprisoning almost every prominent
Social Democrat and trade union leader, and constantly keeping
under Gestapo surveillance all workers' organizations of any kind,
they succeeded in reducing left-wing resistance to local and factory
cells with little regional or national liason between them. Thoroughly
crushed by these methods, it became impossible to plan any independent action from the Left. There only remained the necessity
of survival until some other internal or external force had weakened
the fascist dictatorship sufficiently to permit a renewal of Social
Democrat and Communist activities.

The composition and aims of the Conservative military group
formed by civil servants, ex-Nazis and army officers did not tend to
encourage recruitment from the Left. But realizing that an iron-clad
police state like Hitler's made a revolt amongst the masses almost
impossible, some of the more conservative elements of the Left decided to join the conspiracy which, because of its army component,
seemed to possess the only possible force capable of dealing with the
private S.S. armies of the Nazis. The Socialist leaders did not actively
associate themselves with the plot until 1942, when men like Wilhelm
Leuschner, former Hessian Minister of the Interior, agreed to co-
operate.

Many leading Social Democrats opposed active participation in
the plot since they did not consider it advisable to replace a National
Socialist government by a Conservative military one. The Communists were not ardently encouraged to join the revolt nor did they

show any particular enthusiasm for its aspirations. An attempt to gain their support in June and July 1944 resulted in the arrest of both the Socialist and Communist leaders carrying out the negotiations. The majority of those left-wing members who knew of the plan preferred to remain uncommitted, since they distrusted the leaders of the conspiratorial clique almost as much as they detested Hitler. Instead they made preparations to enter into the national arena and engage in independent political action the moment the putsch had accomplished its purpose.

The church had been in ideological conflict with Nazi totalitarianism from the very beginning of the New Order. It was therefore natural that certain priests and ministers would find their way to the inner circle of conspirators plotting the attempt of 20 July. The Catholic Cardinal Faulhaber of Munich, and Bishop Preysing of Berlin, and the Protestant Bishop Dibelius of Berlin, and Bishop Wurm of Stuttgart, had been informed of the projected attempt, and had given their tacit consent.

Intellectual opposition amongst scholars, who refused to accept the pseudo-philosophical diatribes of Goebbels and Rosenberg, continued to exist in private homes and university circles. Amongst those arrested for contributing vigorous anti-Nazi writings to the conspirators were the historian Gerhard Ritter, and the economists Constantin von Dietze and Adolf Lampe, all professors on the faculty of Freiburg University in Baden. Like the churchmen, with whom they were in close collaboration, these intellectuals represented an ethical and moral revolt against the Nazi program which was lacking amongst most of the other groups participating in the putsch.

Another group which does not fit neatly into the opposition categories already discussed was the Kreisau Circle which met at the estate of Count Hellmuth von Moltke (great nephew of the German military hero of 1871) at Kreisau in Silesia. While essentially Socialist in its nature this group included a large number of the personalities belonging to the more conservative elements of the conspiracy, such as the civil servants, the army and the church. Its leaders were Dr. Carlo Mierendorff and Dr. Julius Leber, both former Social Democrat leaders of the pre-Hitler Reichstag. Amongst its members it numbered young aristocrats like Moltke himself, Count Klaus Schenk von Stauffenberg, who personally carried out the actual assassination attempt, Count Peter Yorck von Wartenburg; civil servants like Adam von Trott zu Solz of the German Diplomatic Service; the Jesuit Father Alois Delp and the Protestant minister Eugen Gerstenmaier and Socialists like Theodor Haubach and Adolf Reichwein.

The subsequent trial of von Moltke failed to establish any concrete evidence of participation by the Kreisau Circle, as a group, in the actual assassination attempt. But there is little doubt that many of its followers were actively involved. In any case they provided a nucleus of philosophical opposition which favored an economic revolution and a strong pro-Russian alliance for any government replacing the Nazis. Naturally such an out-and-out Socialist platform did not find favor with the Conservative elements led by Goerdeler, whose coterie included industrial magnates such as Wilhelm zur Nieden, who controlled the Leipzig electrical industry, and large landowners like Count Heinrich von Lehndorff-Steiner. The result of this conflict was an uneasy compromise between Goerdeler and the left-wing elements, by which the latter provisionally accepted Goerdeler as the prospective Chancellor, but only on the understanding that a programme of socialization of national wealth and a pro-Eastern orientation of the future government would be taken into consideration immediately after power had been seized. It was this fundamental disunity between the right- and the left-wing parties in the conspiracy which augured ill for the life of the prospective government. But despite these deep-rooted differences the desire to destroy the National Socialist government of Adolf Hitler contributed the unifying force which bound the conspirators together.

But the one resistance group, without which the entire plot would have been impossible, came from the officer corps of the German army. Since it possessed the only means of achieving a physical seizure of power it constituted the most important active element concerned with the mechanics of the putsch itself. The steady encroachment of Hitler upon the political independence of the army inevitably left scars which even military victories could not heal. The dismissal of von Fritsch and von Blomberg, which enabled Hitler to assume personal control of the Wehrmacht, was followed by the protests of the General Staff against Hitler's plans to occupy Czechoslovakia. This latter incident resulted in the resignation of Colonel General Ludwig Beck, Chief-of-Staff of the army, and the almost complete subservience of the officer corps to the domination of Hitler. But Beck, unlike von Fritsch and von Blomberg, was unwilling to accept the degeneration of the army's independence as a *fait accompli*. It was Beck who, as early as 1938, began to assemble about him the military figures discontented enough with the Nazi régime to oppose it actively. In him was centered the hope and ambition of the conspirators of 20 July.

Beck, coming from a family of business men and intellectuals, possessed a non-military background which fitted him well for his rôle as a link between the civilian and military elements of the conspiracy. Conscientious and tireless in his activities, he had been greatly respected by the officer corps during his term as Chief-of-Staff, and he was thus able to draw into the plot high-ranking officers who trusted his ability and judgment. Beck's political views were Conservative and neither original nor profound. His hostility towards the Nazis stemmed chiefly from the feeling that they had damaged the prestige and authority of the army and had thereby inflicted upon the German nation a serious wrong which would eventually lead it to disaster.

The other senior officers involved in the conspiracy were motivated . by a variety of special and ideological reasons. Resentment of Hitler's treatment of the Prussian military caste brought in Colonel General Baron Kurt von Hammerstein, who was von Fritsch's predecessor as Commander-in-Chief of the army before he resigned in 1934. His death in retirement in 1943 undoubtedly saved him from the gallows. Personal ambition attracted Field Marshal Erwin von Witzleben, who had retired as Commander-in-Chief of the West in 1942. Vengeance enlisted the aid of Colonel General Erich Hoeppner, who in 1942 was court-martialed and dishonorably discharged for allowing his army to retreat before the Russians against the orders of the Führer. Realization of Germany's hopeless military position stimulated General Friedrich Olbricht to join the movement. As Chief of the Central Army Office of the Home Army, responsible for the supply and training of reinforcements, he was in a position to see the mounting effects of military defeat on German manpower. He received the tacit support of Colonel General Fromm, the Home Army commander, in his activities, and the Berlin offices of the Home Army were frequently used for meetings by Beck, Witzleben and others.

But few of these generals had committed themselves to the plot during the victorious days of 1940 and 1941. It was only after the defeats before Moscow, Stalingrad and El Alamein with the attendant ruthless and autocratic behavior of Hitler, that any large group of officers made known their willingness to help overthrow the régime. In other words it was the spectre of impending defeat, not a sudden surge of moral antipathy to aggression, that drove these men to concrete action against Hitler.

As defeat became more imminent the number of military recruits increased, but they never reached the quantity that one might have expected in view of Germany's helpless position and Hitler's mad determination to stage a Wagnerian Twilight of the Gods. The losses in Russia and North Africa brought in General Heinrich von Stülpnagel, Military Governor of France, and General Alexander von Falkenhausen, Military Governor of Belgium. There is strong, but inconclusive evidence that the disastrous strategy in Normandy also carried into the opposition two of the most important soldiers in the West, Field Marshal Günther von Kluge, von Rundstedt's successor as Commander-in-Chief West,[2] and Field Marshal Erwin Rommel, commander of Army Group 'B.' How far this defection went is not yet completely known, but there is little doubt that they were aware of the existence of the conspiracy. Von Kluge is believed to have made known his willingness to put an end to the war late in June 1944, while Rommel's adherence to the plot was communicated to a liaison officer of the conspirators, a Colonel Cæsar von Hofbacker of Stülpnagel's staff in Paris, about a week before the attempt was made. Again it was the shadow of inevitable defeat, rather than an ideological revulsion, that forced men like von Kluge and Rommel finally to revolt. Even then it was only at the last moment, when no possible hope of victory still remained, that they found courage or disillusionment enough to make such a choice.

There was one other small military clique whose activities must be included in any account of 20 July. This was the Military Intelligence Division of the Supreme Command, or 'Abwehr,' led by Admiral Wilhelm Canaris. As early as the blood purge in 1934 Canaris, an extremely talented and clever man, began to intrigue against the Hitler program. His attitude towards Nazi policies seems to have been dominated by a firm conviction that since Germany was not powerful enough to engage in a major war, any such course could only lead to disaster. Gathering about him men like Major General Hans Oster, Chief of the Central Intelligence Bureau, and Colonel Hansen, Head of the Operational Intelligence Bureau, who succeeded Canaris when the latter resigned in January 1944, the group urged senior army officers to resist Hitler's political and military plans. Thus in the spring of 1939 they prepared the reports designed to prove that an attack on Poland would be certain to lead to conflict with England and France. And in the winter of 1939-40 they were instrumental in establishing contact with Vatican circles in order to initiate peace negotiations with the Western Powers should a projected *coup d'état* against Hitler succeed.[3]

The German victories of 1940 made further efforts along these lines impossible in the immediate future. However, the fiasco at Stalingrad produced the occasion for another attempt, under Abwehr cover, to stage a military revolt. This plan called for all commanders on the Eastern front simultaneously to renounce their allegiance to Hitler. At the last minute several commanders, notably von Kluge, von Manstein and Paulus refused to co-operate and the project fell through. An investigation started by Himmler into this plot was quashed by Field Marshal Keitel, who was convinced Himmler was trying to undermine Keitel's personal position. Abwehr personnel thus escaped the repercussions of their activities, but suspicion was so great that Oster was forced to resign his position in July 1943. The early attempts of Himmler to bring the military intelligence organization under his direct control were now intensified. A constant influx of S.S. and pro-Nazi officers tended to undermine the resistance character of the Canaris group. Nothing has yet been revealed to suggest that this anti-Nazi feeling amongst senior Abwehr officers was the explanation for the many stupid blunders committed by German military intelligence during World War II. The activities of the Canaris group were more concerned with the broad political problems created by Hitler's program rather than a picayune falsification of military intelligence reports. And in any case there were enough Nazis within the branch to make any such juggling with facts extremely dangerous. It is fairly safe to say that the failure of German Military Intelligence was due to the limitations imposed by the inflexible Teutonic mind rather than to any deliberate design.

For the purpose of centralizing the activities of this sprawling alliance of conspirators, a small body containing representatives of each group met frequently in the Home Army offices at Berlin, at various country estates or elsewhere. A provisional cabinet for the new government was drawn up, and although it was frequently changed it attempted to include all elements of the conspiracy. Thus Beck of the army was Chief of State; Goerdeler, the Nationalist, was Chancellor; Leuschner, the Social Democrat, was Vice-Chancellor; Bolz of the Center Party was Minister for Education; Witzleben of the army was Commander of the Armed Forces, and so on.

This government was to assume power after a three-day period of martial law following the assassination, during which time the army would have brought the Nazis under control. The future policies of the government were left intentionally vague since it was obvious that there were no common roots to hold together a coalition of Conservatives, industrialists, Socialists and near-Communists. The immediate plans of the group were concrete enough. The Nazi leaders were to be imprisoned and the party dissolved. A proposal would be broadcast to Germany's enemies offering to lay down arms and withdraw to the Reich's pre-1938 frontier. Germany would make restitution for destruction caused by her, and war criminals would be punished. The question of the occupation of Germany was to be settled by discussion.

At first it was hoped to accomplish the overthrow of the Nazi régime without assassinating Hitler. But the failure to rally leading military personalities to the cause because of the personal oath made to their Supreme Commander, convinced the leaders of the conspiracy that only by eliminating the Führer could any measure of support for their efforts be obtained. As early as the spring of 1943, one of the conspirators, a Colonel von Schlabrendorff, placed an incendiary brief-case in Hitler's plane while he was visiting the Russian front. Because of a mechanical failure the bomb failed to explode on the return trip to Berlin, but the plot was not detected because the unreliable brief-case was retrieved in time.

The man who was personally responsible for the assassination attempt was a comparatively young colonel of the General Staff, Count Klaus Schenk von Stauffenberg. A member of the Socialist Kreisau Circle, he was a Bavarian Catholic who held strong leftist, pro-Russian views which tended to make him unpopular with the Conservative wing of the conspiracy. But it was undoubtedly his personal courage and his sincerity which gave the plot whatever dynamic force it possessed. Baron Gottfried von Cramm, the well-known German tennis player, has claimed that von Stauffenberg was the real guiding spirit of the putsch, although Beck was given the nominal lead because of his prestige and authority.[4]

Von Stauffenberg, having lost an arm in the Tunisian campaign, was given a job as a liaison officer between Hitler's Supreme Headquarters and the Home Army. This had been arranged by the conspirator General Olbricht of the Home Army, and it gave von Stauffenberg an excuse for visiting the Führer personally every few days. Although it would have been preferable to shoot Hitler, von Stauffenberg's wooden arm and the possession of only two fingers on the other hand made this impossible. The alternative of an explosive brief-case was therefore adopted.

In December 1943, it was again decided to try planting the bomb at a proposed conference Hitler was to hold with his generals. At the last minute the conference was canceled, without explanation, and almost simultaneously London newspapers published reports of an imminent revolt in Germany. The increased vigilance of the Gestapo made a further postponement advisable and it was then decided to withhold any further action until the Allied invasion of Europe.

The successful landings in Normandy, together with vehement disagreement by most senior officers with Hitler's conduct of the battle, made the month of July the logical time for another attempt. Von Stauffenberg carried his brief-case to meetings with Hitler on the 6, 12 and 16 of July, but on each occasion the assassin felt that the conditions were not ideal. After this third essay it became imperative to act regardless of risk. On the 16th military forces had actually been set in motion to march on Berlin. When the attempt was not made this activity had to be passed off as an exercise. On 20 July such a manœuvre could not be tried again without arousing suspicion and thus on the fatal day itself troops only started to move after the bomb had actually exploded. As a result they did not reach the War Ministry offices in time to forestall Nazi counter-measures. Another reason for speed was the fact that the Gestapo had on 12 July arrested Leber and Reichwein, two Socialist conspirators negotiating for Communist support, and it was clear that something of the plot was already known by the Nazi authorities.

The plans for the day itself were thoroughly Germanic in the detail with which they had been worked out. Hitler was reviewing four Italian divisions at Rastenberg in East Prussia. Von Stauffenberg was to visit the concrete bunker where the Führer's conference would be held, and place the explosive brief-case under the table beside Hitler. He would then leave the bunker and wait for the explosion. As soon as he was satisfied that all had gone according to plan he was to take off for Berlin in the plane which had brought him to Rastenberg. On landing he was to telephone to Beck, who was waiting in the Home Army offices in the War Ministry, with Generals Olbricht, Hoeppner and others.

Simultaneously with the explosion, General Erich Fellgiebel, of the Signal Corps, was to destroy the central information office, including all communication facilities at Rastenberg. This was designed to isolate Hitler and his aides, so that they would be unable to contact their supporters in Berlin or elsewhere. Thus even if Hitler were not killed the conspirators hoped to have the situation under control before this fact was made known.

When von Stauffenberg had reported the successful completion of his mission to Beck in Berlin, it was then planned to send out orders by teletype to all generals of the Home Army telling them that Hitler was dead, that the army was taking over control and that all Nazis in their areas be arrested. A similar order in the name of Field Marshal von Witzleben was to be sent to all field commanders outside Germany.

Within Berlin itself, General Karl von Hase, the District Commandant, was to guard the Home Army offices at the War Ministry with Berlin troops until the arrival of regular army regiments from the infantry school at Doeberitz. Once all Nazi resistance was liquidated, Beck and Goerdeler were to install their new government and issue their first proclamations.

A combination of precipitate action on the part of von Stauffenberg, nervous incompetence on the part of Fellgiebel and bad luck all round dashed to nothing these carefully conceived plans. Instead of meeting in the concrete bunker underground as had been expected, Hitler held his conference in a light wooden hut above ground. As a result the blast, instead of being concentrated in a small space, burst through the weak roof, which reduced its effect. Hitler, who was reading a wall-map at the time, received severe injuries, which resulted in partial deafness and partial paralysis of his left arm and leg from which he never recovered. Nevertheless in a few hours he was able to carry on with his normal duties and even speak over the radio. Four men in the hut, two of them generals, died as a result of the explosion, while other officers such as Colonel General Jodl, also sustained serious injuries.

Von Stauffenberg, hearing the bomb explode, did not wait to ascertain what damage it had caused but immediately took off for Berlin. On arriving at the airport he telephoned the War Ministry offices in the Bendlerstrasse, where the conspirators were waiting, and reported that everything was under control and to go ahead. The teletype orders to both field and home commands were sent out as planned, and the military forces at Doeberitz ordered to march on Berlin. When von Stauffenberg finally reached the conspirators in person, he admitted that he was not certain that Hitler was indeed dead since he had not waited to find out. To this Beck replied, "For us he is dead," and pressed on with the plans, relying on General Fellgiebel at Rastenberg to prevent news of the assassination from reaching outside sources. This hope was however dispelled when Field Marshal Keitel, not then knowing who was involved in the plot, telephoned through to the Home Army offices and informed all military commanders that the teletype orders were fakes and that Hitler was still alive. The speed with which the news of the failure of the attempt reached Berlin was due to the fact that General Fellgiebel lost his nerve at the last moment and failed to destroy the radio transmitter and the telephone communication system at Rastenberg.

In Berlin itself the commander of the Guards Regiment, a Major Remer, was ordered by General von Hase to surround the War Office and protect it against the S.S. Remer, worried by rumors that Hitler was not dead, neglected to obey these orders, and instead went to Goebbels's office and reported that Hitler was dead and that he had orders to arrest Goebbels. Goebbels immediately called Hitler at Rastenberg, put Remer on the telephone and the Führer personally ordered Remer to arrest all generals in the War Ministry, regardless of the contrary orders he had been given by his senior, General von Hase. Thus, instead of protecting the War Ministry from the S.S. as had been planned, Remer's regiment had by six o'clock that evening arrested all the conspirators in the immediate vicinity who had not yet committed suicide.

The next few days were a mad kaleidoscope of arrests, betrayals, suicides and murders. Beck and three other officers with him killed themselves before they were arrested by Remer's troops. Colonel General Fritz Fromm, commander of the Home Army, who had allowed General Olbricht to use the Home Army offices for further-ing the conspirators' plans, now desperately tried to wipe out all witnesses who might implicate him in the plot. He arrested Olbricht, von Stauffenberg and two others, and summarily had them shot on the evening of the 20th. The attempt to erase his own guilt failed, however, for Fromm was executed several weeks later by the S.S. Witzleben, Canaris, Oster and others were arrested in the early hours of the 21st, while a thorough campaign by the Gestapo managed to bring in most of the remaining conspirators in a few weeks. Goerdeler managed to evade capture until late August.

In Paris, General Heinrich von Stülpnagel had arrested all Nazi personnel on the receipt of the first teletype message, but subsequent reports forced Field Marshal von Kluge to dismiss him the next morn-ing. Stülpnagel was immediately called to Berlin to explain his actions. On the way he attempted to commit suicide, but blinded himself instead. He was subsequently executed. Von Kluge himself was, in late August, asked to explain references to himself which came out during the course of Himmler's investigation into the conspiracy. His reply was to take poison. Men like Rommel paid their debt to Hitler much later still. The Nazis, in a wild frenzy, not only exterminated those connected with the plot, but used the occasion to rid themselves of many who were suspected of animosity towards the régime. No complete figures are yet available as to the total number of executions carried out in this thorough purge. One estimate based on actual names and places puts the death toll at 4980 persons.

The reaction of the non-participating members of the officer corps to this orgy of blood and murder was typical. The plot having failed, their first concern was to save their honor. In an attempt to save the waning prestige of the officer corps senior generals like von Rund-stedt, Keitel, Jodl and Guderian insisted that the army conspirators be court-martialed before being turned over to a People's Court. The subsequent theatrics produced by Goebbels at the trial of Witzleben, Hoeppner, Hase and five other military defendants, on the 7-8 August are already well known to the world. The gruesome pictures of the hanging bodies of the conspirators were shocking reminders of the terror Hitler was still capable of organizing.

The extermination of all resistance was followed by a last-ditch grab on the part of the Nazis to get the remaining political and military power of the Reich into their hands. On 25 July Hitler ordered a total mobilization of the entire country's manpower and industrial resources with Göring and Goebbels as the chief administrators. Himmler was appointed to succeed Colonel General Fromm as commander of the Home Army, and therefore directly in charge of all military training and reinforcements. The final blow to the army came with the issue of the following order dated 29 July and signed by Colonel General Heinz Guderian, who had only recently replaced Colonel General Kurt Zeitzler, as Chief-of-Staff of the army.[5]

Headquarters of Commander-in-Chief, Army.

29 July 1944.

To: *All General Staff Officers.*

Every General Staff officer must be a National Socialist officer-leader, that is not only by his knowledge of tactics and strategy but also by his model attitude to political questions and by actively co-operating in the political indoctrination of younger commanders in accordance with the tenets of the Führer. . . .

In judging and selecting General Staff officers, superiors should place traits of character and spirit above the mind. A rascal may be ever so cunning but in the hour of need he will nevertheless fail because he is a rascal.

I expect every General Staff officer immediately to declare himself a convert or adherent to my views and to make an announcement to that effect in public. Anybody unable to do so should apply for his removal from the General Staff. . . .

By Order,

GUDERIAN.

And so had come to pass the final humiliation of the General Staff of the German army. It no longer resisted Nazism. It preached it. The destiny which its own weakness and ambition had shaped had at last overtaken it. It existed only to act as a puppet of the master who dangled the strings at Berlin. This final, futile, desperate act of rebellion left the officer corps cringing and frightened because some of their number had attempted what they all realized was necessary. And having been beaten and defeated from within and without so often they were now much too weary to do anything but play out the rest of the game fatalistically and without protest.

Chapter XIX

DEFEAT IN NORMANDY

WHETHER Field Marshal von Kluge was involved in the plot of 20 July or not, he exercised all the skill and determination he possessed to carry out successsfully his rôle as Commander-in-Chief in the West. There is no evidence that he failed so miserably in Normandy because of any treacherous behavior on his part, although he would probably have co-operated with the conspirators had Hitler been killed. Von Kluge's responsibility for the fall of France was comparatively small. The major share of the credit for that event must be divided between the excellent generalship of the Allied commanders and the stupid demands of Hitler's intuition.

The Allied strategy of holding the bulk of German armor on the eastern flank, while the Americans prepared to smash out in the west, had succeeded so well in June that it was decided to maintain this pressure during July. Successive attacks by the British at Caen on 8 July, at Maltot on 10 July, at Evrecy on 12 July and at Bourguebus on 18 July kept six panzer divisions constantly in the line trying to hold the vital hinge of the German position.

"Field Marshal von Kluge came to Normandy eager and optimistic," said Blumentritt, who had been retained as Chief-of-Staff despite the firing of his boss, von Rundstedt.[1] "He had received orders from Berlin that the enemy was to be thrown back into the sea and he was determined to do it. He made a thorough inspection of the front and worked feverishly to determine what was taking place, and then slowly his enthusiasm began to cool. He began to see that it was not as easy as it had looked from Berlin. It was essential that a new plan be adopted by us. The Field Marshal sent a detailed and extremely pessimistic report to Hitler stating that it was impossible to prevent the Allied bridgehead from growing stronger, and that either more troops be sent to him or a withdrawal take place. For four days we waited for a reply from the Führer's headquarters and then a teletype message came through. 'Hold your ground and stay where you are,' was what it said."

The dissatisfaction with Hitler's policy of clinging to ground despite the necessity of a strategical withdrawal had also brought him into sharp disagreement with his former favorite, Field Marshal Erwin Rommel. By the end of June Rommel had also seen the danger of dawdling in Normandy with Allied might in the bridgehead increasing hourly. He had shared von Rundstedt's views at the Führer's

conference at Soissons, and recommended either the transfer of some
of the nineteen idle infantry divisions in the Pas de Calais to Normandy, or a retirement to behind the Orne or the Seine River. Both
suggestions were turned down. Hitler's intuition still convinced him
that a second landing would be attempted. He was largely governed
in this opinion by his belief in the devastating effect of the V-weapons
then being launched against England and the necessity of protecting
these firing sites scattered along the Channel coast north of the
Somme River. It was probably this disagreement at Soissons that
resulted in Rommel being passed over when a successor had to be
found for von Rundstedt.

When von Kluge's report setting out the unhappy German situation in Normandy was sent to Berlin, it was accompanied by a
memorandum of Rommel's confirming von Kluge's opinions. This was
followed by a stormy interview between Hitler and Rommel on
9 July, following the fall of Caen, in which the Field Marshal again
demanded permission to withdraw and in which Hitler again refused
it. It was shortly after this interview that Rommel remarked to some
of his subordinates that the only hope for Germany now lay in the
immediate elimination of Hitler. And a few days later he is reliably
reported to have contacted Colonel von Hofbacker, of von Stülpnagel's staff in Paris, and given his support to any action that would
end the hopeless struggle taking place in France. But three days
before the assassination attempt, on 17 July, a low-flying Allied plane
attacked his car near a small Normandy village, ironically enough
called Sainte Foy de Montgommery. The vehicle capsized throwing
Rommel out and fracturing his skull. After hospital treatment he was
sent to his home in Southern Germany where he appeared to be
rapidly recovering. Suddenly in mid-October it was announced to the
world that Field Marshal Rommel had died. He was given a state
funeral and military honors. The Order of the Day issued on 18
October 1944, by his successor as commander of Army Group 'B,'
Field Marshal Model, read in part:

Order of the Day.

Our former Commander-in-Chief, Field Marshal Erwin Rommel, holder
of the Knight's Cross of the Iron Cross, with Swords, Oakleaves and
Diamonds, a Knight of the Ordre Pour le Mérite, died on 13 October of
wounds sustained on 17 July.

In him we have lost a commander with a lightning power of decision, a
soldier of the greatest bravery and of unexampled dash. . . . Always in the
front line, he inspired his men to new deeds of heroism by his shining
example.

He led our army group for one year. In the midst of the decisive struggle
he was called away from his activities for Führer and Fatherland. He will
go down into history as one of the greatest commanders of our nation.

Let us, in the face of his death, prove ourselves worthy of him, and
faithful to his example, stake all for victory.

Long live the Führer and our Great German Reich, united in National
Socialism.

MODEL,
Field-Marshal.

Such was the tinsel gaudily displayed to hide the shabby truth.
The seventeen-year-old son of Field-Marshal Rommel has also issued
a statement about his father's death.[2] Much less flamboyant and
much less stirring than Model's Order of the Day, it is a sworn and
attested declaration providing a far drearier account of the final fate
that had befallen "the greatest commander of our nation." It reads
as follows:

My father, Field Marshal Erwin Rommel, died on 14 October 1944 at
Herrlingen, an unnatural death, received in the following manner at the
order of the Chancellor of the Reich, Adolf Hitler:

My father was severely wounded in the head (four skull fractures and
many splinters in the face), through the explosion of a shell during an
American low-flying attack on 17 July 1944 in France near Livarot
(Calvados). The first dressings were made in a hospital near Paris, and
when he was able to be moved he was transferred in a truck to Herrlingen-
bei-Ulm, his home at that time. There was no danger at all of his dying.
The fracture to his skull could be looked upon as already healed. My
father was already going out for walks. I myself was then drafted out of
the home anti-aircraft battery, to which I had been appointed as an assistant,
to help my father as a reader. My father still suffered from a paralysis of
the left eye. His treatment was in the hands of Professor Albert and
Professor Stock, both of Tübingen University.

On 7 October 1944 I had to return to my battery and came home on
short leave on 14 October 1944. I arrived on the six a.m. train. My father
was already up and we breakfasted together, then I went for a walk with
him till eleven o'clock, during which time he told me that two army generals
and no doubt General Maisel and General Burgsdorf, both of the Army
Personnel Bureau, would be coming.

He said that he did not have much confidence in the meeting and he
did not know whether the stated object of discussing his further employment was not being used as a manœuvre to get rid of him.

At twelve o'clock my father received the two generals. My father asked
me to leave the room. After three-quarters of an hour I met my father
going out of my mother's room. He told me that he had taken leave of my
mother and that he had been given the choice by Adolf Hitler either of

poisoning himself or of being sent for public trial. Moreover, Adolf Hitler had stated that in the event of suicide nothing would happen to his family, but on the contrary, they would be provided for. We observed in the meantime that the house was surrounded by at least four or five armored cars. The cars were apparently occupied by armed civilians, so that the eight men on duty-watch in the house, who had only two machine-guns, would be powerless. After my father had said good-bye to me and the orderly officer, he left the house in uniform, wearing a leather cloak and with marshal's baton and cap. We accompanied him to the car where the generals saluted him with the 'Heil Hitler' greeting. We saw an S.S. man at the wheel of the car. My father climbed in first and took a seat in the back, then the two generals followed.

The car went off in the direction of Blaubeuren. Fifteen minutes later we received a call from the Reserve Hospital Wagner-Schule in Ulm, to the effect that my father had been brought in by the two generals, apparently having had a brain stroke.

In my last conversation with my father he told me the following facts: He had been suspected of complicity in the 20 July 1944 affair. His former Chief of the General Staff — Lieutenant General Speidel — who had been arrested a few weeks previously, had said my father had had a leading interest in the 20 July affair and had only been prevented from a direct share in it by his injury. General von Stülpnagel had made the same statement after his dismissal through Field Marshal von Kluge, and left in the direction of Germany. On the way he tried to shoot himself but only lost his eyesight. The S.S. found him, and gave him blood transfusions in order to restore him to consciousness to extract conclusive statements. Afterwards he was hanged. Moreover, my father had been put on the list of Oberbürgermeister Goerdeler as Minister President.

The Führer did not want my father's standing before the German people to be degraded, and gave him the chance of voluntary death by a poisoned pill, which was given to him on the way by one of the generals. This killed him within three seconds. In the case of a refusal he would have been immediately arrested and put before the High Court of Justice in Berlin. My father chose a voluntary death.

So died Rommel. His career typified the course set and followed by those who had risen to power on the tidal wave of National Socialism; a course that rocketed dizzily upwards from obscurity through ambition to power and spiraled downwards from disillusionment through defeat to disaster. His end provided a fitting postscript to the hopes of 20 July and a prophetic warning to those who had traveled a similar path but had not yet reached the bend in the road.

With the Führer's refusal to withdraw from Normandy, the only alternative left to von Kluge was to hold on bitterly until the Allies or Hitler forced him to do something else. The Allies acted first. By the third week in July the third phase of operation 'Overlord' — the break-out — was to begin. The plan evolved by Generals Eisenhower, Montgomery and Bradley was to drive forward with a left jab on 17 July in the Evrecy area, followed by a hard left blow by the British south and southeast of Caen. This double punch on the left was to keep the German armor off-balance and uncertain. Then on 19 July a right-hand blow was to lash out from the Americans, in a narrow sector west of St. Lô, which would swing westwards to Coutances and then south to Avranches. By this latter manœuvre it was hoped to tear open the German positions at the base of the Cherbourg Peninsula and allow General Bradley's armor to break into Brittany and capture the much-needed ports of Western France. Both of these attacks were to be preceded by an overwhelming concentration of Allied air power laying down the heaviest bombing carpets ever employed in support of ground troops.

Trying to meet this series of successive attacks the tired German armor was shifted from sector to sector like restless London firemen during an incendiary air raid. Each time a new conflagration flared up along the line a panzer division had to be shifted or split or brought up from a rest area it had only just reached. Thus the first feint of 17 July in the Evrecy area pulled into battle against it 9 S.S. Panzer Division which had been trying to recuperate south of Caen, while about forty tanks from 1 S.S. Panzer Division, holding east of the Orne, were detached and rushed west over the river.

Then the main British assault broke east of Caen on 18 July. The two German divisions positioned to meet it, 16 Luftwaffe Field and 21 Panzer, had already been thoroughly weakened in the fighting for Caen on 8 July and could not stand up to the Allied blow. Again 1 S.S. Panzer Division had to gallop to the rescue by detaching its remaining eighty odd tanks and sending them off to help hold the advancing British armor. This time the fire brigade really helped put out the fire. Brigadeführer (Major General) Theodor Wisch, commander of 1 S.S. Panzer Division 'Adolf Hitler,' another youthful fanatical S.S. general who attained his rank because of his early associations with Hitler's personal bodyguard, has described his formation's part in stopping this British assault.[3]

"When the British attacked south of Caen my division was immediately sent into battle once more. My Panther tanks became heavily involved around Frenouville, while my lighter tanks had not yet advanced past Roquancourt. I was on a reconnaissance trip on the evening of 18 July when one of those things happened, which occurs to a soldier only once in a lifetime. Approximately 100 British tanks, having completed their job for the day, had chosen an exposed part of the countryside in which to camp for the night. This mass of armor was lying only a stone's throw from where my own tanks were assembled. I immediately ordered my Panthers to attack from the east and my light tanks to attack from the west. The range was perfect. From my point of view, the manœuvre was highly successful. With my own eyes I saw forty tanks go up in flames during the evening engagement. At dawn of the next morning we went into action again and we must have destroyed another forty tanks. My own losses were twelve Panthers and one light tank." [4]

This blunting of the British armored attack might not have created more than a momentary delay in the advance, since Allied tank replacements were plentiful and speedily available had not the weather conspired against it. A persistent and heavy downpour of rain turned the roads and fields into quagmires effectively preventing any further tank operations. The rain also delayed the start of the American offensive at St. Lô, scheduled for 19 July, since it washed out the planned program of air support by grounding Allied planes. It was not until six days later, on 25 July, that the weather turned fair enough again to enable General Bradley's impatient troops to leave the start-line.

This delay may actually have been a blessing in disguise, for it resulted in 2 Panzer Division, with about 100 tanks at its disposal, being moved from the sector adjoining the coming American attacks to a reserve rôle south of Caen. For on 20 July this formation defending the line at Caumont, less than fifteen miles from St. Lô, was relieved by 326 Infantry Division, one of the first infantry divisions permitted to leave the Pas de Calais. It was the vanguard of the huge stream of infantry that was to follow in the next few weeks, when Hitler had finally decided a second cross-Channel invasion would not take place. The shifting of this strong armored division from in front of the American attack was due to another of the many bad appreciations made by German commanders. The commander of 2 Panzer Division, General Heinrich von Lüttwitz, whose red face, fat body, peaked nose and horn-rimmed glasses belie the forceful energetic personality beneath, had the following to say of his division's movements at this time: [5]

"When 2 Panzer Division was finally relieved in the Caumont sector on 20 July, after having been steadily in the line since 12 June, it did not mean that we were to be given a rest. The British having been stopped in the Caen area on 19 July, it was expected that they would soon start again. To meet this attack my division was moved to Brettville on 24 July, while 116 Panzer Division, newly arrived from the Pas de Calais, was sent to Rouvres. There we waited in reserve, some five miles behind our front line south of Caen, for another attack to begin. The two divisions, 2 Panzer and 116 Panzer, possessed between them about 200 tanks and were comparatively strong. But instead of the offensive coming from the British, it suddenly broke loose on 25 July on the American sector near St. Lô where I had just come from. We had been fooled as to your intentions. By placing this large armored reserve south of Caen we completely wasted it and weakened our front west of the Orne River. Highly chagrined, the High Command quickly moved us back to the St. Lô area on 26 July, but by that time it was too late to prevent the break-through of the Americans."

This bad guessing on the part of the German commanders had provided just the opening that General Bradley needed. It meant that on the day the push at St. Lô began no fewer than seven of the ten German armored formations in Normandy were clustered in a semi-circle south of Caen, waiting for a British attack which did not come.[6] It enabled the Americans to cross the Périers-St. Lô road and swing east as planned with none too severe opposition from the German infantry. By the time 2 Panzer and 116 Panzer Divisions were able to enter the fray, after their wild-goose chase to Caen, it was 28 July, and Coutances had already been taken, sealing off three infantry and two armored divisions north of the town. Some of these managed to escape, but by 31 July Avranches had been captured, over 8000 prisoners had been taken and the moment for General Patton's Third Army dash into Brittany had arrived.

The resulting chaos and concern created by these events has been vividly preserved in the records of the telephone conversations held by Field Marshal von Kluge on 31 July 1944. No one had yet replaced the wounded Rommel as commander of Army Group 'B.' His Chief-of-Staff, Lieutenant General Speidel, who had not yet been arrested for his part in the 20 July affair, was carrying out the direct orders of von Kluge. Seventh Army, now sharing the Normandy front with Panzer Group West, was rapidly disintegrating before the mounting American pressure.

At one o'clock on the morning of 31 July Speidel rang von Kluge to report "the left flank has collapsed." Forty-five minutes later General Farmbacher, commanding a corps in Brittany, stated that he was having difficulty in obtaining the co-operation of the naval and air force units stationed in the ports and airfields of Brittany. This independence of command of the three services had always been a persistent headache to senior commanders. Since the Luftwaffe was responsible only to Göring, and the navy obeyed only Dönitz, no army officer could force the other service to carry out his orders, no matter how critical the situation. This individuality was jealously guarded by all three services, as well as the S.S., who had their direct channels to Himmler, so that generals like von Rundstedt and von Kluge had constantly to obtain Hitler's personal consent to any order they issued to any personnel other than the army.[7] A typical example of the problems created by this rigid, parallel system of independent commands was Farmbacher's inability to have the large forces of the navy and air force help him in his efforts against the advancing Americans.

At nine o'clock in the morning Speidel reported a further deterioration in the situation. He claimed that while the Seventh Army position was 'absolutely unclear,' part of the responsibility for the crisis was due to Seventh Army's decision to break through towards Avranches instead of holding on to their positions to the north of the town. Speidel apparently believed that by holding their line, despite the fact that they had been encircled by the fall of Avranches, Seventh Army would be in a more favorable position to restore the situation. Von Kluge shared this appreciation and countermanded Seventh Army's orders to break-out. This faith in an ability to counteract an Allied tactical *fait accompli* by staying put characterized much of German operational thinking in Normandy, not only on Hitler's part, but on the part of some of his subordinates as well. It was based on a thorough misconception of Allied strength and ability to ensure the success of a bold manœuvre, such as the dash to Avranches, once it had been undertaken.

On 31 July von Kluge, having spoken to all his field commanders, telephoned through to Supreme Headquarters where he spoke to General Walter Warlimont, who took the call as Hitler's representative. The report of that conversation graphically presents the effects of the American break-through at St. Lô on the German Seventh Army.

10.45 hours.

Conversation of Field Marshal von Kluge with General Warlimont.

The Commander-in-Chief West . . . reports that the enemy is in Avranches and may be also in Villedieu. These key positions for future operations must be held at all costs. . . . All available forces from St. Malo were brought up. The idle forces of the navy and air force which are absolutely needed for the decisive fight, the price of which is the future or the end of the situation in the bridgehead, are . . . not obtainable. General Warlimont agrees to refer this question to the Führer. Commander-in-Chief West describes the seriousness of the situation with impressive eloquence. Whether the enemy can be stopped at this point is still questionable. The enemy air superiority is terrific, and smothers almost every one of our movements. Every movement of the enemy, however, is prepared and protected by its air force. Losses in men and equipment are extraordinary. The morale of the troops has suffered very heavily under constant murderous enemy fire, especially, since all infantry units consist only of haphazard groups which do not form a strongly co-ordinated force any longer. In the rear areas of the front, terrorists, feeling the end approaching, grow steadily bolder. This fact and the loss of numerous signal installations makes an orderly command extremely difficult. . . . Part of the responsibility for the present situation rests with the order of Seventh Army for the northern front to break through towards the south and the southeast. Commander-in-Chief West has, as soon as he was informed thereof, changed this order to reconstitute the front with the forces at hand. Fresh troops must be brought up from the Fifteenth Army or from somewhere else. Commander-in-Chief West recalls herewith the World War I example, in which Parisian buses were used to bring up troops to the Allied front. Now, as then, all available means must be exhausted. It is, however, still impossible to determine whether it would be possible to stop the enemy.

And to add emphasis to this dismal report von Kluge might also have pointed out that of about 700,000 Germans committed to battle almost 80,000 of them had become prisoners-of-war since the Allied landings and personnel casualties in dead and wounded were about that much again. Of a total of almost 1400 tanks thrown in against the bridgehead he had already lost some 750. It may be relevant to examine this latter figure because of recent carping criticism about the conduct of the battle of Caen. Against the British on the left side of the Allied front 1 S.S., 9 S.S., 10 S.S., 12 S.S. and 21 Panzer Division were in constant action. Two armored formations, 2 S.S. and 17 S.S. were always used against the Americans. Two others — 2 Panzer and Panzer Lehr — had shifted their attentions between the British and American sectors. The newcomer, 116 Panzer Division, had hardly been committed at all by the end of July. By correlating the statements of German commanders of these divisions and captured documents, it is safe to say that at least 550 of the 750 tanks destroyed in Normandy by this date, met their fate on the Caen front. What better justification for the strategy adopted by Allied planners to attract to the anvil of Caen the bulk of German armor and there methodically hammer it to bits!

PLATE I

Field-Marshal Werner von Blomberg (left) with Colonel-General Hans von Seeckt

At a ceremony in Berlin in March, 1935 are (front row): Field-Marshal von Mackensen, Hitler and Field-Marshal von Blomberg; (rear row): Colonel-General von Fritsch, Göring, and Admiral Raeder

Inspecting a guard during maneuvers in August, 1938 are, from left to right, Colonel-General Blaskowitz, Field-Marshal von Rundstedt, Field-Marshal von Brauchitsch, and Hitler

PLATE II

Colonel-General Franz Halder, Chief-of-Staff of the German Army, September 1938 to September 1942

Field-Marshal Fedor von Bock, Commander Army Group "B" in France (1940) and Army Group South in Russia (1941-1942)

Colonel-General Werner von Fritsch, Commander-in-Chief of the German Army, February, 1934 to February, 1938

Hitler and his Field-Marshals, August, 1940 (left to right): Field-Marshal Keitel, Field-Marshal von Rundstedt, Field-Marshal von Bock, Reichsmarshal Göring, Adolf Hitler, Field-Marshal von Brauchitsch, Field-Marshal von Leeb, Field-Marshal List, Field-Marshal von Kluge, Field-Marshal von Witzleben, and Field Marshal von Reichenau

PLATE III

A STUDY IN VICTORY AND DEFEAT

Top row — Victorious Generals (left to right): Field-Marshal von Rundstedt, Commander Army Group "A" in France (1940), Army Group South in Russia (1941), Commander-in-Chief West (1942-45); Field Marshal von Leeb, Commander Army Group "C" in France (1940), Army Group North in Russia (1941); Field-Marshal List, Commander Army Group "A" in the Caucasus (1942)

Bottom row — Defeated Generals — Field-Marshals von Rundstedt, von Leeb and List as prisoners-of-war

PLATE IV

Field-Marshal Erwin Rommel, Commander "Afrika Korps" (1941-1943), Army Group "B" in France (1944)

Colonel-General Kurt Student, Commander Army Group "H" (1944-45), Commander-in-Chief German Airborne Troops (1943-45)

Adolf Hitler congratulating (from left to right) Admiral Raeder, Field-Marshal von Brauchitsch, Field-Marshal Keitel and S. S. Reichsführer Himmler at Berlin in April, 1941

PLATE V

S.S. Brigadeführer (Major-General) Kurt Meyer, Commander 12 S.S. Panzer Division, "Hitler Jugend"

General Günther Blumentritt, Chief-of-Staff to the Commander-in-Chief West (1942-44), Commander Twenty-fifth Army and First Parachute Army (1945)

Field-Marshal Rommel in May, 1944 inspecting 21 Panzer Division, led by Lieutenant-General Edgar Feuchtinger (extreme right)

PLATE VI

S.S. Oberstgruppenführer (Colonel-General) Joseph "Sepp" Dietrich, Commander Fifth Panzer Army and Sixth S.S. Panzer Army

Colonel-General Heinz Guderian, Commander-in-Chief East (1944), Chief-of-Staff of the German Army, July, 1944 to May, 1945

Field-Marshal Walter Model, Commander Army Group North and Army Group Centre in Russia (1944), Army Group "B" in France (1944-45)

Colonel-General Ludwig Beck, Chief-of-Staff of the German Army (1936-1938), and military leader of the 20 July assassination plot against Hitler

PLATE VII

Field-Marshal Günther von Kluge, Army Group Centre in Russia (1943), Commander-in-Chief West (July-August, 1944)

Field-Marshal Albert Kesselring, Commander-in-Chief South (1942-43), Commander-in-Chief South-west (1944-45), Commander-in-Chief West (March-May, 1945)

Colonel-General Alfred Jodl signing the surrender terms on behalf of the German Supreme Command at Rheims on 7th May, 1945. At the extreme right is Admiral Hans von Friedeburg

PLATE VIII

Wehrmacht, Rear View
Nuremberg, September, 1936

Wehrmacht, Front View
The Elbe, May, 1945

Chapter XX
MORTAIN

THE gloomy report sent by von Kluge to Hitler on 30 July had one important result — the Führer decided to send along his own personal liaison officer to check up on what von Kluge had told him. He chose General Walter Warlimont for the job, and on 31 July Warlimont left Berchtesgaden for Normandy. But before leaving, Hitler warned his representative not to encourage von Kluge in the belief that a withdrawal might be permitted. "If von Kluge questioned me about defense lines," Warlimont said,[1] "I was to reply that Supreme Headquarters would take care of building up any necessary lines in the rear to which the army might have to fall back. Hitler ended his instructions with the acid comment, 'Whenever a line of defense is built behind the front line, my generals think of nothing but going back to that line.' "

However, Hitler did make one concession to his Commander-in-Chief in the West. He gave him permission to start thinning out his infantry divisions in the Pas de Calais and bring them into Normandy. At last, almost seven weeks after the invasion, Hitler's intuition assured him that there was little danger of a second Allied invasion across the Straits of Dover. It had taken the Führer four weeks longer to reach this obvious deduction than was needed by every other responsible German commander on the spot. By the end of July about two infantry divisions had already left their comfortable bunkers in the Pas de Calais and taken up positions in Normandy. More were on the way. But Hitler had no intention of resting these panzer divisions which for the first time since D-Day he was able to pull out of the line. For the Führer now wanted an armored counter-attack.

To Hitler at Berlin the dash of General Patton's armor into Brittany seemed to provide a golden opportunity. If he assembled all the available German armor at Mortain it would be possible to smash the thinly held flank protecting the American tanks speeding to the east and to the south. Once the sea was reached at Avranches the American forces that had broken out of the bridgehead would be cut off. The plan was obvious and simple. Early in August he ordered von Kluge to execute it.

"The plan came to us at the headquarters of the Commander-in-Chief West in the most minute detail," said General Blumentritt.[2] "It set out the specific divisions that were to be used and they were to be pulled out of the line as quickly as possible for this purpose. The sector in which the attack was to take place was specifically identified, and the very roads and villages through which the assaulting forces were to advance were all included. All this planning had been done in Berlin from large-scale maps and the advice of the generals in France was not asked for, nor was it encouraged."

Von Kluge on receiving these instructions realized it would be impossible to carry them out. For in addition to launching a counter-offensive Hitler had also ordered that the German line from Avranches to St. Lô be restored. The object of this attempt to restore the left wing of the German position was to prevent any additional reinforcements or supplies going to the Americans in Brittany and already approaching Le Mans. There were not enough troops available to accomplish this twofold object and von Kluge gave this as his opinion to General Warlimont who was conducting his inspection tour on behalf of the Führer. Nevertheless since withdrawal was forbidden it remained the only course of action left, and the Commander-in-Chief West began to prepare his offensive. It meant a considerable reorganization of the chain of command in Normandy, but German staffs were adept at hasty regrouping of forces. The armored offensive would be conducted by six panzer divisions grouped together in a formation called Panzer Group 'Eberbach' after its commander General Hans Eberbach. On its right flank at Vire carrying out a conforming and protecting attack was to be Seventh Army under Colonel-General Paul Hausser, the first S.S. man ever to be given command of a formation of army size. Holding the Caen front was to be the newly-constituted Fifth Panzer Army under Colonel General 'Sepp' Dietrich, another S.S. favorite of Hitler's. In other words, the two armies in Normandy were now led by tired Nazis who earned their promotions in the S.S. Hitler had stopped trusting the German General Staff.

The first and most formidable problem facing von Kluge was how to get these armored divisions without dangerously weakening his front. He approached 'Sepp' Dietrich south of Caen, and told him that in order to carry out the counter-attack, and still protect the right flank of the operation against the British, he would need at least three panzer divisions from the Caen-Falaise sector. Dietrich claimed that he was horrified at the suggestion.

"I protested with von Kluge for over an hour," said Dietrich, with much feeling,[3] "about the impracticability of such an operation. I used every argument in the book. There was not sufficient petrol for such an attack; if three armored divisions were sent west it would be impossible to hold Falaise; it was impossible to concentrate so

many tanks without inviting disaster from the air; there wasn't sufficient space to deploy so large an armored force; the Americans were
far too strong in the south and such an attack was only wedging one's
way tighter into a trap rather than safely getting out. To each of
my arguments von Kluge had only one reply, 'It is Hitler's orders,'
and there was nothing more that could be done. I gave him what
he wanted."

Once the armor had been collected there remained the choosing
of the appropriate day for the beginning of the offensive. Although
Hitler had originally ordered von Kluge to hurry the attack, he had
now changed his mind. Watching the Americans pouring south
through the Avranches gap, he decided to catch as many of them
as he could by holding off his counter-attack. He was so confident that
his plan would succeed that he ordered von Kluge to carry out his
preparations for the offensive to the last detail before jumping off.
Hitler envisaged that the attack would start on 8 August. But von
Kluge apprehensively observing the flood of American infantry and
armor swirling into Brittany and southern Normandy told General
Warlimont that he could delay no longer without risking the danger
of encirclement. Thus contrary to the Führer's wishes von Kluge
ordered the offensive to begin twenty-four hours before the intuition
of Hitler had ordained it. Even then it was too late.

Assembling six panzer divisions, with a total of about 400 tanks,
near the small town of Mortain, and using two others to help Seventh
Army carry out its covering operation on the right flank of the main
thrust, the first serious German armored offensive in Normandy was
finally launched early on the morning of 7 August.[4] General Paul
Hausser, commander of Seventh Army, dramatically expressed the
hope of the German Supreme Command in the following order
announcing the offensive:

The Führer has ordered the execution of a break-through to the coast
in order to create the basis for the decisive operation against the Allied
invasion front. For this purpose further forces are being brought up to the
army.

On the successful execution of the operation the Führer has ordered
depends the decision of the war in the West and with it perhaps the
decision of the war itself. Commander of all ranks must be absolutely clear
as to the enormous significance of this fact. I expect all corps and divisional
commanders to take good care that all officers are aware of the unique
significance of the whole situation.

Only one thing counts, unceasing effort and determined will to victory.

For Führer, Volk and Reich,

HAUSSER.

But inspiring words were not enough. General Bradley, appreciating just such a German move had deployed his troops to meet it. The only German division that attained even limited success in its attempts to reach the sea was 2 Panzer Division. Its commander, General von Lüttwitz, gave this account of his formation's part in the battle of Mortain.[5]

"We made a swift advance of about ten miles and suffered only three tank losses. 116 Panzer Division, our left-hand neighbor, made only limited progress. The morning of 7 August had dawned bright and clear. It was a perfect flying day. Suddenly the Allied fighter-bombers swooped out of the sky. They came down in hundreds firing their rockets at the concentrated tanks and vehicles. We could do nothing against them, and we could make no further progress. The next day the planes came down again. We were forced to give up the ground we had gained, and by 9 August the division was back where it started from north of Mortain, having lost thirty tanks and 800 men."

The helpful telephone journal of Seventh Army indicates that the experience of Lüttwitz was being shared by the other formations in the offensive. At ten minutes to ten on the night of 7 August von Kluge 'phoned through to Hausser. "How is the situation in your sector tonight?" asked the Field Marshal. To which the Seventh Army commander replied, "No essential changes. Terrific fighter-bomber attacks and considerable tank losses. . . ." And after discussing the future employment of one of the panzer divisions, von Kluge continued. ". . . every commanding officer is aware of the importance of this operation. Each man must give his very best. If we have not advanced considerably by this evening or tomorrow morning, the operation will have been a failure."

Chapter XXI

THE HELL OF FALAISE

MEANWHILE in the Caen sector 'Sepp' Dietrich's warning that it was dangerous to weaken the line protecting Falaise was becoming all too evident. With the withdrawal of most of the German armor to carry out the offensive towards Avranches and to contain the newly-won British bridgehead across the Orne near Thury-Harcourt, there was nothing left to guard this vital hinge of the German position but an inexperienced infantry division fresh from Norway[1] backed by the weakened remnants of the once mighty 12 S.S. Panzer Division

'Hitler Jugend.' This latter formation, after having been in the line since D-Day, had about forty tanks left of an original 214. Using some 1500 heavy bombers to announce their first important offensive operation in Normandy, the First Canadian Army with two infantry and two armored divisions broke through the German defenses south of Caen, which were manned by the fresh troops of 89 Infantry Division. Major General Kurt Meyer, the fanatical young leader of 12 S.S. Panzer Division, hurriedly drove forward to the front-line positions in the early morning of 8 August to see what effect this Canadian attack was having. What he saw was not reassuring. Discounting his tendency to over-dramatize his own activities and to over-emphasize the importance of his own division, Kurt Meyer has given an interesting description of his reactions on the Caen-Falaise road as he watched the results of this latest offensive.

"I got out of my car," said Meyer,[2] "and my knees were trembling, the sweat was pouring down my face, and my clothes were soaked with perspiration. It was not that I was particularly anxious about myself, because my experiences of the past five years had accustomed me to the fear of death. I was afraid because I realized that if I failed now and if I did not deploy my division correctly, the Allies would be through to Falaise, and the German armies in the West would be completely trapped. I knew how weak my division was and the task which confronted me gave me at that time some of the worst moments I have ever had in my life. Before me, making their way down the Caen-Falaise road in a disorderly rabble, were the panic-stricken troops of 89 Infantry Division. I realized that something had to be done to send these men back into the line and fight. I lit a cigar, stood in the middle of the road and in a loud voice asked them if they were going to leave me alone to cope with the enemy. Hearing a divisional commander address them in this way they stopped, hesitated and then returned to their positions."

By the evening of 8 August Field Marshal von Kluge realized that the Canadian attack on Caen constituted a serious threat to his rear. At the same time it was obvious that the Mortain offensive had failed dismally, and that with the American capture of Le Mans desperate measures had to be taken. Speaking to Hausser of Seventh Army that evening von Kluge said:[3] "We have to risk everything. A break-through has occurred near Caen the like of which we have never seen. . . . Preparations to reorganize the attack will have to be made first thing tomorrow. Therefore, we shall not continue the attack tomorrow but make preparations to attack on the following day (10 August)."

But the threat to Caen was not as imminent as it had first appeared. The fanatical fighting of the S.S. who, according to their commander, Kurt Meyer, did not hesitate to leap on Allied tanks with explosives tied about their bodies, and the unexpected appearance of a large quantity of 88-millimetre guns, brought the dashing charge of the new Polish and Canadian armored divisions to an abrupt halt on the edge of the valley of the Liaison River. The presence of these devastating weapons in the Caen sector was explained by tall, young-looking Major General Herman Plocher, of the parachutists, who was Chief-of-Staff of the German air forces in the West.

"Immediately after the landings in Normandy," he said,[4] "we sent about ninety-six heavy anti-aircraft guns to the battle area from east of the Seine River. At the beginning of August we sent another forty of these 88-millimetre guns to Colonel General 'Sepp' Dietrich of Fifth Panzer Army. However, since these guns belonged to the Luftwaffe they were to be controlled by an air force officer, Lieutenant General Pickert, rather than an army officer. We had insisted on these guns being controlled by Luftwaffe officers because the army did not know how to handle such equipment. There was always a great deal of argument about who was to deploy the 88's, but Field Marshal von Rundstedt finally allowed us to choose our own localities. This was necessary in order to prevent the army from squandering both men and equipment. We used to say that the German infantryman would always fight until the last anti-aircraft man."

The other side of the story was feelingly expressed by 'Sepp' Dietrich who said,[5] "I constantly ordered these guns to stay forward and act in an anti-tank rôle against Allied armor. My orders were just as often countermanded by Pickert, who moved them back into the rear areas to protect administrative sites. I asked time and time again that these guns be put under my command, but I was always told by the High Command that it was impossible."

Despite this unhappy chain of command, these long-range powerful 88's did effective work on 8 and 9 August. Well camouflaged and offered excellent targets by the advancing Allied tanks they opened up with devastating results. In less than forty-eight hours the hulks of over 150 Sherman tanks dotted the rolling wheatfields north of the Liaison River. It succeeded in breaking the momentum of the Canadian attack after an advance of about fifteen miles. A pause until tank reinforcements arrived was now necessary. This pause proved fatal to the Germans west of the Orne, for it allayed the fears of von Kluge that he might be encircled. Instead of thinking of retiring he decided to press on with another attack towards Avranches. At half-past three on the afternoon of 9 August, the telephone journal of Seventh Army records von Kluge's words to the Army's Chief-of-Staff:

"I have just had a decisive conference with the Supreme Command. The situation south of Caen having been re-established and not having had the much feared effects, I propose to retain the idea of an attack. Now, however, the attack must be prepared and executed to plan and must not be rushed. The panzer units led by General Eberbach are under your command. . . . Whatever we can get hold of will be thrown in. I consider it improbable that the operation can be initiated before the day after tomorrow. . . ."

And on the morning of 10 August von Kluge is again reported as saying to the Chief-of-Staff of Seventh Army:

"According to instructions from Supreme Headquarters, preparations for an attack do not have to be rushed. It is impossible to set a date now as further reinforcements are to be brought up. . . . I will give you further details when I visit you tomorrow noon. . . ."

Thus we have the incredible situation of a large military force of almost twenty divisions blissfully planning an attack while far behind it an enemy is busily forming a noose with which to strangle it. When it became clear to General Eisenhower that von Kluge did not intend to retire despite the fact that American armor had already, on 9 August, captured Le Mans, some fifty miles east of the German position, the next step was obvious. Instead of continuing on towards the Seine, General Bradley's troops were ordered to move north towards Argentan, where by linking up with the Canadians pushing south from Falaise they would completely encircle the dallying Germans. The danger of just such an Allied move had not been overlooked by most of the senior German commanders. When von Kluge told 'Sepp' Dietrich of Fifth Panzer Army on 10 August, that the attack towards Avranches was to be continued, Dietrich vehemently protested against the decision.

"I warned the Field Marshal," said Dietrich,[6] "that the Canadians had only been stopped on the Liaison River for a short period. Once they resumed the attack Falaise could not be held more than one or two days. Both Hausser of Seventh Army and Eberbach of the Panzer Group had also urged von Kluge to call the attack off and withdraw. But the Field Marshal had received a new order from Berlin insisting that he go ahead. There was only one person to blame for this stupid, impossible operation. That madman Adolf Hitler. It was a Führer's order. What else could we do?"

But instead of the Germans attacking, the Allies did. The Seventh Army telephone journal of 11 and 12 August was black with news of retreats and enemy infiltrations. Items such as "Enemy attacked along entire front ... our forces are too weak ... enemy has penetrated in force ... enemy has broken through," announced a collapse of the German line all along the front. General Warlimont, who had seen the failure of the first attacks, had returned to Hitler's headquarters, now in East Prussia, to report the dismal tidings.

"Hitler listened to me for almost an hour," Warlimont said.[7] "After I had tried to point out the striving by everyone to make it succeed, he only said, 'Von Kluge did that deliberately. He did it to show me that my orders were incapable of being performed!'"

On 13 August permission was finally given for the German forces in Normandy to retire behind the Seine River. It was much too late. The Canadians resumed their attack towards Falaise on 14 August and the Americans had already reached the outskirts of Argentan. Some twenty-five miles separated the jaws of the closing trap. And the Germans had about thirty-five miles to withdraw before they were out. The race was on.

But von Kluge had not been forgiven for his defeat. In the midst of his desperate efforts to extricate his troops from the Falaise pocket, Field Marshal Model arrived from Russia on 17 August, to relieve von Kluge of his command. Model thus became the third Commander-in-Chief West in just over three months after the first landings in Normandy. The nervous strain of fighting both Eisenhower and Hitler, and the humiliation of this new blow were too much for von Kluge. The suspicion that he was being sent back to Berlin to be questioned about the plot of 20 July may also have influenced him in his decision to do away with himself. When the plane carrying him back to Germany arrived at Metz, Field Marshal von Kluge was dead. On 18 August he had written a letter explaining the reasons for his suicide. In that document is reflected the fatalism, the helplessness, the pettiness, the confusion, the fear and the discipline that dominated the mind of a typical product of the German officer corps. The letter reads:[8]

My Führer,

Your decision handed to me yesterday by Field Marshal Model relieves me of the command of the High Command West and Army Group 'B.' The obvious reason for this is the failure of the panzer thrust to Avranches which made it impossible to close the gap up to the sea. My 'guilt' as the responsible commander is thereby confirmed.

Allow me, my Führer, with all respect, to state my point of view. When you receive these lines, which I am sending you by Oberstgruppen-führer (Colonel General) 'Sepp' Dietrich whom I have come to know and appreciate as a brave, incorruptible man in these difficult weeks, I shall be no more. I cannot bear the reproach that I have sealed the fate of the West through faulty strategy, and I have no means of defending myself. I draw a conclusion from that, and am dispatching myself where thousands of my comrades already are. I have never feared death. Life has no more meaning for me and I also figure on the list of war criminals who are to be delivered up.

As regards the question of guilt may I say the following:

(1) The panzer formations were in themselves far too weak in striking power owing to the previous battles, to guarantee success. Even if I had succeeded through cleverer strategy in increasing their striking power, they would never have got to the sea, despite certain initial successes gained by them. The only division which could be described as more or less normal in its striking power was 2 Panzer Division. Its successes cannot, however, be taken as a yardstick in the judgment of the other panzer divisions.

(2) Even if one assumes that Avranches could have been reached, then the gap could certainly have been closed, but the danger to the Army Group would certainly not have been averted — at the most, delayed for a time. A further penetration of our panzer divisions to the north as ordered, a joining up of our other forces in the attack in order to influence the total position, was completely out of the question. Everyone who knew the actual state of our own troops, particularly of the infantry divisions would, without hesitation, agree that I am right. Your order assumed, therefore, a position which did not exist. When I read this decisive order I immediately had the impression that here something was being demanded which would go down in history as a magnificent operation of the utmost daring, but which unfortunately was in practice impossible to carry out, and which would lay the blame conclusively on the responsible army commander.

I did my utmost to carry out your command. I also admit that it would have been better to have waited another day to begin the attack. But that would have altered nothing fundamentally. That is my unshakeable conviction, which I am taking to the grave with me, for the position had developed much too far for anything to have been able to change it. There were already too strong forces on the southern flank of the Army Group which, even if the Avranches gap had been closed, could have been quite easily supplied by air, and have received further support from the forces which had been poured into Brittany. Our own actual line of defense had already been so weakened that it was no longer to be expected that it could hold out for any length of time, especially as now the stream of new Anglo-American formations was thrown directly against it and no longer flowed through the Avranches gap, to the south. When I agreed with the proposal of the panzer commander and of the Seventh Army that they should strike quickly despite my better judgment, it was because we all knew exactly the holding power of the northern front of this army and no longer trusted it very much, even without taking into account the enemy's enveloping movement in the south. It was therefore a question of acting quickly, as the position in the air also demanded quick action. With regard to the position in the air, which almost completely ruled out a daylight battle, the prospects of the hoped-for success were likewise quite small. And the barometer remained high until today.

By reason of these facts I stick to my assertion that there were no chances of success; on the contrary, the attacks ordered were bound to make the all-round position of the Army Group decisively worse. And that is what happened.

The army in the West was in the end almost isolated from a personnel and material point of view. The desperate position in the East forced that. The rapid drop in numbers of tanks, however, and of anti-tank weapons, and the insufficient supply of mortars to the so-called static divisions, produced the situation (made extremely more desperate by the losses in the so-called cauldron), which must be recognized today.

Owing to my strained relations with the new Chief of the General Staff (Colonel General Guderian), who considers me his enemy, I could not approach him, and so there was no possibility of my receiving panzer support for the West which was necessary. All that was decisive for the development of the overall position.

My Führer, I think I may claim for myself that I did everything within my power to be equal to the situation. In my covering letter to Field Marshal Rommel's memorandum which I sent you, I already pointed out the possible outcome of the situation. Both Rommel and I and probably all the other commanders here in the West, with experience of battle against the Anglo-Americans, with their preponderance of material, foresaw the present development. We were not listened to. Our appreciations were NOT dictated by pessimism, but from the sober knowledge of the facts. I do not know whether Field Marshal Model, who has been proved in every sphere, will still master the situation. From my heart I hope so. Should it not be so, however, and your new, greatly desired weapons, especially of the air force, not succeed, then, my Führer, make up your mind to end the war. The German people have borne such untold suffering that it is time to put an end to this frightfulness.

There must be ways to attain this end and above all prevent the Reich from falling under the Bolshevist heel. The actions of some of the officers taken prisoner in the East have always been an enigma to me. My Führer, I have always admired your greatness, your conduct in the gigantic struggle and your iron will to maintain yourself and National Socialism. If fate is stronger than your will and your genius so is Providence. You have fought an honorable and great fight. History will prove that for you. Show yourself now also great enough to put an end to a hopeless struggle when necessary.

I depart from you, my Führer, as one who stood nearer to you than you perhaps realized in the consciousness that I did my duty to the utmost.

Heil, my Führer,

(Signed) VON KLUGE.

Field Marshal.

18 August 1944.

The most curious aspect of this lengthy letter is the fact that it was written by a man who was about to die. As death would have put him well beyond the vengeance of even Adolf Hitler, there seems to have been little need for such elaborate and detailed explanations — particularly since von Kluge was not defending any cause or any group, but merely himself. Why this squabbling about whether the closing of the gap at Avranches would or would not have helped matters? Why this petty quibbling about whether or not it would have been better to attack a day later? Why the repetition of the well-known facts that the divisions in the West were dangerously weak? Why the childish reference to a personal quarrel with Guderian? Why this pathetic submission to the man who had brought it all about? Was the letter written merely to explain von Kluge's military position to the historians of the future? Was von Kluge really so loyal to his Führer that he was willing to absolve Hitler of all blame and assume it all himself? Or was there some other reason?

It is suggested that there might have been. These lengthy excuses, protestations of good faith, and feverish words of devotion to Adolf Hitler may have been written to counteract the discovery of evidence connecting von Kluge with the conspiracy of 20 July. While the Field Marshal himself would be beyond the reach of the Nazi executioner by his suicide, his family would not. He knew that proof of his association with the plot would bring down fearful reprisals on all those closely related to him, and by this letter he probably hoped to avert these consequences. Rommel, when offered the lives of his family for his own, did not hesitate in making his choice. Von Kluge may have seen the same alternative and taken it even though it had not been officially offered to him. It was the one explanation that provides some reason to an otherwise inconsistent and illogical course of action.

The senior officers of the German army in the West were not the only ones who were depressed by the outcome of events in Normandy. This rot in the core of their confidence in an ultimate German victory had also begun to set in amongst the men. As new secret weapons failed to live up to the promises that had been made for them, as still newer and more devastating secret weapons failed to materialize, and as the news of recent retreats in both the East and the West reached the front line troops, doubts as to the invincibility of a National Socialist Germany began to assail the German soldier. It was still too early for any mass feeling of defeatism. But the events of 20 July, the reality of the growing strength of the Allies, and the realization that a German victory was becoming more and more dependent upon a technical or spiritual miracle, were beginning to undermine the faith Goebbels had taken so long to build up. When it became evident, in early August, that Allied forces could no longer be contained within the limited confines of the Normandy bridgehead, defeatist rumors, that bane of all armies, started to circulate madly amongst the troops in France. Initially begun by the physical reality of defeat, these wild tales of disaster were fanned by French Resistance groups and clever Allied propaganda. Sweeping, with the speed of a forest fire, amongst men weary and exhausted after weeks of fruitless fighting, they seared the first scars of doubt into the disciplined mind of the German soldier. The demoralizing effect of these rumors was quickly recognized by the High Command and a series of orders and warnings began to emanate from formation headquarters following the Allied break-through.

Thus on 5 August the men of 276 Infantry Division holding a sector in the region of Villers-Bocage read the following paragraph in an order issued by their commander, Lieutenant General Kurt Badinski:

Latrine rumors circulate in an alarming manner, especially in the rear among the supply columns and services behind the lines. I condemn this irresponsible chatter as sabotage of the worst sort. It is punishable by death. I wish the responsible authorities to investigate every rumor which comes to their notice and to identify the originator or the rumor-monger, as the case may be. I must protect the forward troops fighting the enemy against such traitors and alarmists. . . .

With the collapse of the offensive at Mortain and the subsequent retreat, the panic became more widespread. Even first class troops were falling prey to these tales. Thus a formation like 3 Parachute Division, one of the best in Normandy and containing some of the youngest and most fanatical German troops, was apparently not immune. Having been forced to give up St. Lô after weeks of tenacious fighting, and then to start their trek towards the Seine, its commander, the garrulous fat Lieutenant General Richard Schimpf found it necessary to issue the following stimulating order:

Commander,
3 Parachute Division.   *14 August 1944.*

To all men of the 3rd Parachute Division.

Foul rumors are the same as bad odors, BOTH ORIGINATE FROM THE REAR. I have occasion to point out that contrary to rumors which are brought up to the fighting troops from the rear, there is no reason for concern about the situation. It is rumored that the division is encircled by the enemy. Although I cannot go into details I want to state that all rumors of this kind are false. They are to be classed as enemy propaganda which is designed to discourage our paratroops in battle.

The army, British or American, which can encircle or capture our division does not exist. Even if the enemy should succeed in interrupting our communications for a short time, that is no reason for paratroops, who are trained to jump into the midst of the enemy, to lose heart. . . .

It is certain that we will finish this war victoriously. And it is just as certain that the glorious 3rd Parachute Division will never cease to fight and will do its duty unvanquished to the end of the war.

Whosoever thinks or speaks differently will be slapped across the face.

SCHIMPF.

But despite the vigorous words of Schimpf, 3 Parachute Division was indeed encircled. And not only it, but the bulk of the Fifth Panzer Army, the Seventh Army and Panzer Group Eberbach as well. The Germans had definitely lost their race to safety, for on 17 August the Canadians had captured Falaise and the Americans were in Argentan. Less than fifteen miles separated the two Allied armies, but to the west of the gap the remnants of fourteen German divisions, almost 80,000 men, had still failed to make good their escape.

Up until 18 August the withdrawal had been comparatively orderly although casualties from artillery and air bombardment had been colossal. But it had been much too slow. On that day General Paul Hausser issued an order announcing that he had been "entrusted with sole command of the withdrawal of the forces of Fifth Panzer Army, Seventh Army and Panzer Group Eberbach, at present lying in the salient formed by the Orne, to a position behind the line of the Dives." However, the order pointed out, a deep penetration into the area northwest of the small town of Trun on the Dives River, made it imperative that this territory be retaken by counter-attack. Once this had been done, the intention was to hold a line southeast of Falaise and northeast of Argentan and then "to withdraw the formations lying southwest of the Dives behind the river in two to three nights." The counter-attack against the northern end of the line was to be carried out by two S.S. panzer divisions that had managed to get out of the pocket, while at the same time the trapped Germans would squeeze their way through the narrow opening which would be kept open for them during the next few days.

But the gap was not kept open. The counter-attack failed to do more than alleviate the situation for several hours, and soon nothing remained of the escape route but a thin corridor less than five miles in width, through the three tiny villages of Trun, St. Lambert-sur-Dives and Chambois. Here in the wooded, hilly and close country of the Dives valley the Germans suffered a defeat in blood, men and material equaling in significance such other German defeats as Stalingrad, Moscow and El Alamein.

The carnage and chaos that reigned in the Falaise pocket from 19 August to 22 August can best be described by the men who were in it. The orderly withdrawal that began on the night of 19 August turned into a helpless rout by the morning of 20 August. Each man looked out only for himself, and small tiny groups of tanks and men made individual efforts to break through the curtain of fire laid down by Allied artillery. General Heinrich von Lüttwitz, whose 2 Panzer Division was deep in the middle of the pocket, has given a relatively sober account of his efforts to escape the cauldron.

"On the evening of 19 August," he said,[9] "large numbers of our troops were crowded together in the restricted area of Fourches-Trun-Chambois-Montabord. Some of them had already made repeated attempts to escape to the northwest with vehicles and horse-drawn columns. Quite apart from attacks from the air, the entire terrain was being swept by enemy artillery fire and our casualties increased from hour to hour. On the route leading into St. Lambert-sur-Dives from Bailleul where my division was collected, a colossal number of shot-up horses and vehicles lay mixed together with dead soldiers in large heaps which hourly grew higher and higher. That evening the order was given to force a break-through near St. Lambert. I ordered all my remaining tanks (there were fifteen left of the 120 with which I arrived in Normandy) and other armored vehicles to form a vanguard behind which we intended to break through from Bailleul to St. Lambert, a distance of less than ten kilometres. But ground reconnaissance had established the fact that driving would be impossible in total darkness owing to the large numbers of destroyed vehicles that were lying about. Thus we were only able to start leaving the Bailleul area at four in the morning when there would be more light.

"I had expected that this route would be under such a raking fire that it would be hardly possible to extricate any considerable numbers from the pocket. But for some unknown reason enemy artillery fire had practically ceased on the evening of 19 August and remained quiet until the next morning. In this lull we began to move in the early morning mist of 20 August. As a narrow lane near St. Lambert was known still to provide an escape route across the Dives River, columns

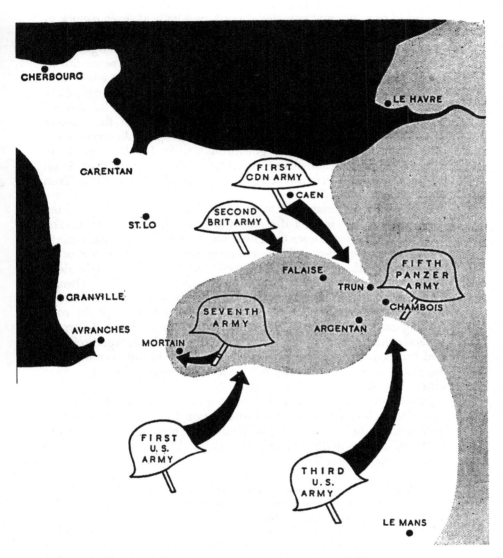

THE FALAISE POCKET — 19th August, 1944.

of all the encircled units were streaming towards it, some of them driving in rows of eight vehicles abreast. Suddenly at seven o'clock in the morning the artillery fire which had been so silent, now broke out into a storm such as I had never before experienced. Alongside the Dives the numerous trains of vehicles ran into direct enemy fire of every description, turned back, and in some cases drove round in a circle until they were shot-up and blocked the roads. Towering pillars of smoke rose incessantly from petrol tanks as they were hit, ammunition exploded, riderless horses stampeded, some of them badly wounded. Organized direction was no longer possible, and only a few of my tanks and infantry got through to St. Lambert. At ten in the morning these elements reported to me that they had cleared an escape route and were providing cover south and north of it at Trun and Chambois.

"By noon I had managed to reach St. Lambert myself, and from the church in the town I directed the evacuation of my men. The crossing of the bridge over the Dives was a particularly ghastly affair. Men, horses, vehicles and other equipment that had been shot-up while making the crossing had crashed from the bridge into the deep ravine of the Dives and lay there jumbled together in gruesome heaps. Throughout the whole afternoon enemy tanks tried to break through again into St. Lambert from Trun, while other tanks kept the road leading northeast from St. Lambert under constant fire. I formed separate small groups of my men, placed them under energetic officers and ordered them to march northeast. At nine in the evening of 20 August I broke out myself, but enemy infantry had by this time entered St. Lambert and the Falaise gap was closed."

The letters and diaries of men written inside the pocket itself confirm the picture presented by General von Lüttwitz. These simple statements of little men reveal with adequate eloquence the reactions of those caught in the inferno at Falaise. The diary of a medical sergeant reads: [10]

17 Aug. 44. We have not seen a German fighter for weeks. . . . I am wondering how the war will end. Nobody believes in a turn for the better. No rest or sleep by day or night, only a lot of work.

20 Aug. 44. For several days now we have been inside the pocket. We are supposed to fight our way out. Two divisions made an attempt, but three kilometres in front of our objective we find ourselves between British tanks. Our comrades of the infantry fall like flies. There is no leadership left. I don't want to fight anyone, it is so useless. God grant that we get out of this alive. I wonder what my wife is doing now.

And another diary belonging to a corporal reports even more tersely: [11]

15 *Aug.* 44. We had to retreat again. All roads are choked with vehicles. It looks as if they are trying to pull the motorized columns out of the pocket first.

16 *Aug.* 44. The British have landed at Toulon. They say that our new turbine-operated fighter planes (Dusenjägers) have brought down 400 enemy aircraft the very first day.

18 Aug. 44. Nothing to eat for two days. . . .

19 *Aug.* 44. Today we moved east under fire. A lot of equipment has been left behind everywhere. The roads are still choked with transport. Only one road out of the pocket is left. The Allies are less than fifty kilometres from Paris.

The letters sent back home expressed much the same sentiments although they were usually more guarded in their tone. A prisoner writing to his parents said:

On 13 August I lost everything but my life and the rags on my back. That night whoever was left of the unit marched back. Marching may not be the proper word for our type of retreat. Two days later we were pocketed. I lived exclusively on raw turnips. Most of my old buddies did not get out of the pocket.

A corporal in a letter dated 18 August wrote to his wife: [12]

. . . We had to retreat in a great hurry. All the other units pulled out without firing a shot and we were left to cover them. . . . I wonder what will become of us. The pocket is nearly closed, and the enemy is already at Rouen. I don't think I shall ever see my home again. However we are fighting for Germany and our children, and what happens to us matters not. I close with the hope that a miracle will happen soon and that I shall see my home again.

Another letter dated 18 August, and written inside the pocket, included much more defeatism than the average German soldier dared reveal in a letter destined for Germany:

. . . Our future looks hopeless, and I think it is only right that I write you that most likely we will be taken prisoner. I know it will be hard on you but I can't help it. At least I have let you know how things are and when you get the notification that I am missing you will know that I am a prisoner, because I don't think I shall be wounded. . . .

The punishing Allied fire made no distinction between rank. Generals and privates ran the same gauntlet of death in their attempts to reach safety. Amongst the prisoners-of-war were a corps commander and two divisional commanders — Generals Elfeldt, Menny and

Badinski. Severely wounded were Colonel General Hausser, commander of Seventh Army, Major General Wisch, commander of 1 S.S. Panzer Division and Major General Dettling of 363 Infantry Division. The dead included Lieutenant General Drabich Waechter of 326 Infantry Division. On foot and in small groups of armored vehicles they desperately sought their way out of this man-made hell. Some managed to escape unscathed. Most did not. When the Falaise pocket was finally eliminated it had yielded up no fewer than 45,000 Germans to swell the bursting Allied prison cages. The total number of German dead and wounded that reddened the green countryside of the Dives Valley with their blood will never be known. The estimated figure is between 10,000 and 15,000.

The fleeing, disorganized remnants of the Seventh and Fifth German Armies were all that now remained of the force that had so confidently advanced against the Allied invasion of the Continent. For disaster in such overwhelming measures, the German soldier could proffer his thanks to the intuitive genius of his Führer. And to share the blame with Adolf Hitler were the arrogant, confident, disciplined products of the German officer corps whose conceit and blindness deluded them into believing that they could successfully carry out the demands of a madman. Normandy proved that they could not.

Chapter XXII

PARIS AND THE SEINE

THE disaster in the Falaise pocket was not the only price the Wehrmacht was to pay for its stupidity in Normandy. It had still to contribute thousands of more German dead and thousands of more German prisoners before it had atoned for its mistakes. Broken and disorganized, the remnants of the fourteen divisions that had succeeded in escaping through the Falaise gap could not hope to do more than continue their headlong rush to the safety of the eastern bank of the Seine. Clogging the roads with their variegated transport they offered Allied air forces the most obvious and most profitable targets since the start of the invasion.

Only on the right wing of the German front was there any semblance of an organized withdrawal. Here the three infantry divisions[1] which had been located north of Falaise, were still relatively healthy. All the British and Canadian effort had been directed southeast of

Caen so that there had been little intense fighting along the Channel coast itself. Following the débâcle at Falaise, these three formations, thanking their stars that they had not been sucked into the whirlpool, stealthily picked up their arms and began to tiptoe back towards the Seine as unobtrusively as possible.

According to Lieutenant General Diestel, the podgy-faced, uninspiring but efficient commander of 346 Infantry Division — one of the three formations concerned — their withdrawal, begun on 18 August, was based upon the rivers Dives, Touques and Risle, which were to be held in turn until the Seine was reached. But, while it was hoped to hold these river lines for a respectable period of time, actually it was impossible to utilize them for a defensive stand of more than two or three days each. "As soon as we were safely lodged behind a river," said Diestel,[2] "we would find that our left flank had disintegrated and that we were in danger of being encircled. We would then move back again. We were never hurried in these movements because of the systematic and thoroughly organized tactics of the Allies. When we had been thrown back during the day, we always knew that there would be a pause at night when the enemy would regroup for the next day's operations. It was these hours of darkness that enabled us to retire without suffering many casualties. Had it not been for the position on our left we would have been able to hold these river lines much longer than we did."

The left wing of the German front, following the defeat at Falaise, had been shattered. General Patton's Third U.S. Army speeding along the southern edge of the German position had in a breath-taking dash captured Mantes-Gassicourt on the Seine on 19 August — the very day the bulk of Seventh Army was trying to break out of the Falaise pocket some seventy miles to the west. It was imperative that something be done to fill this yawning hole on the German left. But where were the needed troops to come from? The bulk of Seventh and Fifth Panzer Armies had been rendered impotent in the Falaise trap. The First and Nineteenth Armies in Southern France had been steadily milked of their divisions by the demands of Normandy during June and July. When the French and American invasion forces landed between Toulon and Cannes early on 15 August, there were available to meet this fresh threat only seven of the fourteen divisions originally designated to guard the Mediterranean coast. This left the Fifteenth Army in the Pas de Calais as the only source of ready reinforcements with which to attempt another stand in France.

But the Fifteenth Army was no longer the mighty formation it had been on D-Day. Once Hitler had made up his mind that a second landing from across the Straits of Dover was unlikely, the infantry which had been uselessly twiddling its thumbs east of the Seine had been sent in a constant flow to aid the forces in Normandy. But this decision had been delayed much too long. Not until late July did any large number of divisions abandon their watching brief in the Pas de Calais and begin to move to the battle zone. The Allied planes, waiting for this exodus to take place, pounced upon the roads and railway lines carrying fresh troops to Normandy, with results similar to those achieved in delaying infantry from reaching the Seine-Loire rectangle in the early days of the invasion.

The short, stocky, red-faced General Eugen-Felix Schwalbe, commander of 344 Infantry Division, has given an account of his formation's experiences in trying to get to Normandy in August 1944. In loud, booming tones, probably due to a serious deafness in one ear, the general explained the reason for his division's tardiness in reaching the front. It was typical of what was happening to most of the divisions attempting to make the relatively short journey to the western side of the Seine.

"On 3 August my division of about 8000 men was finally told to move to Normandy, after having waited just north of the Somme for a second landing since the day the invasion began," shouted Schwalbe.[3] "Our destination was Falaise. I decided that, since speed was essential, my fighting troops would travel from Amiens to Rouen by train, while my supply troops would make a three-day journey on foot by road. I expected that the fighting element of the division would reach Rouen, about 120 kilometres away, in about twenty-four hours. I went off to Rouen in advance to make preparations for my division's arrival, only to find that three days later my butchers and bakers and hygiene men arrived on schedule but my infantry was nowhere to be found. It seems that the first of the twenty-eight trains carrying my division was derailed south of Amiens, and as a result the men were sent by a long circuitous route to Rouen. They were shunted around France for days on end, and it took them no less than nine days to make this 120-kilometre journey by rail. By the time they arrived and were ready to move off again, the battle for Falaise was lost and the retreat of Seventh Army had begun."

It was now clear that no useful purpose could be served in sending the remaining infantry of Fifteenth Army as far west as Falaise. Instead it was decided to use these fresh troops to act as a covering force for the withdrawal of Seventh Army across the Seine. Three new infantry divisions were to provide this protective screen north of Paris, while four other untried divisions of Fifteenth Army were sent south of Paris.[4] But so confused was the entire German position across the river that Schwalbe admitted that he never knew exactly what his division was expected to do on the west side of the Seine until it was explained to him in a prisoner-of-war camp four months after the war was over.

"All I was told at the time," said Schwalbe, "was that the three divisions, 331, 344, and 17 Luftwaffe Field were to take up defensive positions about ten miles south of Evreux. I never knew, until I was shown a captured order by an Allied interrogator, that our task was to cover the withdrawal of Seventh Army to the Seine.

"It would not have mattered in any event, whether I knew this or not, since the life of my division was so short. In trying to cross the Seine, air attacks were so bad that it was only possible to move my formation piece by piece over the river. As a result I was never able to have my complete division together. Nor were we ever properly dug in for a defensive fight. No sooner had we reached our intended positions when we discovered the Allies were already there. We attempted to withdraw but we were new, and chaos resulted instead. The vehicles jammed every road in all directions and planes attacked us constantly. In one of these attacks my own vehicle was destroyed. It was no longer healthy to drive about these roads in a motor car. I therefore was forced to travel between my units with the only safe vehicle I still had — a bicycle. My corps commander was so anxious about Allied air attacks in this area that he used to have two men sitting on the hood of his car and one on the rear bumper to act as aircraft spotters.

"In a little over a week my division ceased to exist as a fighting formation. I lost three-fifths of my men, and two-thirds of the weapons of the formation had to be abandoned. The other two divisions who went over the Seine with me suffered much the same fate. So weak were we all that it was decided to merge the three divisions into one under one headquarters staff, and with this force guard the approaches to the Rouen ferries. I do not know whose plan it was to throw good divisions after bad into the cauldron west of the Seine. These 30,000 to 35,000 men might have performed a useful function organizing the defense of the Seine River itself instead of being dissipated in a few days in a hopeless situation. I had untried troops under my command and my orders were vague and impossible. I never knew exactly where my division was, what its task was supposed to be and what was taking place all about me. Disastrous results under such circumstances were inevitable."

With the collapse of resistance on the west bank of the Seine, the glittering prize of Paris was now within reach of Allied hands. By 19 August American troops had reached Melun to the south of the city and Mantes-Gassicourt to the north of the city, while a frontal attack from Versailles threatened the German garrison from the west as well. The fact that Paris was spared the ravages of a full-scale assault and battle was due to a series of fortuitous circumstances. The happiest of these was the coincidence which placed in the capital of France a group of German officers whose opposition to Hitler had been sincere enough to involve them in the affair of 20 July. One of the most active members of the conspiratorial clique was General Heinrich von Stülpnagel, Military Governor of France, who had under him as commandant of Greater Paris the German nobleman, Lieutenant General Wilhelm von Boineburg-Lengsfeld, whose contempt for Hitler was no less than that of Stülpnagel's. Between them these two men managed to staff the garrison of Paris with a large group of hand-picked anti-Nazis. Most of these officers were members of the German aristocracy, and von Boineburg-Lengsfeld, who took over the Paris post after Stalingrad, was often asked by the Supreme Command to account for the number of noblemen in his staff.

The thin, wiry, bemonocled Thuringian Junker, von Boineburg-Lengsfeld, must have been born with a horseshoe in his mouth and four-leaf clovers clutched in each tiny paw. Incredible luck alone enabled him to live through experiences which brought many of his less fortunate colleagues to their graves. In Russia he had been run over by a tank which broke almost every bone in his body. He survived it. On 20 July 1944 he arrested all the members of Himmler's Security Police and of the Gestapo in Paris. He was not hanged. Four weeks before the end of the war he was brought before a military court inquiring into the surrender of Paris without a fight. The trial was postponed long enough to enable him to travel to Erfurt so that he would be captured by the advancing Americans. The luck of Lieutenant General von Boineburg-Lengsfeld was shared by the Parisians he was charged to command. There were hundreds of other German officers who would have carried out the destruction of the cultural landmarks of Paris without hesitation or regret. But Fate had conspired against the barbarians and Paris was saved.

"After Stalingrad I was deeply depressed," said von Boineburg-Lengsfeld,[5] "I did not relish my new post as commandant of Paris because it would inevitably place me in the limelight which I was attempting to avoid. But I soon learned to love Paris and the Parisians, and eventually the French. I was determined to prevent the destruction of the city if I possibly could. It is true that I designed the so-called 'Boineburg Line' which was to be used in the defense of Paris, but it was an imaginary line that existed only on paper. It was my life insurance since it convinced Berlin that I was actually planning the city's defense.

"On 20 July I was 'ordered' by General von Stülpnagel to arrest General Oberg of the S.S. and the entire Gestapo and Security Police in Paris." The general smiled when he used the word 'order.' "The pretext under which they were arrested was that they had participated in a conspiracy against Hitler. When it was obvious, however, that the putsch had failed, General von Stülpnagel attempted suicide and I was forced to free Oberg and his men. I was saved from any immediate reprisals because of the ridiculous 'order' which I had received from von Stülpnagel.

"Early in August 1944 I received orders direct from Hitler to defend Paris to the last and above all to destroy the bridges over the Seine. I informed my staff that I could not carry out these orders since the troops at my disposal were police forces only and not capable of defending the city against the Americans. The destruction of the Seine bridges, I claimed, was utter military nonsense, since the Seine was not a military obstacle. About ten days before the Allies entered Paris I was relieved of my command because of my activities on and after 20 July. When my successor, Lieutenant General Dietrich von Choltitz arrived, nothing had been prepared for the defense of Paris nor for the destruction of the Seine bridges. I implored von Choltitz to save the city, and since it was much too late to organize a proper defense he agreed to cooperate. Von Choltitz had come straight from the Führer's headquarters when he relieved me. He told me that the rage of the Führer, as a result of the events of 20 July, was inhuman. Said von Choltitz: 'When the Führer told me how he hates generals, a sadistic hatred I can never forget was in his eyes.'"

Von Choltitz kept his word and made no effort to destroy either the Seine bridges or other installations in the city. By mid-August the activities and attacks of the French Resistance Movement became so widespread that the Germans planned a co-ordinated operation against it. But on 19 August General von Choltitz issued a sudden order prohibiting such an attack. About the same time negotiations began between the Germans and the underground forces through the medium of the Swedish Legation. A strange truce was agreed upon whereby certain parts of Paris, such as the Hôtel de Ville, the Palais de Justice, the Palais de Luxembourg, were to be regarded as the territory of the Maquis and all members of the Resistance in this area were to be regarded and treated as soldiers. The other sections of Paris were to be free for German use. The two parties were not to interfere with each other. But the agreement was not observed as no one really knew the exact boundaries, and the clashes continued. Barricades appeared in the streets and rifle shots punctuated the life of the capital in an eerie atmosphere that was neither war nor peace. A German war correspondent, Dr. Toni Scheelkopf, gave the following description of Paris on 22 August to his listeners on the German radio.

"As the front drew steadily nearer to Paris at the beginning of this week, and when we heard the news that conditions in the city itself had considerably deteriorated, we went in again on Tuesday (22 August) to get an idea of the situation. We knew that the garrisons of the strong-points remaining behind in Paris had to fight in every part of the town in ceaseless skirmishes against the followers of de Gaulle on the one hand, and against the Bolshevist-controlled Resistance on the other. We saw barricades in the side-streets, sandbags piled high, vehicles driven into one another, pieces of furniture heaped together to form barriers . . . somewhere a machine-gun chattered from time to time . . . but we came through unchallenged to the well-defended German strong-points and reached the Champs-Elysées. Here the change which had come over this city was even more noticeable. It was a little after midday. But this street, usually crowded at this time of day with people and vehicles, was empty. On the way from the obelisk to the Arc de Triomphe we counted just over fifty people. . . ."

These sporadic skirmishes continued throughout the city for over a week. Von Choltitz, unable to organize an effective defense because he had neither the time, the troops nor the inclination, and unable to retire because of Hitler's order demanding that the city be defended, ended up by neither fighting nor withdrawing. Locking themselves up in the hotels and public buildings of Paris, they offered token resistance to the French underground forces. But when on 25 August the tanks of the French 2 Armored Division led by General Leclerc entered the capital in strength, von Choltitz surrendered the garrison of 10,000 Germans that had been uselessly left behind to carry out Hitler's mad desire to hold or destroy the city he had entered as a conqueror some four years before.

The failure of von Choltitz to carry out the Führer's demands was not forgotten or forgiven in Berlin. General von Boineburg-Lengsfeld reports that in early April 1945 he was called to Torgau as a witness in the court-martial proceedings against von Choltitz. The charge was treason for having surrendered Paris without a fight. Although von Choltitz was safely out of harm's way, being a prisoner-of-war in Allied hands, the trial was being held to establish von Choltitz's guilt. If he were declared a traitor the general's family would have had to pay the penalty on his behalf, since Hitler had decreed that the relatives of a soldier were to be punished for desertion or other treacherous conduct. Fortunately for both von Boine-burg-Lengsfeld and the family of von Choltitz, one of the generals acting as a judge at the court-martial was a good friend of von Boineburg-Lengsfeld. The main witness conveniently could not be found. Proceedings therefore had to be postponed. The war was over before they could be resumed.

By the time Paris had fallen nothing German remained west of the Seine other than a few isolated pockets of resistance, the beleaguered garrisons of the Brittany fortresses and the thousands of disconsolate prisoners-of-war. The defeat of the German armies in Western France was overwhelming and complete. The debit side of their ledger sheet was thick red with blood and destruction. Two armies, Seventh and Fifth Panzer, had been reduced to scattered remnants of fleeing units. Two other armies, First and Fifteenth, had been drained of the bulk of their fighting strength and had been dissipated at Falaise and the Seine River in fruitless efforts to retrieve an irretrievable situation.

About fifty divisions of the Wehrmacht had been committed to battle in Normandy — well over a million men. Fewer than ten of these divisions could still be classed as reasonable fighting formations after the Seine River had been crossed. Of a total of about 2200 tanks and assault guns used in Normandy, almost 1800 of them remained as burnt-out hulks in the rolling fields west of the Seine. About 210,000 Germans had become prisoners-of-war since the invasion, and another 240,000 had been either killed or wounded. In other words almost half of the total number of German troops engaged in the battle of Normandy had appeared on a Wehrmacht casualty list in one category or another.

The losses amongst senior commanders were commensurately as high as those suffered by the men. For in addition to the normal hazards of the battlefields, German generals were also subjected to the tantrums and intuitions of their Führer. Hitler succeeded in dismissing his senior officers almost as quickly as the Allies managed to kill, wound or capture them. By 25 August three field marshals had been eliminated — von Rundstedt had been dismissed, von Kluge had taken poison and Rommel had been wounded. Amongst army commanders, Dollman of Seventh Army had died, his successor Hausser had been severely wounded in the Falaise Gap, Geyr von Schweppenburg of Panzer Group West had been recalled to Berlin, and von Salmuth of Fifteenth Army had been replaced by von Zangen. And farther down the military hierarchy no fewer than three corps commanders and twenty divisional commanders had been killed, captured or wounded. The battle of Normandy had cost the

German Wehrmacht in three months almost twice as many men as they had lost at Stalingrad where 250,000 troops had surrendered to the Russians. And as additional satisfaction to Allied commanders, the Seine had been reached two weeks ahead of schedule and the broad strategical battle had been fought exactly as planned.

Retreat had been well learnt by the Wehrmacht in Russia. In fact, by the end of August 1944, it had almost become a habit. Once the German General Staff was given complete freedom to carry out a straight, administrative task it usually did it well. Having once decided to withdraw behind the Seine, the fact that no bridges existed over the river below Paris constituted a relatively minor problem. Crossing rivers while going backwards was a specialty of staff officers who had been chased back over the Volga, the Don and the Dnieper. With the destruction of the Seine bridges it had been necessary early in the campaign to organize a system of ferries and pontoons for the sending of supplies and reinforcements to Normandy. These well-camouflaged crossing places now did yeomen service in the reverse rôle of transporting the broken units to the comparative safety of the east bank. Harassed by a vigilant Allied air force, almost 300 barges were destroyed or damaged in the seven days preceding 23 August when the exodus was at its height. Although the west bank of the Seine was choked with abandoned vehicles, knocked-out guns and tanks, and frightened horses, thousands of German troops succeeded in crossing the Seine at Rouen, Elbeuf, Caudebec and Duclair.

But once on the other side the protection of the wide expanse of the Seine proved more illusory than real. With an Allied bridgehead established over the river as early as 20 August and with the bridges of Paris intact in Allied hands by 25 August, the Seine no longer constituted a defensive barrier. Field Marshal Walter Model, who had replaced von Kluge in the twin job of Commander-in-Chief West and commander of Army Group 'B,' was at his wits' end trying to bring order out of the chaos that stemmed from the defeat in Normandy.

The square-jawed, square-built, short Walter Model was closer to Hitler in allegiance and background than most senior members of the officer corps. At fifty-four he had attained a field marshal's baton at a much younger age than most of his contemporaries. Like Rommel, he owed his rapid climb to the highest rung in the military ladder to a ruthless energy and an intimate relationship with the Nazi Party. Unlike Rommel, his loyalty to the Führer survived the 20th of July, and his message of faith in the régime, following the assassination attempt, was the first to be received at Berlin from an officer on the Eastern front.

Model's leadership of a panzer division in the early campaigns, and his command of an army in Russia, displayed an impulsive dash and unyielding determination to carry out orders, at whatever cost, which marked him as the kind of officer Hitler wanted. In 1944 he was given an army group in the East and after he had managed to check the Russian summer offensive on the Vistula he was called to France. Model, belonged to that growing group of commanders — Rommel, Dietrich, Student, Hausser were others — who might truly be called 'Hitler's generals,' in that they had achieved prominence by winning the confidence of the Führer rather than that of the officer corps. It was natural, therefore, that he was disliked and resented by the average General Staff officer. His comparatively lowly birth and his coarse manner of speech made him no more dear to them.

Yet this tough exterior, while it repelled the polished products of the officer corps, appealed to many of the men who worked under him. An incident described by his admiring chauffeur, who had been with him for two years, will illustrate this.[6] On 2 January 1945, the Field Marshal's car was held up during a snowstorm in the Ardennes. Several cars were stalled ahead of his, and officers in them sat snugly in their vehicles while a group of other ranks cleared the road for traffic. Suddenly Model, losing patience, became furious and bellowed "Goddammit, what would happen now if Allied fighters were to strafe this road?" He dismounted and began to shovel the snow alongside the men. Just as the first vehicle was cleared, an indignant-looking captain appeared and, not seeing Model, demanded to know what the trouble was. Immediately the Field Marshal snapped at him, "And where have you been while the shovelling was going on?" The captain was forced to reply that he had been sitting in his vehicle. "So," replied Model, "you would let a field marshal clear the road for you while you sit comfortably in your automobile — as from today, Kamerad, you are a private," and with these words Model stripped the officer of his insignia of rank.

These bursts of temperament, coupled with his unbending allegiance, gave to his military career an uneven quality of performance that alternated between brilliant competence and muddled inefficiency. He demanded of his men that all of Hitler's orders be carried out to the last detail. Since these chiefly insisted on positions being held to the last man, many unpleasant complications developed. Although brutal in his insistence on a literal compliance with the Führer's orders, he did not hesitate to object to instructions which did not agree with his own judgment. In this way he did, to some extent, manage to retain some freedom of action. His administrative capacity was not respected by his junior officers, and amongst them the expression 'to Model' was sarcastically used to describe a state of hopeless confusion, while 'to de-Model' was to sort things out again.

By the end of August affairs were properly 'Modeled' east of the Seine. The Allied troops were moving so quickly that conditions were never stable enough for long enough to enable an order to be carried out. Each intention was out-dated before it could be put on paper. General Günther Blumentritt, who was now acting as Chief-of-Staff for his third Commander-in-Chief West since the invasion of France, mournfully described those unhappy days for the Wehrmacht.

"There was no plan available at this stage for an orderly fighting withdrawal," said Blumentritt.[7] "At first it was hoped to fall behind the Seine, but with the Americans already on the outskirts of Paris this had to be abandoned. It was then decided to use the Seine as a midway position to delay the enemy and give the retreating troops sufficient time to build a line on the Somme. The Seine was expected to hold for at least seven days and then defensive positions were to have been taken up on the so-called Kitzinger Line which was to have been built by General Kitzinger across France through Abbeville-Amiens-Soissons-Epernay-Châlons-St. Dizier-Chaumont-Langres-Gray-Besançon to the Swiss border. These defensive positions had been designated as far back as 1943, but the line had only been completed on the right flank between Abbeville and Amiens. Even though this line existed in theory only, nevertheless we had been ordered to hold it. But there were no troops available to man either the Seine or the Somme, and the Allies cut through France with little opposition."

As early as 28 August 1944 Model had already issued detailed instructions for the defense of the Somme. Seventh Army was ordered to take over the front of Fifth Panzer Army on the line Neufchâtel-Beauvais-Compiègne at noon on 31 August. The Army's "first priority task was the construction of the Somme-Oise position . . . in the shortest possible time and to make it capable of defense." It was hoped to hold this intermediate position between the Seine and the Somme until the Kitzinger Line based on the Somme was manned and ready. But the intention showed a complete misappreciation of the strength of the Allied bridgeheads over the Seine, and of the utter weakness of both the Seventh and Fifth Panzer Armies. The capture of Beauvais on 30 August rendered this halfway line impotent a day before Seventh Army was supposed to take it over. The only remaining geographical barrier in France was now the Somme. On 31 August, with the capture of Amiens, this impressive river line was crossed

and the liberation of all France ensured. The sudden collapse of the
Somme position was due to muddled and inept planning on the part
of the German senior commanders. They underestimated the enemy's
strength and overestimated their own — a fatal combination.

Even when it was obvious that the Seine could no longer be held,
the Fifteenth Army in the Pas de Calais was still sitting on the Channel
coast with its eyes glued on the English ports. True, by this time it
awaited a second invasion with only six divisions[8] instead of the
original nineteen it had owned on 6 June, but the possibility of further
landings was still a serious consideration in the minds of German
strategists. This fact was revealed by General Gustav von Zangen,
who had been called from Italy to replace Colonel General Hans von
Salmuth as commander of Fifteenth Army. Von Zangen, who had
been a member of the German Police Force for fifteen years after
World War I, still retained the stolid, unimaginative appearance so
peculiar to those of his profession. Handsome in a dull sort of way
and rather stocky in build, von Zangen was one of those 'reliable'
generals whom Hitler was now sending to the West to replace those
who had not shown themselves keen enough about National Socialism.

"When I arrived in France on 25 August," said von Zangen,[9] "I
found that my army consisted of six divisions. My rôle was to protect
the Channel coast in the event of another landing. At first I thought
I would have to defend the Seine, but this task was given to Fifth
Panzer Army under Colonel General 'Sepp' Dietrich. About 28 August
I was told to abandon the territory west of the Somme, except for the
fortresses and take up a defensive position on the Somme between
Abbeville and Amiens. On my left flank and to include the defense
of Amiens, was to be Seventh Army under General Hans Eberbach.
My army reached its designated sector along the Somme, but Seventh
Army never arrived on my left. Eberbach and most of the Seventh
Army staff were surprised and captured at Amiens. This left all the
troops on my flank without any organized leadership. When the
news of this disaster reached Field Marshal Model he hurriedly
ordered 'Sepp' Dietrich of Fifth Panzer Army to take over this open
front. But Model did not realize how weak 'Sepp' Dietrich was at the
time, and how little there remained of his army. In the resulting confusion no one ever did arrive on my left flank. With no opposition
against them the British took Amiens on 31 August and crossed the
river in force the next day. With an open flank it was useless for me
to hold my ground northwest of Amiens and I gave up my positions
on the Somme."

With the breaching of the Kitzinger Line, not even a theoretical defense line existed to protect the remnants of the Wehrmacht in France. The symphony of collapse was reaching a thundering crescendo of despair. All through France Germans were fleeing, hiding or dying. In wild panic they took to the roads and fields and in disorganized confusion hurried eastwards as fast as they could go. During those early days in September 1944, the vaunted discipline of the Wehrmacht was not enough to hold together a force that had been shattered into isolated, scattered fragments. Where local commanders were firm and able, some manner of organized resistance was possible, but, on the whole, the withdrawal from France consisted of separated formations ignorant of the whereabouts and intentions of both their own and Allied troops.

"During all this chaos," moaned General Blumentritt,[10] who, as Model's Chief-of-Staff, had the unenviable task of piecing together this broken jig-saw puzzle, "the only instructions that came from Berlin were 'Hold! Hold! Hold!' Since it was impossible to carry out this order, we advised units to report any retreat they were forced to make in the following words, 'Thrown back or fought back. Countersteps are being taken.' These were the only terms that would satisfy Berlin that a withdrawal had been necessary and thus save the commander involved from severe punishment for having disobeyed orders."

Cutting through these soft, bewildered remnants, Allied armored columns weaved a pattern of iron and fire amongst the slow-moving marching and horse-driven units. The cities and towns of France and Belgium toppled into the hands of their liberators with the ease and eagerness of long-separated lovers. Names of places that had filled the histories of the first World War flashed across the headlines of the world in quick-changing profusion. Dieppe, Abbeville, Amiens, Albert, Bapaume, Arras, Tournai, Lille, Soissons, Château-Thierry, Charleroi, Mons, Cambrai, Valenciennes, St. Quentin, Sedan, Rheims, Verdun, St. Mihiel — all were tasting freedom again before the first week in September was out. And with each locality there was yielded up a complement of Wehrmacht personnel who had been either too weak, too slow, too stubborn, too fanatical or too disillusioned to make good their escape to the German frontier.

The mounting intake of prisoners was embarrassing the Allied administrative facilities prepared to handle them. In the towns of the Pas de Calais and the Somme valley, exclusive of the Channel fortresses, over 40,000 Germans had been left behind to be picked up by British and Canadian infantry. In a pocket extending from Mons to the forest of Compiègne, where some misguided commanders chose to resist, some 25,000 prisoners were taken in three days by First U.S. Army. On the east bank of the Meuse from Namur to Mézières, twenty-four hours produced another 11,000 exhausted German warriors. General Patch's Seventh Army driving up from the Mediterranean had taken Lyons by 4 September and could already boast of over 50,000 prisoners in its newly-built cages. Thus in less than two weeks after the fall of Paris the total number of prisoners-of-war taken in the West had swollen from 210,000 to the staggering total of well over 350,000. This was still part of the price being paid for the defeat in Normandy.

Morale was degenerating quickly amongst the men of the fleeing Wehrmacht. Their letters to those back home contained the same overtones of resignation and helplessness that characterized the messages written in the pocket at Falaise.[11]

We have no vehicles or guns left, and whoever is still alive will have to fight as an infantryman. But I won't stay with them very long. I really don't know what we are still fighting for. Very soon I shall run over to the Tommies if I am not killed before I get there. . . .

wrote an artilleryman.

And a soldier fighting the Americans described his experiences thus:

We reached Sedan again in a very hasty retreat — much faster than our advances four years ago — but there is only one-fifth of our regiment left. The rest of the men and vehicles do not exist any longer. It is impossible to describe what happened to us during the last five days.

While a German with an ironic sense of humor wrote home:

My total estate now fits into my little bag as I have lost everything else. The words "hot meal" sound like a foreign language. We are gaining ground rapidly but in the wrong direction.

Recognizing the seriousness of this deterioration in the spirit and confidence of the men under his command, Field Marshal Model delivered the following message on 3 September, which for frankness and bold talk is probably a model of its kind:

To the Soldiers of the Western Army.

With the enemy advance and the withdrawal of our front, a great stream of troops has been set in motion. Several hundred thousand soldiers are moving backwards, army, air force and tank units, troops which must reassemble and form new strong-points or lines according to a plan and the orders they receive.

Among them there stream along, together with headquarters now superfluous, columns which have been routed, which have broken out from the front and which for the moment have no firm destination and could receive no clear orders. . . . So, while closely packed columns turn off the road to get themselves sorted out, the stream of the others pushes on. With their vehicles travel idle talk, rumors, haste, inconsiderateness, unnecessary disorder and shortsighted selfishness. They may bring a feeling into the rear areas and into the fully intact bodies of fighting troops which must be prevented, at this moment of extreme tension, with the severest measures.

As your new Commander-in-Chief I direct this call to your honor as soldiers. We have lost a battle but I tell you, we will win this war! I cannot say more now, although I know that there are many questions burning on the lips of the troops. Despite everything that has happened, do not allow your firm, confident faith in Germany's future to be shaken one whit.

I must however make known to you the gravity of this day and hour. This moment will and should separate the weaklings from the real men. Every single man carries now the same responsibilty: when his commander falls out, he must take his place and carry on. . . . [There follows here a series of instructions in which the German soldier is exhorted to report to his nearest headquarters, to stop feeling depressed, to maintain a flawless discipline and a correct outward appearance, to disbelieve "pessimistic rumor and idle talk," and to stop the useless and over-hasty abandonment of weapons, equipment and fortifications. The message ends]:

Take thought then that at this moment everything adds up to the necessity to gain the time which the Führer needs to bring into operation new troops and new weapons. They will come.

Soldiers, we must gain this time for the Führer!

MODEL,
Field Marshal.

But by this time it was obvious to even the most obtuse observer that Model was not of the stuff of which commanders-in-chief are made. The task of defending the Fatherland itself from invasion needed a more experienced and more acute mind than Model possessed. Looking about him to discover the proper man for this unenvied responsibility, Hitler found his available stock of senior officers sadly depleted. Those that had talent couldn't be trusted, and those that could be trusted hadn't the talent. There remained only one exit from this vicious circle — find the man with talent who could be distrusted least. The choice to be made was now plain. Swallowing his pride, Hitler asked von Rundstedt to come back to the West. The old man, having proved his loyalty to the régime by his complete ignorance of, and detachment from, the events of 20 July, wearily agreed. He had sat on the Court of Honor which had tried the military conspirators, because, in his own words, "it had to be done in the best interests of the army." It is likely that his return to the wars was motivated by a somewhat similar reason. Discussing the reappearance of von Rundstedt, the *Intelligence Review* of Field Marshal Montgomery's Twenty-first Army Group, written at the time, made a shrewd and witty analysis of these events.

"Just as von Rundstedt has never been strong enough utterly to disregard the party," it said, "so has his ability (or his reputation) been too convenient for the politicos to ignore. If his own health has improved, the state of his armies has deteriorated in his absence. To bring back the Old Guard implies that the situation is desperate, and since little can be done about it, it may mean that the Old Guard is to take the blame. The return of von Rundstedt is reminiscent of the description of the rôle of cavalry in modern war: 'to add distinction to what would otherwise be a vulgar brawl.' The reappointment is interesting as exhibiting muddle and desperation; but (unlike the cavalry) it doesn't really make much difference. The task of Commander-in-Chief in any German theatre has degenerated into that of local Chief-of-Staff to Hitler and liable to dismissal as much for carrying out quaint orders as for protesting against them. Only Model, it is said, has found the solution: neither to implement nor to criticize, but to promise."

Chapter XXIII
THE RETREAT

THE most spectacular and most significant advance, once the Seine had been crossed, was made by Second British Army in their breakout from their bridgehead at Vernon. In less than four days their armor dashed about 250 miles to capture Amiens, Arras, Tournai, Brussels, Louvain and Antwerp. The sudden fall of Antwerp, on 4 September, with its harbor facilities intact and undamaged, took both Allied and German commanders by surprise. That this huge port with its enormous shipping capacity should fall, like a rich, ripe plum, into Allied hands was beyond the dreams of the most optimistic of planners. Yet, the panic-stricken troops garrisoning the port, frightened and unnerved by the tales of what had happened in France, had hurriedly packed their suit-cases and disappeared, without bothering to blow up this most important prize of the campaign.

The capture of Antwerp presaged an early easing of the Allied supply problem, which was becoming increasingly acute as the distance widened between the front line and the Normandy supply bases at Cherbourg and the Arromanches Mulberry. It achieved a second significant result as well — it had bottled up against the Channel coast the slow-moving units of von Zangen's Fifteenth Army. As has already been explained, the Fifteenth Army's task of defending the right wing of the Somme position had been abandoned when Amiens fell. Its fall had been largely due to a confused understanding of the forces and staffs available in the area on the part of Field Marshal Model, who had still believed that Fifth Panzer Army was capable of undertaking an operational task. In fact it had completely disintegrated after the Seine was crossed, and on Fifteenth Army's left flank was the gaping hole through which British armor had sped in their race to Antwerp.

The original six divisions which von Zangen had received when he had taken over Fifteenth Army on 25 August had been joined, in early September, by the remnants of five divisions escaping from Normandy. Now with the sea to the west and north of them, and with Allied troops south and east of them, this force of almost 100,000 men began a cautious withdrawal movement towards the northeast.

"When we retired from the Somme about 1 September," said von Zangen,[1] "I planned slowly to fight my way back to Brussels and Antwerp and then take up a line in Holland. I had no fear that Antwerp would be taken since it was far behind the front line, and there was a special staff organized to defend it. When I heard on 4 September that it had been captured it came as a stunning surprise. The reason for the fall of Antwerp was the failure of the High Command to appreciate how badly beaten Fifth Panzer Army really was. Instead of an army on my left flank there was an empty gap. It was not yet realized how weak our forces had become.

"My own forces were neither strong enough nor fast enough to get back to Antwerp in time to defend it. We had no motorized equipment and we were constantly being attacked by armored columns. It was only by the greatest of efforts that we succeeded in withdrawing at all. One of my divisions marched ninety kilometres in one day during this retreat. With Antwerp in enemy hands there remained only two courses of action open to me — evacuation by sea or a break-through to the northeast. I decided on the latter course and on 5 September I ordered my troops to assemble in the neighborhood of Audenarde with the object of attacking in the direction of Brussels. However, before this operation could get properly under way I received word from the Commander-in-Chief West on 6 September to abandon this break-through attempt since the enemy line was already much too strong in the area between Brussels and Antwerp.

Instead I was told to make preparations for the evacuation of my army across the Scheldt to the islands of Walcheren and South Beveland."

In this decision to hazard an evacuation by sea, in face of Allied air power, could be seen the tidy, steady hand of the newly-installed Commander-in-Chief West, von Rundstedt. It was a chance that had to be taken if any order was to emerge from the confusion reigning amongst the troops in Belgium and Holland. The plan in its broadest terms was to use Fifteenth Army to deprive the Allies of any more supply bases in France and Belgium, and at the same time occupy the attention of as many enemy troops as possible while the fortifications of the Siegfried Line were prepared for the coming battles for Germany. The method by which this was to be done was to hold tenaciously to the Channel fortress of Le Havre, Boulogne, Calais and Dunkirk and simultaneously by manning the north and south shores of the Scheldt Estuary, deny access to the port of Antwerp. While this was in process the balance of Fifteenth Army, not needed for these priority tasks, would be evacuated through Breskens south of the Scheldt, to the port of Flushing north of the Scheldt. Once safely on Walcheren Island the rescued troops would then march eastwards along this narrow chain of islands until they reached the mainland north of Antwerp. Here a line would be taken up along one of the numerous canals and rivers that striate this part of South Holland. So long as the road through Walcheren and South Beveland to the mainland remained in German hands the plan was feasible. If it fell they would have to think again.

Von Zangen took to his new task with energy and vigor. One division was immediately sent off to Dunkirk to end its days in that unhappy fortress, while other units were designated to remain behind in Le Havre, Boulogne and Calais. He ordered a line to be built along the canal running between Bruges and Ghent, behind which preparations for the crossing of the Scheldt were begun. North of Antwerp itself, to safeguard the strip of land upon which the success of the whole operation depended, he brought down 719 Infantry Division from Northern Holland and all the odd units that could be assembled in the immediate vicinity. The actual responsibility for directing the evacuation of Fifteenth Army across the Scheldt, von Zangen delegated to the serious-minded, deaf General Eugen-Felix Schwalbe. Schwalbe, who had lost his division in the senseless attempt to cover the retreat of the Seventh Army across the Seine, had been unemployed ever since. Now he was given a task which he proudly recalls as one of the most satisfactory achievements of his military career.

"When I was told what my new job was to be," said Schwalbe,[2] "I immediately set up my headquarters in Breskens, from where I could control the situation. Gathering about me as many officers as I could find I sent them along the roads leading to Breskens, where they set up collecting posts for the assembling of the retreating units. They would telephone to me telling me what formation had arrived and was ready to cross, and I would allot it a specific hour when it was to be evacuated. Until that hour it was to remain well-camouflaged and hidden along the roads.

"For the task of crossing the Scheldt I had assembled two large Dutch civilian ships, three large rafts capable of holding eighteen vehicles each, and sixteen small Rhine boats with a capacity of about 250 men each. The trips were made chiefly at night, although, since time was pressing, some crossings had to be made during the day. Allied planes constantly harried the ships and a number of them, laden with troops, received direct hits. However, in sixteen days we managed to evacuate the remnants of nine shattered infantry divisions — 59, 70, 245, 331, 344, 17 Luftwaffe Field, 346, 711 and 712. We left one division in Dunkirk to defend the approaches to Antwerp. In terms of men and equipment we brought to safety by this operation some 65,000 men, 225 guns, 750 trucks and wagons, and 1000 horses. By 21 September my task was completed and the bulk of Fifteenth Army had been rescued from encirclement.

"I was in constant fear that the Allies would cut off the Beveland Isthmus by an advance north of Antwerp and thereby trap such troops as were in the process of moving out. If this had happened our alternative plan was to evacuate the troops by sea through the Dutch islands to Dordrecht and Rotterdam. But such a journey would have been slow and dangerous. It would have meant a twelve-hour voyage by sea rather than the three-quarters of an hour needed to cross from Breskens to Flushing. We could not have hoped to rescue anything but the troops themselves had it been necessary to adopt this course."

If there be one criticism to make of Allied tactics at this stage of the campaign, it was this failure to push on beyond Antwerp shortly after the port had been taken. From 4 September to 21 September no serious effort was made to cover this stretch of twenty miles from Antwerp to the base of the Beveland Isthmus, thereby depriving Fifteenth Army of their only reasonable escape route. True the small British armored spearheads that reached Antwerp were tired after their headlong dash from the Seine, and the long supply haul from Normandy had gravely affected the availability of petrol, food and ammunition for any large-scale operation. Nevertheless with little to

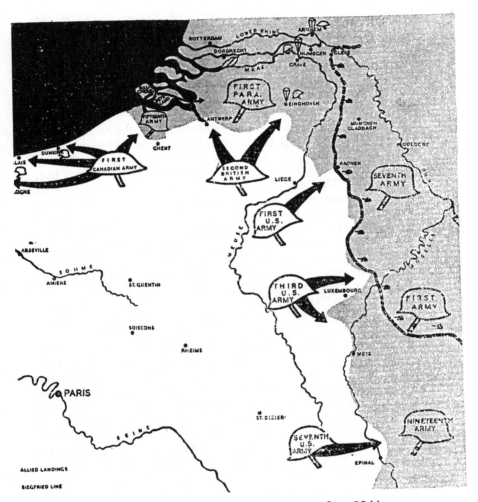

THE RETREAT FROM FRANCE — 17th September, 1944.

oppose them but the hastily assembled infantry troops in Holland, a gamble of this kind might well have paid handsome dividends. Had the Allies bottled up these 65,000 Germans on Walcheren Island or even forced them to take the hazardous sea voyage to Rotterdam, there could never have been an effective German position south of the Maas River. And had this position not existed there might well have been a different outcome to the airborne operation at Arnhem. The fact that no determined effort was made to seal off the escape route of Fifteenth Army is probably a measure of the surprise with which the Allied Supreme Command received the news that Antwerp had been taken.

By the successful evacuation of Fifteenth Army, the establishment of a line north of Antwerp, the holding of the Channel fortresses and the securing of the approaches to the port of Antwerp, the German plan of a continued denial of supply bases to the Allies had been accomplished. The next move was up to the Allies. General Eisenhower in his report to the Combined Chiefs-of-Staff has outlined what that move was to be and the reasons for it.

"It was our plan to attack northeastward in the greatest strength possible," writes the Allied Supreme Commander.[3] "This direction had been chosen for a variety of reasons. First, the great bulk of the German army was located there. Secondly, there was the great desirability of capturing the flying-bomb area, not only to remove this menace to England, but also to deny to the enemy the propaganda which he enjoyed on the home front and in the army from the attacks on London and talk of new weapons which would decide the war. A third reason for the northeastward attack was our imperative need for the large port of Antwerp, absolutely essential to us logistically before any deep penetration in strength could be made into Germany. Fourthly, we wanted the airfields in Belgium. Finally and most important, I felt that during the late summer and early autumn months the Lower Rhine offered the best avenue of advance into Germany, and it seemed probable that through rapidity of exploitation both the Siegfried Line and the Rhine River might be crossed and strong bridgeheads established before the enemy could recover sufficiently to make a definite stand in the Arnhem area."

These aims had only been partly achieved by the end of the first week in September. On the accomplished side were the destruction of a large part of the German forces in the West, the elimination of the flying-bomb sites in Northwestern France and the acquisition of the airfields in Belgium. Yet to be accomplished was the freeing of the approaches to Antwerp, and the establishment of bridgeheads

over the Rhine. Not having sufficient forces or supplies to take on
both these tasks simultaneously, General Eisenhower decided to give
the crossing of the Lower Rhine first priority. In his own words, "The
attractive possibility of quickly turning the German north flank led
me to approve the temporary delay in freeing the vital port of
Antwerp, the seaward approaches to which were still in German
hands." To carry out this intention the airborne operation designed
to capture the bridges over the Maas, the Waal and the Lower Rhine
at Grave, Nijmegen and Arnhem was prepared.

Meanwhile the intelligence staff at the headquarters of the
Commander-in-Chief West was attempting to appreciate just what
the Allied intention would be once the Seine had been crossed. By
making two guesses it got it half right and half wrong. A report
written in late August assessed the most likely Allied course to be an
American thrust through Trier to Mannheim and Darmstadt. The
heavy bombings of cities in the path of such a push, such as Frankfurt-
am-Main, Ludwigshafen and Mainz, together with the fact that
Southern Germany was to be occupied by American troops, were the
reasons for this appreciation.[4]

But simultaneously with this drive into Southern Germany an
airborne landing in the Oldenburg area was predicted. With their
usual tendency to overrate Allied resources, this opinion was based
upon an assessment of five or six airborne divisions believed to be
ready in Britain for such an operation. To meet this possibility troops
had been sent to the threatened area, and they were thus available
when the drop at Arnhem took place.

Having hit upon the correct answer by guessing twice, von Rundstedt's intelligence staff then proceeded to ensure themselves of
infallibility by venturing to suggest a third alternative which the Allies
might take — a push north of Cologne to effect an encirclement of the
Ruhr.[5] On 17 September the Allied airborne troops were dropped at
Eindhoven, Nijmegen and Arnhem to prove that if an intelligence staff
provides enough courses of action it is bound to produce the right one.

There they were confronted by the unexpected divisions of 2 S.S.
Panzer Corps — 9 S.S. and 10 S.S. Panzer Divisions — carrying out
the twofold task of reorganizing their badly beaten units and, at the
same time, standing guard on the Lower Rhine. These experienced
troops, together with a hastily assembled collection of all the available German manpower in Eastern Holland, formed the force which
foiled General Eisenhower's prospects of a speedy advance into the
north German plains. Utilizing the tanks they had managed to
salvage from Normandy and fighting an efficient tactical action, the

Germans finally forced the First British Airborne Division to abandon
the northern bank of the Lower Rhine after eight days of the most
bitter and intensive fighting yet experienced by any Allied troops in
the West. From the German point of view the battle of Arnhem was
the only gleam of light, since the invasion of France, to break through
the rapidly darkening clouds of impending defeat. They tried to make
the most of it. The propaganda merchants shouted themselves hoarse
using Arnhem to prove that Germany was still far from beaten. The
following extracts from an account of the battle of Arnhem by a
German war reporter, Erwin Kirchof, give a reasonable description
of what took place, if one discounts the obvious coloring of many of
the facts.

It was early on the Sunday afternoon of 17 September [the story begins].
The cinemas in the small Dutch towns were slowly filling up, and the streets
and highways, along the canals and small streams, were crowded with
young people on bicycles. And then out of the blue sky roared several
hundred enemy fighter-bombers. Their aim was to attack the German
defensive positions and locate the flak positions. Barely had they disappeared beyond the horizon when, coming from the west across the flooded
coastal areas, appeared the planes and gliders carrying regiments and
brigades of the enemy's airborne army. . . . The first parachute landings
were made on a front of about 70 kilometres and approximately 100 kilometres behind our lines. The troops bailed out from a very low altitude,
sometimes as low as 60 metres. Immediately after that the several hundred
gliders started to land. In those first few minutes it looked as if the down-
coming masses would suffocate every single life on the ground. . . .

Shortly after the landings of the British and American divisions, our
reconnaissance troops went into action. By searching the countless forests
and large parks in that area, cut by numerous small streams, they had to
ascertain where the enemy intended to concentrate his forces; only then
could a basis for our counter-attacks be established. The telephone lines
were cut. The reconnaissance cars could move forward only slowly. Some
of the enemy dug themselves in near their landing places and brought
weapons into position. Others moved up to the houses and barricaded
themselves, using the furniture inside the buildings, From there they tried
to dominate the bridges and beat back our counter-attacks. Elements of the
Dutch population assisted the enemy in their task. . . .

The area in which the landing of the First Airborne Division occurred
had a width of 10 kilometres and a depth of 12 kilometres. In the cold and
rainy night the town of Arnhem was entirely cut off, particularly from the
northwest. On the morning of 18 September the S.S. units arrived from the
north to reinforce the northwestern part of the pocket. . . .

On the right flank, between the railroad tracks and the Rhine, in the residential suburbs of Oosterbeek, the struggle for each building continued for hours. In the narrow streets, hand grenades were thrown from one side of the street to the other. Further down the northern bank of the Rhine the fight for buildings from which the enemy dominated the bridge with his guns, had continued since dawn. Hand-to-hand fighting raged on each floor of the houses. In the power station on the Oost Straat men of the Luftwaffe mounted to the first floor and exchanged hand grenades with the British on the floor above.

In the evening a British radio message was intercepted in which a battalion commander, barricaded with four hundred of his paratroopers in the buildings along the Rhine bridge, asked for the dropping of masonry tools and cement. He intended to build a defensive wall around his positions.

The battles continued deep into the raining night.

19 September. The British airborne division was now encircled in an area of only a few square kilometres, between the railroad line and the Rhine. . . . Artillery and mortar batteries hammered the pocket. Around noon, two British envoys asked for a one-hour armistice to take more than 600 casualties into German hospitals. Their proposal was accepted. A doctor of the Waffen S.S. and a British doctor supervised the transport. Afterwards there were further heavy attacks by the enemy. The number of prisoners rose to 904. Among them was the divisional commander. . . .

20 September. The period of bad weather kept up. Between the railroad track and the Rhine heavy house-to-house fighting continued. . . .

21 September. The British division again received several hundred reinforcements and attempted in desperation to break the ring of iron; but despite this, we compressed the pocket still further. The size of the pocket was now an area of 1200 metres by 750 metres. Mortars, artillery and flak fired into the forests and into the positions in the streets. . . . The number of dead was now extremely high. Our light and medium flak was forced to destroy every single building on the southern bank of the Rhine. . . .

The last hours. In the following days Eisenhower continued to send new parachute battalions and glider units to the encircled remnants of the British division. On the south side of the Lower Rhine, between Nijmegen and Arnhem, a Polish parachute brigade landed with the task of breaking open the ring. Their attack failed. . . . In London they spoke of the crisis of the Lower Rhine, but it was hoped that Dempsey would succeed in saving the remnants of the division. During the night of the 25-26 September, the First British Airborne Division, now only about 400 men strong, attempted to break through from Oosterbeek under cover of American fire and cross the Rhine. The British wrapped rags around their feet and crept upon the asphalt roads to the Rhine bank. Suddenly German mortars caught them. Three, perhaps four, assault boats succeeded in reaching the opposite bank. . . .

Through the Goebbelesque haze of this account, with its obvious distortion of Allied losses, one can nevertheless discern a certain grudging admiration for the fight carried on by the men of the First British Airborne Division. However, that the cost of Arnhem had been high to the Allies is verified by General Eisenhower's own report. According to it, 2163 men of the division managed to escape or withdraw back across the river, while casualties in killed, wounded and missing in this single operation were "some 7000 men."

Officially the German explanation for the Allied defeat at Arnhem is contained in a Luftwaffe intelligence report entitled 'Air Landings in Holland' which was written at the end of October 1944.[6] It recognizes the merit of the plan to seize the principal crossing of the Maas, Waal and Lower Rhine rivers, by asserting that had it succeeded, the Germans would have found it extremely difficult to prevent the Allies from breaking out into the north German plain. It then goes on to give four chief reasons for the failure at Arnhem. In the first place the landings were not concentrated enough: since they were spread out over a period of three days the Germans never faced the entire strength of the British division at one time. Secondly, Allied intelligence was not aware of the location of the 2 S.S. Panzer Corps which was refitting north of Arnhem. Or, if the Allies were aware of this force, they did not make proper dispositions to meet it. The former view, the report believed, was the more likely one. Thirdly, Arnhem was too far from the front; the airborne troops could not hold out long enough for the Allies to break through from the south to link up with them. And fourthly, the bad flying weather following the landings prevented effective re-supply from the air. It also prevented the necessary 'isolation of the battlefield' and direct support of ground operations. If German supply and transport units could have been effectively broken, the Allied force might have been successful.

Yet despite the inability of the Allied troops to take Arnhem, the airborne operation had achieved some useful results. It had driven a wedge into the German northern position, thereby isolating the Fifteenth Army north of Antwerp from the First Parachute Army on the eastern side of the bulge. This segregation from the rest of the German front complicated the supply problem of Fifteenth Army, which was now forced to rely on the inferior crossings over the Maas and the Waal rivers west of the Allied penetration. The capture of these bridgeheads across the Maas and Waal also served as an important base for subsequent operations against the Germans on the Rhine. "The loss of the bridges at Grave and Nijmegen was a great embarrassment to us," said General von Zangen of Fifteenth Army.[7]

"By capturing them the Allies forced us to remain on the defensive in this area in order to prevent this bulge from growing. We were never able to assemble enough troops for a serious counter-attack to retake Antwerp."

Chapter XXIV

THE FORTRESSES

SIMULTANEOUSLY with the decision to drop the Allied airborne troops in Holland, preparations were begun for the clearing of the French ports in Brittany and along the Channel coast. Although the parachute operation had delayed the opening of the port of Antwerp as a main supply base, it had not seriously impeded the plans for the freeing of the subsidiary ports in Northern France. As has already been described, these ports had been designated, long before the invasion, as 'fortresses.' Technically such a term would have been applied only to isolated areas having sufficient concrete, weapons, supplies and men to conduct an all-round defense for a considerable period of time. In practice it came to mean any piece of land which Hitler wanted to be defended "until the last." Few of these ports in France had been properly prepared for their rôle. While strong enough in cement and guns facing the sea, they contained little but hastily-built field defenses to safeguard them from attack from the landward side. And, since it was against their flabbily-protected rear that the Allies concentrated their assaults, the eventual fate of these fortresses was settled with the break-out of the Allied forces from the bridgehead in Normandy.

But the most interesting feature of the battles for the fortresses in France was the reaction of the officers and men locked up within them. With the rapid advance of the Allied columns through France, and the unexpected collapse of all German resistance on the Seine and the Somme rivers, there had been left behind in the ports of St. Nazaire, Lorient, Brest, St. Malo, Le Havre, Boulogne, Calais, Dunkirk and the approaches to Antwerp over 140,000 German troops with no other future but death or a prisoner-of-war camp. In each of these fortresses the commandant had taken an oath, usually in writing, to fight on "until the end." But what 'the end' meant varied with the personality of the commander. To some it meant the end of food, ammunition or adequate weapons with which to fight, to others it meant the end of hope, to still others it meant the end of military logic. To none of them did it mean the end of life itself, even though these very words were used by some of the commanders in the pledges they demanded of the officers under them. At Boulogne, for example, every officer of the garrison signed the following oath before the fortress commander Lieutenant General Ferdinand Heim:

H.Q. Boulogne,
2 *September* 1944.

On 2 September I undertook in the presence of Lieutenant General Heim, commander of the fortress of Boulogne, to hold and defend the strong-point or sector under my command to the end of my life and that of the last man under me.

I am conscious of the great responsibility of my task and of my commitment and I swear to hold and defend the strong-point or sector under my command to the end of my life and that of the last man under me.

Yet despite the twice-repeated vow to die in Boulogne practically every officer whose name appeared on this document turned up hale and hearty in an Allied prison camp — invariably with his personal belongings neatly packed in a conveniently ready suit-case! Along with themselves they brought over 9000 of the men who they had guaranteed were going to die under them.

Whatever aspect of World War II future German historians may attempt to glorify as master feats of arms, the defense of the French ports is not likely to be one of them. The account of the forlorn troops expected to die in the fortresses of Europe displayed none of the heroism, determination and idealism with which Dr. Goebbels tried so hard to clothe it. Rather the story is of lost garrisons fighting a losing cause, and realizing it only too well, and what is more important, not relishing the rôle of martyrs and defenders of the faith which had been suddenly thrust upon them. These men burned with no fierce National Socialist zeal or patriotic Teutonic fervor; they were merely unfortunate troops chosen for this job because they happened to be there. Unable to think for themselves, and capable only of obeying, the quality of their resistance depended chiefly on the ability and fanaticism of the men who led them. Since commandants for lost fortresses were either chosen because they were accidentally in the neighborhood, or someone at Berlin wanted to be rid of them or they could easily be spared, the brand of leadership was not likely to be high. It is in the personality of these men picked to die for the Führer and Germany that some explanation can be found for the uneven quality of the resistance encountered in these so-called fortresses. Let us examine them each in turn.

The fiercest and most stubborn fortress defence was offered by the garrisons of St. Malo and Brest. Assaulted shortly after the break-out from Normandy, the 7000-man garrison of St. Malo had little opportunity to feel itself isolated and besieged. When it was attacked on 14 August substantial German forces were still within rescue distance of the port, for the disaster at Falaise was still a week away. In other words hope had not had time to die, and to continue the fight was therefore natural. The commandant of St. Malo buttressed that hope with orders such as these.

9 August 1944.

To all Soldiers of the Garrison.

From this moment there will be only three types of punishment:

(1) Whoever leaves the corridors of his billets not clean, whoever does not use the W.C. properly, whoever does not take care of his arms, will receive ten to twenty-five strokes on his behind.

(2) Anyone found lacking in interest or showing reluctance in his work, and anyone exhibiting pessimism, will be punished in the following way:

The individual will be chased in broad daylight, without weapons, in the direction of the enemy.

(3) Disobedience and cowardice will be punished by death.

F. AULOCK.

The energetic Colonel Aulock turned out to be much less formidable in a prison camp than he had been in his orders. A tall, be-monocled man with a distinctly Semitic appearance, he persisted in playing the clown amongst his fellow-prisoners, and seemed to find the war and his future prospects an incredibly funny joke. It may well be said that the grim four-day defense of St. Malo, from 14 August to 17 August, was offered in spite of, rather than because of, the activities of the 'mad colonel of St. Malo,' as his men were wont to call him.

The story of Brest was, however, quite different. The Allied assault begun in the last week of August found the going heavy and prolonged. The largest garrison of all the ports, some 30,000 men, was inspired in its stand by the parachute general, Herman Bernhard Ramcke. Like all senior officers in the parachute arm of the service, he was a capable tactician and thoroughly loyal to his Führer. With an exceptional record for bravery, having won the highest award for heroism in the last war, the Pour le Mérite, and done the same again in this one by receiving the Oak Leaves with Swords and Diamonds, Ramcke whipped his men into a frenzy of resistance. His square-jawed, pugnacious face revealed a character that was not loathe to rely on brutality to achieve its ends. It was not until 18 September, after three weeks of house-to-house fighting in the streets of Brest, that the Allies finally gained possession of the port. But the harbor facilities of the city had been so thoroughly destroyed that the Allied plans for its use as a major port had to be abandoned. But even to a man as determined and fanatical as Ramcke, his oath to fight to the end did not really mean to the end of his life. Along with most of the 30,000 men in the garrison, the fortress commandant wended his way to the cold sanctuary of a prisoner-of-war cage. In fact so indifferent was Ramcke to the very letter of his vow that he turned up in Allied hands completely equipped with everything he felt necessary to make his life thoroughly comfortable as a prisoner-of-war. Obviously having been prepared days before the actual capitulation, Ramcke brought along with him into captivity eight large well-packed suitcases, a complete set of delicate china, an elaborate box of expensive fishing tackle together with four long rods, and a thoroughbred setter dog. Hardly the trappings of a man who had resolved to die for his country. To the realistic Ramcke 'the end' was a long way this side of death itself. It probably ranged somewhere between the end of military reason and the end of personal satisfaction.

Before the Seine had been crossed there still remained some visible hope that relief might come to the garrisons of the fortresses of France. But once the front line had been pushed back to the borders of the Reich the possibility of a resurgence of German troops into France, within a reasonable period of time, all but disappeared from the minds of those left behind. Thus morale amongst the troops of Le Havre, Boulogne and Calais, who for the most part had been chased back into their concrete bunkers after experiencing the power of the advancing Allies, was much lower than it had been amongst the men of St. Malo and Brest. The commandants who had been chosen to die with their men in these ports east of the Seine, were not, either by disposition or training, likely to raise that depressed morale.

If you had placed a bowler hat on his head, covered his long thin legs with pin-striped trousers and put a rolled umbrella in his hand, Colonel Eberhard Wildermuth, commandant of Le Havre, would have been indistinguishable from the thousands of bankers, brokers or business men that daily crowd Threadneedle Street. This fifty-five-year-old, tall, skeletal, balding man was primarily a civilian and typified the civilian both in temperament and appearance. Not even the form-fitting, disciplined cut of the German gray-green uniform could make him look like anything else. Between wars, while he had remained an officer on the reserve list, he devoted his activities to a life of business and by 1939 was on the board of directors of one of Berlin's largest banks. After the usual spell of duty on both the Eastern and Western fronts, in which he saw heavy fighting in France, Russia and Italy, he was given a harmless coastal sector to defend in the neighborhood of Venice, Italy. Suddenly on 4 August, for no reason that he knows of, other than the fact that he had been a Social Democrat before the war or had been given four months' leave to recover from battle fatigue and was therefore not considered to be of much further use, he was sent to France for employment as a fortress commandant. On 14 August, hardly two weeks before the city was invested, Wildermuth took over the defense of the bastion of Le Havre.

If the Supreme Command was looking for a fanatical, zealous, feverish young Nazi to inspire German troops to fight to the end, it could have chosen no one less likely to fit the rôle than Colonel Eberhard Wildermuth. He was not young, he was not inspired, he was not a soldier, and what was most important, he was not a Nazi. Nevertheless, the polite, tired, efficient bank director was suddenly shunted from Italy to this fortress in France, and ordered to perform a fight-to-the-death task for the glory of the Fatherland. Small wonder the martyr's crown rested uneasily on his head, and so readily slipped off when events hemmed him in.

A two-divisional British assault, following the dropping of some 11,000 tons of bombs in Le Havre, was launched on 10 September. By noon on 12 September, forty-eight hours later, the port had capitulated and 11,300 German troops had laid down their arms. This, despite the fact that the defenses available were amongst the strongest in Europe, that ammunition was plentiful for the 115 guns in Le Havre, and that sufficient food was on hand to keep 14,000 soldiers for eighty-nine more days. The explanation for this speedy collapse lies in the commandant's personal conception of what 'the end' really meant. "In my opinion it was futile to fight tanks with bare hands," said Colonel Wildermuth.[1] "As early as 9 September I had given orders to all my officers that Allied infantry attacks were to be opposed everywhere, even with the side arms only. But in the event of an attack by tanks, resistance nests which no longer had any anti-tank weapons were then at liberty to surrender."

Thus the Colonel had transformed the Supreme Command's precept of fight to the last man to his own concept of fight to the last anti-tank gun. The difference was fundamental. It marked the civilian from the soldier. For Wildermuth, with his banker's mind, was a soldier only so long as it was reasonable to remain one. Once the cost in blood and pain was too much, he felt it was time to become a civilian again. He was an efficient, able man who carried efficiency and ability into battle with him in much the same way as he would have used them to draw up a balance-sheet. He was not mentally prepared to sacrifice the lives of his men for a philosophy in which he only half-heartedly believed. It is in the personality of the leader of the garrison of Le Havre that lies much of the explanation for the fall of this formidable fortress in less than forty-eight hours.

Having freed Le Havre, the First Canadian Army, which had been given the task of clearing the northern coast of France of these stubborn centers of German resistance, next turned its attention to the port of Boulogne. Here again the garrison was pledged to fight until the last man. Their inspiration in this stand was the professional General Staff officer, Lieutenant General Ferdinand Heim, who at the age of fifty could well be taken for a man ten years younger. With this thin, pinched face and prominent blue eyes he resembled a somewhat larger version of Goebbels.

The presence of a high-ranking officer like Heim in the forlorn job of a fortress commandant illustrates the method by which Hitler disposed of men who had become an embarrassment to him. Heim was first and foremost a careful, methodical staff officer who at the height of his power was undoubtedly a cold and efficient machine. As Chief-of-Staff to General von Reichenau he played an important part in drafting the plan for the invasion of Russia. Having led a panzer division with distinction in the battles for Kharkov and Rostov, Heim, on 1 November 1942, was promoted to the command of 48 Panzer Corps which formed part of the Sixth German Army of Field Marshal Paulus, then besieging Stalingrad.

A few days later the corps was taken from Paulus and attached to the Third Roumanian Army, which was given a sector to defend in the neighbourhood of Kalatz on the Don River. To carry out this task Heim was given two Roumanian divisions and one German division. The Roumanian formations were hopelessly equipped with outmoded weapons and little ammunition. They were particularly weak in anti-tank guns with which to stop the Russian armor, and as a result the Russians broke through Heim's sector and by sweeping south succeeded in encircling the complete German Sixth Army investing Stalingrad. From this military disaster the Wehrmacht never recovered, and the magnitude of the fiasco made it essential that some scapegoat be found to shoulder the blame. Heim was arrested in January 1943 and sent to an Investigation Prison where he spent five months.

"During this period," said the general,[2] "I never saw any formal indictment against me, nor was a sentence ever promulgated, nor an inquiry held, nor an explanation given to me for my being imprisoned. The only document I ever saw was the Führer's order for my incarceration, and the reason for it I only learned subsequently as a result of conversations with high-ranking friends. Apparently, Antonescu, the chief of the Roumanian state, had warned Hitler, prior to Stalingrad, about the inefficiency of the Roumanian divisions and the danger of placing them in a vulnerable spot. After the catastrophe, Hitler felt that some gesture had to be made to Antonescu involving a senior German officer, who could be blamed for the blunder. This would also act as a deterrent to failure in the future. Since the divisional commanders involved were Roumanians their heads could not roll. Since efficient army and army group commanders were becoming scarce, the Supreme Command could not afford the luxury of throwing one of these men into jail. The only person left was the corps commander, and that was me."

Following his five months' internment, the general was suddenly released, still without any explanation, and sent to Ulm where as a comparatively young man he lived the life of a retired officer, drawing all the while the pension of a lieutenant general. Here he remained from May 1943 until August 1944, when he was rudely jolted out of this quiet existence and told to take over command of the fortress of Boulogne. Since this was understood to be a 'defend to the last' task, it was obvious that someone at Berlin had not forgotten Ferdinand Heim.

When Heim arrived at Boulogne in late August, like Wildermuth only a few weeks before the post was cut off and surrounded, he found that little had been done to prepare the fortress for defense against a land attack. He had received instructions from Fifteenth Army to build a defensive zone to a depth of ten kilometres around the town. In this area all bridges were to be blown, buildings torn down and mines laid. So vast a job required hundreds of trained engineers, which Heim did not have. "I merely put a big red circle on my map," he remarked cynically, "to show that the demolitions theoretically had been carried out."

The feelings of the men bottled up in these cement posts can best be described as resigned. Many of them felt they were being uselessly squandered when the same long-term results could have been achieved by effectively destroying the harbor installations. But although they felt embittered and hopeless they were incapable of any form of resistance to their fate other than the muttering of complaints to one another and the writing of depressing letters and personal diaries. The following extracts from a diary written by a German officer during the siege of Boulogne graphically portrays this atmosphere of despondency and stolid fatalism: [3]

7 September 44. Encircled in Boulogne. For days I knew that there was no getting out of it for us. It is very hard to get used to the thought of having one's span of life nearly finished, and not to see one's wife and children again. If Fate is favorable I may become a prisoner-of-war. . . .

9 September 44. Last night was comparatively quiet. Yesterday, late in the afternoon, enemy bombers attacked the forward defensive positions of Boulogne. My God, how long will it be until the town itself will be the target? Can anyone survive after a carpet of bombs has fallen? Sometimes one can despair of everything if one is at the mercy of the R.A.F. without any protection. It seems as if all fighting is useless and all sacrifices in vain. . . .

11 September 44. We have lovely weather again today with a brilliant sun in a cloudless sky. How wonderful life could be for humanity if there wasn't a war. Will there ever be peace again? All day long artillery fire in our outlying strong-points and, in between, attacks by fighter-bombers. The outskirts are being evacuated by the French. I wonder if that means that the real show will start tonight? The morale of the troops is bad, and no wonder. They are mostly old married men and the situation is quite hopeless. . . .

12 September 44. Dear diary, I am glad to have you. It quietens me to put down my thoughts, which usually go out to family and country. The inexorable enemy stands on the borders of the Fatherland. Will it be possible to hold him there? Woe to my country should we lose this war. Life will not be worth living then. What will become of our children?

13 September 44. Alcohol is the only thing which can comfort anyone in our position. . . . This afternoon more heavy air attacks on the outer defenses of Boulogne. Most of the civilians have wandered off with bits of their belongings. What a tragic spectacle. When will tormented humanity have peace again. . . ?

14 September 44. At the harbor command everyone is desperately gay and tries to drown all worries in alcohol. And these filthy jokes which aren't even funny! I'll be glad to get away from there. . . .

15 September 44. I wonder how my family is. No mail from home now for six weeks. That is the hardest of all to take. . . .

16 September 44. Last night I visited Lt. Hauptman with whom I had bunked for so long. He is in the same state of mind as I am — very depressed. . . .

17 September 44. It is nine months today since I last went on leave. What a good time I had. And today what a contrast. I was just ready to go to breakfast when we had to run for shelter and we have been there ever since. The bombardment by bombers and artillery was terrific. It is four o'clock in the afternoon now. I am looking at your pictures, my loved ones. I am

quiet now and resigned to my fate whatever it may be. Farewell, my dear
ones, I pray to God that He may protect and guide you. . . . All afternoon
a heavy artillery barrage fell on our positions. We could not move. Then
we heard tanks approaching and had to surrender. It is a wonder that we
are still alive. . . .

This then was the mood and experience of one of the valiant
defenders of Boulogne who had taken an oath before General Heim
to hold his strong-point "to the end of my life and that of the last
man under me." Nowhere in the document is there that determination
and will to fight to the death that Hitler had demanded of his followers. Rather it sighs an uneasy hope that fate be kind and preserve
the writer for the security of an Allied prisoner-of-war camp. With
this pessimism and lack of enthusiasm permeating the garrison of
Boulogne, it is understandable that when the fortress capitulated on
23 September, after a six-day assault by the Canadians, over 9500
German soldiers had decided that life as a prisoner was better than
death as a martyr. And this decision was arrived at even though the
defending forces had suffered very few dead and wounded, and
when, according to General Heim himself, the total casualties had
been "astonishingly light." Heim vigorously denied that 'defend to
the end' meant to him to defend 'to the last man,' but rather 'to
the last bullet.' This despite the vow he had forced the men under
him to take where the words 'end of my life' were used. When I
decided that the situation was hopeless from a military standpoint,"
said the commandant of Boulogne, "I felt I could lay down my charge
with a clear conscience." Heim also forgot to mention that his personal experiences with National Socialism had made it most unlikely
that he would be burning with any fervent desire to die for that
ideology.

Heim had thought often about this inconsistency between his
oath to die fighting and his decision to live instead. "It is difficult
for us Western people to sacrifice our lives when the situation is hopeless," he said, "and that is the main reason for my troops surrendering
rather than dying in their bunkers. The farther east you go the less
important death becomes. The Japanese have no fear of death at
all, and the Russians have almost none. In England and America life
is very precious, and everything is done in wartime to preserve it
and prevent its needless waste. We Germans stand in the middle."[4]

The next hole to be smoked out along the Channel coast was the
port of Calais. This fortress with its huge 21-centimetre and 38-centi-
metre naval guns had made itself a particular nuisance to the inhabitants of Southern England. Ever since the fall of France these monster
weapons had pestered Allied shipping passing through the narrow

Straits of Dover, and had punctuated life in the city of Dover with the unpleasant sound of whistling shells, haphazard explosions and interminable alerts. Now its turn had also come. The Canadians methodically taking on each port in turn, and thoroughly preparing each assault, were becoming expert at the technique of digging out the reluctant German occupants of these concrete bunkers. To face them at Calais and the neighboring strong-point of Cap Gris Nez were some 9000 members of the Wehrmacht led by Lieutenant Colonel Ludwig Schroeder.

If the presence of Lieutenant General Heim symbolized the defense of Boulogne as a lost cause, the personality of the commandant of Calais presaged a useless one. For it cannot be assumed that much importance was attached to the defense of Calais when so mediocre and accidental a leader as Ludwig Schroeder was designated to hold it. Not only was his rank comparatively low for a large-scale, ideological stand, but he was assigned the rôle merely because he happened to be around and not because he was endowed with any special abilities for it. At forty-three his rather large, long-jawed face was both tired and resigned. After an unimpressive military career in the East he was posted to the 59 Infantry Division in the Pas de Calais. When this division evacuated Calais on 30 August 1944, Schroeder was left behind to carry out the last-ditch defense of the port.

The story of Calais is almost a replica of that of Boulogne and Le Havre. A bag of mail written by the beleaguered troops in Calais was captured on its way to Germany. The letters therein reflect the same mood of apathy and resignation already seen in the other fortresses. The following letter written by a corporal to his parents was indicative of the general tone of these last messages.

4 September 44. I am still alive. Perhaps this is my last letter to all of you. We are in the port of Calais and expect to be encircled very soon. The ring will soon be getting smaller. How we shall all end I don't know — death or imprisonment. Our strong-points have been left in a panic, hence no ink. Demolitions are going on day and night and the town looks like Stalingrad. Yes! the Atlantic Wall is no more. The average soldier is not to blame for this mess. I never thought that things would turn out this way. I would not like to see all those who have been killed. I have seen scenes which can hardly be described. . . .

Thus, when the Canadians launched their assault against Calais on 25 September they met a foe as unwilling to die for the Fatherland as the defenders of Boulogne. A five-day battle and 9100 sound, healthy, somewhat shaken Germans languished behind the barbed wire of a field prisoner-of-war cage.

Like the commandants of Le Havre and Boulogne, Schroeder had not taken his oath 'to fight to the end' literally. "Although it was probably understood that I was to resist to the last man," said Schroeder,[5] trying to hide behind a technicality, "I never actually saw a written order to this effect. I admit that my action in surrendering the port after having suffered so few casualties would likely have rendered me liable to a court-martial for disobeying orders. But I had little ammunition with which to continue firing my guns, and the standard of my troops was too low to have maintained any prolonged resistance." The commandant of Calais neglected to mention, however, that Lieutenant Colonel Ludwig Schroeder was hardly the kind of leader to inspire his men to those heights of sacrifice and valor he so bitterly resented their not having attained.

With the fall of Calais there remained only four surviving outposts of coastal resistance in France — Lorient, St. Nazaire, Quiberon Bay and Dunkirk. The bitter opposition at Brest and the thoroughly demolished state of its harbor facilities when it was taken had deterred General Eisenhower from wasting men, material and time in an effort to reduce the remaining Brittany ports. Although letters and prisoners indicated a somewhat similar state of morale amongst the 12,000 troops in Dunkirk as had been found in the other Channel ports, the Allied Supreme Commander did not feel that more forces should be diverted to acquire another small harbor on the northern coast of France. Instead these remaining remnants of Hitler's ambitious fortress plan were surrounded with sufficient troops to keep them within the confines of their bunkers, thereby locking up another 50,000 men of the Reich almost as effectively as if they had been in Allied hands. They spent the balance of the war listening to their commandants exhorting them not to desert, reading Allied propaganda on how nice it was to desert, sheltering themselves from constant air and artillery bombardment, carrying out sporadic raids to supplement their dwindling food supply, and apprehensively awaiting a large-scale Allied assault. On the whole they would have been much happier in a prisoner-of-war camp.

But the acquisition of a series of small ports, so badly demolished that they would require weeks of repair before they could be put to any use, did not solve the formidable supply problem facing the Allies in late September 1944. The only harbor large enough to sustain adequately a fighting force of over two million men was that at Antwerp. Depending upon rail and road traffic to bring up the food, ammunition and petrol from the bases at Cherbourg and the Normandy beaches was already beginning to slow down the speed of the wide-spread Allied armies. The decision to launch the airborne operation in Holland had already resulted in a delay in the opening of Antwerp, and now General Eisenhower instructed the Northern Group of Armies to undertake such an operation "as a matter of first priority."

Although the German High Command in the West had been thoroughly surprised by the sudden capture of the city of Antwerp with its harbor installations practically intact, they had managed to recover quickly. Taking advantage of the opportunity given them to allow Fifteenth Army to escape across the Scheldt Estuary, the Germans had left behind two infantry divisions to hold the north and south shores of this sea-lane leading into the port itself. With his usual mania for having men die where they stood, Hitler had designated these two areas protecting the approaches to Antwerp as fortresses. This meant, of course, that everyone from the divisional commander down had to swear to defend his position to the last. As a matter of fact the oath taken on Walcheren Island, north of the Scheldt, was even more specific and detailed than usual, with its opening paragraph containing the following words: "I am pledged to hold this fortified sector to the last, even to sacrifice my own life. Even if the enemy should already have broken through on my right and left, I am not empowered to give up this sector or to negotiate with the enemy." It was thus becoming more and more difficult to rationalize about the meaning of the phrase 'to the end.'

This formidable task of rooting out the defenders of the approaches to Antwerp was again allotted to the First Canadian Army. It was a much more severe test than the Channel ports had been, for the ground was criss-crossed with innumerable canals and streams, making the deployment of armor extremely difficult. In addition, extensive flooding was carried on by both sides whenever the tactical situation required it. South of the Scheldt this land, which had been reclaimed from the sea, was inundated by the Germans blowing the dykes, while north of the Scheldt, on Walcheren Island, the Allies breached the dykes by an intensive air bombing program. These flooding operations, designed on the part of the Allies to flush the Germans out of the dangerous coastal bunkers they so securely occupied, resulted in a battle that raged for days in fields almost waist-high with water.

The importance of Antwerp to future Allied operations was not lost upon the German Command. On 7 October 1944, a day after the start of the Canadian attempt to clear the south shore of the Scheldt, General von Zangen of Fifteenth Army issued an order frankly explaining to his troops the significance of the port of Antwerp. The fact that such a message as the following be necessary at all is a measure of the defeatist talk then current amongst the troops given this unhappy assignment.

Commander-in-chief Fifteenth Army.

Army Headquarters,
7 *October* 1944.

ORDERS.

The defense of the approaches to Antwerp represents a task which is decisive for the further conduct of the war. Therefore, every last man in the fortification is to know why he must devote himself to this task with the utmost strength. I have confirmed that so-called 'experts' among the local population are attempting to confuse the German soldiers in this battle task ordered by the Führer.

Whether know-it-alls in some headquarters are participating in such nonsense, which then quickly reaches the troops, I do not know. This, I have reason, however, to fear. Therefore, I order commanders, as well as the National Socialist indoctrination officers, to instruct the troops in the clearest and most factual manner on the following points: Next to Hamburg, Antwerp is the largest port in Europe. . . .

After overrunning the Scheldt fortifications, the English would finally be in a position to land great masses of material in a large and completely protected harbor. With this material they might deliver a death blow to the north German plateau and to Berlin before the onset of winter.

In order to pretend that the battle of Antwerp is unimportant and to shake the morale of its defenders, enemy propaganda maintains that the Anglo-American forces already possess sufficient ports which are intact, with the result that they are not at all dependent on Antwerp. That is a known lie. In particular, the port of Ostend, of which the enemy radio speaks frequently, is completely destroyed. Current delays in the enemy's conduct of the war are attributable in great measure to the fact that he still must bring all his supplies through the improvised facilities of Cherbourg. As a result, he has even had to lay a temporary oil pipe-line from these to the interior of France. . . .

In his last speech, Churchill said again, "before the storms of winter we must bring in the harvest in Europe." The enemy knows that he must assault the European fortress as speedily as possible before its inner lines of resistance are built up and occupied by new divisions. For this reason he needs the Antwerp harbor. And for this reason, we must hold the Scheldt fortifications to the end. The German people is watching us. In this hour, the fortifications along the Scheldt occupy a rôle which is decisive for the future of our people. Each additional day that you deny the port of Antwerp to the enemy and to the resources that he has at his disposal, will be vital.

(Signed) VON ZANGEN,
General of the Infantry.

Inspired by this reasoning and being led by an efficient, ruthless officer, Lieutenant General Eberding, the forces south of the Scheldt desperately resisted Canadian efforts to push them back into the sea. The men who staged this admirable piece of defensive fighting were of a much different calibre to the troops locked in the Channel fortresses. They belonged to the newly-constituted 64 Infantry Division, which was one of a group of formations hastily assembled in Germany and rushed to France to help patch the deteriorating Western front following the break-through in Normandy. It was known as a 'leave' division since the bulk of its members were veterans of the Russian, Italian or Norwegian theatres who were home on leave during the latter part of July 1944. Utilizing their experience to the full they took advantage of the flooded terrain in which they fought and forced the Canadians to rely on the narrow roads and dykes for their forward movement. The morale of the defenders heightened with each day that they continued to resist, and General Eberding succeeded in instilling in his troops that will to fight which had been lacking in the Channel ports. He had not, of course, managed to carry out his oath to the very letter, for 13,000 German prisoners were taken in this long, drawn-out battle, but he had imposed a considerable delay on the Allied plans for the use of Antwerp, and had inflicted considerable casualties on the attackers. This was all that any reasonable man could ask, but reasonableness no longer mattered to the German Supreme Command.

North of the Scheldt, on the islands of Walcheren and South Beveland, one of the most curious collections of men ever assembled together to represent a fighting unit stood ready to meet the Allied shortage that such a formation as 70 Infantry Division should have been given an important rôle to play in the defense of the most significant military prize in the West. For of the 10,000 men which constituted this division almost all suffered from stomach ailments of one form or another. After five years of nervous tension, bad food, and hard living conditions, the Wehrmacht found itself swamped with soldiers complaining of internal gastric trouble. Some of these were real, others were feigned. It was difficult to check.

As defeat became more and more imminent and life at the front more dangerous and more uncomfortable, the rise in the number of men reporting themselves as chronic stomach sufferers became alarming. With the staggering losses in Russia and France, it was no longer possible to discharge this huge flood of groaning manpower from military service. On the other hand their presence in a unit of healthy men was a constant source of dissatisfaction and unrest, for they required special food, constantly asked to be sent on leave, continually reported themselves to the doctor, and grumbled unceasingly about their plight. It was thus decided by the Supreme Command to concentrate all these unfortunates into special Stomach (Magen) battalions where their food could be supervised and their tasks made lighter. It was originally intended to use these troops for rear-area duties only, but as the need for additional men became increasingly critical these units were sent forward for front-line duty as well.

On Walcheren Island, following the Allied invasion, it was decided to replace the previous normal infantry division with a complete division formed from these Stomach battalions. By the beginning of August 1944, the transformation was complete. Occupying the bunkers of the polderland of Walcheren Island and pledged to carry on to the very end were stomachs with chronic ulcers, stomachs with acute ulcers, wounded stomachs, nervous stomachs, sensitive stomachs, dyspeptic stomachs, inflamed stomachs — in fact the whole gamut of gastric ailments. Here in the rich garden country of Holland, where white bread, fresh vegetables, eggs and milk abounded, these men of 70 Infantry Division, soon nicknamed the 'White Bread Division,' awaited the impending Allied attack with their attention nervously divided between the threat of enemy action and the reality of their own internal disorders.

The man chosen to lead this formation of convalescents through their travail was the mild-looking, elderly Lieutenant General Wilhelm Daser. His small, peaked nose, his horn-rimmed glasses and his pink, bald head effectively hid his military identity. Only a firm, loud voice accustomed to giving orders betrayed it. Like the other fortress commanders he was chosen for his final military rôle because he could easily be spared, not because he had any particular qualifications for the task. The tremendous wastage of senior officers incurred by the Wehrmacht in Russia and North Africa was the prime reason for Daser's being called out of semi-retirement in February 1944, to take over a static coastal division in Holland. His last active field command had been in 1941 when he had been sent back to Germany because of heart trouble. The years between had been spent as a military administrator of civilians in occupied territory. Now, at sixty years of age, he had neither the enthusiasm, the zeal nor the ability to make of Walcheren a memorable epic of German arms — but neither had most generals of the Wehrmacht in the declining months of 1944.

Faced with extensive flooding caused by the breaching of the

Walcheren dykes, with synchronized attacks by land along the Beveland Isthmus and by sea at Flushing and Westkapelle, and with the rumblings of their own uneasy stomachs, the men of the 'White Bread Division' hung on to their favorable defensive positions from 24 October to 9 November. Had they been better troops and had they been more inspiringly led it is beyond doubt that these islands, ideally designed for defense, with their only approaches either by sea or through narrow defiles of flooded land, would have presented a much more serious obstacle to the Allied amphibious forces engaged. As it was, the land batteries of the island inflicted heavy casualties on the landing craft of the assaulting British commandos and marines, while the many German strongpoints on both Walcheren and Beveland swept the flat land in front of them with severe and raking fire. When the two-week battle was over another 10,000 German prisoners were making their way back to Allied prison cages and a finish to their diet of noodles, white bread and milk.

Thus ended the major struggle for the fortresses of Belgium and France. On 26 November, after the Scheldt Estuary had been cleared of mines, the first Allied ships began to unload their cargoes on the docks of Antwerp. A steady flow of supplies to the Allied armies for the balance of the campaign in Northwest Europe was now assured. To prevent those supplies from reaching France, the German Supreme Command had sacrificed over 165,000 men, if one includes the 25,000 Germans left behind in the Channel Islands. In return they had managed to inflict about a two-months delay on Allied operations in the West. The question remains — was it worth it? Men like von Rundstedt, Blumentritt, Heim think the same results could have been achieved much more cheaply by thoroughly destroying the harbor facilities of the minor ports, evacuating their garrisons and concentrating on the defense of Antwerp alone. It is difficult not to agree with them.

Chapter XXV

MANNING THE SIEGFRIED LINE

BUT whether or not the price in manpower had been too high, there is no doubt that by the end of September the German Command in the West had succeeded in effectively checking the headlong rush of the Allied armies. In the north the luckily salvaged Fifteenth Army and the newly-formed First Parachute Army constituted a tight girdle around the Allied bulge created by the airborne operations in Holland,

and prevented any further expansion by British and Canadian troops either to the north or to the east. In the center, Seventh Army, which had been speedily reorganized from the new forces acquired in Germany by the latest total mobilization effort of the Nazis, re-occupied the long-vacant bunkers of the Siegfried Line and held the First U.S. Army, which had crossed the German border in the area of Trier on 11 September and near Aachen on 12 September. In the southern sector the improvised forces of the German First and Nineteenth Armies, by using the Moselle River and the Vosges Mountains as delaying barriers, had managed to establish a line ranging from thirty to sixty miles west of the German frontier. Here, although they were early forced to give up the line of the Moselle River south of Metz, these German formations contrived to stop the eastward advance of the Third U.S., Seventh U.S. and French First Armies, which had linked forces in strength on 21 September in the area west of Epinal.

From a German standpoint the situation was more tidy than it had been since the American break-through at St. Lô in July. But to achieve this stabilized front the German armies in the West had lost in prisoners alone, and in the single month of September, the incredible sum of 345,000 men, or an average of almost 11,500 soldiers — a good-sized division — for every day of that month. This brought the total number of prisoners-of-war taken since D-Day to well over the half-million mark. Add to this figure the dead and wounded suffered in France, and Hitler's intuitive strategy had cost the German Reich approximately one million able-bodied men in less than four months.

That the German armies in the West were able to recover their balance after coming so close to toppling over completely, was due to a variety of factors. The first, and foremost, was undoubtedly the difficult Allied supply problem which had not yet been eased by the capture of the port of Antwerp. Instead of being able to maintain a simultaneous offensive of all the mechanized forces of the Allies that stretched from the Swiss to the Dutch borders, it was only possible to ration petrol and ammunition to one group of armies at a time. Thus the Allied forward movement during September and October took on the aspect of a series of alternating, jerking jabs up and down the front, wherever sufficient material had been assembled to ensure a reasonable tactical advance. Using the well-known fire-brigade tactics of Normandy days, the German Command rushed their available reserves to each of these conflagrations in turn, and thereby prevented them from achieving more than limited success.

The second factor that was instrumental in saving the German armies in the West in the fall of 1944 was the Siegfried Line. The construction of this well-publicized system of fortifications had begun in 1936 immediately after the reoccupation of the demilitarized Rhineland, and had been feverishly worked upon until the fall of France in 1940. Closely following the 1939 German frontier, the line extended approximately 350 miles from the Swiss border opposite Basle to the junction of the Belgian, Dutch and German borders at München-Gladbach. From there north to Cleve little had been accomplished in the way of deep concrete shelters, and at this end the line rather tapered off into a series of isolated bunkers and field fortifications.

The Siegfried Line varied in depth, strength and effectiveness from place to place along its entire length. Thus, in the area of the Saar where it was at its strongest, it achieved a depth of nearly three miles. Forts were scattered in profusion in this sector attaining a density of about forty forts per 1000 square yards. In contrast to this, the line along the Rhine from Karlsruhe to Basle was only about a half-mile deep and contained only two rows of forts. In the area of Aachen, where the Allies had first reached this belt of fortifications, the Siegfried Line consisted of two thin strings of forts with little density or depth.

The forts themselves were of different designs, but they were usually manned by either machine-gun or anti-tank gun crews, and sited to produce a closely interlocked zone of fire. The roofs and walls were built of cement some five feet thick, and their average size was about thirty-five feet by forty-five feet. The normal complement of men for such forts was about ten, and they lived a damp and cold existence in them. When a battle was at its height, it was considered suicide to vacate one of these bunkers, because Allied artillery and mortar fire was centered on the entrances. Not daring to leave their shelters, even for the purpose of relieving themselves, unbearable sanitary conditions were soon added to the other discomforts of the inmates.

Although no new work had been done on the Siegfried Line after May 1940, and a large amount of the wire had been removed and the mines lifted in the intervening years, this system of fortifications still presented a formidable barrier in the fall of 1944. When the Allies crossed the Seine, engineers and construction troops were rushed to the German frontier in a feverish effort to renovate and improve the long-disused fortifications. From the Fatherland every able-bodied man was hurried forward to be ensconced in the cement bunkers and there they were exhorted to stem the impending invasion of the Reich. The Siegfried Line was now Germany's last hope. On 15 September Field Marshal von Rundstedt issued the following concise order:

1. The Siegfried Line is of decisive importance in the battle for Germany.
2. I order:
The Siegfried Line and each of its defensive fortresses will be held to the last round and until completely destroyed.
3. This order will be communicated forthwith to all headquarters, military formations, battle commanders and troops.

Note the wording of this order—"to the last man" had been replaced by the more practical "to the last round." And from behind their hastily-occupied concrete forts these new troops fighting well on their own soil managed to check an immediate invasion of the Fatherland. But it is extremely unlikely that their efforts would have been of much avail had Allied supplies been able to keep up with Allied armored columns.

The third factor, along with the Allied supply problem and the Siegfried Line, that contributed to Germany's ability to drag the war in the West into another winter, was the fine methodical hand of von Rundstedt. Having been given *carte blanche* to withdraw his forces to the borders of the Reich, the old man set about his task with the coolness and efficiency of a man who knew what he was about. Deciding that the Maas River in the north, the Siegfried Line in the center, and the Moselle and the Vosges Mountains in the south offered the most effective geographical barriers, he ordered his armies to take up sectors along these lines as quickly as they could. Immediately behind these positions he set to work filling up and reorganizing the shattered remnants of the divisions beaten in Normandy. As soon as a unit was even a semblance of its former self, it was shoved into the West Wall where it completed its training and reformation. By the end of September his front line looked neat enough to pass an examination of the General Staff College.

The Field Marshal himself, however, had no illusions as to the ability of this improvised line to do more than temporarily stabilize the situation. "I realized that when I took over again in September the situation was very serious indeed," said von Rundstedt.[1] "I told those about me that if I was not interfered with and that if I were given the necessary forces I believed I could hold the enemy outside the frontier of the Reich for a while. I knew that a war of position was impossible for any length of time, and that with your superiority in material and manpower you could effect a break-through at any point where you chose to concentrate your forces. I knew there was not a chance of winning the war, but I hoped that if I held out as long as possible some political turn of events might have prevented a complete German collapse. A military victory was out of the question."

Von Rundstedt was equally frank in his estimate of the conduct of Allied operations following the break-through in Normandy. In view of the many post-war criticisms of Allied strategy during this stage of the campaign, his remarks are of considerable interest.

"Any suggestion that the Allies could have advanced faster than they did in September is nonsense," he said.[2] "On the contrary they went much faster than was actually expected. I certainly did not expect you to push into the Reich as early as September or October. There is only one possibility by which things might have been speeded up and that would have been a second landing in the north rather than in the Mediterranean. As far as I was concerned the war was ended in September."

But the question might well be asked where were the new German soldiers coming from to replace those that had been lost? The Russian summer offensive, begun two weeks after the invasion of France, on 23 June, had advanced over 300 miles from Vitebsk to the outskirts of Warsaw by early August. Having paused for breath, the Russian armies had renewed their forward thrust in October, although this time confining their operations to the Finnish and Balkan sectors. These events, in addition to driving the Germans back to within striking distance of their own eastern frontier, had also brought about the defection of three former satellites: Finland, Roumania and Bulgaria. In the process almost fifty German divisions were destroyed.

The Italian theatre offered little more consolation to the Supreme Command. Having abandoned Rome on 4 June, Field Marshal Kesselring had been extremely busy trying to pull his forces back to his next defensive position — the Gothic Line — north of Florence. Florence itself fell on 22 August and in early October Kesselring was using all his ready troops to meet a threatening Allied bulge towards Bologna. He had managed to send along two or three divisions to von Rundstedt in September but anything more would have been likely to have seriously weakened his position.

Thus with both the Russian and Italian campaigns demanding not fewer, but more, German soldiers, the desperate need for men to hold the Siegfried Line had to be met from within the manpower pool still available in the Fatherland itself. Curiously enough this was still relatively large. The new mobilization efforts announced by Goebbels on 24 August 1944 showed that large sections of the population had still been allowed to carry on non-essential activities even though the Reich was desperately fighting for its life. Women, for example, had never been asked to make anything like the effort demanded of them in Great Britain. Some extracts from this announcement show what new funds of manpower Germany was still able to tap.

"The whole of Germany's cultural life has been maintained, even in the fifth year of war, to an extent which the other belligerents did not reach even in times of peace," Goebbels began. "The total war effort of the German people now necessitates far-reaching restrictions in this field as in others. . . . All theatres, music halls, cabaret shows and schools of acting are to be closed by 1 September. All schools of music, academies, art colleges and art exhibitions will be closed down. Only scientific and technical literature, armament and school books, as well as certain standard political works will be published: all other types of literature will be suspended. . . .

"Trade schools of no direct war importance, e.g. domestic and commercial colleges, will be closed. At the universities male and female students who are studying subjects which are not of direct importance to the war will be available for employment in the arma- ment industry. These measures will make available a total of several hundred thousand persons. . . .

"In order fully to utilize all labor, working hours in public admin- istration and offices in industry and trade have been fixed uniformly at a minimum of sixty hours per week. . . .

"In order to bring civilians in line with the soldiers, a universal temporary ban on holidays is ordered with immediate effect. Women who will be 50 and men who will be 65 or over on 31 December are exempt from this ban. . . ."

As a result of this thorough comb-out it was hoped not only to rebuild the divisions destroyed on the Eastern and Western fronts, but also to form between twenty and twenty-five new divisions rather wishfully called Volksgrenadier (People's infantry) divisions. These Volksgrenadier divisions, containing about 8000 men and therefore about half the size of a pre-war infantry division, were formed out of the non-essential factory workers, the small shop-keepers, the petty officials who had been finally forced to take their place in the Wehr- macht after managing for five years to convince the Nazi authorities of their indispensability elsewhere. After a few weeks of elementary training these green formations were sent to fill the bunkers of the Siegfried Line. As fighting material such troops were unlikely to reassure the hard-pressed commanders at the front attempting to stave off the coming invasion of Germany.

As well as forming these new Volksgrenadier divisions, frantic efforts were made to reorganize and refit the divisions that had succeeded in escaping to the German frontier. Some 300,000 men had been salvaged from the holocaust in France, but the bulk of them had made their way back in isolated groups completely cut off from their parent formations. Now it was necessary to reassemble them into proper formations so that some semblance of control could be exercised over this aimless mass of men. Divisional staffs, having been sent to a reforming area, were given complete authority to recruit to their formations any unattached German soldier found in their areas. A staff officer of 17 S.S. Panzer Grenadier Division has given an excellent account of how this was done. Having arrived in Normandy only a few days after the Allied invasion, this division had experienced both the early defeats and the final retreat. After being chased across France from St. Lô to Metz, 17 S.S. Panzer Grenadier Division was ordered to proceed to Merzig in the Saar, where it was to be reformed.

"Only a few bedraggled remnants arrived in Merzig," wrote this officer.[3] "No human account could ever describe the hardship, the sacrifice, the misery the men of this division alone experienced. No one who finished this retreat still alive will ever forget this Gethsemane, because each village, each road, even each bush has seared into his brain the memories of terrible hours, insufferable misery, of cowardice, despair and destruction. . . . In the reforming area all means were employed to get the division back on its feet. Every available officer of the divisional staff, including the divisional commander, went out cruising in the Metz area with instructions to gather troops. The officers would stand at road crossings and shanghai every passing soldier who did not have a ready answer to an inquiry after his destination. In one instance I was directing traffic into the divisional area. The army men, not quite satisfied about the prospect of being impressed into an S.S. unit, circled the area until they hit another road, only to run into me at the road junction again. I redirected the men into the divisional area, rather amused at the merry-go-round. When anti-tank guns were needed, an officer with a few prime-movers at hand would set up shop at a road crossing and wait for passing guns the crews of which were not quite certain about their destination or attachment. The horses would be unhitched, the crews piled into the waiting prime-movers, and the caravan then proceeded into the reforming area. . . ."

Still another source that was called upon to make heavy contributions to the sadly weakened German army was the much-maligned and thoroughly cowed German Luftwaffe. Despite all the efforts

of its patron saint, Reichsmarshal Hermann Göring, to prevent any
depletion of its ranks, the desperate state of the army finally forced
the Luftwaffe to yield up some of the thousands of able-bodied, eager
young men it had been retaining for the day when German planes
would be available again. In one huge convulsion the bulk of the
Luftwaffe training schools in Germany were emptied of their potential pilots, observers, navigators, signalers, and sent west to save the
Fatherland. Arriving either as complete units, or organized into improvised battle groups with an army officer in command, they entered
into the fray with the enthusiasm and will of the young. Although
completely untrained for their new rôle — one battalion of 400 men
had gone into battle after doing one infantry exercise during which
their commanding officer was killed — they nevertheless fought tenaciously and well, making up for their inexperience by their courage
and zeal. This collection of fresh youth, picked from amongst the
best manpower in Germany, had not yet suffered the disillusionment
and carnage of the ordinary infantry soldier. Until they did, they were
to prove a formidable opponent whose presence in the line played
a significant part in slowing down the Allied advance from a gallop
to a slow walk.

The German navy was also called upon to make its contribution,
and this it had done by providing a large percentage of the personnel
constituting the garrisons of the Channel ports. By utilizing these
marines as infantry and artillerymen, it was possible to spare regular
army divisions for other tasks. In addition to those comprising these
coastal garrisons, the navy had been milked to provide manpower
for the Volksgrenadier divisions and, like the Luftwaffe, to stand in
the line as battle groups and hold until army divisions were ready
again to take over.

To supplement the Volksgrenadier divisions and the new recruits
from the German air force and navy, the Supreme Command ordered
into the front line every other military and semi-military unit it could
lay its hand upon. These formations, organized to handle rear-area
duties or to carry out essential civilian services, had only one thing in
common — they all wore some kind of uniform. They constituted the
final scrapings from the German manpower barrel, being either too
young, too old or too sick to have been assigned any duties in a battle
zone. Now the Supreme Command could no longer afford such lux-
uries. Into the melting pot went these bodies as well, to help form the
human wall necessary to protect the Reich from invasion.

The variety of this final category of German personnel was almost
infinite. A few examples should suffice. Stomach or Magen battalions,
similar to those that constituted the White Bread Division on

Walcheren Island, also took their disconsolate place in the Siegfried Line. They were not the only convalescents, however, that the Wehrmacht had pulled out of their beds. There were Ear (or Ohren) battalions as well. To qualify for admission into these exclusive units a recruit had to prove that either he was deaf, had one or both ears missing, had one or both ears badly damaged, or had one ear slightly impaired, together with some minor damage to another physical member, such as a missing finger or stiff joints.

The problems that beset such a formation were practically insurmountable. Verbal orders could only be given by a frantic series of gestures. Inspecting the guard at night was a nerve-racking and hazardous task since the men on duty could not hear anyone approach. Thus when suddenly confronted in the dark they fired first and attempted to find out who it was later. In one Ear battalion, two sergeants of the guard had been killed this way shortly after the unit went into action. Casualties from artillery fire were also inordinately high because the men could not hear the sound of approaching shells and therefore took to shelter much too late.

Amongst the semi-military units that were shoved into the line, could also be found those that comprised men too aged or too youthful to have been used before. The civilian police, composed chiefly of men in their early forties, were given a few weeks' training and put into action wherever possible. The Air Raid Precaution Services were utilized as well, and of a group of forty of these men taken in September, the youngest was 48 and few were under 60. The German Labor Service units, normally employed in road and building construction duties, and composed of youths of 17 and under, were also issued rifles and cartridges and put into the front line.

That a force composed of elements like these had succeeded in holding the Allies on the German border, was a striking testimony to the recuperative power of the German General Staff, as well as to the strength that comes from fighting on the frontier of one's homeland. But there is also little doubt that this stand could never have taken place had it not been decisively aided by the difficult Allied supply problem, the forts of the Siegfried Line and weather conditions which, in the words of General Eisenhower, "created flood conditions along our whole front, reducing the lesser roads to quagmires, and impeding tank operations and vehicular movement." [4]

It must also not be forgotten that to acquire even these troops, the German Supreme Command had to abandon an already largely abandoned German navy, it had to give up all hope for the revival of

a mighty Luftwaffe and, finally, it had to sacrifice a large part of its
dwindling resources of industrial manpower. When these were gone
there would be little else to draw upon, only still older and still
younger age groups and still more essential skilled workers.

It was inevitable that this sudden influx of medically unfit and
badly trained personnel would bring about a serious deterioration in
the morale of the German forces in the West. Although no organized
mass opposition to conditions could be expected to develop — discipline was still too ingrained for that — there was nevertheless a
growing sentiment of depression, resentment and hopelessness which
increased as the outlook for Germany became bleaker and bleaker.
For, while the stabilization of the Western front had slowed down
the Allied advance, it had not stopped it. Everywhere along the front,
Allied armies were carrying out limited thrusts designed to better
their own local, tactical position and to keep the weary German
troops in the line and thus deprive them of a chance to rest or regroup.

A diary of a sergeant of 712 Infantry Division opposing the British
in Holland indicates something of what some German soldiers were
going through at this relatively static period of the campaign.

13 *September* 44. Near Bath a convoy has been shot up by fighter-
bombers. We bandage the wounded and send them back. We have to leave
the dead lying in the street, for with fighter-bombers overhead any unnecessary movement may be fatal. Some of the dead are so mutilated as to
be unrecognizable. One of our mates commits suicide by hanging. During
the night British aircraft drop flares and attack with fighter-bombers. We
are in a hell of a fine place. . . .

25 *September* 44. We march about forty-five kilometres. Everybody
is dead tired.

26 *September* 44. There is not a dry thread on us. The battalion
slummocks along the road.

27 *September* 44. The men are done. They are all old chaps. Unnecessary marching and counter-marching is making them discontented. We
have now been two days without food. Three companies attacked Hees.
Only a few stragglers came back. . . . Poor Germany. Everybody is under
the impression that he is selling his life cheaply.

28 *September* 44. We are again fighting tanks with rifles. . . . We
report to the commanding officer. A fresh attack is to be mounted —
Murder! . . . I go back to my fox-hole.

29 *September* 44. Our battalion is now two kilometres back and is to
cover the retirement of the division. . . . Yesterday, before we started off
we got canteen supplies: two tubes of toothpaste (not one of us poor swine
has a toothbrush on him), one tin of shoe cream (who is still polishing his
boots?) . . . I get the order to take an anti-tank section to the road and act

as a covering party. It is a suicide order from the start. About five o'clock
we hear the noise of tanks coming towards us. One of the monsters comes
up behind us. I take up my anti-tank bazooka (Panzerfaust) but the distance
is too great. There is nothing left now but to surrender. The Britishers,
however, are not taking any prisoners, but open fire on us. Four men are
mown down at once. Now another tank rolls up on our left. We run along
a ditch. Both tanks are firing all their guns. Running forward quickly in
order to get out of the zone of fire, I reach a sheltered spot and lie there
exhausted. The tanks pass by. . . . I don't know how long all this lasted.
I am only surprised at my calmness. We must await nightfall, when the
tanks will move away. We are constantly pressing ourselves against the
side of the ditch. Now the tanks have reached the company. There will
not be much left of our battalion. Who can fight tanks with rifles? . . .

And another diary shows the reactions of a twenty-four-year-old
soldier to the personnel newly recruited to the army:

To-day I was transferred to the 42 Machine-Gun Fortress Battalion, as
a messenger. Destination West Wall. This battalion is composed of Home
Guard soldiers, half crippled — I found many among them quite obviously
off mentally. Some had their arms amputated, others had one leg short, etc.—
a sad sight. 'V-2, V-3' they jokingly call themselves. A bunch of fools.

Despite the best efforts of the Goebbels propaganda machine,
which loudly proclaimed the hastily assembled Volksgrenadier divisions as the ultimate saviors of the Fatherland, morale amongst these
formations was rapidly degenerating. Having been hurried into action
much too quickly, these recently recruited industrial workers, convalescents and disillusioned veterans were a constant concern to their
commanders. The following extracts from an order of Major General
Gerhard Franz, commanding 256 Volksgrenadier Division in Holland,
reveals some of the conditions prevalent in these 'divisions of the
people.'

256 Volksgrenadier Division.   Headquarters,
       Commander.   11 October 1944.
Certain events among units have impelled me to point out that discipline
and *esprit de corps* among the troops must be raised in the shortest possible
time. For this, all formation commanders, in particular company commanders, will be held personally responsible to me. . . .
It cannot be tolerated that a formation commander should get drunk,
then wander about the woods at night shouting and firing his pistol at the
sentry. . . .
It shows little discipline in a company when members of the company
call each other 'cheats' during a discussion about captured loot. . . .

A unit shows little *esprit de corps* if a soldier can declare that owing to difficulty in walking he can no longer serve with the artillery since he could not escape quickly enough if the Tommy arrived. Such a statement is a basis for defeatism and this case should be dealt with by courts-martial.

It shows lamentable carelessness if one soldier while cleaning his arms injures four comrades by sheer negligence and in such a way that they will be unable to do any duty. Before cleaning weapons, in particular new weapons, sufficient instruction must be given in stripping and assembling so that everyone who may have to use these weapons is fully conversant with their use. . . .

During the last eight days no less than eleven desertions have been reported, seven of whom went over into enemy lines. . . . Reports about desertions are lamentable and generally arrive too late. In one particular case a soldier deserted his unit on 29 September 1944, and the official report was not made until 10 October 1944. . . .

FRANZ.

And that a somewhat similar state of morale existed all along the German front is shown by the following paragraph from a confidential report made by war reporter Lieutenant Franz Freckman in November 1944. The document is entitled 'Observations Made in the Sectors of 159 Infantry Division, 161 Infantry Division and 21 Panzer Division,' which formations were at that time located at the southern extremity of the German line in the region of the Vosges Mountains and Belfort Gap.

For the most part our troops are very much fatigued owing to their continuous front-line employment since D-Day [Freckman begins]. Already a motley crew through the constant addition of replacements, the soldiers are to a large extent physically unable to cope with the difficulties of mountain warfare. . . . Generally speaking our troops suffer under the impression that we will not be able to compete with the strong enemy superiority. It is often necessary for company commanders, and particularly for battalion commanders, to muster all their patience and their untiring determination in order to get their obstinately indifferent men to go to work at the front or to undertake any activity whatsoever. Patrols often lack the courage necessary for the accomplishment of their mission. They approach enemy lines, lie low for ten minutes, and then return to their units. . . .

The overwhelming weight of defeat in the West and the East was thus finally beginning to bend the iron-hard discipline of the German soldier. It had not yet broken, but it was being sorely strained. The months of September, October and November 1944 undoubtedly revealed the first serious signs of wear and tear on a machine that had kept going chiefly because it did not know how to stop. All through Normandy the German soldier had loyally suffered a beating the magnitude of which has rarely been surpassed in the annals of war.

He had taken it all because he believed what was being told him, and because he knew nothing else. During the retreat through France, however, his personal experience had slowly opened his eyes to facts that Goebbels had tried so long to hide. With the first glimmerings of truth came doubt, and with doubt came desertion.

The causes that will lead a man to desert are many. But at the basis of them all is loss of faith in what one has been fighting for. It sometimes takes more courage to desert than it does to remain in the line. For a deserter voluntarily accepts the risk of death if he should fail, and the hatred and opprobrium of his countrymen if he should succeed. And when he has succeeded his only reward is the soul-destroying existence of a prisoner-of-war camp. Yet in World War II Germans frequently walked through unfamiliar minefields, swam wide rivers, traveled hundreds of miles on forged passes, and even killed their own sentries to enable them to desert.

The non-German element in the Wehrmacht provided the largest category of deserters. These Poles, Czechs, Russians, Alsatians and others were constantly on the look-out for an opportunity to cross over to Allied lines. But since they had little, or no, faith in the German cause their actions were understandable. With the Germans themselves, however, the circumstances leading to desertion were far more complex. They varied with the individual and his experiences. Inability to put up with conditions in the field, recognition of the fact that Germany had lost the war, dissatisfaction with their officers, 'horror' at finding their unit under S.S. command, long periods of unbroken fighting without rest, inadequate equipment, lack of news from home, personal resentment at some unfair treatment, were some of the long list of explanations advanced for the defection of Germans in the fall of 1944. Few deserters claimed that an ideological disagreement with Nazism had brought about their state of mind, and hardly any blamed Hitler personally, although, the S.S., the party and the Wehrmacht came in for their share of condemnation.

So frequently were desertions now taking place, in an army that had been relatively free from them heretofore, that items such as these could frequently be found in unit orders:

"By 16.00 hours, 20 October 1944, the number of desertions, General Courts-Martial, Regimental Courts-Martial ,and a list of those shot through the head for cowardice since 13 September 1944 is to be forwarded. N.C.O.s and other ranks by number, officers by name."

To prevent this rot in the framework of the Wehrmacht from developing to disastrous proportions, drastic and immediate steps were taken. In an endeavor to prevent the potential deserter from

making good his escape, unit commanders employed the most ingenious devices. Nazi party members liberally scattered among front-line
companies, with the responsibility of reporting any subversive activity. A more ambitious attempt was reported by a German prisoner
who claimed that in his unit all twelve sentries were connected by a
wire tied to their left wrists at night. The wire was given a jerk when
sentries changed, thereby informing the sergeant that all was well.
The purpose of the wire was to keep sentries from deserting, for if a
sentry untied the wire and slipped away without jerking it and
arousing the sergeant, it would be obvious that he had deserted and
had not been carried off by an Allied patrol. In another unit in Holland
all personnel were searched for white handkerchiefs before going
into the line, to prevent them from signalling a willingness to
surrender.

But these direct means of preventing desertion were not enough.
The Supreme Command relied on more wide-sweeping measures
to bring about their desired results. With unyielding intensity they
beat upon the mind of the German soldier such a merciless tattoo of
fear and patriotism that only the very few could fail to be deterred
from thoughts of desertion. This was accomplished by three chief
means: exhortations, propaganda and threats.

The exhortations came from the officers whom the men might still
trust. Orders of the day followed orders of the day pleading, commanding, reasoning, promising, flattering, threatening, the German
soldier in the West. Listen to von Rundstedt:

Commander-in-Chief West.   Headquarters,
                                                  1 *October* 1944.

SOLDIERS OF THE WESTERN FRONT !

You have brought the enemy to a halt at the gates of the Reich. But he
will shortly go over to new super attacks.

I expect you to defend Germany's sacred soil with all your strength and
to the very last. The homeland will thank you through untiring efforts and
will be proud of you.

New soldiers will arrive at the Western front. Instil into them your will to
victory and your battle experience. All officers and N.C.O.s are responsible
for all troops being at all times conscious of their great responsibility as
defenders of the Western approaches. Soldiers of the Western Front!

Every attempt of the enemy to break into our Fatherland will fail because
of your unshakeable bearing.

Heil the Führer!

VON RUNDSTEDT,
Field-Marshal.

And now listen to some of Model. Somewhat shriller but still on the same theme.

14 *October* 1944.

ORDER OF THE DAY.

Soldiers of the Army Group!

The battle in the West has reached its peak. On widely separated fronts we must defend the soil of our German homeland. Now we must shield the sacred soil of the Fatherland with tenacity and doggedness. . . . *The Commandment of the hour is: None of us gives up a square foot of German soil while still alive.*

Every bunker, every block of houses in a German town, every German village must become a fortress which shatters the enemy. That's what the Führer, the people and our dead comrades expect from us. *The enemy shall know that there is no road into the heart of the Reich except over our dead bodies. . . .*

Egotism, neglect of duty, defeatism and especially cowardice must not be allowed room in our hearts. *Whoever retreats without giving battle is a traitor to his people. . . .*

Soldiers! Our homeland, the lives of our wives and children are at stake!

Our Führer and our loved ones have confidence in their soldiers! We will show ourselves worthy of their confidence.

Long live our Germany and our beloved Führer!

MODEL,
Field Marshal.

And when the commanders had paused for breath, Goebbels and his propaganda boys stepped in to continue pumping into the dazed and weary body of the German soldier the synthetic stimulants of fear and faith which alone could keep him resisting. But the propaganda line had undergone a change since the early days of the invasion. Then the emphasis had been on hope — the promise of secret weapons and secret armies which would suddenly appear to crush the Allies in one violent cataclysm. The secret weapons had come and gone and yet the shadow of defeat was closer and darker than it had ever been before. The promise of secret weapons now had to be soft-pedaled. The emphasis was now on fear — fear of the destruction of Germany, of the rape of its womanhood, of the vengeance of the Russian Bolsheviks. Hammering on these themes like some mad musician at an organ, Goebbels pulled out all the stops, reaching a Wagnerian crescendo of frenzied hysteria. One typical example of the propaganda efforts used to frighten or shame the German soldier into staying in the line was a leaflet entitled 'The Watch on the Rhine.'[5] Over the picture of a medieval German warrior, complete with flowing cloak, chain-armor and enormous sword, standing guard on the Rhine, the following words, amongst others, were written:

Comrade, the enemy means to outflank the West Wall at the very point where we are and to cross the Rhine into Germany!

Shall our people, shall our families, have suffered five years in vain?

Shall they suffer misery and starvation amid the ruins of our cities in a conquered Germany?

Do you wish to go to Siberia to work as a slave?

What do you say about it?

Never shall this happen.

Never shall the heroic sacrifices of our people prove in vain!

Therefore, everything depends now on your courage! The struggle against an enemy who at the moment is still superior is tremendously hard. But for all of us there is no other way out than *to fight on with knives if need be.*

It is better to die than to accept dishonor and slavery!

It is better to be dead than a slave!

Therefore — keep the watch on the Rhine steadfastly and loyally.

Or take this less flamboyant, but somewhat similar, illustration of the propagandist at work. This document is called: 'Enemy War Aims'[6] and attempts to present its views in a seemingly logical and detached manner:

In May 1944 [it reads] the Soviet Union offered a plan to her Allies, whereby all members of the German forces would be made prisoners-of-war and organized into labor battalions for forced labor in the Soviet Union. The U.S.A. as well as England agreed to the proposal without restrictions.

On top of that, the U.S.A. demanded that the geographical unity of Germany be dissolved by running corridors through it, which would be inhabited by non-Germans. They intend to distribute these sectors to "a population with more peaceful tendencies" while making Germany defenseless and enslaved.

To destroy German national pride, a complete understanding exists between Moscow, London and Washington.

(*a*) They will not make peace with Germany, but will continuously occupy the country.

(*b*) They intend to intermarry German women with members of the occupying forces.

(*c*) German children will be educated after separation from their parents. . . .

The will to destroy is not directed against National Socialism but, without any doubt, against the entire German nation.

Whoever does not fulfil his duty to the utmost during the coming weeks and months is helping to make these war aims of the enemy a terrible reality.

But pleas and propaganda were alone not enough to discourage the German soldier from abandoning a cause he was beginning to realize was hopeless. A more concrete deterrent was needed. It came in the form of a message from that incredible purveyor of mass death, Heinrich Himmler, who had taken over command of the Home Army following the assassination attempt of the 20 July. The message was brief and to the point: [7]

Reichsführer S.S.   10 *September* 1944.
Certain unreliable elements seem to believe that the war will be over for them as soon as they surrender to the enemy.
Against this belief it must be pointed out that every deserter will be prosecuted and will find his just punishment. Furthermore, his ignominious behavior will entail the most severe consequences for his family. Upon examination of the circumstances they will be summarily shot.
                                        (Signed) HIMMLER.

It is safe to say that this single order did more to keep the German soldier in the line than any conceivable plea to his patriotism and duty. For while a man may risk his own life and reputation in attempting to desert, very few will take that risk with the lives of those he has left behind. The realistic Himmler knew that terror would be much more effective than reason. Having cowed a continent of non-Germans with it, he did not hesitate to use it against his own people as well. And it achieved results. What had threatened to become an uncontrollable situation soon simmered down to manageable proportions. The man with a family and a home gave up his plans for crossing over to the enemy and settled down to a stolid acceptance of a fate that had become too inexorable to resist. But in the later days of the war he eagerly listened to news of the Allied advances and, when he heard that his home town was safely in the hands of the enemy, he packed his bag and awaited the earliest opportunity to desert.   .

But that even a measure as ruthless as Himmler's had not altogether stamped out desertion, was soon obvious. It discouraged it. It did not stop it. Non-Germans and single men with few family ties in the Riech still did not hesitate to take the step. And if conditions became unbearable enough even married men went over. With what increasing violence the problem of desertion was treated can be seen by

the following proclamation read to all personnel of the 18 Volksgrenadier Division fighting in the Eifel against the Americans:

Headquarters,
18 Volksgrenadier Division,
November 1944

Volksgrenadier!
Traitors from our ranks have deserted to the enemy. Their names are:
Volksgefreiter (Corporal) Geiger, Eugen
Volksgrenadier Essmann, Johann
Volksgrenadier Walczkiewitz, Anton
Volksgrenadier Gronalewski, Vincent
Volksgrenadier Kobiela, Paul
Volksgrenadier Wolf, Kasimir.
These bastards have given away important military secrets. The result is
that for the past few days the Americans have been laying accurate artillery
fire on your positions, your bunkers, your company and platoon head-
quarters, your field kitchens and your messenger routes. Deceitful Jewish
mud-slingers taunt you with their pamphlets and try to entice you into
becoming bastards also. Let them spew their poison!
We stand watch over Germany's frontier. Death and destruction to all
enemies who tread on German soil.
As for the contemptible traitors who have forgotten their honor, rest
assured the division will see that they never see home and loved ones again.
Their families will have to atone for their treason. The destiny of a people
has never depended on traitors and bastards. The true German soldier was
and is the best in the world. Unwavering behind him is the Fatherland.
And at the end is our Victory.
Long live Germany! Heil the Führer!
(Signed) HOFFMANN-SCHONFORN,
Colonel.

By these means then was the Siegfried Line manned and held in
the months following the defeat in France. But it did not hold everywhere, nor could all the threats and all the promises of all the
Himmlers and all the Goebbelses prevail against the overwhelming
might of Allied military power. On 21 October 1944 the Americans
forced the surrender of Aachen, the first large German city to fall to
the Allies, after an assault of eight days 'duration. Located within the
belt of the Siegfried fortifications themselves, Hitler had demanded
that the city be held until the last. But like its predecessors on the
coast of France, this fortress fell when the commandant of Aachen
felt he had had enough. In a speech given to his men at the formal
surrender, the emotional commandant of the city, Colonel Gerhard

Wilck, revealed his own personal conception of what 'fighting to the last' meant, in the following words: [8]

DEAR GERMAN SOLDIERS,

This is a painful occasion on which I must speak to you. I have been forced to surrender, as ammunition, food, and water are exhausted. I have seen that further fighting would be useless. I have acted against my orders which directed that I would fight to the last man. . . . I wish you all the best of health and a quick return to our Fatherland when hostilities have ceased so that you may help in the rebuilding of Germany. The American commander has told me that I cannot give you the 'Sieg Heil' or 'Heil Hitler' but we can still do it in our hearts.

The firm resistance now being offered all along the Western front made inevitable a grueling winter campaign. General Eisenhower's plan, adjusted to meet this situation, was to edge up to the Rhine itself and take hold of its west bank "from its mouth to Dusseldorf at least, if not to Bonn or Frankfurt," before any large-scale penetration beyond the river into Germany was attempted. In accordance with this plan First Canadian Army and Second British Army in the north pinched out all enemy resistance south of the Maas by 9 November and west of that river by 4 December.

The First and Ninth U.S. Armies engaged in a bitter campaign east of Aachen in the regions of Geilenkirchen, Eschweiler and the Hürtgen Forest. The atrocious weather, the improved defense works of the Siegfried Line and the German soldier fighting on the frontier of his Fatherland, made the advance both costly and slow. The offensive launched on 16 November did not reach the Roer River until 3 December, and there was still some twenty-five miles of muddy country to cross before the Rhine was reached. An additional complication impeding a further Allied advance was the Schmidt Dams, which were capable of flooding the Roer valley and still remained in German hands. An assault across the Roer under such circumstances would give the Germans a golden opportunity to trap the forces that had crossed the river, by releasing the flood waters and cutting them off from the west. Adopting the more cautious course, First U.S. Army launched an attack on 13 December to capture these dams, but before it had completed this operation it was busy elsewhere warding off the German counter-offensive in the Ardennes.

Farther south the other Allied armies were attempting to conform with General Eisenhower's intentions of reaching the west bank of the Rhine. Third U.S. army, overcoming the fanatical resistance of a German officer cadet school, had finally succeeded in taking the city of Metz on 22 November. Now, in the region of Saarlautern, they had bumped into the toughest point of the Siegfried Line, and the going through the maze of bunkers and forts was exceedingly difficult and painfully slow. In the region of the Vosges Mountains the Allied troops of Sixth Army Group achieved notable success in their drive to the Rhine. The Seventh U.S. Army hit the Rhine itself on 23 November by capturing the city of Strasbourg, while the First French Army repeated the trick by breaking through the Belfort Gap and reaching the river on 20 November. Once on the Rhine, Seventh U.S. Army moved south along the river and First French Army advanced north along it, with the object of squeezing out the German forces still resisting west of the Rhine. By mid-December they had managed to eliminate all resistance in the area, except for a rather large bridgehead in the area of Colmar, which was later to prove an embarrassing thorn in Allied flesh before it was finally removed.

Throughout all these slogging, non-spectacular battles, the German forces in the West had but one object — to hold. "Deny the enemy German soil and gain time" was the slogan. But though the line had held throughout the months of October and November it had not been without cost. Another 175,000 German prisoners had entered Allied cages during the two months — bringing the total taken in the West since D-Day to the bulging figure of 750,000. Attrition of this kind, amounting to some 6000 to 7000 casualties every single day, could not be borne without disastrous effects on morale that had already been worn dangerously thin. Armies cannot feed on defeats alone. They must sometimes be offered a victory — or what looks like a victory. The Supreme Command realized this full well, and under the shadowy protection of November and December cloudy days, furtive, but prodigious, efforts were being carried on apace to provide the German people with just such a victory for Christmas. On 16 December 1944 the German offensive in the Ardennes was launched.

Part VI ⟩ THE COUNTERBLOW

Chapter XXVI

OFFENSIVE IN THE ARDENNES

ORDERS of the day are reserved for momentous occasions. When they follow each other like so many rolls on a drum something significant has happened or is about to happen. "Soldiers of the Western Front, your great hour has struck," trumpeted Field Marshal von Rundstedt, Commander-in-Chief in the West. "At this moment the veil which has been hiding so many preparations has been lifted at last." And simultaneously Field Marshal Model, commander of Army Group 'B,' was shouting, "We will not disappoint the Führer and the Fatherland, who created the sword of retribution. . . . No soldier in the world must be better than we soldiers of the Eifel and of Aachen." While, at the same time, General von Manteuffel, the new commander of Fifth Panzer Army was crying: "Forward, march, march! In remembrance of our dead comrades, and therefore on their orders, and in remembrance of the tradition of our proud Wehrmacht!" What did it all mean?

The four American divisions stretched thin in the Eifel-Ardennes sector on that grim morning of 16 December 1944 could provide part of the answer. Suddenly the cold stillness of the wooded Ardennes had been broken by the rumble of guns, the clatter of tracks and engines, the roar of battle. Out of the heavy mist crept hundreds of tanks and thousands of men. Westwards they moved with such unprecedented power that they quickly shattered the cohesive front line of the astounded American forces. Sweeping past the stubborn knots of American resistance that had refused to yield, the tank columns charged along the narrow, crusted roads, and in less than forty-eight hours had made extensive penetrations, some of them from ten to fifteen miles deep, along a front which extended from south of Aachen to north of Trier, a distance of about fifty-five miles.

At the headquarters of the Allied Supreme Command the first reports presented an incredible picture of vagueness and confusion. Villages that had felt the initial force of the attack were being held while others, far behind, were in German hands; tanks were weaving

westwards unchecked and by the hundred; saboteurs in American
uniforms and American jeeps were scurrying ahead of the oncoming
Germans spreading terror and confusion, parachutists were being
picked up in the most incredible places. One fact was clear, however.
The Wehrmacht had launched a counter-offensive of stunning proportions and were backing their gamble with heavy stakes. For by
midnight of 16 December, Allied intelligence staffs had already
identified and charted ten infantry, five panzer and one parachute
division on their battle maps.[1]

That something was going on behind the screen of the Siegfried
Line had been evident for some time. Air reconnaissance had shown
marked rail and road activity along the Rhine valley all the previous
week; unoccupied artillery positions were being manned; a German
resident of Bitburg in the Eifel reported that she had seen an unusually large number of pontoons and small boats moving westwards
and also that new troops had arrived from Italy on 10 December;
morale amongst freshly captured German prisoners was abnormally
high and many of them spoke of a coming attack between the 17 and
25 of December and of the "recapture of Aachen as a Christmas
present for the Führer." In addition to these bits of information it
was known that the Sixth S.S. Panzer Army, which included 1 S.S.,
2 S.S., 9 S.S., 10 S.S. and 12 S.S. Panzer Divisions, had been reforming
and reorganizing since the retreat from France, and that most of these
formations had been concentrated during the first weeks in December
in the area between the Roer and the Rhine rivers. Reports had also
been received of other infantry and armored formations, last heard
of in Normandy, reappearing behind the Siegfried Line. In fact so
ominous had all these portents become that in a report issued by the
intelligence staff of First U.S. Army a few days before the actual
offensive began, it was appreciated that an all-out counter-attack was
being prepared by the Germans. It was predicted that the operation
would include large armored formations, that it would take place
between the Roer and the Erft rivers, and that the enemy would
support it by "every weapon he can bring to bear." The scope and
character of the Ardennes offensive was thus estimated accurately
enough. The place, however, was too far north.

Thus, on the whole, the Allied Command was caught napping,
not so much by the possibility that such an attack might occur, but
by the fact that the German Supreme Command should be rash
enough to launch it in country that was so conspicuously unfavorable
for large-scale armored manœuvres. This close, wooded country with
its narrow, tortuous roads, thickly covered with snow and mud,

offered perfect conditions for anti-tank defense. For a single tank
stuck in the unyielding mire or knocked out by an opposing gun,
created an effective road-block. To venture on to the soft ground of
the adjoining fields with an armored vehicle was to court certain
trouble. And if speed was to be an essential element of any German
counter-offensive, the Ardennes in winter would hardly be the ideal
place to expect to achieve it.

Allied reasoning in this regard is clearly set out by General Eisenhower in his report. "My headquarters and Twelfth Army Group
had felt for some time that a counter-attack through the Ardennes
was a possibility," records the Allied Supreme Commander,[2] "since
American forces were stretched very thinly there in order to provide
troops for attack elsewhere and because Field Marshal von Rundstedt had gradually placed in this quiet sector six infantry divisions,
a larger number than he required for reasonable security. However,
we did not consider it highly probable that von Rundstedt would,
in winter, try to use that region in which to stage a counter-offensive
on a large scale, feeling certain that we could deal with any such
effort, and that the result would ultimately be disastrous to Germany."
As we shall see, General Eisenhower's opinion did not lack support —
either Allied or German.

For the Ardennes offensive was not the brain child of any of the
senior commanders in the West — von Rundstedt or Model or 'Sepp'
Dietrich. On the contrary they had all protested that it was as unfeasible as Allied strategists had believed it was. But their opinions
were not asked for nor were they favorably received — they were
simply told and they obeyed. For this plan was born of intuition. And
in such a conception the cold logic of military reasoning can play
no part. As Göring has said,[3] "The Führer planned it all himself. His
alone was the plan and the idea."

It was late in September, when the German armies had just reached
the comparative safety of the West Wall, that Adolf Hitler had called
Colonel General Jodl to him and outlined his idea for a counter-
offensive through the Ardennes designed to capture Antwerp. The
Führer had conceived of the plan while recovering from an attack of
jaundice. Students of symbolism may find some significance in this
juxtaposition of events. Jodl thought the idea a sound one, and went
ahead with the task of working out the details. As the plan finally
emerged, it was to consist of an armored dash through the difficult
country of the Ardennes with the object of capturing the bridges on
the Meuse River between Namur and Liége. Once this spurt of over
fifty miles had been completed, and bridgeheads on the west bank

of the Meuse secured, the panzer divisions would continue their advance in a northwesterly direction and seize the cities of Brussels and Antwerp. By this bold manœuvre it was hoped to deprive the Allies of their chief supply base at Antwerp, and, at the same time, trap the entire British and Canadian forces of Field Marshal Montgomery's Twenty-first Army Group, then lining the banks of the Maas. The success of the operation depended upon complete and overwhelming surprise. It was believed that the shock would paralyze American resistance long enough to enable the tank vanguards to reach the Meuse by the end of the second day.

No less than twenty-four divisions were to be used in this ambitious counterblow, of which at least ten were armored. The bulk of the infantry divisions belonged to the Volksgrenadier class and most of their personnel were seeing action for the first time. In fact almost every unit involved had either been refitted and reformed after being thoroughly thrashed in France, or had been organized from the second-rate manpower thrown up by the latest total mobilization effort. The result was a group of inadequately trained divisions entirely unsuited for the difficult task they had been ordered to perform.

Operationally the German order of battle looked like a contest between the S.S. and the army. On the northern half of the sector was to be the recently constituted Sixth S.S. Panzer Army, having under command all the S.S. panzer divisions which had fought in Normandy, together with a parachute division and a number of Volksgrenadier divisions. This army was to be led by Oberstgruppen-führer (Colonel General) 'Sepp' Dietrich, together with an entire staff of S.S. officers. Dietrich had been busy rebuilding this army ever since he had been pulled out of France after failing to hold the fronts at Caen, the Seine and the Somme.

The southern half of the sector was to be the responsibility of the reconstituted Fifth Panzer Army which, like its partner, was composed of five of the panzer divisions that had been reformed after being destroyed in France. It, also, was thickened up with Volksgrenadier divisions whose rôle was to take over the ground by-passed by the armor. This army was led by General Hasso-Eccard von Manteuffel, a lean, sad-looking man whose long, thin face gave him the appearance of a thoughtful priest.

Following along after Fifth Panzer Army, and acting somewhat like a closing zipper fastener, was Seventh Army which was to seal the southern edge of the break-through with infantry divisions, and thus protect the salient from any efforts of General Patton's Third U.S. Army to push north. To help gain vital crossroads, seize important bridges and create confusion in the rear of the Allied line, parachutists were to be dropped, and a special panzer brigade composed of expert saboteurs and English-speaking Germans wearing American uniforms was to be employed. More will be said about these special units later in this part. And, finally, the Luftwaffe was to come out of hibernation at last and give active and vigorous support to the ground forces.

The bulk of the striking power was to be concentrated behind Sixth S.S. Panzer Army, which was to be the first to reach the Meuse and cross the river between Huy and Liége. From there it was to push on to its final destination — Antwerp. This desire to give the S.S. Army the prima donna rôle played a major part in the failure of the complete operation. According to von Rundstedt, the basis of the plan was to execute a turning movement from the south in the direction of Liége and Antwerp. Since Fifth Panzer Army, being the southern army, was on the far side of the wheel it should have been specially strengthened. But since Hitler had more faith in his S.S. troops than in the regular army officers, and since he was anxious that whatever success the offensive attained should redound to the credit of those faithful to the régime, he insisted that the main resources be sent to Dietrich's Sixth S.S. Panzer Army. Not only did the Führer demand that this be carried out at the beginning of the offensive, but even later on when the S.S. divisions were hopelessly bogged down, and the only glimmer of success lay with reinforcing Fifth Panzer Army, Hitler ordered the sending of reserves to Dietrich's aid. In von Rundstedt's own words this was a "fundamental error which unbalanced the whole offensive." [4]

In conception and sweep this plan of Hitler's to catch the Americans off guard in the Ardennes and thereby capture Antwerp was both daring and imaginative. The only thing wrong with it was that by the end of 1944 there was neither enough equipment, enough supplies nor enough trained German troops to carry it out. But the steady drain on German manpower during the battles of October and November had made it evident that to remain on the defensive was not enough. Something had to be done. But what and when? Hitler's ideas had appealed to those Wehrmacht officers who surrounded him in Berlin.

"I fully agreed with Hitler that the Antwerp undertaking was an operation of the most extreme daring," said Colonel General Jodl, in explaining his acceptance of the plan.[5] "But we were in a desperate situation, and the only way to ease it was by a desperate decision. By remaining on the defense, we could not expect to escape the evil fate hanging over us. By fighting, rather than waiting, we might save something."

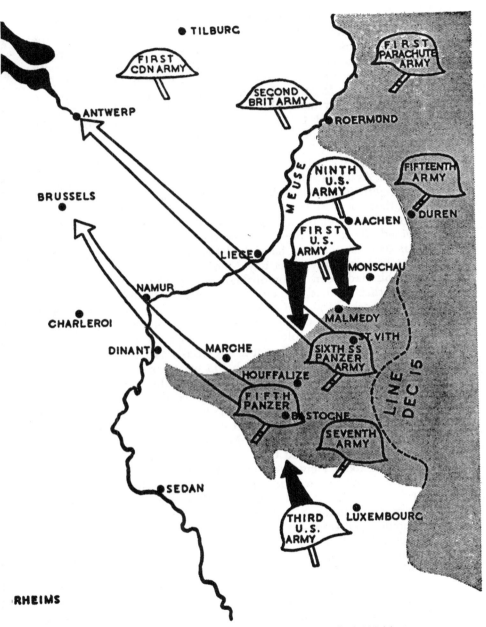

The Ardennes Offensive — *24th December, 1944.*

But those officers at the front, who had been informed of the proposed offensive in October and who were expected to carry it out, were not as sanguine as Hitler and Jodl. Although agreeing with the general principle that an offensive had to be undertaken before the spring, they felt that the scheme put forward by the Supreme Command was far too ambitious for the forces available to them.

"I strongly object to the fact that this stupid operation in the Ardennes is sometimes called the 'Rundstedt offensive,'" said the Commander-in-Chief West.[6] "That is a complete misnomer. I had nothing to do with it. It came to me as an order complete to the last detail. As a matter of fact, once we had retired to the West Wall I had begun preparing a limited offensive of my own. It seemed to me that the American bulge which had been driven towards Cologne in the region of Aachen might well be nipped off by a combined attack from the north and the south. Such a limited offensive, if successful, would have depleted American strength, retaken Aachen and probably offset any Allied plans for a winter offensive. When this had been accomplished we would then think again. I believed that we had sufficient forces for such an operation, and I had even asked my staff to produce a plan along these lines. But this operation was not to be, since Hitler had other ideas.

"When I was first told about the proposed offensive in the Ardennes, I protested against it as vigorously as I could. The forces at our disposal were much, much too weak for such far-reaching objectives. I suggested that my plan against the Aachen salient be used instead, but the suggestion was turned down, as were all my other objections. It was only up to me to obey. It was a nonsensical operation, and the most stupid part of it was the setting of Antwerp as the target. If we reached the Meuse we should have got down on our knees and thanked God — let alone try to reach Antwerp."

Von Rundstedt's views were strongly supported by Field Marshal Model, who, as commander-in-chief of Army Group 'B,' was to supervise the activities of the three assaulting armies. "Model thought Antwerp too far to reach, and beyond our means," Jodl has admitted.[7] "He thought the troops around Aachen would be a danger to our advance unless they were wiped out first. Hitler and I believed we could not wipe out the very strong and well-armed Allied forces around Aachen. We thought our only chance was an operation of surprise which would cut the life-line of the Allied forces at Aachen and in that way alone neutralize them."

But the most eloquent protest of all came from Oberstgruppen-führer 'Sepp' Dietrich who, in the midst of re-equipping and reforming his broken S.S. panzer divisions, was told what his next job was to be. His new army was to attack through the Ardennes, form bridgeheads over the Meuse between Liége and Huy, and then advance in a northwesterly direction along the line St. Trond-Herschot-Antwerp. "I grew so big with these plans," commented Dietrich bitterly,[8] flinging out his arms and puffing out his cheeks to show just how big. "All I had to do was to cross a river, capture Brussels and then go on and take the port of Antwerp. And all this in December, January and February, the worst three months of the year; through the Ardennes where snow was waist deep and there wasn't room to deploy four tanks abreast, let alone six armored divisions; when it didn't get light until eight in the morning and was dark again at four in the afternoon and my tanks can't fight at night; with divisions that had just been reformed and were composed chiefly of raw untrained recruits; and at Christmas time." The crack in Dietrich's voice when he reached this last obstacle made it sound like the most heartbreaking one of all.

Dietrich went with his complaints to Hitler's headquarters, where he saw the army Chief-of-Staff, Field Marshal Guderian and Colonel General Jodl. "I can't do this," Dietrich told them. "It's impossible." But both men shrugged their shoulders and gave him the same reply, "It's the Führer's orders," they said, and that was the end of that.

Once it had been decided that the operation would proceed as originally conceived by Hitler, it was essential that every possible security measure be taken to keep it secret, since its success depended so much on absolute surprise. Every officer involved in the planning stages of the operation was forced to sign a document in which he agreed to accept court-martial if he should, either intentionally or unwittingly, disclose any part of the plan. And to reduce the possibilities of leakage to a minimum, only those immediately concerned with the early preparations were informed of the coming offensive. This mania for security went to such ridiculous lengths that even so senior an officer as Colonel General Kurt Student, commander of Army Group 'H' north of the Ruhr, was not told about it until 8 December, merely eight days before it was to be launched. General Alfred Schlemm, whose First Parachute Army stretched as far south as München-Gladbach, was not given any information until only two days before the offensive, despite the fact that he had been ordered, a week before, to supply Field Marshal Model with all the experienced parachute jumpers he could find.

While these steps succeeded in denying to the Allies any forewarning of the offensive, they also entailed certain unpleasant consequences from a German standpoint. Parachutists were only briefed about the operation a few hours before they jumped, and even then no names of towns were mentioned. As a result many of them had no idea as to where they were or what their mission really was. Front-line officers were notified of their rôle on 15 December, which was insufficient time to acquaint themselves with the ground and to provide their men with a proper understanding of their task. As a result the first day's attack was a masterpiece of confusion and muddle. No one knew when or where the Luftwaffe would appear, since ground troops were apparently not affected by their activities, so that many of Göring's carefully husbanded planes were shot out of the sky by keen German anti-aircraft gunners, who had come to assume that anything in the air was naturally Allied.

There was no dearth of conferences during these days. The head-quarters of the Commander-in-Chief West, which was now at Ziegenberg, was the scene of much poring over maps as von Rundstedt and Jodl and Model discussed the plans which had been worked out for them, to the last detail, at Berlin. Since the only hope of success depended upon weather bad enough to prevent the Allied air forces from getting off the ground, the offensive was first scheduled to begin at the end of November, when flying weather was expected to be at its worst. However, it was soon plain that the reforming panzer and infantry divisions would not be ready by then, and the starting date was postponed to mid-December, when meteorologists assured Hitler of four or five days of thick fog.

On 12 December divisional, corps and army commanders who were to take part in the operation were summoned to von Rundstedt's headquarters at Ziegenberg. This weird conference has been well described by Lieutenant General Fritz Bayerlein, whose re-equipped Panzer Lehr Division was later assigned the task of capturing Bastogne.

"It was at Ziegenberg that I found out about the offensive for the first time," said Bayerlein.[9] "After dinner we were told to attend a special briefing. We were all stripped of our weapons and brief-cases, loaded into buses and then driven about the countryside for about half an hour. Finally we were led into a large room which was surrounded with S.S. guards who watched our every move. Then Hitler arrived accompanied by Field Marshal Keitel and General Jodl.

"Hitler looked sick and broken, and began to read from a long prepared manuscript. The speech lasted for two hours, during which I felt most uneasy. The suspicious looks of the S.S. guards made me afraid even to reach into my pocket for a handkerchief. Hitler started off this briefing as if he were delivering one of his birthday speeches. For about an hour he told us what he and the Nazi party had done for Germany during the past twelve years.

"He then went into the details of the Ardennes offensive, telling us what formations were involved and what they were to do. The object of the attack was to capture Antwerp in fourteen days and at the same time trap Montgomery's Twenty-first Army Group in Holland. The loss of so large a force would cause Canada to withdraw from the war, and thoroughly discourage the United States about continuing the struggle. Hitler also impressed us with the fact that if this offensive did not succeed, things would then be extremely difficult for Germany. At this statement, Keitel and Jodl, who were sitting at the front table, nodded their heads approvingly. The Führer also promised us sufficient petrol, and a fighter support of 3000 planes which would keep the Allies out of the sky. When Hitler had finished, von Rundstedt expressed his loyalty to the Führer on behalf of the generals, and assured him that this time they would not fail him."

But despite the assurances of von Rundstedt the attack did not live up to Hitler's optimistic expectations. Although isolated tank spearheads managed to dart forward in the first few days, the bulk of the forces engaged found the going slow and heavy. Instead of capturing the two vital communication centers of St. Vith and Bastogne on the first day as had been planned, stubborn American resistance held them out of these towns. Instead of Sixth S.S. Panzer Army easily breaking through to Verviers, on the road to Liége, and thus opening up a hole through which a special armored brigade of saboteurs in American uniform and tanks would dash to the Meuse, it became bogged down by its own traffic and by American opposition at St. Vith. Fifth Panzer Army, although having more initial success than its northern neighbor, was still far from having reached the Meuse after forty-eight hours — as had been expected of it.

Nevertheless the Germans had, through sheer weight of numbers, made considerable progress, particularly in the direction of Bastogne, some twenty miles west of the start-line. Recognizing the importance of this road center to any offensive operation in this region of the Ardennes, General Eisenhower had ordered the immediate despatch of 101 U.S. Airborne Division to Bastogne. Refitting at the time near Rheims, about 100 miles from their destination, this division started out at half-past eight on the evening of 17 December and arrived at Bastogne early on the morning of 19 December. Their arrival was none too soon for they had, unknowingly, been competing with Panzer Lehr Division which was racing to Bastogne as well.

Actually the Germans had known that an airborne division had been set in motion to proceed to the Ardennes. General Heinrich von Lüttwitz, who was commanding 47 Panzer Corps responsible for the capture of Bastogne, had found an important message waiting on his desk on the afternoon of 17 December. His signals officer had intercepted an American wireless message which reported that American airborne divisions, near Rheims, had been ordered to the battle area.

"I reasoned that these divisions would be sent to Bastogne," said von Lüttwitz.[10] "But this message also told me much more. Ever since the Arnhem operation our Command had feared another attack by airborne forces. When the message came in, we knew not only that there would be no such attack but that the American army must be extremely short of reserves in the immediate vicinity. Otherwise, it would not commit airborne divisions of such high standing to the battle."

But this information did not make him change his plan, for his own panzer divisions were proceeding to Bastogne as fast as they could, and from the map it appeared that they would easily arrive there before the Americans. Von Lüttwitz had early recognized the importance of Bastogne and when outlining his plan to the divisional commanders of 2 Panzer Division, Panzer Lehr Division and 26 Volksgrenadier Division, which were to form his corps, this large, red-faced general had declared,[11] "Bastogne must be taken. Otherwise it will remain an abscess on our lines of communication. We must clean out Bastogne and then march on." And in furtherance of these intentions, his instructions were that if the town was lightly held the panzer divisions were to attack it at once, if it were defended frontally the tanks were to envelop and attack it from the rear, and if both these courses failed, the panzer divisions were to continue on to the river and leave the task of reducing Bastogne to the 26 Volksgrenadier Division.

Thus, when von Lüttwitz heard that reinforcements were being sent to meet his advance, there was little need to alter his plan for both Panzer Lehr and 2 Panzer Division had reached position less than three miles from Bastogne by the evening of 18 December. Panzer Lehr Division actually started out to reach the town that night, but a series of rumors and bad luck prevented them from covering this short distance before the 101 U.S. Airborne Division arrived.

"We started out at ten in the evening for Bastogne," explained Lieutenant General Bayerlein of Panzer Lehr Division, "but we were misled about the conditions of the road which we took. It was narrow, and deep in mud, and it took us almost three hours to travel less than a kilometre. My forces consisted of a battalion of infantry, fifteen tanks and some guns. When we reached a village about two kilometres from Bastogne a Belgian civilian told me that he had seen an American group of fifty tanks and forty other armored vehicles going east about midnight. It was then two in the morning, and the possibility of so large an enemy force in my rear made me rather uneasy about going on in the night. I therefore took time to protect my rear and did not start off again until five-thirty in the morning. Then my head tank hit a mine and there was another delay of about an hour to clear the road of mines. We started forward again and were almost in sight of Bastogne when enemy fire prevented my infantry from going forward. In the skirmish that followed I lost about eighty men, dead and wounded. I decided to postpone any further attack until I had assembled a larger force."

It was thus that the advancing panzer division made its first contact with a forward element of the 101 U.S. Airborne Division sent out on a reconnaissance mission to find out where the enemy was. The Americans had thus beaten the Germans to Bastogne by a matter of hours. By winning that race, although it did not know it at the time, this crack American formation had done much to thwart Hitler's soaring ambitions for a mighty German offensive. Actually the Belgian civilian had, either intentionally or unwittingly, exaggerated the size of the American force going east, which was in reality merely a few tanks and some armored carriers. But the information had been sufficient to make Bayerlein more cautious and eventually to cause him to recommend that the taking of Bastogne be undertaken by all three divisions in the corps. The corps commander, von Lüttwitz, actually recommended such an attack by his complete force on 17 December, but this request was denied by Fifth Panzer Army. As a result, 2 Panzer Division by-passed Bastogne and proceeded on towards the Meuse with all speed. The remaining divisions, Panzer Lehr and 26 Volksgrenadier, tried on the 20 and 21 December to take Bastogne but by now the 101 Airborne Division was firmly entrenched in the town and prepared to sit it out.

At eleven-thirty on the morning of 22 December the American defenders saw coming towards them a group of four Germans carrying a large white flag. They turned out to be a major, a captain and two other ranks carrying with them a demand for the surrender of the American force in Bastogne. It had been written by General von Lüttwitz, the commander of 47 Panzer Corps. The tone of the demand was what the Germans like to think of as 'very correct.' It read as follows:

22 *December* 1944.

To the U.S.A. commander of the encircled town of Bastogne.

The fortune of war is changing. This time the U.S.A. forces in and near Bastogne have been encircled by strong German armored units. More German armored units have crossed the river Our near Ortheuville, have taken Marche and reached St. Hubert by passing through Homores-Sibret-Tillet. Librimont is in German hands.

There is only one possibility of saving the encircled U.S.A. troops from total annihilation: that is the honorable surrender of the encircled town. In order to think it over, a period of two hours will be granted beginning with the presentation of this note.

If this proposal should be rejected, one German artillery corps and six heavy anti-aircraft battalions are ready to annihilate the U.S.A. troops in and near Bastogne. The order for firing will be given immediately after this two-hour period.

All the serious civilian losses caused by this artillery fire would not correspond with the well-known American humanity.

/s/ THE GERMAN COMMANDER.

The reply of Brigadier General Anthony McCauliffe, the acting commander of the 101 Airborne Division, was simple, terse, undignified, but immortal. It was the one comprehensive word — "NUTS!"

On the northern flank of the attack, Sixth S.S. Panzer Army was faring even worse than von Manteuffel's Fifth Panzer Army. It had failed to capture St. Vith on the first day, as had been scheduled, and when it finally did fall on 22 December the Americans had already taken the necessary precautions to reinforce the Monschau area along the northern edge of the German penetration. In those first few days the remnants of the badly-hit American divisions clung tenaciously to their ground and completely upset the blitzkrieg plan of the Supreme Command. According to von Rundstedt it was not the American resistance alone that stalled the drive of Sixth S.S. Panzer Army to the Meuse. "The bad leadership of the S.S., the difficult terrain and the shortage of fuel also prevented the northern army from making satisfactory progress," said von Rundstedt.[12]

The untried troops and the party officers of the S.S. had not proved up to an offensive operation of this kind. 1 S.S. Panzer Division dashed ahead and soon had its spearheads cut off, surrounded and eliminated. 12 S.S. Panzer Division floundered hopelessly after an advance of only a few kilometers and then had to start battering its way slowly forward. The problem that now beset von Rundstedt was whether the reserves should be shoved in behind Sixth S.S. Panzer Army, as originally planned, or whether they should be directed south to von Manteuffel's army, which was at least making some progress.

But Hitler would not consider committing the waiting 2 S.S. Panzer Corps, with its two S.S. panzer divisions, anywhere but with the S.S. army. Thus, instead of being used to reinforce the limited success achieved by Fifth Panzer Army, these two divisions were kept idly by while they waited for the assaulting 1 S.S. Panzer Corps to break the American positions in the Malmédy-Stavelot sector. This had not been achieved by 22 December. Then, instead of giving up these useless efforts in the north, Hitler threw in 2 S.S. Panzer Corps next to 1 S.S. Panzer Corps in a vain attempt to reach Liége by reinforcing failure. But by this date the Allies were no longer surprised. The shoulders of the penetration — the Monschau area in the north and the Bastogne area on the south — had been well-cemented with American troops. The Germans were now being channeled westwards whether they liked it or not. And on 22 December another significant event occurred. For the first day since the start of the Ardennes offensive, the thick heavy mist which had kept the Allied planes on the ground began to lift. The fighter-bombers took to the air and by taking on the road centers, dumps, bridges and moving vehicles in the battle area, struck a final blow at any lingering hopes of victory that might still have warmed the hearts of the German commanders in the West. On 24 December von Rundstedt recognized that the Ardennes offensive was a wash-out. He wanted to withdraw his forward troops, take up a line from Houffalize to east of Bastogne, and go over to the defensive. Hitler, however, was not discouraged so easily. The attack went on.

Chapter XXVII

THE PARACHUTISTS AND THE SABOTEURS

THE infantry and panzer divisions were not the only formations having trouble in accomplishing their mission. The supplementary troops assigned to the operation for the purpose of striking behind the American front line, were also experiencing their own difficulties. These troops consisted chiefly of two elements — a battalion of parachutists and a brigade of specially-trained saboteurs and tank-men. Both of these units were given a twofold task. They were to seize certain vital localities well to the rear of the American foremost positions, such as bridge and road junctions, and hold them until the advancing divisions of the Sixth S.S. Panzer Army had relieved them. And secondly, they were to spread confusion, terror and fear behind the American line. They failed miserably in both these objects.

On 8 December, eight days before the offensive, Colonel General Student, commander-in-chief of Army Group 'H' and of all the German parachutists, was finally told the secret of the pending operation. The theory that only those directly involved in an operation were to be told about it, had now been carried to such a ridiculous length that an officer holding one of the most senior commands in the West was kept in the dark, until almost the last moment, about so vital an event. And, even at this late date, Student had only been informed because he was to supply a battalion of trained parachutists for the offensive.

The parachute arm of the service was a far cry, in December 1944, from the famed and feared units that had jumped at Rotterdam, Eben Emael and Crete in the early years of the war. For, in addition to the staggering losses incurred in Russia and Italy, the parachutists had suffered from the lack of planes. With the dwindling of Göring's Luftwaffe had come about a commensurate shrinkage in the need for parachutists. But, realizing the value of the parachute tradition, the Supreme Command had organized these youthful, daring men into so-called parachute divisions whose only connection with airborne troops was the Luftwaffe uniform they wore. Actually the parachute divisions, after five years of war, were nothing more or less than infantry troops trying to live up to a reputation that had been established for them when Germany ruled the air. Their fighting quality was convincingly proved at Cassino, Ortona and St. Lô, and was to make itself felt yet again before the war was finally ended.

But while they had quickly learned the business of fighting on the ground, years of disuse had affected their quality as real parachutists. Thus, although General Student had a nominal four parachute divisions in his army group, it was not too easy to find amongst them even one paltry battalion of men who had actually jumped before. He finally managed to assemble a group of about 1200 men, most of them with jumping experience, to carry out the job required in the Ardennes. In command of this unit he placed Lieutenant Colonel von der Heydte, one of his most experienced junior commanders.

Von der Heydte belonged to that soft-spoken, extremely intelligent class of Germans whose protestations of innocence of everything

National Socialist, almost bit off the tongue they held firmly wedged in their cheek. For even while he was disclaiming his connections with the party, he managed to introduce a subtle stream of Nazi propaganda into his talk. Having been awarded, in 1930, a lucrative endowment by the Carnegie Institute to study international law, he professed a natural affinity for the Americans. He was one of the very few German officers whose knowledge of the English language was more than monosyllabic. He had fought with the parachutists in Russia, Crete, Africa and laterly in Normandy and north of Antwerp. In all of these engagements he had displayed both ability and courage, and, by December 1944, von der Heydte was a much-decorated fellow.

On 12 December, von der Heydte visited 'Sepp' Dietrich, whose Sixth S.S. Panzer Army he was to support. The interview was most unsatisfactory from the parachutist's point of view as Dietrich was most vague as to just how von der Heydte's battalion was to be used. After giving the colonel rather vague instructions about cutting the main north-south road in the neighborhood of Eupen, and thus preventing Allied supplies and reinforcements using this route, von der Heydte was assured that his force would be relieved by Dietrich's panzer spearheads by five o'clock on the afternoon of 17 December.[1] Everything went wrong with this operation that could possibly go wrong. Since security regulations had been so stringent, it had been impossible to brief the men about their rôle. Few of them had seen a map before the jump, and they vaguely knew that they were to be dropped some fifty kilometres behind the front and there occupy the crossroads in the vicinity. They had been told that they would get further instructions from their section leaders when on the ground, but even the section leaders only received the bare outlines of what they were to do. Of the 106 aircraft that set out on the night of 16 December only thirty-five reached the correct dropping area. A strong wind helped to scatter the already scattered force, and weapons, supply containers and men were dumped over a wide area. Many of the jumpers incurred broken legs and smashed collar-bones on hitting the snow-covered, pine-wood country of the Ardennes, and died a slow death of starvation, exposure and exhaustion. Confusion as to their whereabouts, their objectives and the location of their own troops, resulted in most of these men being picked up by the Americans before they had fired a shot.

17 December had come and gone and 'Sepp' Dietrich's promised relief had still not arrived. Actually his vaunted S.S. panzer units were then ten to fifteen miles away, battling against the dogged

American defenders in the region of St. Vith. By 19 December the remnants of von der Heydte's force, approximately 300 strong, were still in position east of the main Eupen-Malmédy road, and patiently waiting for the expected armored spearheads which were now two days late. The men were hungry, having had no food for two days, and cold, since their blankets had been lost when they had been dropped. To make matters still worse they had not found any of the radios which had been taken along, and as a result knew nothing of what was going on anywhere about them. When on 20 December Dietrich's tanks had not yet appeared, this small group began to make its painful way eastwards in an attempt to link up with the advancing Germans. In the process most of them including the daring von der Heydte, were captured. Thus ended the last important airborne venture of the German parachutists whose dash had once struck cold fear into the heart of an unprepared world.

Another lieutenant colonel, Otto Skorzeny by name, was having almost as difficult a time as von der Heydte. Skorzeny, Viennese by birth, well over six feet in height, his exploits as Himmler's chief organizer of German sabotage units were already well known to Allied intelligence staffs. Having been trained as an engineer, he joined the S.S. in 1934 and served the early part of the war in France and Russia. His resourcefulness and daring were soon recognized, and he became an important figure in the counter-intelligence services of the S.S. He was instrumental in organizing the German penetration of local resistance movements in the Balkans, and thereby counteracting the efforts of men like Tito in Yugoslavia. Skorzeny led the small body of parachutists that carried out the rescue of Mussolini, following the capitulation of Italy in September 1943. For this feat he was decorated with the Knight's Cross of the Iron Cross, which is one above the Iron Cross, First Class, on the Wehrmacht ladder of awards. There followed a period of sabotage-espionage activity in Southern France and a special job involving the kidnapping of Admiral Horthy of Hungary, and then he was called to Hitler's headquarters in October 1944 and given one of the most vital rôles in the coming Ardennes offensive.

Skorzeny's new assignment was to organize a specially trained panzer brigade, whose job it would be to streak ahead of the Sixth S.S. Panzer Army and seize the bridges on the Meuse River. This unit, containing some 2000 men, was to be equipped with tanks, armored cars and jeeps, most of which were to be American or disguised to look like American vehicles. In addition the men were to be dressed in American uniforms, and as many English-speaking

Germans as possible were to be recruited into the brigade. On 30 October 1944 the following order was issued to the formations engaged in holding the Siegfried Line: [2]

The Führer has ordered the formation of a special unit of a strength of about two battalions for employment on reconnaissance and special tasks on the Western front. The personnel will be assembled from volunteers of all arms of the army and Waffen S.S., who must fulfil the following requirements:

(a) Physically A.1, suitable for special tasks, mentally keen, strong personality.
(b) Fully trained in single combat.
(c) Knowledge of the English language and also the American dialect. Especially important is a knowledge of military technical terms.

This order is to be made known immediately to all units and headquarters. Volunteers may not be retained on military grounds but are to be sent immediately to Friedenthal near Oranienburg (Headquarters Skorzeny) for a test of suitability, but a value will be put on his fighting spirit and temperament.

Captured U.S. clothing, equipment, weapons and vehicles are to be collected and reported for the equipment of the above special troops. Personal wishes of the troops to make use of this kind of captured equipment must take second priority. Details will be notified later. . . .

Under this order about 2000 men were chosen and organized into a unit called 150 Panzer Brigade. The recruits represented every branch of the service but were chiefly parachutists, tank men, signalers and linguists. About 150 soldiers who could speak English, preferably with an American accent, were chosen for special training. The experiences of twenty-four-year-old Corporal Wilhelm Schmidt were typical of what happened to most of the men who took part in this flagrant breach of the generally accepted rules of warfare.

"Early in November 1944 I reported to an S.S. camp at Friedenthal," said Schmidt,[3] "where I was examined as to my linguistic ability by a board consisting of an S.S., a Luftwaffe and a naval officer. I passed this test but was ordered to refresh my English. For this purpose I spent three weeks at prisoner-of-war camps in Küstrin and Limburg, where large numbers of American troops were being held. I was then sent to Grafenwohr where the training of 150 Panzer Brigade was being carried on. The linguists, of whom forty were officers, were then organized into a separate unit and given a special course.

"Our training consisted of studying the organization of the American army, identification of American insignia, American drill and linguistic exercises. We were given courses in demolitions and radio technique. Then our unit was divided up into an engineer group, a communications destroyer group and a radio group. The task of the engineers was to destroy headquarters and headquarters personnel, the communication destroyers were to eliminate message centers, radio stations and communication routes, and the radio group was to reconnoitre behind the American lines and keep the advancing Germans informed of Allied intentions and dispositions.

"At the beginning of December the first weapons and uniforms arrived together with about thirty American jeeps. This was our first indication of what our job was to be. To my knowledge none of the men protested. On 12 December we arrived at Münstereifel, east of Monschau, where we were all given American uniforms, drivers licenses and paybooks. I was told a number of details about the 5 U.S. Armored Division which I was to use in answering questions. The mission of 150 Panzer Brigade was to create confusion and disorder in the American rear areas, thereby aiding the advance of the main German forces.

"Our jeep, which only contained three men instead of the normal four since one of the crew had gone sick at the last moment, was given the task of infiltrating through the American lines and reporting the condition of the Meuse bridges and of the roads leading to these bridges. We were to make our reports by radio, and to remain near the Meuse until German troops had arrived. We had no difficulty penetrating the American line and reached the bridge at Aywaille, about twenty-five miles behind the front, in just over half an hour. Here we were stopped by an American military policeman who asked us for the password. Not knowing it, we were arrested."

All along the front similar groups of English-speaking Germans were being picked up by the fast-recuperating Americans. Approximately seventy tanks of the panzer brigade which were to exploit the break-through created by 'Sepp' Dietrich's forward elements never got started, because no real hole in the American line was made in the north during the first two days. And the attempts to create panic amongst the Americans failed as badly as did the more orthodox armored tactics. Many ingenious devices for causing confusion had been planned. One was to have the American-clad Germans start surrendering in wild disorder at the climax of a battle. Another was to 'retreat' along the vital routes and then by turning around or simulating breakdowns block all traffic on the narrow roads. Another was to spread wild stories of the strength of the advancing Germans, by fleeing westwards and shouting all the while to American troops that the Germans were only a few thousand yards behind.

But these tactics only prevailed for the first few hours. For the quick-witted Americans soon found answers to this novel type of warfare. It was evident that the members of the panzer brigade would be using special signals to identify each other, and these were soon discovered and passed to all American troops in the area. Thus any G.I.s wearing pink or blue scarfs, jackets open at the second button, flashing blue or red flashlights at night, or knocking twice on their helmet, usually turned out to be members of Skorzeny's band. In addition to passwords, American troops were told to ask any suspicious soldiers simple questions which only the indigenous American could possibly answer correctly. Thus the Ardennes was filled with thousands of Americans inquiring of each other the capital of their home state, who won the World Series, who had the best football team in the U.S.A., what was Dewey's first name, and what was the name of the 'Windy City.' These methods soon resulted in the capture or death of most of this group of carefully trained saboteurs.

According to a number of prisoners taken from Skorzeny's unit, the object of 150 Panzer Brigade was not confined to the Ardennes alone. It included an ambitious plan to reach Paris, whence a small group of men, headed by Skorzeny himself, were to set out to find and assassinate General Eisenhower, Field Marshal Montgomery and whatever other high-ranking Allied officers they might find on the way.[4] This story has been strenuously denied by Skorzeny himself, but the fact that a number of these pseudo-G.I.s were found in Paris and that the same account came from a variety of different sources, probably indicates that it would have been tried had things gone differently. In any event the threat alone was enough to provide Allied security officers with some exceedingly anxious hours during those uneasy days.

By the end of the first few days of fighting in the Ardennes it was evident that Skorzeny's panzer brigade had failed in its mission. But so had almost everyone else associated with the abortive offensive. Faced with the inevitable consequences of their flagrant disregard of the rules of warfare, the unhappy Germans sentenced to death for wearing the uniform of the enemy were not so defiant and faithful as their Führer would probably have wanted them to be. The following appeal for reprieve, made by seven Germans captured in American uniforms, was addressed to the Commanding General of the First U.S. Army early in January 1945. It provides an apt epilogue to the Skorzeny episode of the Ardennes offensive!

This morning [it reads][5] the undersigned were notified of their death sentence for having entered the American zone of operations in American uniforms in contravention of the Geneva convention. The undersigned

beg to be allowed to present this appeal for reprieve to the Commanding
General with the request for mercy and a re-examination of the motives
for the act. It may be repeated that the act was not voluntarily committed
but was done because of orders from above, and that the undersigned, in
the truest sense of the word, were driven into certain death. The personal
ambition of a single man is responsible for this criminal action. We were
taken out of our old units because we knew English and with the understanding that we would be interpreters, which is an honorable assignment.
Only shortly before our commitment were we informed of the criminal background of the whole enterprise. One of our comrades who
refused to obey the order was court-martialed and undoubtedly sentenced
to death. Therefore we could no longer escape death. We were captured
by American troops without having fired a shot, because we did not want
to become murderers. We were sentenced to death and are now dying for
some criminals who have not only us, but also — and that is worse — our
families on their conscience. Therefore, we beg mercy of the Commanding
General: we have not been unjustly sentenced, but we are *de facto*
innocent.

Meanwhile all along the Ardennes front the German position was
becoming more and more grim. Not only had there been a failure
to make any spectacular progress, but Allied resistance had now
hardened into an impenetrable wall. Allied planes were in the air
again, making large-scale German movement on the ground impossible, and General Patton's drive from the Arlon-Luxembourg
area to relieve the defenders of Bastogne, begun on 22 December,
was rapidly making significant progress. Only one element of the
entire three German armies had come to within even striking distance
of the Meuse. This was a lone armored battalion of 2 Panzer Division,
which, having by-passed Bastogne, had lunged ahead of its support
and reached Celles, only four miles from the river, by 24 December.
This was destined to be the closest that any German unit came to
achieving the hopes expected of them. For at Celles, while they
waited for their supplies to catch up with them, an entire tank battalion ran out of petrol. Here they waited for another forty-eight
hours but no supplies were able to get through. Finally they were
ordered to abandon and blow up their vehicles, and make their way
back, rather ingloriously, on foot.

Previous to the decision to forsake this spearhead of 2 Panzer
Division it had been decided to make one more attempt at capturing
Bastogne. Reinforcements had been sent to von Manteuffel's Fifth
Panzer Army for the purpose, and on Christmas morning another
concerted attack was made to dislodge the stubborn American air-
borne troops. But the combined efforts of the newly arrived 15 Panzer
Grenadier Division, the badly shaken 26 Volksgrenadier Division,

and elements of the Panzer Lehr Division were of no avail. After a morning of intensive fighting by charging tanks loaded with German infantrymen, the attackers reeled back bloody and broken. At noon, the world was sitting down to its Christmas dinner, General Heinz Kokott, leading this attack against Bastogne, asked for permission to stop the slaughter and to retire to lick his wounds. He was ordered to go on. This he did, but Bastogne was impregnable. On 26 December armored forces of General Patton's Third U.S. Army burst through from the south and the gallant defenders of Bastogne had been relieved.

In the northern part of the Ardennes sector the forward armored columns of Sixth S.S. Panzer Army were also finding themselves well beyond the main mass of their army still struggling to reach them. Getting forward much slower than von Manteuffel's Fifth Panzer Army to the south, one battle group of 1 S.S. Panzer Division had nevertheless reached La Gleize, about twenty miles west of their start line, on 19 December. On 23 December this group, of regimental size, was still there, having been unable to push either north or west. The commander of this force, the handsome, twenty-nine-year-old S.S. officer, Lieutenant Colonel Feodor Pieper, then received his orders to abandon his forward position and retire eastwards and rejoin the main German forces. The story of that retreat has been vividly told by an American officer, Major H. D. McCown, who had been captured by Pieper's troops on 21 December. McCown's account realistically describes what these forward German spearheads had to experience once their first sharp attacks were blunted, and promised reinforcements failed to materialize.

"Late in the afternoon of 23 December I was called once more to Colonel Pieper's headquarters," writes McCown.[6] "He told me that he had received orders from the commanding general to give up his position and withdraw to the east to the nearest German troops. He said that he knew it would be impossible to save any of his vehicles — that it would be a foot withdrawal. . . . All during the night of 23-24 December plans were laid for the evacuation of La Gleize. About three o'clock in the morning the foot columns began to move . . . Colonel Pieper told me that he had 800 men to evacuate . . . and this number was correct according to my estimate.

"We crossed the L'Ambleve River near La Gleize on a small highway bridge immediately underneath the railway bridge and moved generally south, climbing higher and higher on the ridge line. At five o'clock in the morning we heard the first tank blow up and

inside of thirty minutes the entire area formerly occupied by Colonel
Pieper's command was a sea of fiercely burning vehicles, the work of
the small detachment he had left behind to complete the destruction
of all of his equipment. . . .

"Colonel Pieper, his staff and myself with my two guards spent
all day of the 24th reconnoitring for a route to rejoin other German
forces. No food was available at any time after we left La Gleize;
the only subsistence I received was four small pieces of dried biscuit
and two swallows of cognac which one of the junior officers gave
me. . . . At five in the afternoon, just before dark, the column started
moving again on the selected route; we pushed down into a valley
in single column with a heavily armed point out ahead. The noise
made by the entire 800-man group was so little that I believe we
could have passed within 200 yards of an outpost without detection.
As the point neared the base of the hill I could hear quite clearly
an American voice call out 'Halt! Who is there?' The challenge was
repeated three times, then the American sentry fired three shots. A
moment later the order came along the column to turn around and
move back up the hill. The entire column was halfway back up the
hillside in a very few minutes. A German passed by me limping, who
was undoubtedly leading the point as he had just received a bullet
through the leg. The colonel spoke briefly to him but would not
permit the medicos to put on a dressing; he fell in the column and
continued moving along without first aid. The point moved along
the side of the hill for a distance of a half-mile, then again turned
down into the valley, this time passing undetected through the
valley and the paved road which ran along the base. . . . I could tell
that Colonel Pieper was basing his direction of movement on the
explosion of American artillery fire as the probable location of his
friendly forces. His information as to the present front lines of both
sides was as meager as my own as he had no radio and no other
outside contact. He continually consulted his map, thus proving that
he was thoroughly lost. We continued moving from that time on
continuously up and down the rugged hills, crossing small streams,
pushing through thick undergrowth and staying off and away from
roads and villages. . . . All of the officers were constantly exhorting
the men to greater effort and to laugh at weakness. I was not carrying anything except my canteen, which was empty, but knew from
my own physical reaction how tired the men with a heavy weapons
load must have been.

"I heard repeated again and again the warning that if any man fell
behind the tail of the column he would be shot. I saw some men
crawling on hands and knees. I saw others who were wounded but

who were being supported by comrades on either side up the steep slopes; there were fully two dozen wounded in the column, the majority of whom were going along quite well by themselves. There was one captain who was severely wounded, the colonel had told me, who moved along supported by another officer and a medical N.C.O. and was still with the unit the last I saw of him.

"We approached very close to where artillery fire was landing and the point pushed into American lines three times and turned back. . . . I was firmly convinced this time that they did not know where they were on the map as there were continuous arguments from among the junior officers as they held their conferences. At around midnight of the 24-25 December the condition of the men was such that a halt would have to be given, as well as warmth and food provided. . . .

"Suddenly tracer bullets flashed all around us and we could hear the machine-gun bullets cutting the trees very close over us. . . . Mortar fire fell all around on the German position. . . . I could hear commands being shouted in both German and English with the latter predominating. . . . After some time I rose cautiously and began to move at right angles from the direction of the American attack, watching carefully to my rear to see if anyone was covering me or following me. After moving approximately 100 yards I turned and moved directly towards the direction from which the American attack had come. I can remember that I whistled some American tune but I have forgotten which one it was. I had not gone over 200 yards before I was challenged by an American outpost of the 82 U.S. Airborne Division."

Thus instead of a resounding victory to put before the German people on Christmas Day, Hitler could only offer them promises and propaganda of better things yet to come. But the commanders on the spot were not so sanguine. They had already seen their forces stalled and wallowing in the snow and mud of the Ardennes. They had already lost about 10,000 men as prisoners-of-war and at least that much again in dead and wounded. They had by this time committed almost all of their reserves and were still unable to break the hardening crust of American resistance. They had begun to feel the overpowering weight of Allied air power and the pressure of General Patton's army driving towards Bastogne.

To von Rundstedt the next course was already very clear — take up a line from Houffalize to east of Bastogne and attempt to hold on to what had been won. Von Manteuffel of Fifth Panzer Army was a little more optimistic. The retention of Bastogne having blocked the flow of reinforcements to his forward troops trying to reach

the Meuse, von Manteuffel also realized it would be impracticable
to carry on with the original scheme of a drive to Antwerp. But he
had one alternative plan.

"About 25 December I saw that it would now be impossible for
us to attempt a crossing of the Meuse," said von Manteuffel.[7] "I felt
however that we could still carry out a limited operation east of
the river. I recommended that my army be turned in the direction
of Liége, instead of carrying straight on to Namur, thus using the
Meuse to cover my left flank. A battle east of the Meuse would
thus have developed for which I believe our forces were strong
enough. Such a thrust of Fifth Panzer Army in a northwesterly direction might have opened up other possibilities. We felt that if we
labeled the project a move 'to help 6 S.S. Panzer Army forward' it
would be favorably looked upon by the Supreme Command. But the
Führer refused to accept any change from the original plan."

Another week of dogged fighting took place with the twenty-four
German divisions wedged tight into a salient that was forty-five
miles wide at its base, from Echternach to Monschau, and which
reached westwards almost sixty miles to a thin tip at Celles just four
miles from the Meuse. But try as they might, the jammed German
forces could neither widen nor deepen this penetration. By the turn
of the year von Manteuffel had abandoned any hopes for even his
own limited plan. He now agreed with von Rundstedt that it was
necessary to get back to a more favorable defensive position as soon
as possible. On 2 January von Rundstedt asked for permission to
abandon the attack, and recommended, as essential, a withdrawal
of his forces to the German frontier. In reply the usual 'stand and
fight' order was received from the Führer, and more men and tanks
and guns were wasted in a senseless attempt to hold this vulnerable
position.

On 3 January General Hodges's First U.S. Army opened its own
offensive on the northern side of the salient directed towards Houffalize, while on 9 January General Patton's forces reopened their
push from the Bastogne area also aimed at Houffalize. It was only
then that Hitler finally gave his reluctant consent to the withdrawal
of the German troops to their original start-line. The withdrawal,
considering the circumstances, was relatively successful. The armored
elements formed the rearguards, while the infantry divisions slowly
took up a new line of resistance each day. Owing to lack of fuel
a huge mass of tanks and motor vehicles of all types had to be left
behind. By 16 January, a month after the vaunted Ardennes offensive
had begun, the First U.S. Army and the Third U.S. Army had joined
forces at Houffalize. The last violent convulsion of the dying Wehr-

macht had passed. It was still to suffer other spasms before it died, but none so dangerous as this one.

Future military historians, both German and Allied, will undoubtedly spend much time endeavoring to determine just why the final offensive effort of the Wehrmacht was such a dismal failure. To help them in their task, Field Marshal von Rundstedt, who had undertaken the operation with the deepest of misgivings, has suggested no fewer than nine factors that contributed to the thwarting of Hitler's ambitions for a march to Antwerp. According to von Rundstedt[8] the Germans lost the battle of the Ardennes because, in the first place, the forces were incorrectly employed by the Supreme Command; second, too few divisions were made available for the task in hand; three, the Germans lacked sufficient fuel and the fuel that was available did not come up in time; four, the complete air superiority of the Allies; five, the failure to capture Bastogne; six, the strength of Allied reserves, their motorization and their abundance of fuel and ammunition; seven, German transport facilities lacked the tractors and motor vehicles needed for fighting in the difficult country of the Ardennes; eight, German panzer units had not been sufficiently well trained for armored warfare in close, wooded country; and, finally, the newly organized Volksgrenadier divisions were badly trained and of small fighting value.

"It must be remembered," concluded the Field Marshal, summing up his views of this colossal German failure, "that the Ardennes offensive was planned in all its details, including formations involved, time schedules, objectives and so on, by the Führer and his staff. All counter-proposals were rejected. Under such circumstances, there could be little faith in its success. Even during the attack the Supreme Command conducted the operations by means of liaison officers and direct wireless orders to the armies involved. I received few reports from 'Sepp' Dietrich of the Sixth S.S. Panzer Army, and what I did receive was generally a pack of lies. If the S.S. had any problems they reported them directly to the Führer, who would then make them known to Model. The execution of the operation was also made much more difficult by the strict order from above that every place, including sectors that had been cut off, was to be held. And even towards the end, when Fifth Panzer Army was being attacked by superior enemy forces from both the north and south, any and every proposal made by me for a timely withdrawal to a defense line was flatly turned down."

Chapter XXVIII

ELATION AND DESPAIR

THE cost in German blood of the fiasco in the Ardennes had been terrific. The allies had taken about 50,000 prisoners-of-war in this month-long battle, and the total serious casualties suffered by the Wehrmacht in the Ardennes was in the neighborhood of 120,000 men. In addition almost 600 tanks and assault guns were destroyed and countless motor vehicles abandoned. Another crippling blow was the loss of over 1600 planes. It was the price the Luftwaffe had to pay for daring to challenge Allied air supremacy. And it was also the final humiliation and defeat of the German air force. For it never seriously appeared in the sky again.

To offset these losses the Wehrmacht had little to show. They had gained no ground at all, being back to where they had started from by the end of January 1945. They had inflicted about 50,000 total casualties on the Allied forces in the Ardennes, but had paid twice as much in manpower to do it. Their only real achievement was the fact that they had checked the pending Allied operations against the Ruhr and the Saar, and set them back almost six weeks. But it is safe to say that by depriving themselves of the resources in men and material consumed in the Ardennes, the Wehrmacht had so weakened themselves for the battles both east and west of the Rhine that, in the long run, they had shortened the eventual duration of the war by many months.

Another loss suffered by the Wehrmacht through the collapse of the counter-offensive — a much more intangible, but, nevertheless, a very real loss — was the deep disillusionment which now gripped the average soldier in the West. His faith, strained to the breaking point by what it had been through in Normandy and the slogging battles of the Siegfried Line, had been called upon to believe in a new set of promises and to hope for a new series of miracles. But when these hopes and these promises proved as illusory as the rest, when the familiar sensation of defeat all too soon replaced the one fleeting moment of victory, then despair in full measure flooded in upon the German armies in the West.

This reaction could be seen in the letters and diaries written by the soldiers in the Ardennes. The dizzy sensation of advancing instead of retreating, the satisfaction of seeing the enemy dying and in captivity, the thrill of feeling victory in the air, had brought morale

amongst the attacking troops to a pitch of eager expectation un-
equalled since the early triumphant years.

Yes, you are surprised that we are again in Belgium [wrote a soldier
on 24 December 1944],[1] but we advance every day. Well, what does
father say to that? I had a conversation with him last time about the war
and he was not very convinced then that we should be able to do such a
thing. And what do you yourselves say to that? What do you think our
morale is like? Everyone is enthusiastic as never before.

And a Lieutenant Rockhammer, writing to his wife, on 22 December, really let himself go.

This time we are a thousand times better off than you at home [said
Rockhammer].[2] You cannot imagine what glorious hours and days we
are experiencing now. It looks as if the Americans cannot withstand our
important push. Today we overtook a fleeing column and finished it. We
overtook it by taking a back road through the woods to the retreat lane
of the American vehicles; then, just like on manœuvres, we pulled up
along the road with sixty Panthers. And then came the endless convoy
driving in two columns, side by side, hub on hub, filled to the brim with
soldiers. And then a concentrated fire from sixty guns and one hundred
and twenty machine guns. It was a glorious bloodbath, vengeance for our
destroyed homeland. Our soldiers still have the old zip. Always advancing
and smashing everything. The snow must turn red with American blood.
Victory was never as close as it is now. The decision will soon be reached.
We will throw them into the ocean, the arrogant, big-mouthed apes from
the New World. They will not get into Germany. We will protect our
wives and children from all enemy domination.
If we are to preserve all tender and beautiful aspects of our lives, we
cannot be too brutal in the deciding moments of this struggle. . . .

Another letter written on 24 December, although less bloodthirsty
than Rockhammer's, still exudes optimism.

We shall probably not have another Christmas here at the front [wrote
this soldier],[3] since it is absolutely certain that the American is going to
get something he did not under any circumstances reckon with. For the
'Ami' as we call him, expected that he would celebrate Christmas in Berlin,
as I gather from his letters. Even I, as a poor private, can easily tell that it
won't take much longer until the Ami will throw away his weapons. For
if he sees that everybody is retreating he runs away and cannot be stopped
any more. He is also war-weary, as I myself learned from prisoners.

But by Christmas this unanimous mood of exultation had begun
to ebb. Some still were confident, but others were far less sure.

Thus on 25 December a German soldier wrote to his wife:[4]

We have been on our way through Belgium from the 11 to 24 December without a break. No rest or sleep at all. My Christmas presents, after twelve days, consisted of washing, shaving and five hours sleep, but we are on our way again. The main thing is that the Americans are on the run. . . . We cleared an enemy supply dump. Everybody took things he wanted most. I took only chocolate. I have all my pockets full of it. I eat chocolate all the time, in order to sweeten somewhat this wretched life. . . . Don't worry about me. The worst is behind me. Now this is just a hunt. The Americans hardly get to fire a round and the American prisoners say that they are war-weary, and don't want to hear anything more about the war. Things might move very quickly in the West. . . .

That all Germans in the Ardennes were not faring so well on Christmas day, however, is evident from the following entry, in a captured German diary, made on 25 December.

Slept last night in a barn [it reads].[5] At eleven in the morning enemy attacked with planes and tanks. It can hardly be worse in hell. At five in the afternoon we moved out again. Our driver burned to death in his car. The Lord saved me. We are in a village encircled by the enemy. Hundreds of people have had to lose their lives today. I can hardly understand how it was possible for me to escape from the barrage. . . .

And as the power of the Allies grew with each passing day pounding a steadily increasing torrent of fire and death into the ranks of the stalled German armies, and as the snow fell thicker, and the nights grew longer and colder, the mirage of victory faded farther and farther into the bleak forests of the Ardennes. By the New Year, the glowing promises and the renewed hopes had died. All that remained was empty disillusion. The letters from the Ardennes now struck quite a different note from what they had reached only two weeks before.[6]

If you actually saw me you would lift your hands in dismay [wrote one German to his wife on 2 January 1945]. I am ragged and filthy. I have had the same underwear on for five weeks. If one doesn't get lice it's a miracle. If only the war were over soon; it has lasted long enough already.

On 5 January another soldier in the Ardennes wrote to his family:

I have already got my present. I have frozen both my legs. I am in very great pain and I can't sleep at night. . . . I know well what it means to be frozen. Many are learning to pray here, if they could not already. One should not forget dear God; he will not forget us.

Another letter from the Ardennes, dated 6 January, reads:

I'm still getting along very well. Only my feet worry me. Two of my comrades had to go to the hospital because of second-degree freezing.

Besides my platoon leader, whose right hand I am, told me that I keep quivering every night. I suppose it's nerves, strained by overwork.

The process that transformed the eager hope of victory to the somber reality of defeat can be seen in the following extracts from the diary of an artillery lieutenant of 18 Volksgrenadier Division.[7] It illustrates how the German soldier was carried from exultation to wonder, to doubt, to frustration, to apathy and finally to despair in just one month.

16 *December*. First day of attack. The sky was lit up along the whole front. By noon reports of the first successes came in. The population of Duppeln is very enthusiastic.

17 *December*. Our fighter planes still control the air in the morning and afternoon.

18 *December*. The infantry is before St. Vith. The men hear the wildest rumors of successes. . . .

19 *December*. Endless columns of prisoners pass; at first, about a hundred, half of them negroes, later another thousand. Field Marshal Model himself directs traffic. He's a little, undistinguished-looking man with a monocle. Now the thing is going. The roads are littered with destroyed American vehicles, cars and tanks.

20 *December*. . . . The American soldiers have shown little spirit for fighting. Most of them often said, "What do we want here? At home we can have everything much better." That was the spirit of the common soldier. If the officers thought that way . . . ? ? ? A rumor has been started that Eisenhower was taken prisoner. It will probably prove to be only a rumor.

21 *December*. Roads still clogged, but traffic continues. Vehicles are almost exclusively captured American equipment. It was a tremendous haul. St. Vith has fallen. . . .

24 *December*. Dive-bombers attack and hit a house in front of me. Two metres more and it would have been me. We take our car and race towards St. Vith. Here dive-bombers attack again and strafe all the roads. During the night more bombs fall.

25 *December*. On the road to Hinderhausen a dive-bomber starts for us. We are able to stop the lorry in time to get off the road as the bullets start flying about us. Nothing is to be seen of our airforce. Where is it . . . ? Our anti-aircraft guns knock down two bombers. The pilots parachute down but the dogs are lucky and the wind drives them toward the west. They actually regain enemy territory. If they had landed in our lines we'd slay them; in the evening we see the fires in St. Vith. I could cry from rage and tear the prisoners apart.

26 *December*. During the afternoon we undergo the second large-scale attack on St. Vith. . . . The house shakes, and the windows break! The terrorized family seeks refuge in the cellar. Babies cry but the bombers keep coming. . . . There's nothing left of St. Vith. . . .

10-13 *January*. Our position is under continuous artillery fire. On the 12th at eight o'clock, the Americans laid down a heavy concentration of fire. Then the enemy infantry attacked. . . .

14 *January*. Almost every house in the village has been hit. The barrage lasts all morning. . . .

16 *January*. Four weeks ago, our attack started. How quickly everything has changed! Now everything looks hopeless. . . .

It was natural that this immersion into the cold waters of defeat, after having been brought to a fever-pitch of triumphant expectation, would bring about a reaction that might have a disastrous effect on the morale of the German armies in the West. When the offensive was going well the Goebbels boys had almost blown themselves purple puffing up this latest propaganda balloon. The operation was hailed as a triumphant vindication of Hitler's leadership, a demonstration of the strength that was still Germany's, a justification of the ideals of National Socialism, and a manifestation of the fighting spirit of the Third Reich. The press and the radio blared out a series of promises of Aachen for Christmas, Antwerp by New Year, the destruction of Montgomery's armies in the north, and a final victory before the end of 1945.

By mid-January this effervescence had simmered down considerably. Now the Ardennes operation was described as "an offensive defensive" designed primarily to disrupt Allied plans for a winter offensive; that its purpose was to drive home to the Allies, Germany's determination not to capitulate at any price; and that Allied losses had been so great that the threat to the western frontier of the Reich had been averted. The following pamphlet,[8] entitled "Western Warriors, This is Your Achievement," is an admirable example of this new propaganda line adopted to explain away the defeat in the Ardennes.

When Germany opened its offensive on 16 December 1944 [it begins], only a few of you knew what was occurring. Today you are informed. The Americans and the British were preparing to launch their final great drive. They intended to break through Aachen and Cologne into the Ruhr, and to smash through Strasbourg into Southern Germany. There they expected to force a decision.

At the critical moment our offensive hit them. The surprise was perfect. The enemy armies were forced to fall back and go on the defensive. The danger to the Fatherland was averted. This, Western Warriors, was your achievement. You have transcended all difficulties of terrain and weather to prove that you are tougher than the enemy. Your leaders and your country know that they can place their faith in you. . . .

Casualties suffered by American troops in Belgium and in Alsace-Lorraine between 16 December and 15 January were:
over 160,000 dead.
    50,000 wounded.
    35,000 prisoners-of-war.
    2,000 tanks.
      460 heavy and medium artillery pieces, a countless number of anti-tank, anti-aircraft guns, mortars and other infantry weapons.

The enemy was forced to commit all his reserves. Sixty-five per cent, of all enemy forces on the Continent were rushed to the salient. After the airborne divisions had been smashed, the intended American assault towards Cologne and the Ruhr was impossible.

The danger of a Western offensive co-ordinated with the huge Bolshevist drive was averted.

But even this 500 per cent exaggeration of Allied losses could offer little consolation to the weary, dreary German soldier back in the cold comfort of his bunker in the Siegfried Line. He needed no Goebbels to tell him what had happened. He had seen it himself. Having been lifted to the heights he knew how it felt to be dropped with a vigorous thud. The old familiar sensation of hopelessness and despair was more burning and more bitter for having tasted, if only for a moment, the sweetness of victory. Like a sensitive violin string that had been pulled too tight and snapped under the pressure of a heavy bow, so had German morale, raveled and worn by events, broken under the weight of this latest defeat. What little faith the German soldier might still have had, before the battle of the Ardennes, he now had lost. But nothing had come to take its place — neither hate, nor resentment, nor lust for revenge. Whereas other men might have turned upon their leaders and demanded a halt to the senseless slaughter, the men of the Wehrmacht were too ignorant, too disciplined and too terrified to generate anything more than apathy. From now on the German soldier merely waited and waited. He no longer waited for victory. He only waited for an end.

Chapter XXIX
THE THUNDER OF COLLAPSE

But while all this excitement was transpiring on the central sector of the Western front, it did not mean that the northern and southern sectors were sitting quietly by and watching. To prepare for the Ardennes offensive a considerable amount of shuffling amongst

German higher commands had been necessary. In November this shifting had begun, and when it was finished it found the German defense line neatly divided into three army groups. The most northern one, Army Group 'H' under Colonel General Kurt Student, consisted of the newly-constituted Twenty-Fifth Army and First Parachute Army. Student, who combined his operational rôle with his other task of organizing and training all the German parachutists, was responsible for the defense of Holland and the Maas River as far south as Roermond.

Field Marshal Model, commanding Army Group 'B,' was given the central sector from Roermond to the area of Luxembourg. To enable him to carry out the offensive in the Ardennes and protect the flanks of that operation as well, he had under command Fifteenth Army, Sixth S.S. Panzer Army, Fifth Panzer Army and Seventh Army. In the extreme south was Army Group 'G,' under Colonel General Blaskowitz, responsible for the protection of the Saar and the land of the Vosges Mountains. For this task Blaskowitz had two armies, the First and the Nineteenth. When the offensive was at its height the nominal total of German divisions in the West was approximately eighty. But since few of the divisions were over 8000 men in size and since few were properly equipped, it was estimated by Allied intelligence staffs that the actual strength of this force was roughly equivalent to some fifty normal divisions. By the time the battle in the Ardennes was over this strength had been still further reduced.

When Colonel General Kurt Student was finally let in on the secret of the coming Ardennes offensive, the attack was only eight days away. Student was not one to be left out of a party of such proportions. Having led the paratroopers in Holland and Crete and Russia, he felt that his own First Parachute Army should have been given some rôle in so vital and daring an operation. But since he had not been included, other than by being asked to supply a single battalion of jumpers under Lieutenant Colonel von der Heydte, he decided that he must take some steps not to be left out. Student therefore suggested to the Supreme Command that if the goal of the offensive was Antwerp, his forces sitting north of the Maas River were the most likely troops to use since they were only some fifty miles away from the port. This was a far shorter route than the proposed one of over 120 miles through the Ardennes.

"I asked that I be given ten infantry divisions and four panzer divisions, and I would guarantee the seizure of Antwerp from the north," Student said.[1] "I counted on the poor weather to cover my preparations and also to protect me from serious attacks from the air.

But the plan for the Ardennes offensive was well under way by this time, and my scheme was turned down."

This rebuff, however, did not completely discourage Student. The prospects of a rapid push to Antwerp by German forces in Holland seemed particularly bright to him because of the fact that only one Allied formation, the Polish Armored Division, was then patrolling almost twenty miles of the southern bank of the Maas River. Student pressed so eagerly for such an attack that finally on 17 December he was told to organize an offensive operation to be directed against Antwerp. The immediate object of the attack was to split Allied strength by holding Canadian and British troops in the north while 'Sepp' Dietrich's Sixth S.S. Panzer Army isolated them by driving to the sea from the Ardennes.

"For this operation I was allotted three infantry divisions, two parachute divisions and 150 armored vehicles," said Student.[2] "The infantry divisions were to make the initial assault and establish bridge-heads over the Maas, and then the parachute divisions would be used to follow through. The armor was to be ferried across the river on special tank ferries, since no bridges were available in the area east of Dordrecht. I was also going to use a parachute battalion of about 1000 men who were to be dropped in the woods north of Tilburg, and thereby neutralize the Canadian artillery position which was assembled there. I had hoped to start this assault on 24 December, but since preparations would not be ready in time, it was postponed until 27 December. But the exact date was largely dependent upon the success of Model's offensive in the Ardennes. My troops were scheduled to cross the Maas the moment that either one of Dietrich's or Manteuffel's armies reached the Meuse River in the Ardennes. Since this was not reached by the New Year I was forced to abandon my plans."

The responsibility of carrying out this offensive was given to General Eugen-Felix Schwalbe, who had been brought up from Alsace for the purpose. Schwalbe, who had been peacefully commanding a division up to 23 December 1944, was suddenly ordered to proceed to Holland and take over 88 Corps. He arrived at the headquarters of General Student and, before he had time to catch his breath, was told that he would be leading an assault across the Maas in three days' time.

"Although the divisions to be used were already assembled along the river south of Gorinchem," said Schwalbe,[3] "I was not told how these troops were to be supplied once they had reached the south bank of the Maas. General Student was very vague about such details, and he seemed to think it could be done by means of ferries which

were just then being built. A great deal of reliance was also placed
on continuing bad weather which would keep Allied planes from
interfering with the crossing-places. Our chief hope of success lay
in the absolute surprise with which we could launch the attack. But
the difficulties involved in such an operation were so great, in view
of Allied air superiority and artillery power, that I could hardly
believe it was seriously being undertaken. When I awoke the day
after I had been told of the plan, I had to ask myself: Are we really
going to cross the Maas or did I dream it all!"

But if Student's hopes for a lightning drive to Antwerp were based
on the surprise which he could achieve, the operation was doomed
to failure. For the intelligence staff at First Canadian Army had
assessed Student's plans down to the actual crossing-places he was
going to use. With the help of hundreds of reports from Dutch agents
and civilians, the concentration of the German divisions north of
the Maas had been carefully watched since the start of the Ardennes
offensive. On Christmas Eve the Canadians quietly deployed their
tanks and guns south of the river so that had Student come across
on 27 December, as he had planned, he would have lost a great
deal more than just surprise.

To celebrate the New Year the southern German armies in the
Saar also decided to go over to the offensive. Driving south from
the region of Saarbrücken, with the apparent design of pinching
off the Allied salient which was lodged between the Vosges Mountains and the Rhine River, were some six Volksgrenadier divisions
and two S.S. divisions.[4] This attack, begun on 1 January, was followed six days later by the establishment of a German bridgehead
on the west bank of the Rhine, a few miles north of Strasbourg.
Simultaneously another push north was attempted by the German
formations in the Colmar pocket, which was to be, but had not been,
eliminated in November. All in all some fourteen to sixteen divisions
were involved in this series of attacks, but since they were all far
below strength and relatively new in the line, the small amount
of ground that they gained was only made at a disproportionate cost
in German blood.

Actually General Eisenhower had realized that the German
Supreme Command might attempt an operation of this kind in the
Saar, since he had weakened his position there when he had transferred a number of divisions to take part in General Patton's southern
drive against the Ardennes salient. Unwilling to take such a risk the
Allied Supreme Commander had actually ordered a general withdrawal to the line of the Vosges Mountains. This move would have

necessitated the abandonment of Strasbourg, which the French, for political reasons, were unwilling to allow. "As I studied the French views," said General Eisenhower in his report,[5] "it became evident that the execution of the original plans for withdrawal might have such grave consequences in France that all our lines of communication and our vast rear areas might become seriously affected through interference with the tasks of the service troops and through civil unrest generally. Clearly, the prevention of such a contingency became a matter of military as well as of political necessity."

But this offensive in the south was as unprofitable as had been its parent offensive in the Ardennes. Standartenführer (Colonel) Hans Lingner, who was given command of 17 S.S. Panzer Grenadier Division in the Saar at the extremely youthful age of twenty-nine, admitted that this operation failed chiefly because the Wehrmacht was far too weak to carry on simultaneously two offensives in the West.

"When the break-through in the Ardennes had been stopped by the Allies," said Lingner,[6] "it was realized that several Allied divisions had been sent north to aid the Americans in their defense. It was therefore decided to launch an attack against what we felt was sure to be a weak position. This offensive was only given very limited objectives and I believe it was undertaken on the theory that an attack was the best means of defense. We apparently miscalculated Allied strength in the Saar for we were very surprised by the number of divisions still opposing us. As a result the operation only achieved very limited success."

With the abandonment of Student's proposed assault across the Maas, with the withdrawal of the Ardennes salient back to its startline, with Strasbourg still safely in Allied hands in the south, and with the elimination of the Colmar pocket west of the Rhine by the end of January, it was obvious that the German offensive plans for the winter of 1944-45 had been thoroughly thwarted. Their efforts in December and January had cost them 110,000 men in prisoners-of-war alone, bringing this single casualty item to the soaring figure of well over 800,000 Germans captured since D-Day. Adding the killed and seriously wounded to this total meant that the Wehrmacht had already lost over 1,500,000 men in the West in less than eight months.

But defeat in such generous helpings had not been confined to the West alone. The Russians could also boast of having inflicted at least another 1,500,000 casualties upon the German armies in the East. This meant that in one year the Third Reich had lost well over 3,000,000 men.

The first weeks of the new year promised little surcease from this debilitating drain on German manpower. Not only was the aftermath of the abortive Ardennes offensive taking a daily toll of thousands, but on 12 January 1945 the Russians crashed forward with one of their mighty, carefully prepared offensives. In Poland and East Prussia a series of synchronized attacks by Marshals Koniev, Zhukov and Rokossovsky tore through the 150 weak German divisions standing guard in the East, and in less than a week had broken through along 250 miles of the German front. In Poland, Radom, Warsaw, Lodz and Cracow fell in less than a week, while the traditional East Prussian fortresses of Tilsit, Insterburg and Tannenberg gave in by 21 January. By the end of the month the momentum of the Russian drive had carried them to the east bank of the Oder near Breslau. The capture of Gleiwitz and Katowice by 28 January meant that the coal, steel and oil resources of Upper Silesia were no longer available to help maintain the creaking German war machine. Only the shattered industries of the Ruhr now remained to supply the needs of Hitler's dying armies. They were not enough.

But Germany's losses in the East were not merely geographical and industrial. The casualty lists were staggering. By 24 January the Russians announced that their twelve-day-old offensive had already accounted for 200,000 killed and 75,000 prisoners-of-war. It is interesting to note that whereas in the West prisoner figures were always twice or three times as high as the number of Germans dead and seriously wounded, in the East the 'killed' totals were invariably at least double the number of those taken alive. The explanation for this difference undoubtedly lies in the more personal and more bitter nature of the fighting on the Russian front. It produced a German soldier more determined to resist, and a Russian soldier less likely to be bothered with the niceties of taking prisoners.

Early in the year an event occurred which sent Allied intelligence staffs scurrying to their commanders. The second-rate 711 Infantry Division, last located in Holland, had been reported in action against the Russians in Hungary. The news was of vital significance for it meant that, for the first time since the Allied landings in Normandy, a divisional formation had been shifted from the West to the East. That it was unlikely to go alone was immediately realized, and sure enough by the end of the first week in February no fewer than seven armored and three infantry divisions were making their way from the frying pan of the West to the fire of the East. Included in this caravan were the S.S. panzer divisions of 'Sepp' Dietrich's Sixth S.S. Panzer Army sent from the Ardennes to stand guard at the approaches to Vienna.

More significant even than the fact that this exodus reduced the number of nominal divisions available to hold the Rhine from eighty to seventy, was the fact that it revealed how bankrupt German manpower resources had become. For now it was clearly evident that no central pool of reserve German divisions existed in the Reich itself and that the Supreme Command was resorting to a frantic switching of formations from theatre to theatre wherever the need was greatest. As Göring subsequently admitted, there was at this stage no overall plan for the shifting of divisions between the Eastern and Western fronts. "The troops were sent wherever there was a fire," said the Reichsmarshal.[7] "For instance, if the Eastern Command wanted troops for an anticipated action and the West desired troops to check an attack already in progress, the troops were usually sent west. But it was the same principle as a fire department. Hitler, of course, made the final decisions."

With the threat of the Russian offensive looming darker each day and with the forces in the West being stripped of their reserves to meet it, there remained nothing for von Rundstedt to do but fall back on the defensive. His command, now down to seventy weak divisions with barely the strength of forty normal divisions between them, could hardly hope to withstand an Allied force three to four times as large in personnel alone. And there was little left within Germany itself to replenish the urgent manpower needs of both the Eastern and Western fronts.

We have already seen what steps were taken to fill the empty bunkers of the Siegfried Line after the Allied break-through in France. The navy and air force were sucked dry of their best troops, and industries were combed out to produce every non-essential worker for the war fronts. But it was realized that even these stratagems would not be enough. Therefore, on 18 October 1944, Hitler announced a gigantic *levée en masse* of the entire German people designed to bring every able-bodied man to the defense of the Fatherland.

The proclamation declared that in every district of the greater Reich, a German Volkssturm would be set up comprising every man between the ages of sixteen and sixty capable of bearing arms. These units would be led by the most capable organizers and leaders of "the well-proven bodies of the party, the S.A., the S.S., the National Socialist Motorized Corps and the Hitler Youth." Although the Volkssturm would not wear uniforms, but merely arm-bands with the words 'Deutscher Volkssturm,' they were nevertheless soldiers within the meaning of the army code. Service in the Volkssturm was to have priority over duty in any other organization, and the formation, training and equipment of the Volkssturm was to be the responsibility of the S.S. Reichsführer Heinrich Himmler. "The Volkssturm will be sent into the field according to my instructions by the Reichsführer," ordered Hitler.

"Every mile that our enemies advance into Germany," said Himmler in a speech accompanying this proclamation, "will cost them rivers of blood. Every house, every farm, every ditch, every tree and every bush will be defended by men, women and children. . . . Never and nowhere must or may a man of the Volkssturm capitulate. . . ."

Brave words, however, were not enough to turn this untrained citizenry into soldiers overnight. It takes training, weapons and time to make a soldier. The Volkssturm could be given very little of each. By the turn of the year its members were still only civilians with arm-bands. The following letter dated 11 January 1945, written by an oldster to his son in the army, might well have been written by one of Britain's Home Guard after Dunkirk:

"Every German male up to the age of sixty is liable for service, as is well known. Those who are unfit for military service and those who have been discharged from the Forces are included, if they are fit for office or similar work. Uncle Kurt has to do duty as company clerk in spite of being a hunchback. . . . As we have no equipment or weapons, training presents considerable difficulties, especially during the present weather. Last Sunday week, as we were practicing description of terrain, judging distances and deployment in extended order beside and behind the water-tower (with the high tank), our men suffered very much from the cold. Another point is that the drill is new even for the old soldiers of the last war, whilst many of our men have never been soldiers before. There is need, therefore, for a considerable amount of patience, skill, and above all, time, in order to achieve definite results. Last Sunday we had an army-training demonstration team here, to give our men their first glimpse of the present-day infantry weapons and to explain them in general terms. Much water will have to flow down the Lengenfeld Brook before we receive our own fire-arms and are allowed to take them home."

But time was the one thing that both the Volkssturm and von Rundstedt did not have. For the coming battle of the Rhine the Volkssturm could not possibly be of any use. Von Rundstedt knew that the Allies were already girding their loins to carry out the offensive they had been forced to postpone because of the adventure in the Ardennes. Standing west of the Rhine, the Commander-in-Chief West awaited apprehensively the next Allied move. He could no longer retire behind the river itself since the loss of Silesia made it essential to cling for as long as possible to the industrial resources of the Saar and the Ruhr. With the destruction of the German railway system in the interior of the Reich, the Rhine was also becoming increasingly important as the one available transportation route for shipping the coal of the Ruhr to the North German ports of Hamburg, Kiel and Bremen. On 13 February 1945, von Rundstedt issued the following order of the day to the German armies in the West:

Soldiers of the Western Front.

The enemy is on the march for a general attack on the Rhine and the Ruhr. He is going to try with all the means in his power to break into the Reich in the west and gain control of the Ruhr industry. You know what that signifies so soon after the loss of Upper Silesia. The Wehrmacht would be without weapons, and the home country without coal.

Soldiers, you have beaten the enemy in the great battles of the autumn and the winter. Protect now your German homeland which has worked faithfully for you, for our wives and our children in face of the threat of foreign tyranny. Keep off the menace to the rear of the struggling Eastern front, so that it can break the Bolshevist onslaught and liberate again the German territory in the East.

My valiant fellow-combatants. The coming battles are going to be very hard but they demand that we stake our utmost. Through your perseverance the general attack of the enemy must be shattered. With unshakeable confidence we gather round the Führer to guard our people and our state from a destiny of horror.

/s/ VON RUNDSTEDT,
Field Marshal.

Having spoken his piece, there was nothing left for von Rundstedt to do but to emulate his soldiers and wait for an end. In his own case he did not have long to wait.

Part VII ⚹ THE END

Chapter XXX

DEFEAT WEST OF THE RHINE

In the early hours of 8 February 1945, General Alfred Schlemm, commander of the First Parachute Army, was awakened by the ominous rumbling of artillery in the Reichswald Forest. The sound was much too intense to be normal. He had only heard its like before during the mighty battles on the Russian front. The first reports from his forward troops confirmed his worst suspicions. They indicated over 1000 Allied guns firing into his position at the northern extremity of the Siegfried Line. "I smell the big offensive," reported General Schlemm to Army Group 'H,' his next senior formation.[1]

And Schlemm's olfactory sense had not betrayed him. It was, indeed, the big offensive. Or, at least, the start of it. Having allowed the German armies in the West to dominate the Christmas season with their intentions, the Allies were now in a position to resume their own. These intentions embodied nothing less than the complete and utter destruction of Germany's military power by the summer of 1945. In the words of General Eisenhower this was to be done in three distinct phases: "first, the destruction of the enemy forces west of the Rhine and closing to that river; second, the seizure of bridgeheads over the Rhine from which to develop operations into Germany; and third, the destruction of the remaining enemy east of the Rhine and the advance into the heart of the Reich."[2] Since it was also realized how vital a part the industries of the Ruhr played in the maintenance of the German war economy, it was decided that the main Allied effort should be designed to eliminate this industrial region. This was to be achieved by concentrating the maximum effort for the crossing of the Rhine against the favorable terrain north of the Ruhr. A supplementary operation from the Mainz-Karlsruhe area was to accompany the strong northern thrust with the object of achieving a gigantic double envelopment of the entire Ruhr area and the troops that would undoubtedly be left there to defend it.

The initial phase of this strategic plan, the closing up to the Rhine in order to seize suitable crossing places north of the Ruhr, was to be done in three steps. The first step was an advance to the Rhine as far south as Düsseldorf. This was to be accomplished by an attack of the First Canadian Army, with divisions of the Second British Army under command, in a southeasterly direction through the Reichswald Forest, combined with an assault of the Ninth U.S. Army across the Roer River towards Neuss on the Rhine.

Then like a series of fire-crackers on a string the next two steps of phase one were to follow in rapid succession. The First U.S. Army would attack across the Erft River towards Cologne and clear the west bank of the Rhine north of its confluence with the Moselle River. And finally the Third U.S. Army, Seventh U.S. Army and First French Army would start their movement eastwards so as to complete the task of reaching the Rhine along the entire length of its left bank.

What General Schlemm heard on the morning of 8 February 1945, were the opening salvos of this strategic plan. General Crerar's First Canadian Army, with seven infantry and four armored divisions under command, was striking at the one German infantry division[3] holding the northern edge of the Reichswald Forest between the Rhine and the Maas rivers. It was hoped that if the ground were dry enough the armored columns would swiftly smash the thinly-held sector north of the forest and quickly be in a position to disrupt the German rear areas.

But the ground was anything but dry. ". . . the weather conditions could hardly have been more unfavorable," reads General Eisenhower's report;[4] "January had been exceptionally severe, with snow lying on the ground through the month, and when the thaw set in at the beginning of February, the ground became extremely soft and water-logged, while floods spread far and wide in the area over which our advance had been planned to take place. The difficulties thus imposed were immense, and the men had sometimes to fight waist-deep in water. . . . Under such conditions it was inevitable that our hopes for a rapid break-through should be disappointed, and the fighting soon developed into a bitter slogging match in which the enemy had to be forced back yard by yard." But in addition to the trying weather conditions, the rapid exploitation of this attack was prevented by two other factors — the fanaticism and tenacity of the German parachutists, and the skill of General Alfred Schlemm, commander of the First Parachute Army.

Nazi race-purists would have had an embarrassing few moments attempting to explain the presence of Alfred Schlemm on an Aryan General Staff. For with his rather short body, his broad Slavic face, his large, bulbous nose and his dark, almost chocolate skin, he looked the antithesis of what Hitler and Rosenberg would have us believe was the true German type. He had been General Student's Chief-of-Staff at Crete, had led a corps at Smolensk and Vitebsk in 1943, and had been responsible for containing the Allied bridgehead at Anzio in Italy in January 1944. His record, coupled with an orderly mind and a keen grasp of tactical problems, placed him amongst the more able generals still available in the Wehrmacht. The contrast between his non-Teutonic physical appearance and his undoubted military ability may not be very significant, but it is interesting.

Early in November 1944, Schlemm was transferred from Italy to take over the First Parachute Army, which was then holding a sector of the Western front from the junction of the Rhine and the Maas rivers to Roermond with four divisions. Following the collapse of the Ardennes offensive, it was obvious that a major Allied attack would soon be forthcoming. For, despite the propaganda pap being fed to the German civilian and soldier about the inability of the Allies to launch an offensive after their terrible losses in the Ardennes, every responsible senior German commander realized that Allied ability to carry on with their plans had been little affected by the fighting in December.

There now began a period of speculation amongst German staffs as to how, when and where the next Allied move would take place. German military intelligence, already long discredited by its many strategic blunders, was barely existent by early 1945. With no aerial reconnaissance to provide them with evidence of Allied movements, with few trained agents to garner them reports and with wide rivers preventing extensive patrolling, intelligence officers could offer little in the way of an accurate estimate of enemy intentions. Left to their own devices, each senior commander based his appreciation on what he himself would have done had he been in Allied shoes. Since clairvoyance of this kind can at best be only fifty per cent correct, some got it right and others got it wrong. The result was a rather sensitive hesitation all along the front, with reserves being spread thin to meet all emergencies and rarely being committed boldly if the Allied operation did not correspond with the commander's appreciation of what he expected it to be.

Thus while most generals thought the first Allied move would be north of the Ruhr, there was wide disagreement as to just how it would be done. Schlemm's personal view was that the big blow would come southeast through the Reichswald Forest as it eventually did. But this was opposed by Colonel General Johannes Blaskowitz, who had in January 1945 taken over from Colonel General Student as commander of Army Group 'B.' Blaskowitz — and he was supported by von Rundstedt in this appreciation — believed that the Allied offensive would begin by an American assault south of Roermond followed in a few days by an attack by Second British Army from the neighborhood of Venlo.[5]

As a result the two divisions, 15 Panzer Grenadier and 116 Panzer, which constituted the armored reserve of Army Group 'H,' were kept opposite Roermond, while the infantry reserve division, 7 Parachute, was sited across from Venlo. But despite his failure to convince both von Rundstedt and Blaskowitz of the impending threat to the Reichswald, Schlemm ordered his troops to build a series of defensive lines facing northwest to meet any attack from that direction. Thus when, on 8 February, the First Canadian Army launched its offensive, there was little opposition encountered for the first forty-eight hours. But the two main roads leading through the Reichswald soon became such a nightmare of water, ice, mud and holes, that it effectively delayed an immediate Allied exploitation of the surprise that had been achieved. In the interval Schlemm had been able to convince his superiors that this attack was the real thing, and that he should be given all available reserves to deal with it.

Thus although the town of Cleve fell on 12 February and the Reichswald Forest itself was cleared by the 13th, the defense lines constructed under Schlemm's orders were now fully manned. Repeating the tactics he had used at Anzio in Italy, where he had built up a force from nothing to eight divisions in a few weeks, Schlemm began to bring up division after division as the pressure from the Canadian and British troops grew more and more severe. By 19 February, following the fall of Goch, a town some fifteen miles southeast of the Allied start-line, Schlemm had increased his force to nine divisions, three of which were infantry, three parachute and three armored.[6] These formations, holding a front about twenty miles from the Maas to the Rhine rivers, forced the British to engage in what General Eisenhower has described as "some of the fiercest fighting of the whole war."

Schlemm's orders were simple — to hold. "Once the battle was joined," said the general, "it was obvious that I no longer had a free hand in the conduct of the defense. My orders were that under no circumstances was any land between the Maas and the Rhine to be given up without the permission of the Commander-in-Chief West, von Rundstedt, who in turn first had to ask Hitler. For every withdrawal that I was forced to make due to an Allied attack, I had to send back a detailed explanation."

But it was not Schlemm's foresight or the horrible ground conditions alone that stalled the British drive. The resistance of the parachute divisions was as grim and relentless as anything yet seen in the West. In these young, indoctrinated Nazis, fresh from a Luftwaffe that had ceased to exist, the faith in their Führer and in their own cause had not yet died. As has already been explained, they had been rushed into the rôle of infantry troops following the Allied victory in Normandy. Not having personally felt the sickening impact of defeat, they had not yet given way to the despair and hopelessness that by now had gripped most of the Germans fighting in the Siegfried Line.

The parachutists in the Reichswald were that in name only. They had never been taught to jump from an aeroplane. The bulk of them had received no more than three months' infantry training. But they possessed two other compensating virtues — youth and faith. Over seventy-five per cent of them were under twenty-five years of age, and together with the S.S. the parachutists contained the best remaining products of young German manhood. And they were nurtured on the deeds of their predecessors — the men who had landed at Crete, broken the Maginot Line at Sedan, and held Cassino. They developed an *esprit de corps* which the regular army divisions had long since lost. When they took their places in these new parachute divisions, hastily being formed to take advantage of this spirit, they were given speeches such as this, delivered by Lieutenant Colonel von der Heydte to the men who had just been sent to his regiment: [7]

"I demand of every soldier the renunciation of all personal wishes. Whoever swears on the Prussian flag has no right to personal possessions! From the moment he enlists in the paratroops and comes to my regiment, every soldier enters the new order of humanity and gives up everything he possessed before and which is outside the new order. There is only one law henceforth for him — the law of our unit. He must abjure every weaker facet of his own character, all personal ambition, every personal desire. From the renunciation of the individual, the true personality of the soldier arises. Every member of the regiment must know what he is fighting for.

"He must be quite convinced that this struggle is a struggle for the existence of the whole German nation and that no other ending of this battle is possible than that of the victory of German arms. . . . He must learn to believe in victory even when at certain moments logical thinking scarcely makes a German victory seem possible. . . . Only the soldier who is schooled in philosophy and believes in his political faith implicitly can fight as this war demands that he shall fight. This is the secret of the success of the Waffen S.S. and of the Red Army — and lack of this faith is the reason why so many German infantry divisions have been destroyed."

This call for faith in a National Socialist Germany did not go unanswered amongst the young recruits of the new parachute divisions. Aided by the flooded fields, the broken roads and a narrow battlefield hemmed in by two flanking rivers, Schlemm's troops fought skilfully and tenaciously from forest to forest and from defense line to defense line. By 23 February Schlemm could well survey his position south of the Reichswald Forest with some satisfaction. He had stabilized his front and, although his losses had been heavy, he had done what had been expected of him. He had held. But on that day the second part of the operation to reach the Rhine north of the Ruhr was begun by Ninth and First U.S. Armies. This was an attack across the Roer River between Julich and Düren with the Ninth U.S. Army heading for Neuss on the Rhine, and then advancing north to meet the British troops pushing south.

General Eisenhower's original plan had been to have Ninth U.S. Army cross the Ruhr on 10 February, two days after the First Canadian Army attack. However, the dams which controlled the height of the Roer had been opened by the retreating Germans on that day, causing a four-foot rise in the water level. This had forced a postponement of the crossing until 23 February, when, aided by a moonlight night, the assault elements of General Simpson's Army struck the four weak infantry divisions of the German Fifteenth Army patrolling the river.[8] The two weeks' delay in launching this assault had resulted in a weakening of the whole German position along the Roer. For as the demands of the battle in the Reichswald grew heavier, the reserve formations that had been kept back pending just such an attack had been forced to move north to help General Schlemm's hard-pressed troops.

By 26 February the American bridgeheads over the Roer had erupted and armored columns were streaking east. To meet this new threat to his rear Schlemm sent south two armored divisions and one infantry division[9] which did nothing to relieve the broken Fifteenth Army and severely weakened his own front facing the British. By 2 March München-Gladbach, Roermond, Venlo and Dulken had all fallen, while the Rhine had been reached at Neuss. This meant that Schlemm's First Parachute Army was completely encircled and that the only way out was a withdrawal over the Rhine. Hitler's voice was again heard from Berlin. There was to be no withdrawal! Instead Schlemm was ordered to build a bridgehead west of the Rhine, from Krefeld to Wesel, and to hold it at all costs.

"It was explained to me," said Schlemm,[10] "that this bridgehead was needed to maintain shipping traffic along the Rhine. This particular area was vital for the passage of coal from the mines of the Ruhr, since it was shipped along the river to the Lippe Canal, south of Wesel, and from there it was sent up the Dortmund-Emms Canal to the northern ports of Hamburg, Bremen and Wilhelmshaven. I could see the need for protecting this route, since it was the life-line upon which the German navy relied to carry on its U-boat warfare against the Allies."

Despite Schlemm's frantic efforts to defend this area the armored power of the Americans was irresistible and Krefeld fell on 2 March. This meant a further contraction of the bridgehead which was now less than twenty miles long along the Rhine. In this area ten divisions attempted to stave off the constant attacks from the north and the south.

It was at this stage, while he was trying desperately to carry out the impossible rôle that had been assigned to him, that Schlemm was sent a series of utterly stupid and incomprehensible orders. These decrees radiating straight from the Führer himself succeeded in so hamstringing and bewildering Schlemm that he was forced to command an army with men and equipment he did not want, and with the constant fear of a court-martial and a death penalty hovering over his head.

The first of these orders came to the commander of the First Parachute Army following the fall of Krefeld. Under no circumstances was any bridge over the Rhine to fall into Allied hands. If a bridge was captured intact, he Schlemm, was to answer with his head. No excuses or explanations of any kind would be accepted. But to complicate the matter still further, bridges were only to be blown at the very last moment. This was to ensure supplies and reinforcements reaching the troops in the bridgehead and also to enable as much industrial machinery as possible to be evacuated to the east bank of the Rhine. "Since I had nine bridges in my army sector," said Schlemm, "I could see my hopes for a long life rapidly dwindling." He moved his headquarters to Rheinberg, where he established wireless communications with each of the bridges in his area. He thus hoped to be able to give the order for the destruction of the bridges, whenever he felt that they were imminently threatened.

One of the first bridges to be menaced, following the fall of Krefeld, was the road bridge at Homberg. Schlemm waited until he thought the Americans were close enough, and then, by wireless, ordered the bridge to be blown. After waiting about ten minutes he called back to ask if his instructions had been carried out. "No, sir," came the reply, "there is a colonel here who has forbidden us to blow the bridge." Schlemm shouted into the mouthpiece, "Who the devil is a colonel to countermand my orders? I am an army commander and I order you to blow the bridge immediately." There was a moment's pause, and then the voice came back. "The colonel claims that he is not under your command, sir, but that he is under Field Marshal Model. He therefore insists that the bridge is not to be destroyed." At this answer, Schlemm claims, he completely lost his temper. He yelled down the speaker as loudly and deliberately as he could that the blowing of the bridge was the Führer's order and that if it was not destroyed forthwith, Schlemm himself would personally come down to the bridge and not only shoot the colonel, but anyone near the bridge. They then blew the bridge.[11]

The second order that restricted Schlemm's freedom of command was the insistence of Hitler that not a single man or a single piece of equipment was to be evacuated across the Rhine without the army commander first obtaining the special permission of the Führer himself. With the fall of Krefeld and Homberg the original purpose for the maintenance of the bridgehead had lost its significance, since shipping on the Rhine was now dominated by American artillery on the western bank. This latest decree from Berlin meant that the contracting bridgehead was cluttered up with all the abandoned junk and useless personnel of an army that had just been through a heavy, losing action. There were damaged tanks that could no longer run, car-parks jammed with fuelless transport, artillery without ammunition and supply personnel of both First Parachute Army and Fifteenth Army with no jobs to do in so confined a space. This heap of twisted metal, broken horse-carts and purposeless personnel had to be pushed off the roads into hiding, where it rested as a futile gesture to a stupid order.

"By the beginning of March," said Schlemm, "this rubbish had so increased in volume that it seriously handicapped operations in the bridgehead. I reported to General Blaskowitz that unless I was permitted to get rid of some of this useless material I could not be responsible for what was likely to happen. Blaskowitz finally received Hitler's consent to evacuate a specific limited list of personnel and equipment west of the Rhine. This list included vehicles which were damaged or had no petrol, guns without ammunition and supply personnel who were physically unfit to carry on fighting. To make sure that no man still capable of bearing arms was sent east of the Rhine, each commander had to sign a certificate stating that the men they were sending back were too weak to continue fighting."

Plagued by this third nonsensical restriction, Schlemm was forced
to contract his bridgehead under the mounting pressure of the
British and American forces surrounding him. By 8 March the bridgehead at Wesel quivered rather uncomfortably in an area a little more
than fifteen square miles in size. In this postage-stamp sector, because
of Hitler's mad refusal to permit the withdrawal of any fit men, there
were jammed no less than nine divisions, three corps headquarters
and an army headquarters. So crowded were these staffs that one
sugar refinery alone housed the headquarters of three divisions. Here
these troops, who had fought an exhausting battle for a full month
without a rest, were pounded relentlessly from the air and from the
massed guns of the tireless Allied artillery.

"It was only sheer luck that the bridge at Wesel had not yet been
hit well enough to destroy it," said Schlemm. "I told General Blaskowitz that if the bridge were destroyed there would be no other escape
route for my men trapped on the west bank of the Rhine. I also
pointed out that if this force of fighting men was lost there would
be no experienced troops left in this area to prevent an Allied crossing of the Rhine itself. I urged Blaskowitz to tell the Supreme Command at Berlin that if they did not believe my reports, the least
they could do was to send a representative to Wesel and see the
situation for themselves."

This latter plea worked, and on the morning of 9 March a lieutenant
colonel from the Führer's headquarters came to see what was happening. Schlemm described this observer as a dapper officer, all fresh
and crinkly in his best new uniform. "I made him get down on the
ground," said Schlemm, "and crawl forward with me to our further-
most positions, amidst one of your intensive bombardments. After he
had had his fill of shells, and had got himself nice and dirty, he agreed
that the position was hopeless and the bridgehead should be withdrawn. He sent this recommendation back to Berlin, and permission
to send my troops east of the Rhine was finally granted. On the night
of 10 March I pulled back my last remaining infantry and blew
the bridge at Wesel."[12]

Once again the German casualty list represented a staggering
waste of manpower. The Allies had taken another 50,000 prisoners
from 8 February to 10 March, and the total German losses, in this
bitterly contested struggle, were between 90,000 and 100,000 men.
But this was only part of what the Wehrmacht was yet to lose before
it had been pushed back over the Rhine. For while the battle north
of the Ruhr was reaching its closing stages, the second phase of
General Eisenhower's plan to clear the western bank of the Rhine had
begun. The First U.S. Army, which had crossed the Roer at Düren

on 23 February, was making rapid progress to Cologne, and entered the city on 7 March. Third U.S. Army, forming the southern arm of this pincer movement designed to squeeze out all German opposition north of the Moselle, began their drive to the Rhine on 4 March with two spearheads aimed at Andernach and just north of Coblenz. Less than a week later these objectives, almost sixty miles from the start-line, had been reached. By 11 March the left bank of the Rhine, north of the Moselle, had been freed of German forces and another 50,000 German prisoners-of-war had trooped into Allied cages.

The speed with which this second phase of the Allied plan to reach the Rhine was accomplished, indicates how weak German opposition had now become. It had taken over a month of intensive punishing battle to clear the Reichswald, but in that month the Wehrmacht had lost the only troops it still possessed capable of offering the Allies anything more than token resistance. The defeat of First Parachute Army and Fifteenth Army, north of the Ruhr, had meant the end of anything resembling reserves in the West. For, in a situation remarkably analogous to the battle of Caen in Normandy, the cream of von Rundstedt's forces had been sucked northwards to the Reichswald to meet Montgomery's British troops where — to continue the metaphor — it had been thoroughly whipped. This had deprived the divisions defending the Cologne plain of the bulk of their armored reserves, and the American armies found the remaining infantry divisions relatively soft pickings.

In effecting this second push to the Rhine the Allies had succeeded in mauling another twenty-five German divisions, chiefly belonging to the Fifth Panzer and Seventh Armies, which had been responsible for the sector from Cologne to the Moselle River. Their orders had been the same as Schlemm's — to hold and under no circumstances to withdraw. But not having the spirit of the men in the First Parachute Army, and not having a narrow, restricted sector to defend, they collapsed much more readily than their comrades north of the Ruhr.

As had occurred in the Reichswald, permission to retire to the Rhine had been received much too late. The result was a badly disorganized front once the American armored columns had broken through. The story of 5 Parachute Division, as told by its commander, Major General Ludwig Heilmann, was typical of what had happened north of the Moselle.

"My final order from corps was to form a main defensive line about thirty kilometres west of Coblenz," said Heilmann.[13] "But because of the rapid Allied advances from the south it was impossible to carry this out. An alternative line was chosen but everything was too dis-

organized to allow another move to take place. Eventually each subordinate unit had to make its own way to the Rhine. By the time
my first troops reached the river the ferries had been destroyed and
the small assault boats still operating were of little use. Most of the
roads to the Rhine were now blocked, and finally I tried to make
my way east on foot. Utterly exhausted I tried to rest in a local farm-
house but was captured by an American patrol. I do not believe that
more than 500 of my fighting men ever reached the east bank of the
Rhine."

Another senior officer taken in this operation was the talkative,
fat Lieutenant General Richard Schimpf, who fell into American
hands west of Bonn. Schimpf was particularly bitter about his last
days with the Wehrmacht. "I had ample time to cross the Rhine if I
had wanted to," he declared after being captured,[14] "but I remained
behind because I had orders to that effect from General Püchler, my
corps commander. Püchler insisted that I stay behind with my division
so that other units could be saved. If the Wehrmacht thinks that
they have sufficient experienced generals and General Staff officers,
it is all right with me. Püchler and Model messed this thing up
anyway — they are amateurs."

Because men make wars and because men are human no strategist
can guarantee the infallibility of his predictions. Fate or luck or, if
you will, the unreliability of man often takes a hand to upset the best
calculations of the most scientific of planners. On 7 March fate interfered in the battle of Germany. A small armored spearhead of the
9 U.S. Armored Division reaching the crest of a hill overlooking
Remagen, was astonished to see below it, still standing and apparently undamaged, the Ludendorff railway bridge spanning the Rhine.
With the dash and courage of men who make history, an American
platoon charged into the town and made its way to the bridge. Hardly
had they reached it when two of the demolition charges exploded
damaging the easternmost span of the bridge but leaving the roadway
intact. Despite these warnings the American infantry continued on
over the bridge, while engineers quickly cut the wires controlling
the remaining charges. At four o'clock that afternoon First U.S. Army
had crossed the Rhine!

The story of the German defenders delegated to destroy the
Ludendorff railway bridge combines the elements of incompetence,
confusion and bewilderment which characterized most German
operations in the closing months of the war. Under pain of death,
a special engineer regiment had been made responsible for seeing
that the bridge was blown up before the Americans theatened it.

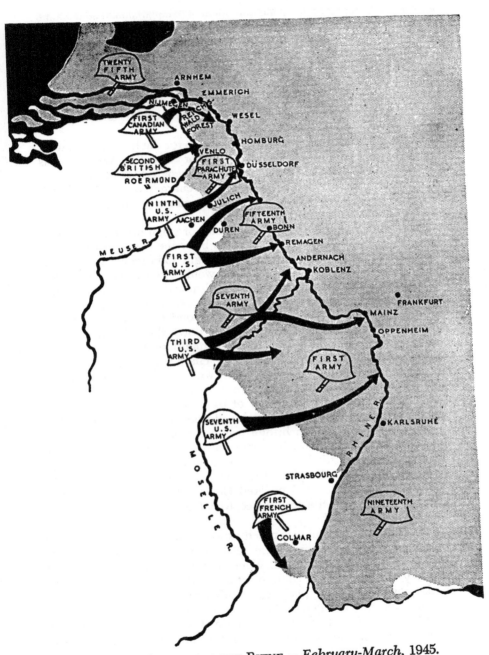

THE ALLIED ADVANCE TO THE RHINE — *February-March, 1945.*

But, as in the case of General Schlemm in the Reichswald, no bridge was to be demolished too soon since fleeing German units would otherwise be cut off from their final escape route. At Cologne a bridge prepared for demolition had been prematurely blown up by bombs falling in the neighborhood, and as a result a large German force had been trapped and captured west of the river. It had therefore been ordered that no charge was to be placed on a bridge until the very last moment.

On 7 March the senior officer responsible for the bridge was away, and his place had been taken by a Major Schoeller. When it was finally decided that the bridge should be prepared for demolition, it was suddenly discovered that the proper charges were not in hand. Frantic efforts were made to improvise effective charges but the final product was entirely inadequate.

Even when Schoeller heard the sound of small arms fire in Remagen, he still considered it too early to blow the bridge. Although it was expected that American infantry might soon reach the western bank, it was not anticipated that tanks would also appear — since the approaches to the bridge had been well mined and blocked. When, however, Sherman tanks unexpectedly turned up sweeping the opposite bank with fire, the situation was beyond remedy. The fire cut some of the ignition cables and pinned down the defending troops on the other side. The last-minute demolitions were not enough seriously to affect the bridge, since the charges were too weak. Surprised and dumbfounded the Germans watched the Americans pouring across the Rhine too helpless to do anything but gape.[15]

When the news of the capture of the Ludendorff bridge reached the Allied Supreme Commander he did not hesitate in deciding to exploit it. "The Remagen bridge was not in a sector from which it had been intended to launch a major thrust eastward," reads General Eisenhower's report,[16] "but I at once determined, at the expense of modifying details of the plan of campaign, to seize the golden opportunity offered to us. . . . I ordered General Bradley, when he telephoned me to report the occurrence, to put not less than five divisions on to the far bank."

The German reaction was much slower. The only troops available on the east bank were some local anti-aircraft units and the engineer regiment of about 1000 men. None of these units were equipped to carry out an effective counter-attack, and they possessed no anti-tank guns of any kind. The regular infantry divisions that had been passing over the bridge for three days had headed into the wooded country east of Remagen for the purpose of reorganizing and refitting. Communications on the right bank of the Rhine were also extremely poor, and news of this disaster did not at once reach the proper authorities. As a result opposition on the 7th and during the daylight hours of the 8th was provided by a wide variety of units scraped together from the surrounding countryside. It was not until after dark on 8 March, almost thirty-two hours after the crossing had been made, that the Americans identified 11 Panzer Division, rushed south after having itself withdrawn over the Rhine near Cologne. But by then it was much, much too late.

In the race to Remagen the Germans were far behind. In contrast to the speedy build-up of the Allies, which went on so quickly that even the ultimate collapse of the Ludendorff bridge on 17 March did not affect it, the Germans arrived in the piece-meal fashion now so much a part of their tactics. Although within ten days the elements of almost ten divisions, including three panzer divisions, had been thrown against the expanding bridgehead, the total force was still much too weak in men and equipment to do more than annoy the determined Americans. This stripping of personnel from the defenses along the river, north and south of Remagen, in a fruitless effort to meet this threat, had a disastrous effect on the eventual battle for the Rhine itself. "It made a long Rhine defense impossible," said Göring,[17] "and upset our entire defense scheme along the river. The Rhine was badly protected between Mainz and Mannheim as a result of bringing reserves to the Remagen bridgehead. All this was very hard on Hitler."

But things were soon to become much harder still. The third phase of the Allied plan to clear the left bank of the Rhine began on 15 March. Like its predecessors this manoeuvre was a co-ordinated drive by the Third U.S. Army attacking south from bridgeheads over the Moselle and the Seventh U.S. Army pushing north from the Saar between Saarbrücken and Hagenau. To meet this attack were the Seventh and First German Armies lying in a wide semi-circle along the Moselle and Saar rivers. They contained about twenty-six divisions, two of which were armored, while the others were chiefly the recently formed Volksgrenadier divisions. Using the bunkers of the Siegfried Line to protect them these formations hoped to carry out Hitler's edict to hold the left bank of the Rhine. But in a battle that was as swift, as astounding and as catastrophic as anything yet seen in the West, this huge mass of German soldiery fell into Allied hands as if it had been eagerly waiting for the opportunity. Having assumed that the Third U.S. Army would continue across the Rhine at Remagen and break out from the bridgehead there, the sudden assault of Patton's armor from the north caught Seventh Army completely off-guard. With nothing but isolated bits of resistance to restrain them Allied columns cut through the untrained, surprised Volksgrenadiers, and by 25 March, ten days after the operation had started, the west bank of the Rhine, along its entire length, was cleared of German troops. And in the process General Patton's men had also made another crossing of the Rhine south of Mainz to further complicate the Supreme Command's future plans for the defense of the river.

During the course of these battles to edge up to the Rhine, German resistance had grown progressively worse in each succeeding phase. North of the Ruhr the First Parachute Army had fought tenaciously and well and had withdrawn in good order despite all the efforts of Hitler to prevent it. Between the Ruhr and the Moselle, opposition had been less fierce, but some modicum of system still existed during the retreat across the river. But between the Moselle and the Saar there had been neither resistance nor order — only chaos. In less than two weeks almost 120,000 prisoners-of-war were taken and over 4000 square miles of German territory captured. The fighting element of thirteen of the twenty-six divisions engaged surrendered almost to a man with hardly a gesture of defiance. No wonder Göring moaned.[18] "We could not believe that these fortifications had been penetrated. That break-through and the capture of the Remagen bridge were two great catastrophes for the German cause."

March was not yet out and von Rundstedt now faced the coming struggle for the Rhine with almost half a million men fewer than he had at the beginning of February. The vast bulk of these troops had found life as a prisoner-of-war more attractive than death as a fanatic fighting for a lost cause, for almost 350,000 Germans had raised their hands in defeat in the battles west of the Rhine. The total German losses since the Allied landings in Normandy had thus risen to the staggering figure of 2,000,000 men.

The decision to risk these troops on the wrong side of the Rhine had been made by Hitler alone. He had been warned by his commanders in the field of what might happen, but he had listened only to his intuition. "Field Marshal Model asked the Führer time and time again to rescind the order that the Siegfried Line be held at all costs," said Model's senior intelligence officer,[19] "but these requests bore no fruit. Model then recommended that at least twenty divisions be sent back to prepare the defense of the Rhine and to act as a rallying-point in case of a withdrawal, but this was also refused. At this time the staff at Hitler's headquarters gave the impression of being completely at sea, and of having lost all control of the situation."

Model was not the only general whose advice was being refused. Von Rundstedt, completely fed-up with his rôle as a receptacle for the Führer's incomprehensible demands, was rapidly becoming a figurehead who held his job merely to remind the German people of the Wehrmacht that used-to-be. Since Hitler was making all strategical and tactical decisions, and since the details were being worked out by von Rundstedt's new Chief-of-Staff, the efficient Lieutenant General Siegfried Westphal, there remained little for the old man to do. In any case he was too disgusted and too weary to want to do very much. If someone was still going to save the Third Reich, it was painfully evident that von Rundstedt was no longer the man. In mid-March, for the third and last time, the Field Marshal was asked to give up his command. To take his place came Field Marshal Albert Kesselring, the former Commander-in-Chief Southwest. As von Rundstedt made his dignified, but halting, exit from the military stage he might well have found some consolation in the fact that, though he had failed to halt the Allies in the West, he had at least done better than anyone else. And for a man of seventy there must have been some satisfaction in the knowledge that an end had come at long last.

Chapter XXXI

DEFEAT EAST OF THE RHINE

THE ultimate disintegration of the German forces in the West had been inevitable since the collapse of the Ardennes offensive. That defeat was now staring the Third Reich full in the face was plain for everyone to see. The one man, however, who kept his senses tightly shut against this verdict of history was Adolf Hitler. And since he was the only man in the Third Reich who mattered, the Germans kept on fighting — automatically, fitfully and hopelessly. It required no diaries or letters of soldiers at the front to reveal the state of morale of the troops defending the Rhine. One needed merely to study the parades of German prisoners steadily filing into the Allied cages to see how badly shattered the German spirit really was. In March over 10,000 prisoners had been taken every single day which, in terms of manpower, was an even greater disaster than the losses incurred in the month of September in France. Few armies could stand two such bleedings in so short a time. The Wehrmacht, after five years of war, obviously could not.

Of the new troops that had been scraped together by the *levée en masse* of the autumn of 1944, only the young parachutists succeeded in living up to the glowing promises proclaimed for them. The Volksgrenadier divisions, untrained and unenthusiastic, had collapsed under pressure with little more than a dismal sigh. South of the Moselle, sixteen of these divisions had provided the most desultory and feeble opposition yet encountered in the West. The Volkssturm, that other standard-bearer of Teutonic steadfastness, just faded away. These old and sick men, the Home Guard of Germany, with their only uniform a white arm-band, hardly appeared at all in the fighting west of the Rhine. The commanding officer of the 41 Volkssturm Battalion described what occurred when his formation was sent into battle early in March. His story was representative of what was happening to these last-ditch units all along the front.

"I had 400 men in my battalion," he said, "and we were ordered to go into the line in our civilian clothes. I told the local Party Leader that I could not accept the responsibility of leading men into battle without uniforms. Just before commitment the unit was given 180 Danish rifles, but there was no ammunition. We also had four machine-guns and 100 anti-tank bazookas (Panzerfaust). None of the men had received any training in firing a machine-gun, and they were all afraid of handling the anti-tank weapon. Although my men were quite ready to help their country, they refused to go into battle without uniforms and without training. What can a Volkssturm man do with a rifle without ammunition! The men went home. That was the only thing they could do."

Again the Wehrmacht adopted all sorts of stratagems to keep the troops fighting. One device was to issue a flood of military awards designed to bolster this rapidly flagging morale. In addition to a lavish distribution of Iron Crosses of all classes, the Führer offered a brand new decoration to all soldiers who had fought their way out of enemy encirclement. This award, which had been first announced in October 1944, was now available to almost every member of the German forces in the West. For in the words of the order itself it was to be given to all "troops who have fought their way back to their own front after having been encircled by the enemy or after their units have been smashed during withdrawal actions, whether they arrive singly or in small groups. . . ." By April 1945 the only German soldiers who could not fall into that category were either dead or in an Allied prisoner-of-war camp.

Then another curious reward for skill and courage in battle was the offer of pin-up photographs of Field Marshal von Rundstedt. A diplomatic, but somewhat peevish, letter written by the commander of 47 Volksgrenadier Division to his corps commander on 4 February 1945, rather pointedly expresses what the men thought of awards of this type: [1]

"The Division reports that so far it has had no experience with the awarding of autographed pictures of Field Marshal von Rundstedt to individual infantry fighters. No requests for this award have been submitted.

"At the present time the Division does not expect an award of this type to promote infantry shooting. The troops can only be induced to shoot better by the creation of more equal fighting conditions. . . . In the opinion of the Divisional Commander the choice of the type of award is an unfortunate one. The soldiers cannot carry the picture of the Field Marshal into the line. . . ."

Obviously such inducements were having small effect on the morale of the German soldier, and the Nazi chiefs resorted to harsher and more terrifying methods as the end loomed nearer and nearer. Fear was still the weapon that was most effective in cowing the masses, and Goebbels wielded it with abandon. The bogy of Bolshevism was raised every where to frighten the nation into submission. On 16 March 1945 the following directive was issued to the National Socialist indoctrination officers of Twenty-fifth Army in Holland. These officers performed a similar function in German units to the rôle carried out by Communist commissars in Russian units, but with far less success. This document illustrated the propaganda line to be adopted in talks to the men and consisted of a series of warnings of catastrophes that would befall the German people "in the event of capitulation."

"As a natural consequence of the reparations demanded by the Reparations Commission in Moscow," it reads, "the whole German agricultural potential is to be at the disposal of Moscow, and hunger, calculatingly produced, will be applied as a means of oppression, at any time.

"German labor will be used as 'reparations production'; as a natural consequence Moscow will deport German slave-labor to Siberia by the million. German industry will then profit only Germany's enemies.

"Moscow will tear asunder all families by deportation, slave-labor, etc., for ever, with the full intention of destroying the family as the basis of the life of the race. . . .

"The German women will be raped by beasts in human guise, dishonored and murdered. . . .

"German children will be torn from their parents by force, deported and brought up as Bolsheviks.

"The German people as an organic community will be literally murdered. Germany will become a vast graveyard. Whoever survives has nothing more to hope for in this life. . . .

"The want and suffering of the present war situation are nothing compared to the aims of extermination by our enemies. These will be carried out in the event of capitulation. The entire German people has risen against this fate and fights as a single armed Nazi army."

But the greatest deterrent of all was still the threat of death. What had begun as a severe punishment for the most heinous of crimes was becoming a blanket punishment for the most trivial of misdemeanors. Death, in flaming capital letters, appeared in each succeeding order, in each succeeding exhortation. It was the last despairing measure to save a cause that was well beyond all saving.

There was death for neglecting to blow a bridge on time, for being related to a deserter, for withdrawing without orders, for failing to fight until the end. On 12 February 1945 Field Marshal Keitel decreed death for forging passes: [2]

In the name of the Führer the following is ordered:
. . . Any officer who aids a subordinate to leave the combat zone unlawfully, by carelessly issuing him a pass or other leave papers, citing a simulated reason, is to be considered a saboteur and will suffer death.

Any subordinate who deceitfully obtains leave papers, or who travels with false papers, will as a matter of principle be punished by death. . . .

/s/ KEITEL,
Field Marshal.

And on 5 March 1945, Colonel General Blaskowitz of Army Group 'H' doled out death for stragglers: [3]

As from midday 10 March, all soldiers in all branches of the Wehrmacht who may be encountered away from their units on roads or in villages, in supply columns or among groups of civilian refugees, or in dressing-stations when not wounded, and who announce that they are stragglers looking for their units, will be summarily tried and shot. . . .

/s/ BLASKOWITZ,
Colonel General.

And on 12 April 1945, Heinrich Himmler announced that the penalty for failing to hold a town was still more death.[4]

"Towns, which are usually important communications centers," decreed Himmler, "must be defended at any price. The battle commanders appointed for each town are personally held responsible for compliance with this order. Neglect of this duty on the part of the battle commander, or the attempt on the part of any civil servant to induce such neglect, is punishable by death."

But no conceivable number of threats could save the German nation from its inevitable fate. Standing on the left bank of the Rhine with a force of 4,000,000 men was a triumphant Anglo-American-French force pawing restlessly at the ground for the final lunge into Germany. To make things still easier for the Allies two bridgeheads over the Rhine had already been seized and by the last week in March these were swollen with expectant American troops.

The unenviable task of stemming this mounting tide was given to Field Marshal Albert Kesselring, whose blunt jaw and stocky figure bespoke a stubborn and resolute man. Kesselring had gained his reputation as a defensive military genius by his expert handling of the German armies in Italy. There, behind the Hitler and Gothic Lines, he had conducted a magnificent delaying action which had cost the Allies much blood and much time. Now he was expected to achieve the same results along the Rhine. But where von Rundstedt had failed Kesselring was hardly likely to succeed. His one order was to hold, and for the purpose he had a nominal sixty-five divisions with a real strength of less than half that number.

On 23 March 1945 he must have realized full well that the order would be impossible to obey. For on that day the second phase of the great strategic plan for the defeat of Germany was set in motion. General Dempsey's Second British Army and General Simpson's Ninth U.S. Army crossed the Rhine in force north of the Ruhr. At Wesel, Rees and south of the Lippe Canal Allied bridgeheads were formed, and landings by two airborne divisions took place in the region of Wesel.

Ready to meet this new assault was the First Parachute Army, not yet recovered from the losses it had sustained in the Reichswald, but by far the most effective fighting force still available on the Rhine. But the nine to ten divisions lining the river north of the Ruhr were no match for the masses of flesh and steel thrown against them. The left wing of the army was torn free from its flanking formation, Fifteenth Army in the Ruhr, and with a completely open left flank the First Parachute Army began retiring in a north-easterly direction towards the German ports of Hamburg and Bremen. On 27 March 1945 General Günther Blumentritt, von Rundstedt's former Chief-of-Staff and now the commander of Twenty-fifth Army in Holland, was ordered to take over the leadership of First Parachute Army. The matter was urgent, he was told, since General Schlemm had been wounded and was unable to continue directing the affairs of the Parachute Army.

"I reported to Colonel General Blaskowitz at Army Group 'H,'" reports Blumentritt,[5] "and he and his Chief-of-Staff both agreed that once the Rhine had been crossed the situation, with the forces at our disposal, was past repair. But since orders from above were to continue resisting I was to do the best that I could. When I took over my new command on 28 March I found that there were great gaps in my front, that I had no reserves, that my artillery was weak, that I had no air support whatever and hardly any tanks. My communication and signal facilities were entirely inadequate and there was one corps under my command that I was never able to contact. The reinforcements that still came to me were hastily trained and badly equipped, and I never used them so that I could save needless casualties.

"Nevertheless, orders from the Supreme Command were still couched in the most rigorous terms enjoining us to 'hold' and 'fight' under threats of court-martial. But I no longer insisted on these orders being carried out. It was a nerve-racking time we experienced — outwardly putting a bold face on the matter in order to do one's duty as one had sworn to do — while we secretly allowed things to go their own way. On my own responsibility I gave orders for lines to be prepared in the rear ready for a retreat. By 1 April I had decided to direct the fighting in such a way that the army could be withdrawn in a more or less orderly manner and without suffering any great casualties, first on both sides of Munster and then behind the Ems Canal and finally to the Teutoburger Forest."

A week after their crossing, the Allied armies north of the Ruhr had already picked up another 30,000 prisoners-of-war. But this was as nothing compared to the rewards awaiting them still farther south. From these two bridgeheads at Remagen and Oppenheim, south of Mainz, the Americans had driven into the Frankfort Corridor, collecting thousands of prisoners all the way. Having secured a base of operations which stretched from the Neckar River in the south to the Sieg River in the north, and eastward for a depth of about fifty miles, the grand double envelopment of the Ruhr was to be undertaken. By 29 March this lodgment area had been seized. With Ninth U.S. Army charging east from their bridgehead at Wesel, and with First U.S. Army striking northwest from Marburg, the two American armies joined hands at Lippstadt on 1 April to effect the "largest double envelopment in history." [6]

Here in the heart of industrial Germany amidst the coal mines and steel factories and ammunition works of Essen and Düsseldorf and Dortmund and Wuppertal, lay the complete force of Field Marshal Model's Army Group 'B.' In a circle about eighty miles in diameter two armies, the Fifteenth and the Fifth Panzer, were trapped, containing between them some twenty-one divisions. Model had realized all the while what was happening, said his senior intelligence officer, but his requests to evacuate the Ruhr had been quashed.[7] Model had then taken steps to blunt the attack of First U.S. Army advancing along the southern edge of the Ruhr, but had been unsuccessful.

"I differed with Field Marshal Model in the way he tried to stop this rapid advance south of the Ruhr," said Kesselring.[8] "In my personal opinion he should have started his attack farther to the east, thereby cutting off the relatively weak points of your advance and restoring a north-south line, rather than allowing his flank to be turned as it was. By attacking too far west, Model ran into a much thicker column and was unsuccessful. It is the point at which you strike that makes the difference. One battalion striking at the right point can do far more than a division at the wrong point."

Once it was clear that the encirclement was complete, Model made desperate efforts to break out at Hamm in the north and Siegen in the south. Hardly had these been thrown back when Hitler took charge of matters. The Ruhr was to be held as a fortress, he ordered, and no withdrawal was to take place. "The troops in the Ruhr were given instructions not to surrender under any circumstances," said Göring.

And to make doubly sure that nothing of any value fell into Allied hands should the Ruhr be taken, Hitler also ordered the complete destruction of this entire industrial center. This demand was in furtherance of the scorched-earth policy already laid down on 19 March 1945. At that time Hitler had ordered that "all things of value — military installations, transport, communications, industrial and food supply installations within the Reich, which could be of any immediate or future use to the enemy for the continuation of his fight, will be demolished." But this futile gesture Model refused to carry out. Again according to his intelligence officer, he had been persuaded by Speer, the Reich Minister for Armament and Munitions, that such destruction would be useless and a crime against future German generations. He therefore only ordered a partial destruction of vital installations and prohibited the local Nazi party leaders from carrying out Hitler's orders to the letter.[9]

At Berlin Hitler was already preparing new areas of resistance. Having made the Ruhr into a fortress, he assumed it would hold out long enough to enable him to think up something else. According to Göring, the Führer thought the Ruhr would occupy twenty Allied divisions and thus prevent them from moving on elsewhere.

General Eisenhower, however, had no intention of launching an all-out attack against the complex, built-up area inside the pocket.

Rather the plan was slowly to compress the trapped formations into a smaller and smaller area until lack of ammunition and food forced them to surrender. And to carry out this operation only a limited number of Allied divisions would be used, while the rest pressed eastwards. Inside the Ruhr conditions worsened steadily. Trapped along with Model's Army Group were the millions of civilian inhabitants of these industrial cities. Attacked and strafed regularly by Allied planes, the communication facilities inside the pocket soon broke down. It became impossible to send ammunition where it was needed, and food was soon a problem in many districts. But despite these difficulties the German forces in the trap might well have made of the bricks and walls and factories of the Ruhr another Stalingrad. . Had they had the spirit and will to resist they might have created here a burning pyre to their Führer and their faith. But this they did not have. They were beaten and finished, and to most of them being encircled by American troops was the easiest and quickest way of getting out of the war.

"The continuation of resistance in the Ruhr pocket was a crime," said General Friedrich Köchling, the commander of 81 Corps, one of the encircled formations.[10] "It was Model's duty to surrender the pocket since he was an independent commander once his Army Group had been cut off. Only the danger of reprisals against my family prevented me from taking this step myself. My staff listened eagerly for news of American advances, and we congratulated each other when we learned that the Americans had occupied another town where members of our families were living. You see, the occupation of these towns made men, free men, of us again."

Lieutenant General Fritz Bayerlein, commanding 53 Corps in the Ruhr, was more practical than Köchling. Instead of merely moaning about his fate he decided to do something about it. Getting together with one of his divisional commanders, Major General Waldenburg of 116 Panzer Division, they began negotiations with 7 U.S. Armored Division for the surrender of the complete corps of four divisions. The matter had to be very delicately handled since two of the divisional commanders, Hammer and Klosterkemper, wanted to continue fighting. Bayerlein managed it by ordering his two stubborn generals to report to his headquarters. While they were on the way to him he sent out orders to the divisional staffs to assemble their units in preparation for surrender. When the two officers arrived at corps headquarters, they were confronted with a *fait accompli,* and shortly afterwards were whisked off to an American prison-camp. Thus Bayerlein in mid-April 1945 became one of the very few German

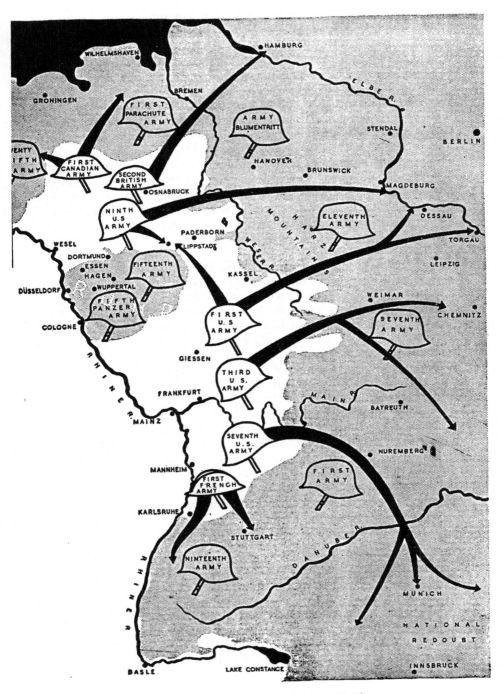

THE FINAL COLLAPSE — *April-May,* 1945.

senior officers in the West with enough personal courage to risk the vengeance of Hitler, by daring to organize the surrender of his command when it was obvious that further resistance could only lead to useless and wasteful bloodshed.

With this kind of morale amongst those on top, it was inevitable that opposition in the Ruhr would not last long. By 13 April prisoners began to turn up in such quantities that Allied facilities for handling them were taxed to the limit. On 14 April the capture of Hagen split the pocket in two. According to Jodl, when this occurred, Berlin ordered the troops to reassemble into small groups and hold out individually as long as possible. If this was impossible, then they were to get out as best they could, reorganize and attack the rear of the Allied lines! How far removed the Supreme Command was from the realities of the fighting front is best revealed by this statement of Jodl's.

On 16 April 80,000 Germans gave themselves up within twenty-four hours. Two days later the final collapse came — eighteen days after the Ruhr had first been encircled. Even to Allied staffs accustomed to handling vast quantities of captured Germans, this latest haul was staggering. No less than 325,000 troops, including thirty generals, crawled out from under the rocks of the Ruhr when the count was taken. They represented two complete German armies, the Fifteenth and the Fifth Panzer, seven corps, twenty-one divisions, and an innumerable amount of independent artillery, engineer, supply and replacement units. The one person, however, who did not turn up was Field Marshal Walter Model.

"On 21 April 1945 Field Marshal Model shot himself in my presence in a wood near Duisberg," said the senior intelligence officer at Army Group 'B,'[11] "I buried him, and I am, as far as I know, the only person who knows where his grave is. He chose death, because he had been accused of being a war criminal by the Russians. In the course of conversations I had had with him over a period of days, I expressed my opinion that the Western Powers would hand him over to the Russians — and it was this which decided him."

Chapter XXXII

RESISTANCE THAT NEVER CAME

WHILE the process of reducing the garrison of the Ruhr was in progress, the remaining Allied forces were anything but idle. Once the Ruhr had been encircled, the third and final phase of General Eisenhower's strategic plan for the defeat of Germany was undertaken. This was to consist of a major thrust by the First, Third and Ninth U.S. Armies through Central Germany towards Leipzig and Dresden. Simultaneously Field Marshal Montgomery's Army Group was to strike in a north easterly direction towards Bremen, Hamburg and the Elbe, while General Dever's Army Group in the south was to push on to Nuremberg and Austria, and prevent any concentration of German resistance in the mountainous terrain of the Austrian Alps. By this combined operation it was hoped to cut Germany first into two longitudinal slices, after which each half would be dealt with separately.

But whereas the Allies knew exactly where they were going and how they were going to get there, the Germans knew neither. After the collapse of the Ruhr, Jodl admitted, the Supreme Command had no overall plan. "From that time," he said,[1] "we could no longer talk of a general conduct of the war. We had no reserves and could exert no control over the situation." And the intelligence staff at SHAEF headquarters echoed these sentiments when, on 8 April, they wrote, "And so the enemy faces disaster but seems unwilling to face the fact. Assaulted by armies everywhere in men and material ten times as effective as his own, he fights on. National surrender seems out of the question, but individual surrender increases. The first five days of April disgorged 146,000 prisoners. Only the German High Command knows what it is doing. No one else does. Presumably a miracle is expected. But what: a secret weapon more potent than Kesselring. That is the only conclusion one can draw. With present aids there can be no hope. . . ."

It needed no military genius to assess the German position as desperate. One had only to look at a map. By the end of the first week in April the First Parachute Army had been pushed back to the Weser River at Minden and the Twenty-fifth Army was about to be trapped west of the Ijssel River and securely locked in the newly-designated "Fortress of Holland." The disappearance of Fifteenth and Fifth Panzer Armies into the rubble of the Ruhr left a gaping hole in the German center between Hanover and Kassel, with American armored columns already east of this latter city. In the south Seventh and First Armies had been thrown back to the Main River and they possessed nothing but the remains of the divisions broken in the Saar-Moselle débâcle to save them from being pushed back still farther. Only Nineteenth Army still hugged the right bank of the Rhine, south of Karlsruhe, and that was because no one had yet attempted to dislodge it.

The prisoner total rose like a sensitive barometer. By the middle of the month over 50,000 Germans were surrendering daily, and well over 500,000 had fallen into the Allied net in the first fortnight of April alone. Generals followed their men behind the barbed wire of a prison cage, but none could provide a clue as to when it was all going to end. Strategically the situation was lost, tactically it was hopeless, spiritually it was broken. "We are little men," explained the captured senior officers. "We do not know what is happening. Although everything is hopeless, we must obey. To a soldier a command is holy." And from above came neither leadership nor inspiration. The only command was still the same — continue to fight. "We did not discuss a general surrender until after Hitler's death," said Jodl.

Thus, baffled, disorganized, lost, the scattered remnants of the Wehrmacht hid in the woods until they were overrun, fought until they were overwhelmed, or waited until they were overtaken, depending upon the ability, fanaticism or common sense of their officers. While in the one place that mattered, a man turned mad wildly tried to keep the smashed bits of his armies together. But like blobs of mercury, they shattered at each succeeding touch, and tumbled farther and farther apart. The wind that the Führer, ignorance and discipline had sown continued to produce its whirlwind. "Hold on till the end," ordered the Führer, and there was only one course open — to obey. Or try or pretend to obey.

And thus it was that at this anti-climactic stage of the war two final gestures of resistance were attempted. The first was the organization of the Werewolves and the second was the preparation of defenses in the National Redoubt.

Sinister and weird is much of German mythology. Replete with mysterious and magic symbols, these legends have always appealed to the deep-rooted fascination for the supernatural which grips the German mind. The neo-pagan religions with their worship of the swastika and their revival of the rites and festivals for old German gods had their foundations in these myths of the ancient Teutonic tribes. The Werewolf movement was also designed to exploit this German love of mysticism. A werewolf was a human being which on occasions changed its appearance into that of a wolf. And along with the idea came all the trappings of the legend. The movement could use as its symbol the 'wolfsangel' or wolf hook and the convenient superstition that a house with such a sign marked on it would be immune from the haunting of werewolves.

When it became apparent that the final battles of World War II would be fought on German soil, it was decided that civilian resistance groups behind the fighting fronts in both the East and West would be needed. The Werewolf movement, organized by the S.S.

for that rôle, first began to function in Upper Silesia against the Russians. The Hitler Youth were given an important part in the enterprise, and as early as 22 February 1945, Wehrmacht personnel were also being assigned for Werewolf activities. In an order of that date, divisions in the East were told "to select a number of men whose homes are in territories now occupied by the enemy. These men must be of outstanding ability, experience and courage, and must be suitable to become leaders of Werewolf troops."

It was not until 1 April 1945 that the Werewolves made their official appearance in the West. A radio message proclaimed its aims and methods in a rather frenzied opening announcement: "The Werewolf is an organization born of the spirit of National Socialism," it ranted. "It does not heed the restrictions which are imposed upon combatants in our regular forces. Any means is good enough to harm the enemy. The Werewolf has its own jurisdiction which decides over life and death of our enemies as well as of traitors to our nation, and which also has the necessary power to ensure the execution of its verdicts. Every Bolshevik, every Briton and every American on German soil is fair game for our movement. Wherever we have an opportunity to extinguish their lives we shall seize it gladly without regard for our own lives. Any German, whatever his station and occupation, who offers his cooperation to the enemy will know our revenge."

With studied German thoroughness a series of schools was set up by Himmler to teach the most effective technique for carrying out guerrilla warfare. The many years of suppressing resistance movements in Occupied Europe had undoubtedly shown them the best methods to use, now that they had to form a resistance movement of their own. How far these investigations had gone, and an insight into the means that the Werewolves planned to adopt in carrying out their aims, can be seen in the following letter written on 23 February 1945 by a Dr. Widmann to S.S. Colonel Panzinger.[2] The subject is the employment of poisons.

"During my stay in Danzig," it reads, "S.S. Major Goertz received among other things a delivery of poisons to be employed by the Werewolf organization. I objected to the delivery of arsenic powder because Goertz told me that, according to instructions he had received, the arsenic was supposed to be used to poison alcohol. Arsenic is insoluble in pure alcohol and dissolves only slowly in dilute alcohol. Arsenic is suitable for poisoning food such as bread, cake, etc., but not for poisoning alcohol as was planned in this case.

"Suicide tablets were also delivered in Danzig. Goertz informed me that they contained veronal. My opinion in this matter is the following: the lethal dose for veronal amounts to about five to eight grams. It is often quite difficult to swallow such an amount in the form of tablets. This difficulty can hardly be overcome by instructions to let the tablets crumble in the mouth and to swallow them only in case of emergency. The deadly effect of veronal tablets is relatively slow, so that there is a possibility of calling a man back to life by pumping out his stomach. It must be assumed that the enemy will make use of such methods. A man who has been recalled to consciousness after severe narcotic poisoning is weakened to such an extent that he can easily be interrogated and will give all the desired information. It is therefore not a satisfactory suicide tablet. . . ."

But the Werewolf movement turned out to be all preparation and propaganda. A few isolated bands built underground dugouts in the forests and sallied forth to blow up small Allied food and petrol dumps. Groups of Hitler youths caused some annoyance by stretching wire across country roads and scattering glass and nails on busy highways. An occasional German was shot for collaborating with the Allies. Nothing else happened. No spontaneous uprising, no bitter underground campaign, no serious sabotage, no hard knots of fanatical resistance. Passively and with a kind of sullen relief, the German watched the Allied columns taking possession of his Fatherland. Everyone was sick of war. No one wanted to be a werewolf. A resistance movement presupposes a faith worth fighting for. One month before the end of the war the German people no longer possessed that faith. The vaunted howls of the Werewolf finally emerged as bleats from a sheep in werewolf clothing.

The story of the National Redoubt is even less heroic than that of the Werewolves. Since late 1944 a steady stream of reports from erratic agents, prisoners and a few air photographs seemed to indicate that large-scale defensive preparations were in progress for a last-ditch stand amongst the mountains of the Bavarian Alps. Here, in an area some 240 miles long and eighty miles deep bordering on the Swiss and Italian frontiers, it was expected that a final ideological demonstration of National Socialist resistance would be made. As the Allies drove deeper and deeper into Central Germany, this view gained credence amongst Allied intelligence staffs since, whether by coincidence or design, the remaining S.S. divisions had drawn back to the edge of the Redoubt in their defense of Vienna, and since the bulk of the German jet fighter planes were located in the south. Coupled with its unlimited facilities for natural defense amongst the narrow, winding roads and the icy, mountain crags, was the fact that Hitler's very own retreat at Berchtesgaden was centered in the area. The prospect of an up-to-date version of Brunhilde riding her horse into a blazing pyre would probably have appealed to a man of Hitler's mentality. In any case it appealed to Allied intelligence officers, and the possibility of its taking place was too dangerous to risk. It was partly to ensure the speedy elimination of any centers of resistance in this difficult terrain that prompted General Eisenhower to press forward into Western Austria as quickly as possible and destroy this potential Nazi haven.

If Hitler indeed planned to carry out such a last act of defiance, he kept the secret well. As late as January 1945 Jodl in a letter to Himmler opposed the idea of fortifying an area of the Swiss frontier, and made no mention of the Redoubt. Most of the Wehrmacht generals had never heard of the Redoubt, and those that had heard rumors could only shake their heads and agree that nothing was beyond Himmler and Hitler. In any case, they asserted, if such a plan was to be put in force, the army divisions would have been expected to carry out delaying actions while the S.S. divisions hurried to the safety of their Alpine defenses. Lieutenant General Kurt Dittmar, the official spokesman of the Wehrmacht, claimed that although some preparations had been made, the idea was mainly confined to paper.

By mid-April most of the key ministries from Berlin had been moved to the Berchtesgaden area, taking their documents and administrators with them. All but a small part of the staff of the Supreme Command had also been transferred to the Redoubt area. But the one man who might have made such a stand possible did not come. Whatever plans Hitler might have had for an impressive Götterdämmerung had, by mid-April, been outstripped by the Allies. Hardly had the Ruhr collapsed when the Russians were already biting into the rim of the Redoubt in the east, and American armored columns were charging towards Munich in the west. By April 20 Hitler had decided to remain in Berlin and defend it to the last. With that decision the National Redoubt, like the Werewolves, disappeared into the limbo of forgotten last stands.

In the West a front line no longer could be said to exist. The third week in April saw Allied spearheads 200 miles east of the Rhine and careering through Germany almost at will. While German battle-maps still indicated over sixty divisions opposing the American, British and French thrusts, the remnants of these hollow formations constituted hardly a third of this strength. The number of prisoners taken in twenty-one days had swollen from 500,000 to well over one million, including forty generals, and there was no indication that this rate of collapse was likely to decrease. New 'shadow' divisions were formed from the convalescents, the Volkssturm, the stragglers, the

feeble and the very young. With no training, few weapons and little
spirit these make-shift formations were flung helter-skelter wherever
the need seemed most pressing. And to make up for this lack of experience and material the 'shadow' divisions were given brave, colorful names instead of ordinary prosaic numbers. Potsdam, Clausewitz,
Scharnhorst, von Hutten, Jüterbog, Nibelungen, Hamburg were the
banners under which these new formations made their way into
battle, but the ghosts of Frederick the Great, Wagner and Bismarck
shouting in unison could not have inspired these sad imitations of
fighting units to further resistance.

To fill the great gap in the line created by the encirclement of the
Fifth Panzer and Fifteenth Armies in the Ruhr, the Supreme Command was creating a new army, the Eleventh, under General Walter
Wenck. Amidst the pine forests of the Harz Mountains about five
divisions were frantically being assembled to help bolster the torn
front. This was the bottom of the barrel after it had been scraped
clean. There was nothing more. "We had a few engineer and cyclist
units," said Jodl.[3] "Improvised forces, all these, to use in localized
operations under the defense commands. Wenck's was the only real
force."

It was at first hoped that the Eleventh Army would be used in a
counter-attack westward with the object of relieving Army Group
'B' in the Ruhr pocket, but General Bradley's troops had moved much
too quickly for such an effort. Utterly unaware of the speed and
strength of the American advance columns, the Supreme Command
ordered Wenck to attack towards the Thuringian Forest near Eisen-
ach. Before this move could be made the Eleventh Army was well
pocketed in the Harz Mountains. Ninth U.S. Army forming the northern arm of the pincer had taken Magdeburg on the Elbe on 18 April
after three days of unexpected opposition from the new 'shadow'
divisions. The southern arm of the pincer, formed by First U.S. Army,
south of the Harz, had little difficulty in reaching Dessau on 14 April,
which left a narrow gap between the two American armies through
which Wenck's 10,000 trapped men tried to escape. For four days the
Germans sought to hold these relentless jaws apart, but on 18 April
they snapped together and Hitler's final army had met its inevitable
fate — in a pocket.

One last attempt was made to relieve Wenck. In the region of
Soltau, over sixty miles to the north, the recently assembled von
Clausewitz Panzer Division was being put together out of the remains
of two panzer divisions and a panzer brigade destroyed on the Eastern
front. With Wenck's troops surrounded, the Supreme Command

ordered the von Clausewitz Division to go to the rescue. As the last serious offensive effort of the dying Wehrmacht in the West, the story of this formation's dash to the Harz Mountains is of some interest.

"The von Clausewitz Panzer Division was hurriedly organized from various units and contained between 5000 and 6000 men and about eighty tanks and assault guns," said its commander, Lieutenant General Martin Unrein,[4] a sharp-faced keen fellow of about forty. "My task was to push down to the Harz Mountains and relieve the troops under command of General Wenck. At the same time as I proceeded south I was to harass and attack the rear of the American divisions advancing on Magdeburg. I divided my division up into two battle groups and, striking where I assumed the boundary between British and American troops would be, I made very rapid progress. Meeting first British and then American forces I succeeded in destroying over 150 Allied vehicles of all kinds. I had little difficulty getting as far south as Brunswick, some sixty kilometres from where I began, and I even rode on the highways at night with all the lights of my convoy burning. I met the balance of my division in some woods south of Brunswick, and here we were found by American forces. After a severe artillery bombardment which caused heavy casualties, and a loud-speaker address warning us to surrender, most of my men gave in. I personally left the woods in a small car which I abandoned later and made my way east on foot. By pulling off the buttons of my coat and slipping on a pair of civilian trousers I attempted to pose as a French worker, but I was soon caught.

"Although my division did not reach the Harz Mountains as it was hoped, it did cause the enemy considerable damage and I believe that it drew two or three American armored divisions away from the Magdeburg area. My command of the von Clausewitz Panzer Division, at such a time, I considered a special honor, for with the complete German army in full retreat I was the one division that was able to attack."

The failure of this spectacular attempt to reach the Eleventh Army meant that most of the encircled troops, along with their would-be rescuers, were swept into the bursting Allied prisoner bag. Wenck himself managed to escape, and was hardly out when he was given a new task. He was to command another hastily assembled army, this one called the Twelfth, and take up a sector on the Elbe, between the Blumentritt Army on his right, also just formed, and Seventh Army on his left. But while his two neighboring armies faced west to meet the Anglo-American forces, Wenck's Army was to face *east* and attack in the direction of Potsdam. In other words the two fronts had now been pushed back to back so that they had been merged into one. And in the center, between Lauenberg and Stendal, where the fusion had taken place, the Supreme Command had decided to concentrate against the Russians. Thus, like a Siamese twin looking apprehensively in opposite directions at once, the Wehrmacht spent its final hours waiting for Hitler or Destiny to make up its mind.

And on 25 April 1945, at four-forty in the afternoon, at Torgau on the Elbe, the Siamese twin was severed in two when forward elements of the American 69th Infantry Division and the Russian 58th Guards Division met and shook hands before the press photographers of the Allied world. There was little that still remained of Hitler's Third Reich. Cities that had echoed to the full-throated roars of massed Nazis, that had proclaimed the victorious goose-step of the conquering Wehrmacht, that had toiled and sweated and smoked to produce the tools of war, were now shattered and still. Amidst the dust of their factories, the rubble of their homes and the stench of their dead, the Germans of Bremen and Hanover and Magdeburg and Leipzig and Stuttgart and Nuremberg heiled and marched no more.

Chapter XXXIII
DEFEAT

DEVELOPMENTS along the Eastern front had been just as sweeping. In Prussia Königsberg had fallen and in Austria Vienna had been abandoned. Danzig, Stettin, Potsdam, Küstrin were no more. Only Berlin remained, encircled and besieged, to carry out the vow of a fight to the very end. Within the charred and skeletal remains of the capital a heterogeneous force of tired battle groups, fanatical S.S., inexperienced Volkssturm, numbering some 250,000 strong, prepared to carry out the dictates of their Führer. While in his bunker beneath the Reich Chancellery, Adolf Hitler feverishly continued to plan the resurrection of an empire that already lay crumbled at his feet. On 23 April the Russians reached the outer suburbs of Berlin and the Führer's last stand had begun.

From a military standpoint Germany had been well defeated weeks before. The leaders of the Wehrmacht, however, had been so cowed and frightened by the twin shadows of Hitler and Himmler that they were incapable of organizing any independent action of their own to bring about an armistice. Only the few faithfuls surrounding the Führer himself still believed that some miracle might avert the impending collapse. And, as we shall see, the corroding influence of constant defeat was even beginning to undermine the allegiance of those that had remained loyal until now.

For once Hitler had decided to end his days in Berlin, the question of who was to don his fallen mantle began to trouble his most likely successors — Göring, Himmler and Bormann. Strangely enough there still seems to have been some earnest rivalry for the unattractive and thankless job of Führer of a fallen Third Reich. The only possible explanation for such keenness appears to be the potential bargaining power for personal immunity that might accrue to the man who finally brought about a formal surrender of Germany. Although Göring had been designated as Hitler's successor as leader of the state, Martin Bormann, Reichsleiter and the Führer's secretary, was to take over Hitler's other job as head of the National Socialist Party. Between Bormann and Göring existed a deep hatred which only Hitler's presence prevented from breaking out into open warfare.

According to Colonel Werner Grothmann, Himmler's personal adjutant,[1] this question of succession was further complicated by Hitler's decision to appoint a deputy Führer in the event of Germany's being split in two by the Americans. The responsibility of the deputy Führer was to be primarily military. Thus if Hitler were isolated in the north by the American drive, Kesselring would deputize for him in the south, and if he were cut off in the south then Gross-Admiral Dönitz would carry on the struggle in the north. But the appreciation was not complete enough. The third possibility, that Berlin might be surrounded and that Hitler might thus be unable to control either North or South Germany, was not even contemplated. It was unthinkable that the Russians would ever take Berlin. Hitler would see to that. It was this confident arrangement, coupled with the death or defection of the other three most likely Nazi princes, that resulted in Hitler's battered crown finally being plunked upon the balding head of Karl Dönitz.

Göring was the first of the heirs-designate to be renounced by the Führer. According to his own story[2] Göring left Berlin for Southern Germany on 21 April, having been informed that Hitler had decided to stay and die in Berlin. On 23 April, at three o'clock in the afternoon, Göring sent a telegram to the Chancellery announcing that in view of his position as Hitler's successor he would take over the duties of Reichsführer unless he received orders to the contrary by ten o'clock that night. Göring claims that he was encouraged in this action by a remark attributed to Hitler: "I shall never negotiate with the Allies, Göring can do it much better." But the Führer's reaction was quite different from what the Reichsmarshal had expected it to be. Göring suspects that Bormann, who received the telegram, interpreted it to Hitler as an act of treachery on Göring's part. In any case, before the ultimatum had expired Göring had been arrested by S.S. troops. Another telegram from Hitler then arrived asking the Reichsmarshal to resign all his offices. Göring, construing the wording literally, assumed that this order only applied to his titles as Prime Minister of Prussia, President of the State Council, President of the Reichstag and a half-a-dozen others — but not to his position as Führer-designate. Still another telegram that came much later sentenced Göring and his family to death. This message the Reichsmarshal considers to have been posthumous and he asserts that the signature should have read "Bormann" and not "Führer." Göring's sentiments towards Bormann were no less vindictive. "Everybody knew my first move would have been to liquidate Bormann," said the Reichsmarshal.

The account of Göring's rescue from this plight unfolds like the final reel of a Hollywood thriller when the United States marines arrive to save the hero just in the nick of time. As he stood surrounded by the S.S. troops, who had arrested him on 23 April, part of a Luftwaffe signals regiment passed by. The Luftwaffe easily outnumbered the S.S., and Göring, thinking quickly, ordered his troops to rescue him. The airmen charged and the S.S., being in no mood to argue, willingly gave up their prisoner. Recalling the occasion, the Reichsmarshal still glowed with satisfaction. "It was one of the most beautiful moments of my life," he said,[3] "to stand there in front of my troops and see them present arms to their Commander-in-Chief."

The retirement from Berlin of the Wehrmacht chiefs, Keitel and Jodl, did not have as dramatic a sequel as Göring's departure. On 23 April Jodl was told to make his way north and attempt to carry out the Führer's last tactical orders. These still spoke grandly of armies that existed nowhere else but on Hitler's battle-maps. Wenck's Twelfth Army was to attack east towards Potsdam, the Ninth Army surrounded north of Kottbus was to break out and drive north towards Berlin to join Wenck, while parts of Army Group Vistula were to attack south from Oranienburg to Spandau. Thus was the encirclement of Berlin to be broken, and its garrison relieved. Keitel was to be in charge of this Herculean effort.

Jodl set off for Flensburg in Schleswig-Holstein, where he hoped to organize further resistance. After a harrowing journey, chiefly at night, in which he was constantly evading first Russian and then British troops, Jodl reached his destination. But with no communication facilities at his command he could not assemble any forces. In constant touch with Hitler by high-frequency radio, Jodl received his last message from the Führer on the night of 29-30 April. Hitler was still juggling his imaginary formations, "How is the attack going at Oranienburg?" asked Hitler.[4] "Where is Wenck's advance column? What is the situation of the Ninth Army? . . ." Jodl's answers offered small consolation to those still trapped in the capital of the Reich.

Deep in the shelter of his bunker beneath the Chancellery at Berlin, Hitler was playing out the final scene of his rôle as a doomed dictator. The best report of those last days of the German Führer has been given by Hanna Reitsch, the well-known test pilot and aeronautical research expert. Her account, which is considered to be reliable, was published in the 19 November 1945 issue of *Interim*, the Intelligence Review of the British army of the Rhine. The extracts reproduced here are from that account.[5] It is a fascinating story by one of the last persons to get out of the shelter alive. Its straightforward reporting throws a revealing light on the personalities that had ruled and ravaged a continent for so long.

On 24 April Colonel General Ritter von Greim in Munich received a telegram ordering him to report to the Reich Chancellery. Taking along Hanna Reitsch, his personal pilot, they arrived in Hitler's bunker on the evening of 26 April after an exciting trip, during which they had twice been forced down by Russian fighters and in which von Greim's right leg had been shattered by Russian fire. While von Greim was having his leg tended by Hitler's personal physician, the Führer came into the sick-room.

"Do you know why I have called you?" said Hitler to von Greim.

"No, mein Führer," said von Greim.

"Because Hermann Göring has betrayed and deserted both me and his Fatherland," said Hitler. "Behind my back he has established connections with the enemy. His action was a mark of cowardice. And against my orders he has gone to save himself at Berchtesgaden. From there he sent me a disrespectful telegram. He said that I had once named him as my successor and that now, as I was no longer able to rule from Berlin, he was prepared to rule from Berchtesgaden in my place. He closes the wire by stating that if he had no answer from me by nine-thirty on the date of the wire he would assume my answer to be in the affirmative."

With eyes hard and half-closed and in a voice unusually low he went on: "I immediately had Göring arrested as a traitor to the Reich, took from him all his offices, and removed him from all organizations. That is why I have called you to me. I hereby declare you Göring's successor as Commander-in-Chief of the Luftwaffe. In the name of the German people I give you my hand."

Later that first evening Hitler called Reitsch to him in his room. She remembers that his face was deeply lined and that there was a constant film of moisture in his eyes. In a very small voice he said: "Hanna, you belong to those who will die with me. Each of us has a phial of poison such as this," with which he handed her one for herself and one for von Greim. "I do not wish that one of us falls to the Russians alive, nor do I wish our bodies to be found by them. Each person is responsible for destroying his body so that nothing recognizable remains. Eva and I will have our bodies burned. You will devise your own method. Will you please inform von Greim?"

Reitsch sank to a chair in tears, not, she claims, over the certainty of her own end, but because for the first time she knew that the Führer saw the cause as lost. Through the sobs she said, "Mein Führer, why do you stay? Why do you deprive Germany of your life? When the news was released that you would remain in Berlin to the last, the people were amazed with horror. 'The Führer must live so that Germany can live,' the people said. Save yourself, mein Führer, that is the will of every German."

"No, Hanna; if I die it is for the 'honor' of our country; it is because as a soldier I must obey my own command that I would defend Berlin to the last. My dear girl, I did not intend it so. I believed firmly that Berlin would be saved at the banks of the Oder. Everything we had was moved to hold that position. You may believe that when our best efforts failed I was the most horror-struck of all. Then when the encirclement of the city began the knowledge that there were 3,000,000 of my countrymen still in Berlin made it necessary that I stay to defend them. By staying I believed that all my troops of the land would take example through my act and come to the rescue of the city. I hoped that they would rise to superhuman efforts to save me and thereby save my 3,000,000 countrymen. But, my Hanna, I still have hope. The army of General Wenck is moving up from the south. He must and will drive the Russians back long enough to save our people. Then we will fall back to hold again."

It appeared almost as if he believed this himself and as the conversation closed he was walking about the room with quick, stumbling strides, his hands clasped behind him and his head bobbing up and down as he walked. Although his words spoke of hope, Hanna claims that his face showed that the war was over.

The next morning Hanna Reitsch was introduced to the other occupants in the elaborate shelter. On 27 April they numbered Goebbels and his wife with their six children; State-Secretary Neumann; Hitler's right hand, Reichsleiter Martin Bormann; Eva Braun; S.S.

Obergruppenführer (General) Fegelein as liaison between Himmler and Hitler and the husband of Eva Braun's sister; Dr. Lorenz, of the German press; one or two officers representing each of the armed services; Hevel, from Ribbentrop's office; Hitler's personal pilot, two of his female secretaries and his personal physician; and various S.S. orderlies and messengers. Reitsch claims that these comprised the entire assembly.

Late in the afternoon of the 27th Obergruppenführer Fegelein disappeared. Shortly thereafter it was reported that he had been captured on the outskirts of Berlin disguised in civilian clothes, claiming to be a refugee. The news of his capture was immediately brought to Hitler, who instantly ordered him to be shot. The rest of the evening Fegelein's betrayal weighed heavily on the Führer and in conversation he indicated a half-way doubt as to Himmler's position, fearing Fegelein's desertion might have been known and even condoned by the S.S. leader.

Reitsch describes Goebbels as being insanely incensed over Göring's treachery. He strode about his small, luxurious quarters like an animal, muttering vile accusations concerning the Luftwaffe leader and what he had done. The precarious military situation of the moment was Göring's fault. Their present plight was Göring's fault. Should the war be lost, as it certainly now seemed it would be, that, too, would be Göring's fault.

One of the last things Reitsch remembers hearing from the lips of the propaganda master was: "We shall go down for the glory of the Reich, so that the name of Germany will live for ever." Even Reitsch was moved to conclude that the Goebbels display, in spite of the tenseness of the situation, was a bit overdrawn and out-and-out theatrical. She claims that in her opinion Goebbels, then as he always did, performed as if he were speaking to a legion of historians who were avidly awaiting and recording every word. After listening to these tirades she and von Greim often asked each other with a sad, head-shaking attitude: "Are these the people who ruled our country?"

Frau Goebbels, as described by Reitsch, was a very brave woman who represented the epitome of Nazi indoctrination. Desperately concerned about the fate of her children in the event of a collapse, Frau Goebbels said to Reitsch: "My dear Hanna, when the end comes you must help me if I become weak about the children. You must assist me to help them out of this life. They belong to the Third Reich and to the Führer, and if those two things cease to exist there can be no further place for them. But you must help me. My greatest fear is that at the last moment I shall be too weak."

It is Hanna's belief that in the last moment she was not weak.

The Goebbels children numbered six. Their names and approximate ages were: Hela, twelve; Hilda, eleven; Helmut, nine; Holde, seven; Hedda, five; Heide, three. They were the one bright spot of relief in the stark death-shadowed life of the bunker. Reitsch taught them songs, which they sang for the Führer and for the injured von Greim. Their talk was full of being in 'the cave' with their 'Uncle Führer,' and in spite of the fact that there were bombs outside, nothing could really harm them as long as they were with him. And anyway, 'Uncle Führer' had said that soon the soldiers would come and drive the Russians away and then tomorrow they would all go back to play in their garden. Everyone in the bunker entered into the game of making the time as pleasant as possible for them.

It seemed to Reitsch that Hitler's girl friend, Eva Braun, remained studiously true to her position as the 'show-piece' in the Führer's circle. Most of her time was occupied in finger-nail polishing, changing of clothes for each hour of the day, and all the other little feminine tasks of grooming, combing and polishing. She seemed to take the prospects of dying with the Führer as quite matter of fact, with an attitude that seemed to say ". . . Had not the relationship been of twelve years' duration and had she not seriously threatened suicide when Hitler once wanted to be rid of her. This would be a much easier way to die and much more proper. . . ." Her constant remark was: "Poor, poor Adolf, deserted by everyone, betrayed by all. Better that 10,000 others die than that he be lost to Germany."

In Hitler's presence Eva Braun was always charming, and thoughtful of his every comfort. But only while she was with him was she completely in character, for the moment he was out of earshot she would rave about all the ungrateful swine who had deserted the Führer and that each of them should be destroyed. All her remarks had an adolescent tinge and it appeared that the only 'good' Germans at that time were those who were caught in the bunker and that all the others were traitors because they were not there to die with him. The reasons for her willingness to die with the rest were similar to those of Frau Goebbels. She was simply convinced that whatever followed the Third Reich would not be fit to live in for a true German.

Martin Bormann moved about very little, but kept instead very close to his writing-desk. He was "recording the momentous events in the bunker for posterity." Every word, every action went down on his paper. Often he would visit this person or that to scowlingly demand what the exact remark had been that passed between the Führer and the person he had just had an audience with. Things

that passed between other occupants of the bunker were also carefully recorded. This document was to be spirited out of the bunker
at the very last moment so that, according to the modest Bormann, it
could "take its place among the greatest chapters of German history."

Throughout Hanna's stay in the bunker Hitler's manner and physical condition sank to lower and lower depths. At first he seemed
to be playing the proper part of leading the defense of Germany
and Berlin. And at first this was in some manner possible as communications were still quite reliable. Messages were telephoned to
a flak-tower and from there were radioed out by means of a portable,
balloon-suspended aerial. But each day this was more and more
difficult, until late on the afternoon of the 28th and all day on the
29th communications were almost impossible.

Occasionally Hitler still seemed to hold to the hope of General
Wenck's success in breaking through from the south. He talked of
little else, and all day on the 28th and 29th he was mentally planning
the tactics that Wenck might use in freeing Berlin. He would stride
about the shelter, waving a road map that was fast disintegrating
from the sweat of his hands and planned Wenck's campaign with
anyone who happened to be listening. When he became over-excited
he would snatch the map from where it lay, pace with a quick nervous
stride about the room, and loudly 'direct' the city's defense with
armies that no longer existed.

But despite Reitsch's evident high esteem of the Führer, she was
shocked by the apparent mismanagement she observed and learned
about in the bunker. For instance, Berlin had been depleted of arms
to hold the Oder. When that line fell it appeared that no coherent
defense plan of Berlin had been prepared, certainly adequate arrangements had not been made to direct the defence from the bunker.
There was no other communication equipment available than the
telephone that led only to the flak-tower. It appears that only in
the last moment had he decided to direct the battle from the shelter
and then did not have the first tools with which to operate. No maps.
No battle plans. No radio. Only a hastily prepared messenger service
and the one telephone were available. The fact that, unknown to
Hitler, the Wenck army had been destroyed some days before was
only one example of the inadequacies. All of which resulted in the
Führer of Germany sitting helplessly in the cellar impotently playing
at his table-top war.

On the night of the 27th to the 28th the Russian bombardment
of the Chancellery reached the highest pitch it had yet attained. As
this indicated that the Russian ground troops would overrun the

area at any moment, another suicide council was called by the Führer. All plans as to the destruction of the bodies of everyone in the shelter were gone over again. The decision was that as soon as the Russians reached the Chancellery grounds the mass suicide would begin. Last instructions were given as to the use of the poison phial.

The group was as hypnotized with the suicide rehearsal and a general discussion was entered into to determine in which manner the most thorough destruction of the human body could be performed. Then everyone made little speeches swearing allegiance again and again to the Führer and to Germany. Yet, through it all, still ran the faint hope that Wenck might get in and hold long enough to effect an evacuation. But even on the 27th, Reitsch claims, the others paid lip-service to the Wenck hope only to follow the lead of the Führer. Almost everyone had given up all thoughts of being saved, and said so to each other whenever Hitler was not present.

Then, on the 29th, fell the greatest blow of all. A telegram arrived which indicated that the staunch and trusted Himmler had joined Göring on the traitor list. It was like a death-blow to the entire assembly. Reitsch claims that men and women alike cried and screamed with rage, fear and desperation, all mixed into one emotional spasm. Himmler, the protector of the Reich, now a traitor was impossible. The telegram message was that Himmler had contacted the British and American authorities through Sweden to propose a capitulation to the San Francisco conference. Hitler had raged as a madman. His color rose to a heated red and his face was virtually unrecognizable.

Later came the anti-climactic news that the Russians would make a full-force bid to overrun the Chancellery on the morning of the 30th. Even then small-arms fire was beginning to sprinkle the area above the shelter. Reitsch claims that everyone again saw to their poison.

At one-thirty on the morning of 30 April, Hitler, with chalk-white face, came to von Greim's room and slumped down on the edge of the bed. "Our only hope is Wenck," he said, "and to make his entry possible we must call up every available aircraft to cover his approaches." Hitler then claimed that he had been informed that Wenck's guns were already shelling the Russians in Potsdamer Platz.

"Every available plane," Hitler said, "must be called up by daylight; therefore, it is my order to you to return to Rechlin and muster your planes from there. It is the task of your aircraft to destroy the positions from which the Russians will launch their attack on the Chancellery. With Luftwaffe help Wenck may get through. That is the first reason why you must leave the shelter. The second is that Himmler must be stopped," and immediately he mentioned the S.S. Führer his voice became more unsteady and both his lips and hands trembled. The order to von Greim was that if Himmler had actually made the reported contact and could be found he should immediately be arrested.

Both von Greim and Reitsch protested vehemently that the attempt would be futile and that they preferred to die in the shelter, but Hitler was adamant. "This is the only chance of success that remains," he said. "It is your duty and mine to take it."

Preparations were quickly made. Everyone gave the departing pair some token, something to take back into the world. Everyone wrote quick, last-minute letters for them to take along. Thirty minutes after Hitler had given the order they left the shelter.

A small armored vehicle took them through the flaming city to where an Arado 96 was hidden near Brandenburger Tor. Reitsch claims that she is certain this was the last craft available. The possibility of another plane having come in and out again with Hitler as passenger she dismisses as highly unlikely, as von Greim would certainly have been informed. In addition Russian fire was much too intense.

After a harrowing trip through Russian anti-aircraft bombardments and Russian fighters, they landed at Rechlin where von Greim ordered all available aircraft to the aid of Berlin. They then flew to Dönitz and there they met Himmler, who confirmed the truth of the report Hitler had received. Moreover, Keitel told them that Wenck's army had long ago been destroyed or captured, and that he (Keitel) had sent word of this to Hitler the day before (30 April). A few hours later the announcement of Hitler's death was received. On 24 May, von Greim, after being captured, committed suicide, using his phial of poison. Reitsch decided to remain alive for one reason only. "To tell the truth," she said. "To tell the German people the truth about the dangers of the form of government that the Third Reich gave them."

And thus ends the story of Hanna Reitsch. The tailpiece was told at Nuremberg when Erich Kempka, Hitler's chauffeur, filled in the missing details. Hitler had died, swore Kempka, at two or three o'clock in the afternoon of 30 April after shooting himself through the back of the mouth. He admitted that he had not seen the entire body itself, but that he had seen Hitler's legs protruding from the blanket in which the body had been rolled. But this glimpse of Hitler's boots had been sufficient to enable Kempka to declare "that Hitler is dead is something I can say with certainty." His evidence of the death of Eva Braun, whom Hitler had married in the bunker, was more direct and conclusive. Kempka testified that he had himself carried her body into the grounds of the Reich Chancellery and there doused it in petrol and burned it.[6]

Martin Bormann's death did not occur until 2 May, said Kempka. It had taken place a few yards in front of him when both men were walking beside a tank fighting its way out of Berlin near the Friedrichstrasse and the Weidendamm Bridge. Between two and three o'clock in the morning anti-tank gunfire had blown up the tank, temporarily blinding Kempka. Before he lost consciousness, however, he had seen Bormann collapse in the flames about the tank.

On 1 May, at Flensburg, the surviving leaders of the German Reich received the news of Hitler's death in a radio message from Bormann. The first message addressed to Grand Admiral Dönitz read: "Führer died 3.30 p.m. yesterday." It was shortly followed by another message, again sent to Dönitz, which, according to Jodl, read: "Hitler provided for you to be President, Goebbels Chancellor, Seyss-Inquart Foreign Minister, Bormann Interior Minister. Leave it to you to tell the people. Will try to get to you." It was signed jointly by Goebbels and Bormann.[7]

At thirty-seven minutes past ten o'clock on the night of 1 May Dönitz broke the news to the German nation by the following announcement over Radio Hamburg:

German Wehrmacht! My comrades! The Führer has fallen. Faithful to the great idea of preserving the peoples of Europe from Bolshevism he had consecrated his life, and died a hero's death. One of the greatest heroes in German history has passed away. We lower our flags in proud reverence and sorrow. The Führer had appointed me to succeed him as Head of the State and Supreme Commander of the Wehrmacht. I take over the command of all branches of the German Wehrmacht in the determination to continue the struggle against Bolshevism until the fighting troops and the hundreds of thousands of families in Eastern Germany have been preserved from enslavement or destruction. I must continue to wage war on the British and Americans in so far and for so long as they hinder me in the prosecution of the fight against Bolshevism. The situation demands of you, who have already accomplished such great historical feats and now long for the end of the war, further unconditional service. I demand discipline and obedience. Only by the unquestioning execution of my orders can chaos and the downfall of Germany be avoided. He who now shirks his duty, thus bringing death and enslavement upon German women and children, is a coward and a traitor. The oath pledged by you to the Führer now applies for each one of you to me as the successor appointed by the Führer.

German soldiers! Do your duty! The life of our nation is at stake!

DÖNITZ.

But German generals were not having anything more to do with oaths. They had had enough of being tied to a vow and now that they had finally been released they were going to do what fear and discipline had prevented them from doing for many months. They were going to surrender — Dönitz or no Dönitz. The first mass capitulation took place in Italy. Curiously enough, here, where the front had been most stable, negotiations for surrender had begun as far back as mid-February 1945. Then Obergruppenführer (General) Karl Wolff, the chief S.S. officer in Northern Italy, had begun overtures for a capitulation of all German troops in the Mediterranean theatre. Since Wolff was bargaining for terms and the Allies would accept only unconditional surrender, no progress was made.

According to Colonel General Heinrich von Vietinghoff, who had taken over command of all German forces in Italy when Kesselring was sent to replace von Rundstedt, the later stages of these negotiations were carried on with Vietinghoff's full consent. "When I last saw Hitler in mid-March 1945," said von Vietinghoff,[8] "I realized how mad the man had become. His statements to me were all lies and made no sense. He told me that he intended to kill himself but that nevertheless he expected us to keep on fighting to the end. In mid-April Oberstgruppenführer Wolff sent some envoys to Field Marshal Alexander, but they were told that all negotiations would have to be carried on with General Eisenhower."

By that time, however, the Allied offensive to break the Gothic Line was in full swing. On 21 April Bologna fell, on the 23rd the Po was reached, on the 26th Milan was taken by partisans. In the process almost 150,000 prisoners had been taken in less than three weeks, which was an unprecedented figure for this theatre. These prods served to stimulate the Germans into renewed approaches for surrender. This time there were no more arguments. On 29 April the Germans agreed to the unconditional surrender of all the forces in Italy — close to 1,000,000 men — and to the cessation of all hostilities on 2 May. By signing these terms, von Vietinghoff became the first German theatre commander to risk surrendering his forces while Hitler was still alive. Even though he only managed it by one day, this act of common sense was, nevertheless, somewhat of a feat for a Wehrmacht general, the vast bulk of whom were still either too filled with fear, too blinded by ignorance, or too corroded by discipline to act on their own.

On Hitler's death the front — it could no longer be divided up into eastern and western halves — consisted roughly of four large but rapidly dwindling pockets. In Holland the Twenty-fifth Army under Colonel General Johannes Blaskowitz sat behind the Grebbe Line, east of Utrecht, waiting for the next Allied move. From Emden to just west of Stettin, in an elongated strip which contained the North German ports and all of Denmark, was another pocket containing the remnants of First Parachute Army and Army Blumentritt, linked together in an army group under Field Marshal Ernst Busch, west of the Elbe. East of the Elbe, in the same northern pocket, were what was left of the Heinrici's Army Group Vistula and the bits of Schorner's Army Group Centre that had escaped north. A third pocket formed in Czechoslovakia held most of Army Group Center and part of Rendulic's Army Group South. The fourth and final pocket being shaped south of the Danube in Austria and Northern Yugoslavia was accumulating in it all the flotsam and jetsam that was being pushed into it by the Americans from the north and west, the Russians from the east and the Yugoslav partisans from the south. It contained what was left over of Army Group South from Russia, Army Group 'G' from Germany and Army Group 'E' from the Balkans.

Resistance amongst all these broken forces existed in name only. During the thirty days of April the Western powers had taken over 1,650,000 prisoners. Included in the collection were those who had risen with the Wehrmacht to its pinnacle of power, and fallen with it to its present depth — Field Marshal von Kleist, von Leeb, Weichs, List, and finally von Rundstedt himself.

This brought the total number of prisoners taken in the West since the Allies first landed on the beaches of Normandy to the astronomical figure of almost 3,000,000 men. To those who are interested in such things, this meant that an average of 9000 Germans had surrendered to the Allies for each day of these eleven months. And all this while their Führer was still alive. To anyone who claims that Germany was not defeated in World War II such statistics should provide the perfect answer.

Sporadic negotiations for surrender were taking place all along the front during the last days in April, but these were usually conducted on a divisional or lower level. Except for those that had been forced to surrender in the Ruhr, no officer commanding an army or an army group was yet prepared to follow von Vietinghoff's example. Typical of this stubborn, unthinking, automatic adherence to a code was the behavior of Colonel General Blaskowitz in Holland. A man of sixty-two years with a flattened frog-like jaw, broad nostrils and thinning hair, Blaskowitz was a sterling product of the German General Staff. His forces in Holland had been pushed back to the Grebbe Line by the Canadians and were obviously incapable of resisting much longer. However Blaskowitz, and his superior civilian authority, Arthur von Seyss-Inquart, still held one trump-card in their hands.

They controlled the dykes protecting the Netherlands from the waters of the North Sea and the Zuider Zee. Should the Canadians continue their advance, it was quite simple for the Germans to open the dykes and flood the countryside with salt water. Such an action would have been an incalculable disaster, for the fertility of the swamped land would have been destroyed for years to come.

In an attempt to prevent the Germans from carrying this out, and also to arrange for the sending of food and supplies to the starving populations of Western Holland, General Eisenhower sent his Chief-of-Staff, Lieutenant General Bedell Smith, to talk to Seyss-Inquart and Blaskowitz on 30 April. After some quibbling the Germans agreed to the delivery of Allied food to the Dutch, but when it came to the question of the surrender of the Twenty-fifth Army in Holland both men refused to shoulder the responsibility. Although realizing that their plight was a hopeless one, that the military situation was beyond repair, and that further resistance could only mean the needless suffering of millions of Dutch civilians, neither Seyss-Inquart nor Blaskowitz would yield. The Nazi commissioner shifted the burden neatly to Blaskowitz by stating that such a decision was one for the military commander alone, and Blaskowitz shrugged it off by answering that he could not consider capitulation so long as any further resistance continued in Germany. The mechanical doll that had been built only to obey could do nothing else even though its spring was fast unwinding and it found itself goose-stepping off the table.

But once the news of Hitler's death reached the front, the senior commanders, like children just released from school, tumbled over each other in their eagerness to make an end. The experiences of General Blumentritt, whose army was defending a sector between Bremen and Hamburg, reveals how the preliminary negotiations for a final armistice were brought about.

"On 1 May I was summoned to Field Marshal Busch," said Blumentritt,[9] "and told that the Führer was dead, that Grand Admiral Dönitz was his successor, and that my oath of allegiance was to be transferred to him. I objected to this and told the Field Marshal that I would not take the oath nor would I allow my troops to do so. Following this interview I was contacted by Lieutenant General Dempsey of Second British Army to discuss matters. I was anxious to do so and informed Field Marshal Busch to this effect. The Field Marshal got in touch with Dönitz who informed him that no negotiations were to be conducted by me since Dönitz himself intended to contact Field Marshal Montgomery.

"Surprisingly enough after this discussion I was ordered to defend

Hamburg. I immediately drove back to Busch's headquarters and pointed out to the Field Marshal the madness of attempting to carry out such an order. I told him that it could only cause senseless slaughter and ruin what was left of Hamburg. The Field Marshal telephoned to Dönitz again and after some deliberation it was decided to declare Hamburg an open city.

"I at once left for Hamburg and on my arrival I heard that Dönitz was wavering again, and had apparently changed his mind about giving up Hamburg. I, however, refused to let this interfere with my decision. At noon on 2 May the British were contacted and the arrangements for the evacuation of the city agreed upon. At the same time I informed Field Marshal Busch by telegram that I now considered it necessary to bring the war to a conclusion, and that I was acting with the full concurrence of all my generals in this request. My answer was that Dönitz was already preparing to send a deputation to Field Marshal Montgomery."

Thus, with Hitler's death, the tottering structure of the Third Reich quickly began to collapse. In each of the remaining pockets independent negotiations for surrender were started. Frightened by their own propaganda and by their own conscience, those who held nominal command over the remnants of the Wehrmacht made frantic but unsuccessful efforts to drive a wedge between the Russians and the Anglo-American forces by offering to surrender only to the Western Powers. Himmler had already tried this ruse through the Swedish Government. On being rebuffed he had no other solution to offer. He waited aimlessly and uselessly for the end. A fortnight after the war was over he was dead having committed suicide by biting a poison capsule. Dönitz and Keitel, however, had not yet given up the attempt to split the Allies.

When Admiral Hans von Friedeburg, representing the Supreme Command, arrived at Field Marshal Montgomery's headquarters he asked to be allowed to surrender three German armies facing east, so as to avoid surrendering them to the Russians. This was turned down. During an interval in the discussion von Friedeburg was asked if he knew what the military situation was. He replied that he was fairly well in the picture, but could not claim to be strictly up to date. When shown the true situation he burst into tears. Von Friedeburg was now so anxious to get back and make his report to Dönitz, that he became very agitated at a slight delay in the preparations to send him back. Finally he beckoned to an officer and said in English, "Hurry up, hurry up — time is money." The next day von Friedeburg returned with the necessary authority to surrender all the German forces in Northwest Germany, the Frisian Islands and Heligoland,

Holland, Schleswig-Holstein and Denmark. It was signed at twenty minutes past six on the evening of 4 May.

Another bit of the Wehrmacht to surrender before the official end was Army Group 'G' under General Schultz, whose First and Nineteenth Armies laid down their arms in the Austrian Alps. On 5 May Admiral von Friedeburg, becoming an expert by now, arrived at General Eisenhower's headquarters in Rheims. Again he attempted to surrender only the forces facing the Western Powers. But it was obvious that the Admiral was now merely playing for time. The longer the negotiations could be dragged out the more German forces would be saved from becoming prisoners of the Russians. Again von Friedeburg was shown how helpless the German situation was, again he burst into tears, and again he made his report to Dönitz. This time he was told General Jodl would be arriving to help him out.

Jodl arrived on the evening of 6 May and promptly entered into von Friedeburg's game. He was willing to surrender to the Western Allies but not to the Russians. When this was refused he asked for a forty-eight hours' adjournment before signing, on the pretext that the time was needed to get the order down to outlying units. General Eisenhower was now fed up with these tactics. He bluntly told Jodl that unless the Germans agreed to his terms, the Allied front would be sealed off in forty-eight hours and further westward movement by German civilians or soldiers would be prevented, by force if necessary. This convinced Jodl that the end had come and he wired Dönitz to that effect. The necessary acceptance of Allied terms finally arrived from Dönitz, and at forty-one minutes past two on the morning of 7 May Jodl, on behalf of the German Supreme Command, signed the act of surrender. At midnight of the 8-9 May 1945, Europe was once more officially at peace.

Chapter XXXIV
THE VANQUISHED

THERE remains only to assess what is left. In Germany it is very little. Physically and spiritually the Reich is a broken land. Its wounds are so deep and grievous that they cannot possibly be healed within a generation of time. To compare the Germany of 1918 with the Germany of 1945 is nonsense. No basis for comparison exists. For then, even after the demands of Versailles, Germany still remained one of the strongest industrial countries in Europe. With the factories of Silesia undamaged and the coal mines of the Ruhr intact the German people held within their grasp the tools with which to forge their weapons of revenge. They needed only a leader and a cause to busy them at converting this economic wealth to the production of the machines of war.

Today what still remains in Germany is barely sufficient to feed her scattered millions, let alone clothe and house them. Beneath the mountains of rubble that were once Berlin, Cologne, Düsseldorf, Nuremberg, Stuttgart, Hamburg, Frankfurt, Essen, Munich lie the power and strength of what was once the Third Reich. Until it is rebuilt Germany will remain a poverty-stricken liability to those that conquered her. Under the most favorable conditions the task of reconstruction alone can be measured in decades. In a world anaemic from the losses of six years of destruction, and in which Germany's requirements will undoubtedly be given last priority in any distribution of capital goods, it is reasonably safe to predict that Germany's war-producing potential has been emasculated for a period of time far beyond the foreseeable future.

This, of course, is not to say that Germany's ability to constitute a threat to world peace no longer exists. There are too many Nazi industrialists, administrators and officers still at large, too many fanatical youths poisoned forever with the virus of Hitlerism, to warrant such an optimistic assumption. But the Reich alone, purely on the basis of its physical incapacity to rebuild its shattered economy, cannot play a dominant rôle in another major world conflict for many years to come. However, even though the German nation will not be fit enough to undertake the prima donna rôle in a future war, she can very profitably become a valuable military assistant to whatever country succeeds in enlisting her aid. It is in this rôle of a pawn, available to the highest and most attractive bidder, that constitutes Germany's greatest menace. To be on the winning side, even as a junior partner, is better than constantly losing by one's self. Those Germans that still burn for revenge realize that within their lifetime this fact constitutes their one remaining trump-card. Even now they are beginning to play it for all it is worth.

What part in a political game of this kind can the German military caste have? If they are allowed to, quite an important one. For while they are now a dismembered group of broken and embittered individuals, it needs little encouragement to get them back to the planning table where they can once more practice the art they know and love so well. Organize them into a Free Corps or a 100,000 army and you have the nucleus of another Wehrmacht. To plant the tiniest seed of militarism in German soil is to grow the inevitable weeds of war.

This does not mean that all Germans are incurable militarists. A nation that has produced a Goethe, a Beethoven and a Thomas Mann is capable of leading the world upwards as well as down. But before the present generation of Germanic people can be cleansed of the iron that has settled in their soul through the teachings of Frederick the Great, Bismarck, Nietzsche and Hitler, they must be isolated for at least a generation or two from the germ of Teutonic domination that has been nurtured within them for so long. Disband all military organizations, forbid the production of weapons, ban the teaching of military science, prevent the wearing of uniforms, and you have gone most of the way towards eliminating German militarism. To claim that belligerence is inherent within the German is flying in the face of all anthropological and sociological evidence to the contrary. It is as spurious and unscientific a contention as the blood theories of the Nazis themselves. But one other step must be taken before a new German generation will be relatively free of infection. The worst-contaminated of the lot, the men whose lives have been corroded with the rot of militarism, hate and revenge, must be either cured or segregated from the rest of their countrymen. Those diseased by Nazism, of course, belong to this class of problem men. The other large group needing special attention is the German officer class.

The only striking feature of German generals as a group is their normality. They look like anyone else. The bemonocled, bescarred, bullet-headed prototype of a Prussian officer belongs to Hollywood and the popular magazines. In reality these men, who represent the final stage in the evolution of a caste, look and act like any other representative group of middle-aged bankers, brokers, clerks, teachers, tradesmen that one might find in England, United States, Russia or France. They are blond and swarthy, tall and small, thin and fat, stupid and clever, stolid and energetic, eager and listless, polite and rude, good and bad. They are loyal, treacherous, vain, petty, humble, courageous, officious, domineering, weak, strong and any other adjective that might be used to describe the average man.

A story told to me by an American colonel in charge of one of the early prisoner-of-war camps for senior officers — appropriately enough called 'Ashcan' — may illustrate this point. The plumbing facilities at 'Ashcan' were not lavish, and in the prisoners' wing only one bathtub existed for a number of generals, colonel generals and field marshals. This hygienic prize, however, was awkwardly situated, since it adjoined the largest bedroom in the house which, because he was the highest-ranking officer at the camp, had been assigned to Field Marshal Keitel. There had been no love lost between Keitel and many of those generals to whom he had sent impossible orders from the Führer's headquarters during the war. To most of the General Staff he was contemptuously referred to as 'nick-Keitel' because he always 'nodded' like a yes-man at everything the Führer said.

Since the only way to reach the bathroom was through Keitel's room it meant that a constant stream of officers would have to invade the Field Marshal's privacy to have a bath. Keitel, standing on his dignity and his seniority, forbade any of the officers from entering his room and thus deprived them all of their one opportunity to bathe. Like docile children, the others accepted this ruling, even though they resented it bitterly. Realizing that to openly break Keitel's authority in such a matter would only worsen, rather than alleviate, the situation, the Allied camp authorities devised an ingenious solution to the problem of keeping their wards clean. They brought to 'Ashcan' Field Marshal von Rundstedt, who not only keenly disliked Keitel but was one of the few officers in the Wehrmacht senior to him as well. It was therefore logical that von Rundstedt should be given the best room in the camp, which included the troublesome bathroom, and Keitel be sent to occupy one of the less pretentious quarters. Taking over his new quarters von Rundstedt immediately laid down a new set of rules. All officers were free to pass through his chamber to the bathroom whenever they liked — with one exception. The exception was Field Marshal Keitel.

While the tale may have gathered some flourishes in the re-telling, human pettiness of this kind was just as prevalent amongst the German Generals of the Wehrmacht as it might have been amongst the lowliest clerks in an insurance company. Only in their unbending adherence to the discipline of their caste — even as prisoners-of-war — and in their attendant loss of a ready sense of humor, did they differ on the surface from those who had captured them. It is important to realize this, I feel, in order to discount the notion that German officers were somehow 'different' from normal men. For it was because of this presupposed difference in their make-up that the world was ready to credit them with a reputation of military omnipotence which had little basis in actual fact.

German propaganda, and it was inadvertently helped by the press of the world in this regard, succeeded in building up the German officer as a superhuman military machine towering above all others in his profession, both in ability and performance. Many Germans will attempt to perpetuate this myth in the coming years by offering varied excuses for the defeat of the Wehrmacht. They will blame it on Hitler's interference, on the overpowering strength of Allied material, on the stupidity of Nazi politicians, on dozens of other reasons some of which did and some of which did not contribute to the downfall of the Third Reich. But one reason that they will rarely or never offer for their defeat was the fact that, in addition to these other weaknesses in their national effort, they were also beaten on the battlefield. The Russians did it time and time again; the Western Powers did it time and time again. If this book has proved anything, I trust that it has proved that as well as making strategical blunders of the first magnitude in the early years of the war, the German generals also made far-reaching mistakes of their own design in the battles of the West.

These mistakes, some made with Hitler's help and a large number made without it, undoubtedly brought about Germany's military defeat. The German General Staff will attempt to duck and squirm out of taking their share of responsibility for the military collapse of the Third Reich. Having done it after World War I they will try it again after World War II. But the facts are irrefutable. Despite their longer study of, their fuller experience in, and their greater passion for the art of war than any of their opponents, they nevertheless managed to lead their country to the most overwhelming defeat in modern times. That alone should be enough to tear away the martial halo from above their brows.

But if that were not enough, the sight of these martinets stripped of their uniforms and their authority would complete the disillusioning process. For they are not all hard, calculating, learned, keen men — these generals of the Wehrmacht. A few — a very exceptional few — are. The bulk are so ordinary that I was constantly amazed that anyone should ever have been in awe or fear of them. There was Straube, a wizened, wrinkled corps commander who was the picture of dejection and self-pity; there was Schack, who couldn't remember the numbers of the three regiments in his division; there was Dietrich, who had studied to be a butcher and who could not get beyond sergeant's rank before Hitler came on the scene; there was Fiebig, who looked and talked like a Park Lane playboy, and many others who would have lived out their lives as mediocrities and unknowns had not Hitler and war puffed them up to look like giants and geniuses.

As a group post-war generals fall into three categories — the fanatics, the disillusioned and the converts. No one better represents the fanatics than Brigadeführer (Major General) Kurt Meyer. Now serving a sentence of life imprisonment for having incited his men to shoot Canadian prisoners-of-war, Meyer is typical of the kind of German it would be most dangerous to let loose in Germany once again. A devoted disciple of Nazism and all that it stands for, his mind is so distorted by pseudo-philosophy, military jingoism and bald lies that no possible experience could ever purify it of its beliefs. Along with my fellow-interrogator I visited this thirty-four-year-old ex-commander of the 12 S.S. Hitler Jugend Division about three months after the war had ended. It was a time when most senior officers were letting their hair down about the treatment and degradation they had undergone under National Socialism. His first words to us were, "You will hear a lot against Adolf Hitler in this camp, but you will never hear it from me. As far as I am concerned he was and still is the greatest thing that ever happened to Germany."

During a two-day discussion with Meyer about the activities of his division in Normandy, I had an opportunity of seeing what went on in the mind of this representative product of Hitlerism. At first Meyer scrupulously refrained from talking about anything other than the military problems of his formation. But once he felt assured that our visit was concerned only with historical facts, and had nothing to do with the war crimes with which he was charged, Meyer became more expansive in his speech. When he began to wander into the political and philosophical field, it might have been the reincarnation of Hitler and Goebbels voicing their cant.

"Germany fought this war for the preservation of Western culture and civilization," Meyer assured us. "The menace of the East was always appreciated by the Führer, and his one object was to save Europe from the menace of Bolshevism. We had no quarrel with the English or French, but these countries, unfortunately, had no idea of the Russian system of life and its people. The peoples of the East want to sweep away all of Western culture as we know it, and set up in its place their own half-developed, animal-like existence. This Germany tried unsuccessfully to prevent."

According to Meyer this Eastern threat was not confined to Russia alone. It was a question of the European peoples attempting to stem the advance of the barbaric Asiatic peoples. "So seriously do I believe in this menace," continued Meyer, "that I have spoken to many of my young S.S. officers who are in this camp with me." (The camp was classified as a 'black' camp containing the most dangerous Nazis amongst German prisoners-of-war.) "They have all agreed with me that this Eastern danger must be dealt with first, and this in my opinion includes Japan as well as Russia. I am therefore prepared to offer to the Allied authorities my services, and those of the other S.S. officers in Allied hands, in helping them fight the Japanese." (The war with Japan was not yet over at the date of this discussion.) "My proposition is that I be given permission to recruit one S.S. division of about 23,000 men from amongst the German prisoners-of-war. This formation will be named the 'S.S. Division Europa,' and it is to be equipped with German weapons and equipment. I will have no difficulty in raising the men for such a unit to take part in the struggle against the East. We will then show you how Germans can fight."

That talk of this kind should come from a German divisional commander a few months after the end of the war shows how successful Nazi propaganda had been in deluding a generation of Germans as to what the non-Germanic world was thinking. To Meyer's distorted mind it seemed perfectly logical for British and American troops to welcome as allies an S.S. division which represented everything that they had been fighting against for so long. Perhaps better than the hundreds of books that have been written on the subject, this one speech of Meyer's reveals how difficult, and perhaps even hopeless, the task of re-educating this brand of young Nazis will be.

The fanatics are not only confined to the young. There are a number of the older officers who still cling to their faith in National Socialism. But they are usually more cautious in expressing their views than was Meyer. Thus one day Colonel General Kurt Student, Commander-in-Chief of the German parachutists and confidant of the Führer's, was sitting with some fellow-prisoners and a British officer in one of the prison camps. To pass the time away, a mock local government under the democratic system was instituted and Student impatiently assumed the rôle of Bürgermeister. His irritation at the discussions was evident, and at last, unable to control himself any longer, he burst out: "Enough of this democratic twaddle!" There was a frightened silence, but with a hasty glance at the British officer, he added, "I mean, of course, *German* democratic twaddle."[1]

The second category of German senior officers, and by far the largest one, are the disillusioned members of the Wehrmacht. These are chiefly the older men who have been through two wars and know how it feels to lose twice. Because of their age and because of their experience, a large number of them are fed up with soldiering, and from behind the barbed wire of their prison camps express a longing to begin fresh careers in the peaceful pursuits of farming or business or art. Since the bulk of these men are well over fifty their yearning for a life of quiet is understandable. But to presume from such sentiments that they would be willing to renounce the profession to which their whole life had been devoted, should the opportunity ever arise to practice it again, is a wishful and dangerous deduction. The majority of German generals still believe that there was nothing wrong in why Germany fought World War II, but only in how she fought it. To them the Führer's great crime was not that he waged an aggressive and immoral war, but that he lost it. For that sin, both National Socialism and Adolf Hitler will never be forgiven by the German General Staff.

Further salt was rubbed into the grievous wound of defeat by the callous, brutal and contemptuous manner with which Hitler handled his military leaders. This ruthless trampling upon the dignity and pride of his senior officers even managed to alienate from the Führer the loyalty and respect of some of those men who had been closest to him. One of these was Oberstgruppenführer (Colonel General) 'Sepp' Dietrich, who rose from a crude, uneducated butcher to become the most popular military figure in the Waffen S.S. But although Dietrich owed his entire fame to the Führer's patronage, the bitter and chastening experiences of his last days as one of Hitler's generals thoroughly dampened his fanaticism. It was at Vienna in the final days of World War II that Dietrich met his disillusionment.

The S.S. divisions that had been destroyed in Normandy and then rebuilt only to be badly pommeled again in the Ardennes, had been sent off to Hungary at the end of January 1945, to hold back the rapidly-advancing Russians. Dietrich, as Commander-in-Chief of the Sixth S.S. Panzer Army, soon found that battles in the East were just as difficult to win as they had been in the West. Slowly retiring before the Russians, Dietrich, in March, was ordered by Berlin to stand in front of Vienna and under no circumstances was he to withdraw into the city. "But there were almost sixty Russian divisions against us," said Dietrich, "and we finally had to fall back into Vienna itself." As a result of this failure to carry out orders a wireless message from the Supreme Command was sent to Dietrich on 27 March. "The Führer believes that the troops have not fought as the situation demanded," it read, "and it is ordered that the divisions 1 S.S. 'Adolf Hitler,' 2 S.S. 'Das Reich,' 4 S.S. 'Totenkopf' and 9 S.S. 'Hohenstauffen' be stripped of their arm-bands." Furthermore, the message went on, all promotions in the Sixth S.S. Panzer Army, which were to be announced on Hitler's birthday, were canceled.

The arm-bands to which the order referred had always been the proud emblem of these élite Nazi divisions. They bore the name of the division of the wearer, and these names, such as Adolf Hitler, Hohenstauffen, Frundsberg, Götz von Berlichingen, identified the formation with some great patriotic figure of Germany's past or present. To deprive these divisions of the names with which they had been associated all through the war was equivalent to divesting a British Guards regiment of its title 'Guards.'

Dietrich's reaction to this order was violent. He first got drunk and then went to sleep for three hours. "When I awoke," he said, "I asked myself, 'Am I crazy or are they crazy? But I'm not crazy, therefore they must be!'" He summoned the four S.S. commanders to his headquarters, and throwing the message on the table, said, "There's your reward for all that you've done these past five years." He told his commanders not to take down their arm-bands, and wrote a flaming message to the Führer's headquarters in which he announced that rather than carry out this order he would shoot himself. Dietrich waited for about a week, and when no reply had come, he bundled up all his decorations, from the Iron Cross to the Oak Leaves with Swords and Diamonds, and sent them back to Adolf Hitler. Before any repercussions to such defiance could be felt Hitler was dead and the war was over.

The disillusioning process experienced by Dietrich was felt in a greater or less degree by almost every senior officer who had come into contact with the tantrums and temperament of the Führer. Some of them, like Beck, von Witzleben, Rommel, von Kluge, had paid with their lives for trying to take some effective action, even though late, to rid Germany of their mad leader. Others, like von Brauchitsch, Halder, von Rundstedt, had thrown up their hands in disgust at the course of events, and as a result ended the war either in retirement or in a concentration camp. But most of them, like Keitel, Jodl, Warlimont, Blumentritt, continued to obey their Führer until the very end, even though that obedience led them to sanction crimes and horrors that have shamed Germany in the eyes of the world for decades to come.

The third category of generals, and this is by far the smallest group, are the truly converted. While many of these officers profess to believe in democracy, a few moments' conversation with them soon reveals that these protestations are but lip-service to a philosophy they cannot possibly comprehend. However, there have been some who have genuinely come to understand the concept of freedom of thought and speech, and who are sincerely anxious to help lead the German people back to some sane and dignified system of government. Allowed to return to their Fatherland, and encouraged to express their views, these men, discouragingly few in number as they are, might well find a useful function in the shaping of a new and enlightened Germany.

If then the converted are sent back to Germany, and the fanatics are kept out of Germany, the problem of the future of the vast bulk of the others remains unsolved. The judgment at Nuremberg, by refusing to declare the German High Command and the German General Staff criminal organizations, has thereby implied that those members of these organizations who are free from war crimes are entitled to their liberty on the same basis as any other prisoner-of-war. Will it be dangerous, then, to return these ex-officers to their Fatherland once more? The answer is an unsatisfactory yes and no. Yes, if there is any semblance of a military organization left within the Reich. No, if all military institutions in Germany are effectively disbanded, and kept disbanded, for their lifetime at least.

Since Germany's threat to world peace lies not in her own capacity to wage an independent war within the next quarter of a century, but in her value as a partner in any future world conflict, it is important that her bargaining power as such a partner be kept to a minimum. The complete demilitarization of Germany is an essential prerequisite in any such policy. For once any form of militarism is permitted to function in the Reich then beware of the ex-officers of the Wehrmacht. They will flock to any organization that allows them to wear a uniform, as they flocked to the Free Corps and the 100,000 army after World War I. And in uniform these men are dangerous — first, because they know only the art of warfare; secondly, because they fear, distrust and hate, primarily, Russia, and to a lesser extent the Western Powers; and thirdly, because their minds are disciplined to obey blindly whatever demagogue is next allowed to dominate and lead the German people.

It is reasonable that men should want to do what they know best, and not only do the ex-members of the German General Staff know the business of making war best, but they know nothing else. Deprive them of weapons to play with, maps to mark, men to command and orders to be obeyed and they may become useful and peaceful members of society. Convince them that they are not, and never were, supermen superior in blood and race to those about them and they may lose their insensate fear of Russia and their unreasonable contempt for the Western Powers. Teach them disobedience, as Gertrude Stein once said, or more constructively teach them how to think for themselves, and they may then be able to distinguish right from wrong on the evidence of their own conscience, and not only on the orders of a Führer.

But, conversely, give them an army, no matter how small, encourage their suspicions of the Russians or their disrespect for Western parliamentary institutions, or prevent them from ridding themselves of a disciplined mentality that will only accept democracy if it is 'ordered' to do so, and the German High Command and the German General Staff and the entire German Wehrmacht, by whatever name they are then called, will be neck-deep in another world war, whether they are fighting with the West against the East because they are frightened, or with the East against the West because they are ambitious. And should another generation of German officers steeped in the Prussian military tradition of Frederick the Great, Bismarck and Hitler, be brought before another international tribunal to be tried for their crimes in a third world war, then there is little doubt but that the judgment of that tribunal will contain similar words and findings to those delivered in the verdict at Nuremberg.

"They (the officers of the German General Staff and the High Command) have been responsible in large measure for the miseries and suffering that have fallen on millions of men, women and children. They have been a disgrace to the honorable profession of arms. Without their military guidance the aggressive ambitions of Hitler and his fellow-Nazis would have been academic and sterile. Although they were not a group falling within the words of the Charter, they were certainly a ruthless military caste. The contemporary German militarism flourished briefly with its recent ally, National Socialism, as well as, or better than, it had in the generations of the past.

"Many of these men have made a mockery of the soldiers' oath of obedience to military orders. When it suits their defense they say they had to obey; when confronted with Hitler's brutal crimes, which are shown to have been within their general knowledge, they say they disobeyed. The truth is they actively participated in all these crimes, or sat silent and acquiescent, witnessing the commission of crimes on a scale larger and more shocking than the world has ever had the misfortune to know. This must be said."

APPENDIX A

SENIOR GERMAN OFFICERS INTERVIEWED
BY THE AUTHOR

(All appointments are those held in Northwest Europe and Italy)

Field Marshal Karl Gerd von Rundstedt, Commander-in-Chief West.

Colonel General Joseph 'Sepp' Dietrich, Commander 1 S.S. Panzer Corps, Fifth Panzer Army, Sixth S.S. Panzer Army.

Colonel General Kurt Student, Commander German Airborne Troops, Army Group 'H,' First Parachute Army.

Colonel General Heinrich von Vietinghoff, Commander Army Group 'C,' Tenth Army.

General Günther Blumentritt, Chief-of-Staff to Commander-in-Chief West, Commander Twenty-fifth Army, First Parachute Army.

General Hans Eberbach, Commander Seventh Army, Panzer Group 'Eberbach.'

General Richard Heidrich, Commander 1 Parachute Corps, 1 Parachute Division.

General Heinrich von Lüttwitz, Commander 47 Panzer Corps, 2 Panzer Division.

General Eugen Meindl, Commander 2 Parachute Corps.

General Alfred Schlemm, Commander First Parachute Army.

General Eugen-Felix Schwalbe, Commander 88 Corps, 719 Infantry Division, 344 Infantry Division.

General Leo Geyr von Schweppenburg, Commander Panzer Group West.

General Otto Sponheimer, Commander 67 Corps.

General Erich Straube, Commander 86 Corps.

General Gustav von Zangen, Commander Fifteenth Army, 87 Corps.

Lieutenant General Wilhelm Daser, Commander 70 Infantry Division.

Lieutenant General Erich Diestel, Commander 346 Infantry Division.

Lieutenant General Edgar Feuchtinger, Commander 21 Panzer Division.

Lieutenant General Ferdinand Heim, Commandant 'Fortress Boulogne.'

Lieutenant General Wolfgang Pickert, Commander 3 Flak Corps.

Lieutenant General Hermann Plocher, Commander 6 Parachute Division.

Lieutenant General Erwin Sander, Commander 245 Infantry Division.

Major General Kurt Meyer, Commander 12 S.S. Panzer Division.

Major General Theodor Wisch, Commander 1 S.S. Panzer Division.

Colonel Eberhard Wildermuth, Commandant 'Fortress Le Havre.'

Lieutenant Colonel Ludwig Schroeder, Commandant 'Fortress Calais.'

APPENDIX B

BIBLIOGRAPHY
DOCUMENTS

War Office Intelligence Reviews.
SHAEF Weekly Intelligence Summaries.
Twenty-first Army Group Intelligence Reviews.
Twelfth Army Group G-2 Reports.
First U.S. Army G-2 Reports.
Second British Army Intelligence Summaries.
First Canadian Army Intelligence Summaries.
Third U.S. Army G-2 Reports.
Seventh U.S. Army G-2 Reports.
Ninth U.S. Army G-2 Reports.
Interim, British Army of the Rhine Intelligence Reviews.
SHAEF Psychological Warfare Reports.
Twenty-first Army Group Psychological Warfare Reports.
War Office Interrogation Reports on Field Marshal von Rundstedt, Colonel
General Halder, General Blumentritt, General von Manteuffel.

PUBLICATIONS

W. E. D. Allen and Paul Muratoff. *The Russian Campaigns of 1941-43.
The Russian Campaigns of 1944-45.*
Lieutenant General Walter Bedell Smith. 'Eisenhower's Six Great Deci-
sions,' *Saturday Evening Post.*
Captain Harry C. Butcher. *Three Years with Eisenhower.*
K. C. Chorley. *Armies and the Art of Revolution.*
Winston Churchill. *Secret Session Speeches.*
General Dwight D. Eisenhower. *Report by the Supreme Commander to
the Combined Chiefs-of-Staff on the Operations in Europe of the
Allied Expeditionary Force, 6 June 1944 to 8 May 1945.*
W. E. Hart. *Hitler's Generals.*
Ralph Ingersoll. *Top Secret.*
B. H. Lidell Hart. 'The German Generals,' *The New English Review.*
General G. A. Marshall. *Biennial Report of the Chief-of-Staff of the United
States Army, 1 July 1943 to 30 June 1945, to the Secretary of War.*
Colonel S. L. A. Marshall. *Bastogne: The First Eight Days.*
Field Marshal Bernard L. Montgomery. *Normandy to the Baltic.*
Colonel C. P. Stacey. *The Canadian Army in Normandy.*
General H. Maitland-Wilson. *Report by the Supreme Allied Commander
Mediterranean to the Combined Chiefs-of-Staff on the Italian Cam-
paign, 8 January 1944 to 10 May 1944. Report by the Supreme Allied
Commander Mediterranean to the Combined Chiefs-of-Staff on the
Operations in Southern France (August 1944).*
The Trial of German Major War Criminals. Proceedings of the Inter-
national Military Tribunal Sitting at Nuremberg, Germany. London,
1946.

NOTES

PART I — THE CAUSES

Chapter II — HITLER

[1] This incident is reported by a lieutenant colonel of the historical section of the OKW who was responsible for keeping the war diary at the Führer's headquarters, First Canadian Army Intelligence Summary, 1 May 1945.

[2] SHAEF Weekly Intelligence Summary, 1 April 1945.

[3] This speculation is not meant to imply, of course, that the political head of a democratic state could never have overruled his military leaders. Churchill often did, or tried to, particularly in the early desert campaigns undertaken by Field Marshal Wavell. But it is contended that there was much more give-and-take between Allied political and military personalities than could have been possible in a dictatorship. A striking illustration of this ability of a military leader to insist on his course of action being taken despite the pressure of political opposition is reported in Captain Butcher's book, *Three Years with Eisenhower*. He there records that on 5 August 1944, Prime Minister Churchill spent a complete afternoon attempting to convince General Eisenhower to cancel the impending invasion of Southern France. "Ike said no," writes Butcher, "continued saying no all afternoon, and ended saying no in every form of the English language at his command." The Allied Supreme Commander was supported in his stand by Admirals Ramsay and Tennant. In Hitler's Germany such opposition to the Führer's views would have meant instant dismissal.

Chapter III — DISCIPLINE

[1] First Canadian Army Intelligence Summary, 1 May 1945.

[2] 12 British Corps Intelligence Summary, No. 6.

Chapter IV — IGNORANCE

[1] *La Lanterne*, Brussels, November 1945.

[2] Personal interview, General Schlemm, October 1945.

[3] Personal interview, Colonel General Student, October 1945.

[4] Personal interview, General Schlemm, October 1945.

[5] Fifth U.S. Army G-2 Report, No. 274.

[6] 'File on Colonel M,' *Interim*, British Army of the Rhine Intelligence Review.

PART II — THE BEGINNINGS

Chapter V — THE WEHRMACHT IS REBORN

[1] Quoted by Bénoist Méchin, *Histoire de l'armée Allemande*, vol. i, p. 131.

Chapter VI — HITLER VERSUS THE GERMAN GENERAL STAFF

[1] 'The Officers and the Corporal,' *Interim*, British Army of the Rhine Intelligence Review.

[2] *Ibid.*

[3] 'The Trial of German Major War Criminals.' Proceedings of the International Military Tribunal Sitting at Nuremberg, Germany. Part I, London, 1946, p. 156 *et seq.*

4 Reproduced from a SHAEF report in First Canadian Army Intelligence Summary, 30 April 1945.

5 *Ibid.*

6 'The Officers and the Corporal,' *supra.*

Chapter VII — The Phoney War

1 'The Officers and the Corporal,' *supra.*

2 'The Trial of German Major War Criminals,' *op. cit.,* p. 166 *et seq.*

3 'The Officers and the Corporal,' *supra.*

4 *Ibid.*

5 'German Naval Preparations in the West,' *Interim,* British Army of the Rhine Intelligence Review.

Chapter VIII — Victory — and Defeat

1 'The Officers and the Corporal,' *supra.*

2 Personal interview, Field Marshal von Rundstedt, October 1945.

3 War Office Interrogation, Colonel General Halder, September 1945.

4 War Office Intelligence Review, November 1945.

5 'Wir Fahren Gegen England,' *Interim,* British Army of the Rhine Intelligence Review.

6 *Ibid.*

7 On 23 April 1942, Prime Minister Churchill said: "Moreover in 1940 an invading force of perhaps 150,000 picked men might have created mortal havoc in our midst." 'Secret Session Speeches,' London, 1946, p. 52.

8 War Office Intelligence Review, November 1945.

9 Personal interview, General Blumentritt, February 1946.

10 'The Officers and the Corporal,' *supra.*

PART III — THE MISTAKES

Chapter IX — The Early Mistakes — Gibraltar and Crete

1 Report, Nuremberg Trial, *The Times,* London, 10 January 1946.

2 Report, Nuremberg Trial, *The Times,* London, 8 December 1945.

3 Report by Ossian Goulding, *Daily Telegraph,* London, 15 October 1945.

4 Seventh U. S. Army Report of Interrogation of Reichsmarshal Hermann Göring, 19 May 1945.

5 Report, Nuremberg Trial, *The Times,* London, 16 March 1946.

6 Interview, Field Marshal Keitel, *Daily Graphic,* London, 17 September 1946.

7 Personal interview, General Meindl, February 1946.

8 Interrogation of Colonel General Student, War Office Intelligence Review November 1945.

9 *Ibid.*

Chapter X — The Greatest Mistake — Russia

1 'The Trial of German Major War Criminals,' *op. cit.,* p. 176.

2 Report, Nuremberg Trial, *The Times,* London, 12 February 1946.

3 Report, Nuremberg Trial, *The Times,* London, 11 December 1945.

4 War Office Interrogation, Colonel General Halder, September 1945.

5 Personal interview, Colonel General Dietrich, September 1945.

6 Personal interview, General Schlemm, October 1945.

7 War Office Interrogation, Field Marshal von Rundstedt, July 1945.

8 Personal interview, General Blumentritt, February 1946.

9 War Office Interrogation, Field Marshal von Rundstedt, July 1945.

[10] *Ibid.*

[11] Personal interview, General Blumentritt, February 1946.

[12] War Office Interrogation, Field Marshal von Rundstedt, July 1945.

[13] War Office Interrogation, Colonel General Halder, September 1945.

[14] Personal interview, Lieutenant General Pickert, July 1946.

[15] W. E. D. Allen and Paul Muratoff, *The Russian Campaigns of* 1941-43, London, 1944, p. 132.

Chapter XI — THE DECISIVE MISTAKE — UNITED STATES

[1] 'The Trial of German Major War Criminals,' *op. cit.,* p. 73.

[2] *Ibid.*

[3] 'The Trial of German Major War Criminals,' *op. cit.,* p. 178.

[4] War Office Intelligence Review, December 1945.

[5] Report, Nuremberg Trial, *The Times,* London, 10 January 1946.

[6] According to Ciano's diary, produced at Nuremberg, the Japanese Ambassador in Rome saw Mussolini on 3 December 1941, and informed him that Japanese-American relations were at a dead-end. He asked for, and received, complete assurance that Italy would declare war on the United States immediately after the outbreak of hostilities. Ciano also records the fact that Berlin's reaction before the event was extremely cautious. This would seem to contradict Göring's assertion that the attack on Pearl Harbor came as a complete surprise. Yet Jodl, at Nuremberg, also agreed with Göring that the attack was unexpected. Jodl testified that Hitler himself was genuinely surprised the night of Pearl Harbor for he had come into Jodl's map-room in the middle of the night to inform Keitel and himself of the news. The answer would seem to be that while the Germans expected Japan to take action against the United States, they had not been informed of either the manner in which, or the time when, such hostilities would begin.

[7] War Office Intelligence Review, December 1945.

Chapter XII — THE FINAL MISTAKE — EL ALAMEIN

[1] War Office Interrogation, Colonel General Halder, September 1945.

[2] Interview with General Cramer, *The Times,* London, 26 October 1945.

[3] Interview with Field Marshal Keitel, *Daily Graphic,* London, 17 September 1946.

[4] 'German Naval Preparations in the West,' *Interim,* British Army of the Rhine Intelligence Review.

[5] Personal interview, Colonel General Student, October 1945.

[6] Personal interview, Colonel General von Vietinghoff, August 1946.

[7] *Ibid.*

[8] 'The Officers and the Corporal,' *Interim,* British Army of the Rhine Intelligence Review.

PART IV — THE INVASION

Chapter XIII — THE ATLANTIC WALL AND THE MEN BEHIND IT

[1] War Office Interrogation, General Blumentritt, September 1945.

[2] Personal interview, General Blumentritt, February 1946.

[3] Personal interview, Field Marshal von Rundstedt, October 1945.

[4] *Ibid.*

[5] First Canadian Army Intelligence Summary, 24 November 1944.

[6] Personal interview, Field Marshal von Rundstedt, October 1945.

Chapter XIV — WATCHING AND WAITING
[1] Personal interview, General Blumentritt, February 1946.
[2] Personal interview, Field Marshal von Rundstedt, October 1945.
[3] Quoted by Lieutenant General Walter Bedell Smith, *Sunday Express*, London, 9 June 1946.
[4] Personal interview, General Blumentritt, February 1946.
[5] Quoted by Lieutenant General Walter Bedell Smith, *supra*.
[6] The six armored divisions north of the Loire were 1 S.S., 12 S.S., 2, 21, 116 and Panzer Lehr Divisions. South of the Loire were 2 S.S., 9 and 11 Panzer Divisions and 17 S.S. Panzer Grenadier Divisions. Under Rommel's direct command were 2, 21 and 116 Panzer Divisions.
[7] Personal interview, Lieutenant General Feuchtinger, August 1945.

Chapter XV — THE FIRST DAYS
[1] Personal interview, Field Marshal von Rundstedt, October 1945.
[2] Telephone Journal of Seventh Army, First Canadian Army Intelligence Summaries, 27 August, 22 and 28 September, 27 October 1944.
[3] Personal interview, Lieutenant General Feuchtinger, August 1945.
[4] *Ibid.*
[5] Personal interview, Brigadeführer Meyer, August 1945.
[6] Personal interview, Colonel General Dietrich, September 1945.
[7] Telephone Journal of Seventh Army, *supra*.
[8] 'As a German General Saw It,' *Saturday Evening Post*, 20 October 1945.
[9] Telephone Journal of Seventh Army, *supra*.
[10] 'As a German General Saw It,' *supra*.

Chapter XVI — THE BATTLE OF THE BRIDGEHEAD
[1] 858 Grenadier Regiment of 346 Infantry Division.
[2] Account of 2 Panzer Division as told by General von Lüttwitz in personal interview.
[3] 276 Infantry Division.
[4] Personal interview, Colonel General Dietrich, September 1945.
[5] Personal interview, Field Marshal von Rundstedt, October 1945.
[6] *Ibid.*
[7] 9 S.S. and 10 S.S. Panzer Divisions.
[8] Field Marshal von Rundstedt, *supra*.
[9] These seven formations were: 1 S.S., 9 S.S., 10 S.S., 12 S.S., Panzer Lehr, 2 and 21 Panzer Divisions.

Chapter XVII — THE GERMAN SOLDIER STILL HOPES
[1] Second British Army Intelligence Summary, 11 July 1944.
[2] Second British Army Intelligence Summary, 7 July 1944.
[3] Personal interview, General Blumentritt, February 1946.
[4] *Ibid.*
[5] Personal interview, Field Marshal von Rundstedt, October 1946.

PART V — THE DECLINE

Chapter XVIII — JULY TWENTIETH
[1] 'Political Implications of the 20th of July,' *Interim*, British Army of the Rhine Intelligence Review.
[2] Amongst senior German officers opinion seems to be divided as to whether or not von Kluge was in the plot. General Geyr von Schweppenburg, who was

himself approached to take part, asserts definitely that von Kluge had agreed to co-operate with the plotters.

[3] 'The German Intelligence Branch and 20 July,' by Franz Maria Liedig of the Naval Intelligence Branch of the Abwehr, *Interim*, British Army of the Rhine Intelligence Review.

[4] Interrogation of von Cramm, 13 U.S. Corps G-2 Report.

[5] SHAEF Weekly Intelligence Summary, 23 September 1944.

Chapter XIX — DEFEAT IN NORMANDY

[1] Personal interview, General Blumentritt, February 1946.

[2] War Office Intelligence Review, August 1945.

[3] Personal interview, Brigadeführer Wisch, August 1945.

[4] A short account of this action from the Allied viewpoint is contained in *Canada's Battle in Normandy*, by Colonel C. P. Stacey. In part it reads: "The 8th British Corps, composed of three armored divisions, had crossed the Orne low down, where, thanks to the airborne troops, both its banks had been in our hands from the beginning. The armor now lunged southward, hoping for a break-through. In the first instance things went well; but on the edge of the higher ground about Bourguebus, some four miles south-east of Caen, and on the plain to the east, a formidable screen of anti-tank guns put an abrupt period to the advance." Apparently it was Wisch's tanks rather than 'anti-tank guns' that did the damage.

[5] Personal interview, General von Lüttwitz, April 1946.

[6] The seven armored divisions were 1 S.S., 9 S.S., 10 S.S., 12 S.S., 2, 21 and 116 Panzer Divisions. Opposing the Americans on 25 July 1944 were 2 S.S. Panzer, Panzer Lehr and 17 S.S. Panzer Grenadier Divisions.

[7] These private armies of the individual services were one of von Rundstedt's pet peeves. While all German manpower in France was ostensibly under von Rundstedt's command, Göring, Himmler and Dönitz insisted on their right to reject any operation they did not like. "This arrangement not only made a unified command impossible," von Rundstedt told me, "but it seriously affected the morale of the ordinary Reichswehr divisions. For while the army formations were constantly told that equipment and reserves were scarce, the S.S. units received the latest weapons and best clothing, the Luftwaffe Field and parachute divisions were supplied with constant reinforcements, and the navy was stocked with better rations. This created resentment and suspicion amongst the men who had suffered the brunt of the fighting in France and Russia, and did not make the problem of command any more simple or harmonious."

Chapter XX — MORTAIN

[1] Quoted by Lieutenant General Bedell Smith, *Saturday Evening Post*, 15 June 1946.

[2] Personal interview, General Blumentritt, February 1946.

[3] Personal interview, Colonel General Dietrich, September 1945.

[4] The six armored divisions in the attack were: 1 S.S., 2 S.S., 10 S.S., 2, 9 and 116 Panzer. The two armored divisions helping protect the right flank of the offensive were 9 S.S. and 21 Panzer.

[5] Personal interview, General von Lüttwitz, April 1946.

Chapter XXI — THE HELL OF FALAISE

[1] 89 Infantry Division.

[2] Personal interview, Brigadeführer Meyer, August 1945.

[3] Telephone Journal of Seventh Army, *supra*.

[4] Personal interview, Major General Plocher, April 1946.

⁵ Personal interview, Colonel General Dietrich, September 1945.
⁶ *Ibid.*
⁷ Quoted by Lieutenant General Bedell Smith, *Saturday Evening Post*, 15 June 1946.
⁸ 'Von Kluge's Last Letter,' *Interim*, British Army of the Rhine Intelligence Review.
⁹ Personal interview, General von Lüttwitz, April 1946.
¹⁰ First Canadian Army Intelligence Summary, 23 August 1944.
¹¹ *Ibid.*
¹² *Ibid.*

Chapter XXII — PARIS AND THE SEINE
1 272, 346 and 711 Infantry Divisions.
2 Personal interview, Lieutenant General Diestel, September 1945.
3 Personal interview, General Schwalbe, September 1945.
4 The three divisions north of Paris were 331, 344 Infantry and 17 Luftwaffe Field, while the four divisions south of Paris were 47, 48, 348 Infantry and 18 Luftwaffe Field.
5 Interrogation, von Boineburg-Lengsfeld, First U.S. Army Report, April 1945.
6 Interrogation, Herbert Sauer, Model's chauffeur, Ninth U.S. Army Report, April 1945.
7 Personal interview, General Blumentritt, February 1946.
8 The six divisions in Fifteenth Army at this time were 59, 64, 70, 226, 245 and 712 Infantry Divisions.
9 Personal interview, General von Zangen, July 1946.
10 Personal interview, General Blumentritt, February 1946.
11 First U.S. Army G-2 Report, September 1944.

Chapter XXIII — THE RETREAT
1 Personal interview, General von Zangen, July 1946.
2 Personal interview, General Schwalbe, September 1945.
3 'Allied Supreme Commander's Report to the Combined Chiefs-of-Staff on the Operations in Europe of the Allied Expeditionary Force,' London, 1946, p. 77.
4 Interrogation of member of intelligence section of Commander-in-Chief West, SHAEF Intelligence Notes, 7 April 1945.
5 *Ibid.*
6 First Canadian Army Intelligence Summary, 26 February 1945.
7 Personal interview, General von Zangen, July 1946.

Chapter XXIV — THE FORTRESSES
1 Personal interview, Colonel Wildermuth, December 1945.
2 Personal interview, Lieutenant General Heim, December 1945.
3 First Canadian Army Intelligence Summary, 21 September 1944.
4 Personal interview, Lieutenant General Heim, December 1945.
5 Personal interview, Lieutenant Colonel Schroeder, December 1945.

Chapter XXV — MANNING THE SIEGFRIED LINE
1 War Office Interrogation, July 1945.
2 *Ibid.*
3 Third U.S. Army Interrogation Report, November 1944.
4 Allied Supreme Commander's Report, *supra*, p. 86.
5 Second Army Intelligence Summary, 4 October 1944.
6 First U.S. Army G-2 Report, September 1944.

▬▬

[7] Third U.S. Army G-2 Report, December 1944.
[8] First U.S. Infantry Division G-2 Report, No. 124.

PART VI — THE COUNTERBLOW

Chapter XXVI — OFFENSIVE IN THE ARDENNES
[1] Infantry and Volksgrenadier divisions were 12, 18, 26, 62, 272, 276, 277, 326, 352 and 560. Armored divisions were 1 S.S., 12 S.S., 2, 116 and Panzer Lehr. Parachute division was 3.
[2] Allied Supreme Commander's Report, *supra*, p. 92.
[3] Quoted by Lieutenant General Bedell Smith, *Saturday Evening Post*, 22 June 1946.
[4] War Office Interrogation, September 1945.
[5] Quoted by Lieutenant General Bedell Smith, *supra*.
[6] Personal interview, Field Marshal von Rundstedt, October 1945.
[7] Quoted by Lieutenant General Bedell Smith, *supra*.
[8] Personal interview, Colonel General Dietrich, September 1945.
[9] First U.S. Army Interrogation Report, April 1945.
[10] Colonel S. L. A. Marshall, *Bastogne*, Washington, 1946, p. 179.
[11] *Ibid.*, p. 177.
[12] War Office Interrogation, September 1945.

Chapter XXVII — THE PARACHUTISTS AND THE SABOTEURS
[1] First U.S. Army G-2 Report, December 1944.
[2] First Canadian Army Intelligence Summary, 30 November 1944.
[3] First U.S. Army G-2 Report, December 1944.
[4] *Ibid.*
[5] 12 Army Group G-2 Report, January 1945.
[6] First U.S. Army G-2 Report, December 1944.
[7] War Office Interrogation, General von Manteuffel, September 1945.
[8] War Office Interrogation, Field Marshal von Rundstedt, September 1945.

Chapter XXVIII — ELATION AND DESPAIR
[1] Twenty-first Army Group Psychological Warfare Summary, January 1945.
[2] 101 U.S. Airborne Division G-2 Report, January 1945.
[3] Twenty-first Army Group Psychological Warfare Summary, January 1945.
[4] First Canadian Army Intelligence Summary, 20 January 1945.
[5] *Ibid.*
[6] Twenty-first Army Group Psychological Warfare Summary, January 1945.
[7] First Canadian Army Intelligence Summary, 30 January 1945.
[8] 2 U.S. Infantry Division G-2 Report, February 1945.

Chapter XXIX — THE THUNDER OF COLLAPSE
[1] Personal interview, Colonel General Student, October 1945.
[2] Personal interview, Colonel General Student, October 1945. The divisions to be used in this proposed offensive were 346, 711 and 712 Infantry Divisions, and 6 and 7 Parachute Divisions.
[3] Personal interview, General Schwalbe, September 1945.
[4] The S.S. divisions were 17 S.S. Panzer Grenadier and 6 S.S. Mountain. The Volksgrenadier divisions were 36, 245, 256, 257, 361 and 559.
[5] Allied Supreme Commander's Report, *supra*, p. 99.
[6] Seventh U.S. Army Interrogation Report, January 1945.
[7] Quoted by Lieutenant General Bedell Smith, *Saturday Evening Post*, 29 June 1946.

PART VII – THE END

Chapter XXX – Defeat West of the Rhine
1 Personal interview, General Schlemm, October 1945.
2 Allied Supreme Commander's Report, *supra*, p. 100.
3 84 Infantry Division.
4 Allied Supreme Commander's Report, *supra*, p. 107.
5 Personal interview, General Schlemm, October 1945.
6 These were 84, 180, and 190 Infantry Divisions, Panzer Lehr, 15 Panzer Grenadier and 116 Panzer Divisions, 6, 7 and 8 Parachute Divisions.
7 30 British Corps Intelligence Summary, September 1944.
8 59, 176, 183 and 406 Infantry Divisions.
9 15 Panzer Grenadier, Panzer Lehr and 84 Infantry Divisions.
10 Personal interview, General Schlemm, October 1945.
11 *Ibid.*
12 *Ibid.*
13 First U.S. Army Interrogation Report, March 1945.
14 *Ibid.*
15 Interrogation Report, Captain Friesenhahn of 12 Landes Engineer Regiment, First U.S. Army, March 1945.
16 Allied Supreme Commander's Report, p. 111.
17 Quoted by Lieutenant General Bedell Smith, *Saturday Evening Post*, 29 June 1946.
18 *Ibid.*
19 'File on Colonel M,' *Interim*, British Army of the Rhine Intelligence Review.

Chapter XXXI – Defeat East of the Rhine
1 SHAEF Weekly Intelligence Summary, 14 April 1945.
2 Ninth U.S. Army G-2 Report, March 1945.
3 30 British Corps Intelligence Summary, March 1945.
4 First Canadian Army Intelligence Summary, 14 April 1945.
5 Personal interview, General Blumentritt, February 1946.
6 Allied Supreme Commander's Report, *supra*, p. 128.
7 'File on Colonel M,' *Interim*, British Army of the Rhine Intelligence Review.
8 Quoted by Lieutenant General Bedell Smith, *Saturday Evening Post*, 6 July 1946.
9 'File on Colonel M,' *supra.*
10 First U.S. Army Interrogation Report, April 1945.
11 'File on Colonel M,' *supra.*

Chapter XXXII – Resistance that Never Came
1 Quoted by Lieutenant General Bedell Smith, *Saturday Evening Post*, 6 July 1946.
2 First Canadian Army Intelligence Periodical, May – June 1945.
3 Quoted by Lieutenant General Bedell Smith, *Saturday Evening Post,* 13 July 1946.
4 12 British Corps, April 1945.

Chapter XXXIII – Defeat
1 'Twelfth-Hour Politics,' *Interim*, British Army of the Rhine Intelligence Review.
2 *Ibid.*

3 *Ibid.*

4 Quoted by Lieutenant General Bedell Smith, *Saturday Evening Post*, 13 July 1946.

5 These extracts from the Reitsch account in *Interim* are reproduced verbatim.

6 Report, Nuremberg Trial, *The Times*, London, 4 July 1946.

7 Quoted by Lieutenant General Bedell Smith, *supra*.

8 Personal interview, Colonel General von Vietinghoff, August 1946.

9 Personal interview, General Blumentritt, February 1946.

Chapter XXXIV — THE VANQUISHED

1 'Democratic Twaddle,' *Interim*, British Army of the Rhine Intelligence Review.

INDEX OF PERSONAL NAMES

INDEX OF GEOGRAPHICAL NAMES

CPSIA information can be obtained at www.ICGtesting.com
Printed in the USA
BVOW06*0859080715

407676BV00011B/24/P